DAILY INSPIRATION FROM
THE LION'S DEN

Devotionals to help you
Stand Strong Through The Storm

Paul Estabrooks

Library of Congress Cataloging-in-Publication Data
ISBN: 978-0-901644-22-0

All Scripture quotations, unless otherwise indicated, are taken from
THE HOLY BIBLE, NEW INTERNATIONAL VERSION®, NIV®
Copyright © 1973, 1978, 1984, 2011 by Biblica, Inc.™
Used by permission. All rights reserved worldwide.

Other Scripture quotations taken from:

LB Living Bible (Wheaton, IL: Tyndale House Publishers, 1979).

Msg The Message (Colorado Springs: Navpress, 1993).

NCV New Century Version (Dallas: Word Bibles, 1991).

NLT New Living Translation (Wheaton, IL: Tyndale House Publishers, 2007).

TEV Today's English Version also called Good News Translation
(New York: American Bible Society, 1992).

J.B. PHILLIPS The New Testament in Modern English
(New York: Harper Collins Publishers, 1962)

Front Cover Photo © The Walters Art Museum, Baltimore, Maryland, USA

Graphics, layout, cover design and printing by
Inscapes Creative Design and Print, Oakville, Ontario, Canada

Printed in Canada

INTRODUCTION

It has been a joy to produce these daily devotionals from the Scriptures and our global training program Standing Strong Through The Storm (SSTS). Most of the stories and illustrations come directly from the Persecuted Church. I have learned so much myself from the reports and true life situations of each one.

The process began with a request in 2010 from Michele Miller of our Open Doors-USA team to produce a daily devotional to be sent from their office daily by e-mail. I started with great trepidation at the prospect of finding 365 applicable stories. But like most large projects, one day at a time ultimately brings completion.

This has been truly a team effort. Our Open Doors "field communicators" around the world have provided most of the stories and interviews. In addition, I have relied on other writers on the Open Doors team—especially my favorite authors and good friends, Brother Andrew and Ron Boyd-MacMillan.

Beginning with the year 2014, the reader will need to adjust the dates of Holy Week readings from Palm Sunday to Easter Sunday. They are dated March 24-31 in this volume.

The daily Scripture passages are taken from the New International Version (NIV) of the Bible with exceptions noted.

Standing Strong Through The Storm is an Open Doors published book which gives the basic curriculum of three-day seminars taught around the world, often in areas of conflict. A Second Edition of the book is scheduled for release in early 2013. One-day Saturday seminars are also available on request for North American churches. In addition, an Open Doors team has produced and taught from this material a Seminary graduate-level course titled "Theology of Persecution and Discipleship" or TOPAD.

Our prayer is that these daily glimpses into application of the Word of God will strengthen and encourage you to stand strong too!

Paul Estabrooks
Senior Communication Specialist
Open Doors International
December 31, 2012
paule@od.org

January 1

BE A LIGHTHOUSE

I have come into the world as a light, so that no one who believes in me should stay in darkness.
John 12:46

One of the strongest images of standing strong in a storm is the lighthouse. In the era before radar, satellite navigation and GPS systems, lighthouses were vital to protect ships from crashing onto rocks, shoals and shores. Building lighthouses can be considered one of man's most noble endeavors. Since the beginning of seafaring, families and friends have lit bonfires at night to guide sailors home.

George Bernard Shaw said, **"I can think of no other edifice constructed by man as altruistic as a lighthouse. They were built only to serve."**

And evangelist D.L. Moody commented, **"Lighthouses don't fire cannons to call attention to their shining—they just shine."**

Jesus used this imagery of light to describe our role in His kingdom. We are the light of the world, He said, after claiming Himself to be the true light. Therefore we function much like a lighthouse, both internally and externally.

The first design for a lighthouse is the internal function of generating light. Early lighthouses used a literal fire that had to be constantly fed and watched. Later electric lights were utilized and ultimately laser lights. But this light still has to be **internally projected**.

So we too as followers of Jesus project internal light, the outer expression of the inner life under the control of the Holy Spirit.

The other aspect of a modern lighthouse is that it also is an **external reflector**. Over the years of improvements, revolving lenses have been developed to reflect that internally generated light further into the darkness.

As the moon reflects the light of the sun, so we reflect the light of the Son in a world of darkness.

And finally, lighthouses remind us of God's love. Like the bright shining beam of a lighthouse, His love reaches out…piercing through the darkness of any storm.

RESPONSE:
Today and throughout this year I will be a lighthouse for Jesus, projecting His inner light and reflecting His light externally.

PRAYER:
Lord, may Your love and Your light pierce the darkness of the world around me as I stand strong and faithful for You like a lighthouse, today and through the year ahead.

Our desire and prayer is that these devotionals will create reaction and interaction.

Each day there is white space in this area for your own written personal notes, questions, reflections, insights, actions plans and prayers.

We encourage you to journal your responses and reactions here in this space each day.

Jan 1/14

Siento que mi luz se apaga, me queda lo que le queda a una vela al final, ayúdame Señor, estoy muy triste y sólo quiero dormir, no estoy bien, te necesito Señor, ayúdame por favor a pasar de mi pesar, en el nombre del señor Jesucristo, amén.

quiero ser un faro que refleje tu luz, dame vida en abundancia en el nombre del Señor Jesucristo.

2

January 2

STORMS CAN COME FROM OBEDIENCE

That day when evening came, he [Jesus] said to his disciples, "Let us go over to the other side." Leaving the crowd behind, they took him along, just as he was, in the boat. There were also other boats with him. A furious squall came up, and the waves broke over the boat, so that it was nearly swamped.
Mark 4: 35-37
(Read Mark 4:35-41)

From the disciples experience we see that storms can arise just by following the path of obedience. We know that when Jesus says, "Let's go to the other side," we **will** reach the other side in spite of any storms.

Ahmad was a respected Muslim leader and a brilliant scholar. While studying for his doctorate in comparative religions he began reading the New Testament and ultimately gave his life to Jesus. When *Sharia*, the law of Islam, became the law of the land, Ahmad was called in for questioning. When he admitted to being a Christian, he was arrested, put in chains, and thrown into solitary confinement.

The first night in prison, the authorities tried to kill him. Unexplainably, however, they could find no gasoline for their car to drive him to the place of execution. The next day, he was to be arraigned before the Islamic High Court. A lawyer friend urged him to renounce his faith publicly and just keep it secretly in his heart. Ahmad refused. "Jesus is my only defence," he said. "I cannot deny Him."

Ahmad was sentenced to six months in prison, stripped of his military rank, and fired from his teaching position. His wife had already divorced him. He also lost his four children, his car, house, and bank account.

If at the end of his sentence he still refused to return to Islam, the judges said, he would spend six more months behind bars. Ahmad organized small Bible studies and prayer groups throughout the prison. "By the end of three months," he said, "there were more than three hundred known Christians in our prison, at least seven from Muslim background."

One night, the guards threw Ahmad into a truck with orders to drown him in the river. But as the truck neared the river, it stopped mysteriously. Terrified, the guards and driver refused the officer's orders to kill Ahmad. Soon after, he was released.

RESPONSE:
Today I will live in the awareness that <u>storms are a normal part of</u> life in this world and the wise <u>disciple prepares for them.</u>

PRAYER:
Pray that you will be cognizant of the storms you face which simply result from your obedience to Jesus.

Enero 2/14

Padre,
Ayúdame a prepararme
para las tormentos que resultan
de la obediencia hacia ti.
Tormentas son parte de
nuestra vida en este mundo,
ayúdame con esta que
estoy pasando y por favor
ayuda a mi mamá y
hermanos. En el nombre
poderoso del señor Jesus,
Amen.

JESUS' PRESENCE DOESN'T GUARANTEE OUR COMFORT

A furious squall came up, and the waves broke over the boat, so that it was nearly swamped. Jesus was in the stern, sleeping on a cushion. The disciples woke him and said to him, "Teacher, don't you care if we drown?
Mark 4:37-38

Many times storms can make it seem like Jesus doesn't care. In this story Jesus' humanity is evident. He was so tired he was sleeping through a storm which caused the disciples—some even professional fishermen—to fear for their lives.

Without warning, Muslim background believers, Gulshan and Latifa, found themselves caught in a dangerous storm of opposition from local police—all because they had accepted an invitation to a Christian woman's home to meet with several women who were not believers.

While they were drinking tea and chatting, the police arrived and searched the house. When they could find no incriminating materials, the officers left. But a short time later, other policemen started filming all the ladies. Accusing the two Christian ladies of holding a religious meeting, the police took them into custody. They escorted them to a police station where they were pressured to admit involvement in "illegal missionary activities."

When they refused to sign, police detained and abused them for six hours. Gulshan was beaten so badly that she suffered a concussion. Only after their pastor intervened did the police let them receive treatment for their injuries.

Gulshan and Latifa left their hometown and sought refuge in one of Open Doors' "Safe Houses" in another region of their country. For a month they were able to escape the brunt of the storm, staying in the "Safe House" until the pressures abated. Meanwhile, the judge hearing the women's case fined them in absentia seven times the minimum monthly wage—more than a half year's salary.

"We were very happy to spend time away from all the tumult," the two believers said as they later left the "Safe House" to return home. "We were able to learn more about spending time with God and being quiet before Him. To meet with other believers was a blessing and really encouraged us. And thank you so much for assisting us in paying these huge fines. You are a blessing!" the two women concluded.

Though it seemed at first that Jesus did not care for or about them, those who were the hands and feet for Jesus came to the rescue and the storm was weathered with encouragement resulting in more boldness.

RESPONSE:
Today I will live in the awareness and peace that Jesus is in the storm with me. His presence doesn't guarantee comfort, but it builds faith that He will ultimately calm the storm.

PRAYER:
Pray that all those feeling that Jesus doesn't care about their storm will realize the power and comfort His presence can bring.

Enero 3/14

"Gracias señor porque tu estás siempre conmigo!"

January 4

FAITH AND FEAR

Jesus was in the stern, sleeping on a cushion. The disciples woke him and said to him, "Teacher, don't you care if we drown?" He got up, rebuked the wind and said to the waves, "Quiet! Be still!" Then the wind died down and it was completely calm. He said to his disciples, "Why are you so afraid? Do you still have no faith?"
Mark 4:38-40

Storms often bring out our true spiritual condition. Jesus was in the boat but the disciples still feared for their lives. He chastised them for their fear and their *little faith!* Thus our greatest need is not for the storm to end but to be freed from fear and have faith in Him while the storm rages.

At a Standing Strong Through The Storm (SSTS) seminar in Central Asia, our translator looked at us at the close of our three-day session and commented, "Thank you for teaching us how to stand strong. God spoke to me a lot through this seminar. I was afraid to die but not anymore. I have peace to go and spread God's Word." She is now serving the Lord in a dangerous but strategic mission in her region.

A middle-aged man in North Korea was arrested after the police found a Bible in his home. terribly beaten, he was certain he would die. A Christian friend shared, "When he came to faith, he made the decision that one day he would die for Christ. Every Christian in North Korea has made that choice. Every Christian in the country has the spirit of martyrdom in him. If you lose that spirit for one second, you cannot carry the burden of being a follower of Jesus."

A significant factor in dealing with fear—especially fear of dying—is realizing that we are *already dead* in Christ (Galatians 2:20). Former Open Doors colleague, Hector Tamez, says that this concept is clearly seen in the lives of Christians living in war zones of Latin America. The Christians who were caught in the civil war between the government and Shining Path guerrillas in Peru, are a classic example for us. Here is how Hector expresses their commitment:

They know that they are going to be killed. And they say, "In order to be a Christian here, you have to recognize that you are already dead in Christ. Once you recognize this, then any day that passes by in your life is a gain."

In some countries, surviving one day or one year means that you have one God-given day or year to testify not only with your words but with your deeds. Fear should not control your life! Christ should control your life!

RESPONSE:
When storms come my way, I will affirm God's power to overcome fear and live by faith.

PRAYER:
Ask God to forgive you for your times of fearfulness and lack of faith. Pray that all members of the Persecuted Church would have faith in Jesus like these Peruvian believers.

January 5/14

Para mi vivir es Cristo y morir es ganancia. Ayúdame señor a ser libre del miedo y crecer en la fe. En el nombre del Señor Jesucristo. Amén!

January 5

STORMS REVEAL NEW THINGS ABOUT JESUS

He [Jesus] said to his disciples, "Why are you so afraid? Do you still have no faith?" They were terrified and asked each other, "Who is this? Even the wind and the waves obey him!"
Mark 4:40-41

Thankfully storms ultimately do come to an end! We learn this as another insight from this passage of Scripture. And the storms often reveal something **new** about Jesus. Here the disciples express their amazement that He even controls the winds and the waves. They had already spent considerable time with Jesus yet this experience actually **terrified** them. They had known Jesus as fully human to this point in their relationship. And now they are confronted with His being also fully divine—something that *really* terrified them.

There is always something more to learn about Jesus and sometimes this happens in the storms of life. Twenty-three-year-old Maria fled with her parents from Bagdad, Iraq to the Kurdish north of the country because they had been threatened as Christians living in the capital.

"I really struggled the first year," she says. "But I knew I had to go on. I could not crawl up and mourn the things I had lost…Because I went to college, it was pretty easy to find a job. And what I really like is that I am safe here."

Maria had to leave everything behind but did not give up. She concludes, "Start with something small and you will slowly move on."

We received a report of a Christian arrested for selling Bibles in front of a university in another middle east Islamic country's capital. He was repeatedly interrogated during six weeks of imprisonment. In a final effort to intimidate him, his captors brought his wife to the prison and threatened to execute him unless he renounced his Christian faith.

"If I have to choose between my wife and children or Jesus Christ, then I choose Jesus," he reportedly told his captors. When this and

9

other attempts failed to coerce him to renounce his faith, he was finally released from prison. He was forced to sign a letter agreeing not to sell Christian literature, although he continued to actively evangelize in parks and other open-air areas.

"I don't know why, but I cried the whole day," he said upon release, adding that he wished he could have been martyred for his faith. "I felt very close to heaven in prison. I was happy that the Lord had heard my prayers for my love to be a sacrifice in that small prison cell. But it seems that the Lord wished me to be alive and active in His work again."

RESPONSE:
Today I will be thankful that the storms in my life will come to an end. I will deliberately seek to discover something new about Jesus.

PRAYER:
Pray that you—and believers everywhere—will have spiritual eyes and ears to see, hear and learn new lessons from Jesus in the storms of life.

Enero 5/14

Amado Padre, por favor indícame que aprender de esta tormenta de perder físicamente a mi papá. Ayúdame Padre a aprender más de ti, en el poderoso nombre sobre todo nombre, Jesucristo, Amén!

January 6

THREE FOLD PREPARATION

*Put on the full armor of God so that you can take your
stand against the devil's schemes.*
Ephesians 6:11

In the 1980's, an Open Doors co-worker visited Pastor Tu in
Vietnam—leader of the fastest growing house church network at that
time. The pastor learned from a member of his house church that
the authorities were threatening to imprison him. Pastor Tu told our
colleague, **"I know it is coming. I have prepared my people for my
imprisonment. I am ready for prison."**

Shortly after that, Pastor Tu did spend three years in prison. When
he was released, he found his house church network had grown three
hundred per cent in his absence.

I received a Christmas card from him the following year that read:
**"...God greatly gives our church 20,203 more new believers this
year. Hallelujah!"**

The pastor's comment to our colleague reveals three areas of
preparation for coming storms:

- **Intellectually** – "I know it is coming."
- **Practically** – "I have prepared my people for my imprisonment."
- **Spiritually** – "I am ready for prison."

1. Preparation **intellectually** involves:
   - understanding what the Bible teaches about persecution
   - understanding what is God's purpose in persecution
2. Preparation **practically** involves:
   - practicing the **do's and don't's** so not to invite persecution
     unnecessarily
   - knowing what programs and forms to undertake so the church
     can continue to function under pressure and persecution
   - knowing your rights as a citizen (Acts 22 & 25)

11

3. Preparation **spiritually** involves:
    - engaging in activities that stress the importance of fighting
      the spiritual battle

RESPONSE:
Today I will prepare intellectually, practically and spiritually for
any coming storms.

PRAYER:
Pray that Christians in all restricted countries will understand
these three aspects of the spiritual battle and preparation.

Enero 7/14

Padre enséñame quien eres, por favor. Quiero crecer en ti en cada aspecto de mi vida.
En el nombre del, señor Jesús, Amén!

12

January 7

CAN YOU SLEEP WHILE THE WIND BLOWS?

Do not be anxious about anything, but in every situation, by prayer and petition, with thanksgiving, present your requests to God. And the peace of God, which transcends all understanding, will guard your hearts and your minds in Christ Jesus.

Philippians 4:6-7

During a recent hurricane storm, the following story circulated on the Internet:

A farmer on the Atlantic seacoast constantly advertised for hired hands. Most people were reluctant to work on farms along the Atlantic because of the awful storms that wreaked havoc on the buildings and crops. One applicant for the job was a short, thin man, well past middle age.

"Are you a good farm hand?" the farmer asked him.

"Well, I can sleep when the wind blows," answered the little man.

Although puzzled by this answer, the farmer, desperate for help, hired him. The little man worked well and kept busy from dawn to dusk. The farmer felt satisfied with the man's work.

Then one night the wind howled loudly from offshore. Jumping out of bed, the farmer grabbed a lantern and rushed to the hired hand's sleeping quarters. He shook the little man and yelled, "Get up! A storm is coming! Tie things down before they blow away!"

The little man rolled over in bed and said firmly, "No sir. I told you, I can sleep when the wind blows."

Enraged by the response, the farmer was tempted to fire him on the spot. He hurried outside to prepare for the storm. To his amazement, he discovered that all of the haystacks had been covered with tarpaulins. The cows were in the barn, the chickens were in the coops, and the doors were barred. The shutters were tightly secured. Everything was tied down. Nothing could blow away. The farmer then understood what his hired hand meant, so he returned to his bed to also sleep while the wind blew.

13

When you're prepared for storms, spiritually, mentally, and practically, you have nothing to fear. Can you sleep when the wind blows through your life? The hired hand in the story was able to sleep because he had secured the farm against the storm.

We secure ourselves against the storms of life by soaking ourselves in the Word of God, being obedient to it and then placing our faith and trust in God's goodness. We don't need to understand, we just need to hold His hand to have peace in the midst of our storms.

RESPONSE:
Today I will prepare myself practically, mentally and spiritually so that I can sleep when the storms blow in my life.

PRAYER:
Thank You, Lord, for the peace only You can give when the strong winds try and wreak havoc in my life and daily situations.

Enero 7/14

Ayúdame Padre a estar preparada para la tormenta y durante la tormenta. Ayúdame a crecer en ti durante esta tormenta de ya no tener a mi papá en la tierra. En el nombre del señor Jesús, Amén.

14

FAITH THAT BRINGS HOPE

*...for everyone born of God overcomes the world. This is
the victory that has overcome the world, even our faith.*
1 John 5:4

We often think that faith is our duty, or something we can give
back to God. In reality, we cannot even do that on our own. There is
nothing we can give to God. We must rely on Him for everything —
even our faith. When we accept it as His precious gift, we find victory
over sin and trials. We could never have this victory if we relied only
on our own tenuous faith. "Faith does not always provide exemption
from suffering, but it does keep us from being defeated at the hands of
suffering."

Carl Moeller, former Open Doors' USA President says, "I met
secretly with a courageous believer who had been forced to hang from
his ankles or wrists every day, subjected to repeated beatings and was
crammed in a three-foot square box for three weeks.

Racked by memories of the agony he'd been through, Aran had been
looking at me with a pained expression until I asked the question,
"What were you thinking or feeling during that time?"

His face completely changed. A huge smile broke across it, and he
gave me two thumbs up.

What was he thinking...?

Aran simply said, "That I was counted worthy to suffer for Jesus
Christ."

A Christian leader in another restricted country shared the situation
there in these words:

In our country, we live in the midst of a pressure cooker. To
survive as Christians, we must have a pressure cooker faith. Our
young people decide for Christ not because He offers them the
most, or because it is fashionable, but because they consider
that here is One worth dying for. That may even be what their
discipleship may have for them.

Standing Strong Through The Storm examines persecution and the results of persecution — suffering and martyrdom. Satan wants to dishearten us and create hopelessness because of persecution and suffering. We will expose Satan's lies and show how by faith we can experience God's restoration of our hope — "the oxygen of the human spirit."

RESPONSE:
Today I will rely on the Lord to walk by faith and not by sight, no matter what happens.

PRAYER:
Lord, help me to ignore Satan's lies and live victoriously today by faith in the hope which only You can give and restore.

January 9

BOLDNESS, LOVE AND NON-VIOLENCE

Do not repay anyone evil for evil. Be careful to do what is right in the eyes of everybody. If it is possible, as far as it depends on you, live at peace with everyone.
Romans 12:17,18

A few years ago I was leading a group from my home church in Canada on a mission trip to Cuba. The church in Cuba had experienced a significant revival movement and the fast-growing house church movement was overflowing with new believers.

In Havana we visited the Baptist Seminary and were delighted to have some time with its then elderly president, Dr. Leoncio Veguilla. He spoke perfect English and shared with us how he had spent five years in Castro's prison system in the 1960's just because he was a Christian pastor. He further itemized the pressures the church had experienced at the hand of the regime over the past five decades. Then he smiled and in his very positive style of expression concluded, "But we have learned three things through all of this. **We learned not to fear, not to hate and not to harm!"**

I have meditated on this statement for some time and concluded that it expresses very succinctly the biblical essence of standing strong through any storm. And although his three point outline is stated negatively, there are very positive aspects of each:

- learning **"not to fear"** infers a development of boldness and courage
- learning **"not to hate"** implies a focus on love, forgiveness and grace
- learning **"not to harm"** indicates a commitment to the biblical principles of non-violence and aggressive love

Dr. Veguilla summed it up perfectly and as you continue to read these devotionals, you will see dozens of specific applications for all aspects of discipleship in following our Lord Jesus.

RESPONSE:
Today I want to live in boldness, love and non-violence. I am committed not to fear, not to hate, and not to harm anyone.

PRAYER:
Lord, this kind of living is counter-culture. I need Your strength and power to live this way. Help me — as well as Your Persecuted Church — to keep this in focus.

January 10

GOD HAS EVERYTHING UNDER CONTROL

When the storm has swept by, the wicked are gone, but
the righteous stand firm forever.
Proverbs 10:25

Throughout the Bible, God reveals that He is always in control over His vast universe and even our seemingly insignificant lives. Here is a true-life story from a member of the Persecuted Church:

"I was the only convert of a man who died thinking he was useless to God. Both our crimes were for violent robbery and we actually shared a prison cell together.

"He told me about how—by mistake—he had been placed into a cell with a group of Christians. They were singing hymns at night and praising God together. He saw them as a soft touch and robbed them of their food parcels. He even beat them to show who was boss. For the first time in years he felt powerful again. But somehow they were not afraid of him and repeatedly shared their faith in Christ.

"One day in a fit of anger he took his knife to kill one of them. But something—or Someone—blocked him from bringing down the knife. For the first time, he was up against a force more powerful than himself, and one he could not understand.

"At that moment he put his trust in Christ. The prison authorities realized he had been allocated to the wrong cell and they moved him to solitary confinement. There he pleaded with God, 'Lord, let me witness to Your power and love before I die.'

"One night the prison was overcrowded and I was put into his cell. I could see he was far-gone, barely conscious. He beckoned me close to his lips told me all about Jesus and how He loved me and wanted to save me.

"When I woke up in the morning, he was cold and dead. I was to be moved to a hard labor camp that day but the truck that was to take me there broke down. So I ended up in another cell—the one full of Christians.

"My truck was delayed a week. In that time the Christians told me

19

the whole story about this man. They were delighted to learn he had witnessed to me before he died. The night before I was moved, I too trusted Christ.

"That's the strength of suffering for Christ. It kept a dying man going because he wanted to witness. It kept those Christian prisoners buoyant all through their captivity. It gave me hope when I looked ahead at eight years of hard labor camp. I would have died if not for Christ."

RESPONSE:
Today I will live in the awareness and peace that God has everything under control — no matter what storms I face.

PRAYER:
Pray that all those living in conditions as described above will also understand God's purposes for their lives and realize the strength and meaningfulness in suffering for Christ.

THIS IS GOOD

And we know that in all things God works for the good of those who love him, who have been called according to his purpose.
Romans 8:28

A tribal king had a close friend with whom he grew up. The friend had a habit of looking at every situation that ever occurred in his life (positive or negative) as well as the lives of others and remarking, **"This is good!"** He based it on two Scriptures: one that says that it is God's will that we be thankful for ALL circumstances (1 Thessalonians 5:18); and Romans 8:28 which assures us that God can turn every situation (good or bad) into ultimate good. The king loved his friend's positive outlook and took him with him wherever he went.

One day the king and his friend were out on a hunting expedition. As the king fired his gun at a pheasant that flew up from the long grass, the rifle backfired and blew off his right thumb. Looking at the king's bleeding hand, his friend remarked as usual, "This is good!"

The king was angry and replied, "No, this is NOT good!" and proceeded to send his friend to jail for his insensitivity.

About a year later, the king was hunting all alone in an area that he should have known to stay clear of. Cannibals captured him and took him to their village. They tied his hands, stacked some wood, and were going to cook him in a big pot. As they set fire to the wood, they noticed that the king was missing a thumb on his right hand. Being very superstitious, cannibals never eat anyone who is less than perfect. So they released the king.

Walking home he kept staring at his right hand without a thumb. "This IS good!" he said out loud. He was reminded of the event that had taken his thumb and felt remorse for his shabby treatment of his friend. So he went immediately to the jail to speak with his friend.

"You were right," he said, "it was good that my thumb was blown off." And he proceeded to tell the friend all that had just happened. "And so, I am very sorry for sending you to jail for so long. It was bad for me to do this."

21

"No," his friend replied as usual, "This is good!"

"What do you mean, 'This is good?' How could it be good that I put my friend in jail for over a year?"

"Well," replied his friend, "if I had not been here in jail, I would have been out there with you!"

In our SSTS seminars we share this story early in the sessions and for the rest of the time together holding up four fingers on the right hand (with a hidden thumb) communicates clearly the message: THIS IS GOOD!

RESPONSE:
Today I will focus by faith on the potential good that God wants to bring out of the negative challenges I face in my life.

PRAYER:
Pray that all persecuted Christians will respond to their daily challenges with this faith perspective.

January 12

GOD IS IN CONTROL

The stone the builders rejected has become the cornerstone; the LORD has done this, and it is marvelous in our eyes.

Psalm 118:22-23

Co-worker Ron Boyd-MacMillan writes in his epic volume, *Faith That Endures*, "Your life's purpose may remain a mystery to you, as may the events of your world, but that's okay. God is in control. We are relieved of the responsibility of understanding everything and the need to change it."[1]

R. J. Thomas was a Welsh missionary with a burden for the xenophobic hermit kingdom of Korea in the middle of the nineteenth century. In 1865, while in China, the opportunity he had been waiting a lifetime for arrived. An American ship, the *SS General Sherman*, was going to steam up the Taedong River to the capital, Pyongyang, in hopes of luring the Koreans into trade. Thomas bought a berth on the ship, hoping to meet some scholars in Pyongyang who spoke and read Chinese, and took as many Chinese Scriptures with him as he could carry on board.

When they reached Pyongyang, they were not welcomed. They got stuck on a sandbank and the ship was set afire. As the crew waded to shore, they were killed by the waiting Koreans. Thomas also waded to shore. Before he could speak, a club swung with murderous force dashed his brains into the water, but his killer noticed he had emerged with books. He picked up a couple of the sodden books. Drying them off, he separated the leaves and saw that they were nicely printed. He could not read but decided to paper the outside of his house compound with the pages, as was the custom at the time.

Imagine his astonishment when he returned from the fields a few weeks later to find a clutch of scholars earnestly reading his walls. One of these scholars became a Christian by reading a Gospel portion

---

1 Ronald Boyd-MacMillan, *Faith That Endures* (Grand Rapids: Fleming Revell, 2006), p. 315.

plastered onto the wall. A generation later his nephew assisted in the first translation of the New Testament into Korean in Shenyang, China under the supervision of another little-known missionary, John Ross from Scotland.

R.J. Thomas never lived to see the fruit of his labor or his prayers for Korean people. He died, his life's purpose unfulfilled, his potential unrealized. For anyone aware of Thomas's death, his life was a mystery for years afterward.

But his life was not in vain. The meaning of life does not consist in what we make of it, but in what God makes of it. Success is not about achievement or what we make of ourselves. It's about placement, or what God makes of us. We take the lesson from the Persecuted Church that it is okay to die quite unaware of our life's meaning. We can rest in trust that God, in His mercy, has used us to help build His eternal kingdom.[2]

RESPONSE:
Today I leave my placement, my purpose, my potential in the hands of a good and loving God.

PRAYER:
May I ever realize that You are in control and thus truly allow You to be Lord of my life.

---

2 Ibid, p. 314.

January 13

NO FEAR WHEN THE HEAT COMES

"But blessed is the one who trusts in the LORD, whose confidence is in him. They will be like a tree planted by the water that sends out its roots by the stream. It does not fear when heat comes..."
Jeremiah 17:7-8a

Trees were not plentiful in Israel and most grew by sources of water like an oasis or a stream. Jeremiah's simile indicates a person with confidence in the Lord is like a deep-rooted tree by the stream (see Psalm 1 also) that is not afraid of heat.

Samuel Lamb is a well-known house church pastor in southern China in the city of Guangzhou. He spent time in prison for his faith as a young pastor on two occasions totalling almost twenty years. He was forced to work in a coal mine where the work was hard and dangerous. He is convinced that God's protection is the only reason he survived.

Upon his release after the second imprisonment, he returned home to find out that his dear wife had just passed away. Now in his seventies, he threw himself fully into the ministry again opening an unregistered house church on the second and third storey of his home while the local police utilized the ground floor for their office. His congregation grew rapidly. He could pack in two hundred sitting shoulder-to-shoulder on the third floor where he preached and another two hundred listening via a speaker system on the second floor. Soon he had to have five services a week to get everyone in. Each person had to walk past the police post to climb the stairs to his meeting.

He soon became the best-known unregistered house church pastor in China. United States President Ronald Regan sent him a monographed pen set. Billy and Ruth Graham visited the location with many photos taken.

Because of his refusal to register with the government Three Self Patriotic Movement Church, the authorities were constantly irritated. Unhappy with his boldness and the growth of his church, they harassed him repeatedly and often threatened to return him to prison. Each time this threat occurred, Samuel Lamb would hold up two fingers and say, "I've been to prison twice already. My bag is packed and I'm ready to go again!" Intimidation would not work against him as he had no fear and his trust was completely in the Lord. And each time the authorities would leave to consider what other tactics they could use against him.

Pastor Lamb continues his unofficial, growing church ministry to this day. As an elderly pastor, he does not fear when the "heat" comes.

RESPONSE:
Today I will trust completely in the Lord and rely on His wisdom when pressures arise.

PRAYER:
Pray other pastors in China will have the fearlessness and church growth of Samuel Lamb.

January 14

LEAVES ARE ALWAYS GREEN

"But blessed is the one who trusts in the LORD, whose confidence is in him. They will be like a tree planted by the water that sends out its roots by the stream...its leaves are always green..."
Jeremiah 17:7-8b

Trees were not plentiful in Israel and most grew by sources of water like an oasis or a stream. Jeremiah's simile indicates a person with confidence in the Lord is like a deep-rooted tree by the stream whose leaves never die but are always green.

Aunty Esther was the first Christian I met inside China thirty years ago. She was a diminutive elderly Chinese medical doctor with a soft, kind voice that masks the many years of suffering through which she has passed.

"During the Cultural Revolution," she says, "I was called in by my superior one day. At that time I was in charge of eight large pediatric wards in my hospital.

"The communists were cracking down on people who did not toe the current party line. My superior warned me that I should deny my faith and join the communist party or I may have to face the serious consequences of job demotion and salary reduction.

"A few days later, I was rudely awakened by four nurses who roughly pulled me from my bed and marched me to the hospital. En route they stopped at a barbershop and shaved off half of my hair. In front of the rest of the staff, I was confronted to renounce my faith in Christ and join the communist party.

"I responded, 'I can't deny Jesus. I love Jesus!' At the mention of His name they threw me down on the ground and cursed. Later, the communist cadre at my hospital tore the stethoscope from my neck and said, 'You are no longer Esther; you are now The Fool.'

Esther continues. For the next eleven years she lived in the basement of the hospital and obediently submitted to her new task — cleaning the floors and toilets of the hospital wards that she previously headed.

27

Her already meagre salary of 50 dollars per month was reduced to 15 dollars. And she had to buy the cleaning materials from it. The rest was used up on food.

But Esther practised the presence of Jesus in her job. She sang as she toiled. With a twinkle in her eyes she adds, "My hospital had the cleanest floors and cleanest toilets in all of China!"

Hospital staff would come to her and with great envy question her source of joy in spite of her troubles. Esther responded, "When you have Jesus in your heart, it doesn't matter what job you do or what position you have. It only matters that you love Him and are faithful and loyal to Him!"

When the Cultural Revolution period ended, Aunty Esther was reinstated in her original job and given back pay for all that she had been deprived during those eleven years. This amount enabled her to send one of her children for higher education. She faithfully carried on her public witness for Jesus until the day she died in her late nineties.

RESPONSE:
I will allow my roots to grow deep in the Lord so that my leaves will always be green.

PRAYER:
Lord, thank You for the example of faithful Aunty Esther whose life reflected Your love.

28

January 15

NO WORRIES IN A YEAR OF DROUGHT

"But blessed is the one who trusts in the LORD, whose confidence is in him. They will be like a tree planted by the water that sends out its roots by the stream...It has no worries in a year of drought..."
Jeremiah 17:7-8c

Trees were not plentiful in Israel and most grew by sources of water like an oasis or a stream. Jeremiah's simile indicates a person with confidence in the Lord is like a deep-rooted tree by the stream which has nothing to worry about even when a whole year goes by with no rain.

A young Christian boy in Iraq shares this insight after the bombing of his church in late 2010:

I always imagine having a special cape, like superman wears, as I run in and out of my sister's bedroom. The cape is gold with red print just like the curtains in our dining room. I think of myself as a protector of the royal realm and my sister as a princess to guard — well, okay, when she isn't making me mad.

I used to play outside, but when the war started we had to play inside all the time. When we do go outside we take the car, but I help my dad check under the car first for bombs. We are always checking things around the house and everyone is very nervous when we travel even short trips around the city. We even have some suitcases stuffed with things in case we have to leave in the middle of the night. I wonder if any of my toys will fit in those bags.

A really, really bad thing happened at our church and I lost a lot of my friends. They were all killed. I didn't see it, but I heard most of the stories. I think lots of things will never be the same and that I need to take the role of protector and guardian of the realm. If I have this special cape I can protect my family.

At night before my sister goes to bed my parents pray with her. I can hear my sister now. She is praying, "God help that they don't bomb another church and that there are no car bombs. Stop the blood."

She has been very scared since the bad thing happened in the church and my mom often comes to her at night to pray with her again after nightmares. She didn't used to have these things.

Then my dad comes to pray for me. He tells me that Jesus will take care of us and I mustn't worry. He tells me that God even loves the people who hurt us. He tells me that Jesus is love — and that it is something like my special cape.

With confidence in the Lord, we can have no worries even when the drought lasts a year or more.

RESPONSE:
Today I will place my trust and confidence only in God asking Him to bear my worries.

PRAYER:
Lord, give courage, peace and confidence to those of our family living in areas of violence.

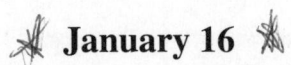 **January 16**

NEVER FAILS TO BEAR FRUIT

"But blessed is the one who trusts in the LORD, whose confidence is in him. They will be like a tree planted by the water that sends out its roots by the stream...and never fails to bear fruit."
Jeremiah 17:7-8d

Trees were not plentiful in Israel and most grew by sources of water like an oasis or a stream. Jeremiah's simile indicates a person with confidence in the Lord is like a deep-rooted tree by the stream that bears fruit faithfully year after year in all kinds of weather.

The most remarkable report I've heard from China is about a Christian lady in prison during the "anti-spiritual pollution campaign" in the mid-eighties. She spent her time in prison hand carving Scripture verses in miniature lettering with a sharpened end of a toothbrush on the walls and even on the frame of the cot in her cell. Years later she actually met another person who subsequently spent time in the same cell and came to Christ through reading those verses over and over.

One year when visiting Christians in the north of China, I asked the whereabouts of Aunty Mei Bo. This short octogenarian medical doctor, I was told, was away on a missions outreach in spiritually needy Tibet. The next summer she was home and very anxious to hear of our group experience in Tibet—the rooftop of the world—since she was planning another mission trip there soon. She concluded, "Jesus is saying, 'Hurry up and get the job done so I can come back again!'"

Aunty Mei Bo often stored Bibles from foreign couriers in her home where she lived alone. One day the Public Security Police raided her home and confiscated all the Christian materials they found. Later in the day she found a *JESUS* video they had missed. So off to the police station she headed with the video.

The young lady at the desk looked askance in her direction. "I want to talk to the Chief of Police!" Mei Bo demanded firmly. "Today his men were at my house and they did not see this," she said waving the video tape in the air. The receptionist ushered Mei Bo into the police chief's office. He acted oblivious to her arrival yet grunted a question of intent.

"Sir," Mei Bo began slowly. "Earlier today your men raided my house and took all the Bibles I had stored there. I understand that they were just doing their job. But after they left, I noticed that they missed this video tape. I need to know from you if this is acceptable material or not. Would you and your staff check it for me?"

"Very well, come back in two weeks," he muttered dismissing her with a wave of the hand. Mei Bo almost skipped out the door with overflowing joy as she headed toward home. "Thank you Lord! How else could I get the Beijing chief of police with his staff to watch the JESUS video?"

Aunty Mei Bo led many to the Lord all through her long life and spent her time in discipling them. She never failed to bear fruit.

RESPONSE:
I want to be a tree that bears fruit without fail, regardless of age and weather conditions.

PRAYER:
Lord, may my deep rootedness in You cause me to never fail to produce lasting fruit.

January 17

THE POWER OF LIFE AND DEATH

"See now that I myself am He! There is no god besides me. I put to death and I bring to life, I have wounded and I will heal, and no one can deliver out of my hand.
Deuteronomy 32:39

January 17 will remain a vivid memory in the mind of forty-six-year-old Ali Moses for a very long time. The almost fatal attack on Ali's life in central Nigeria turned out to be a powerful testimony destined to touch many more lives.

On the afternoon of that day, Ali was heading home to his family after a long day's work. He got paid that day and like many previous pay-days had something special planned for the family.

On his way home Ali heard gunshots. Panic made him turn around with an urgency to get back to his working place as quickly as possible. But before Ali could make it back there, he ran into a group of irate jihadists. The incited protesters were proclaiming the name of Allah in Arabic, shouting profane slogans, insulting the Christian governor of Jos and called on the killing of Christians as infidels.

Within seconds Ali found himself surrounded by the violent mob. Brutal blows were raining down on him.

More than eighteen hours later, Ali woke up in the hospital. His swollen body was throbbing and covered with bruises. Open Doors representative, Isaac, went to visit Ali in the hospital shortly after the incident to bring encouragement and assistance and learned about his near death encounter with the Muslim radicals. Considering the course of events, it appears the assailants buried Ali alive while in a state of unconsciousness.

Ali refers to the person who came to his aid as the "Samaritan."

On the morning following the incident, Ado was passing by what looked like a new grave. He noticed movement in the pile of sand and went closer to inspect. To his astonishment, he could tell from the motion that it was in fact a person. The man immediately called for help.

Military police dug Ali from the shallow grave and rushed him to the hospital. At first, the medical staff found it very hard to believe that he could still be alive after his eighteen-hour ordeal. But hearing Ali's testimony gave sceptics food for thought. After spending some time in hospital he made a complete recovery.

"I am grateful to God Almighty for saving my life from the hole, it is a miracle. God rescued me in a special way…Now I believe that the power of life and death lies in no-one's hand but the Lord's. All thanks belong to Him," shared Ali from his hospital bed.

RESPONSE:
Today I will live victoriously in the realization that my life and my death are in the hands of my loving Lord.

PRAYER:
Pray for many Christians in hot spots of the world—like central Nigeria—who face death and death threats on a regular basis. Pray they will have the same assurance as Ali about God's power and protection.

January 18

SATAN'S TACTICS

Submit yourselves, then, to God. Resist the devil, and he will flee from you.
James 4:7

Satan called a worldwide convention. In his opening address to his evil angels, he said, "We can't keep them from reading their Bibles and knowing the truth. We can't even keep them from family values. But we can do something else. We can keep them from forming an intimate, abiding experience in Christ.

"If they gain that connection with Jesus, our power over them is broken. So let them go to church, let them have their conservative lifestyles, but steal their time so they can't gain that experience in Jesus Christ.

"This is what I want you to do, angels. Distract them from gaining hold of their Savior and maintaining that vital connection throughout their day."

"How shall we do this?" shouted the evil angels.

"Keep them busy in the non-essentials of life and invent unnumbered schemes to occupy their minds," he answered.

"Tempt them to spend, spend, spend, then borrow, borrow, borrow. Persuade the wives to go to work and the husbands to work six or seven days a week, ten to twelve hours a day, so they can afford their lifestyles. Keep them from spending time with their children. As their family fragments, soon their homes will offer no escape from the pressures of work.

"Overstimulate their minds so that they cannot hear that still, small voice. Entice them to keep the TV, the DVD, and their CD's going constantly in their homes. Tempt them to spend more time on their computers, especially watching internet pornography.

"Fill their coffee tables with magazines and newspapers. Pound their minds with the news twenty-four-hours-a-day. Invade their driving moments with billboards. Flood their mailboxes with junk mail, sweepstakes, mail order catalogues, and every kind of newsletter and promotional offering, free products, services and false hopes.

"When they meet for fellowship, involve them in gossip and small talk so that they leave with troubled consciences and unsettled emotions. Crowd their lives with so many good causes they have no time to seek power from Christ. Soon they will be working in their own strength."

RESPONSE:
Today I will live in awareness of Satan's subtle tactics to keep me from victory. I will stand against him and he will flee.

PRAYER:
Lord, help me remain close to You today and not allow the "things" and "busyness" of life to crowd You out.

January 19

ONE BIG FAMILY IN CHRIST

The righteous perish, and no one takes it to heart; the devout are taken away, and no one understands that the righteous are taken away to be spared from evil. Those who walk uprightly enter into peace; they find rest as they lie in death.
Isaiah 57:1-2

I was reading this Scripture on January 19th, 1994, the day Bishop Haik Hovsepian-Mehr mysteriously disappeared en route to the airport in the capital of Iran. He had spoken out courageously against the persecution of Iranian Christians and the closure of the Iranian Bible Society as well as the closing of a number of churches across Iran. He had campaigned vigorously for the release of Rev. Mehdi Dibaj from prison and had acted as substitute father for Mehdi's four children during his imprisonment in addition to his own four children. Days later his dead body with multiple stab wounds was identified.

Iranian Christians reported that the bishop was a brave and humble man who was much loved and respected by the church community in Iran. They added that in his last few weeks of life, he would often speak about his possible martyrdom for which he was prepared. At his memorial service one of his taped sermons was played which spoke about giving your life for the sake of Jesus. One of his statements regarding the possibility of losing his life was made to Brother Andrew just weeks before he died, **"I will not die a silent death!"**

Today's verses from the Bible gave me great encouragement as to the purpose of God in allowing martyrdom among His people. They rest in peace. But what about their families?

This day and event changed the life of Haik's son, Andre, forever. He says, "As a pastor's son growing up in Iran, I got used to the fact that sometimes my dad would be gone for a day or two for interrogation. But then on that dreadful day in January '94, my father left the house and never came back."

Looking back, Andre testifies that God used the love and support of the body of Christ to bring the Hovsepian family courage during the dark days following his father's murder. "It meant a lot to me that someone I didn't know from another country was praying for me and was caring for me."

Andre and his mother, Takoosh, now live in the United States where they use their freedom to continue ministry to Iran via satellite. They produce programs, movies, teaching materials and music to air in all the Persian-speaking nations like Iran, Tajikistan, Afghanistan and Pakistan.

Andre and his family really value your prayers as, following in the footsteps of Haik himself, they work to advance the kingdom in those countries where still today faith costs the most.

He concludes, "I learned we are one big family in Christ—and I think that was the number one thing which gave us courage and helped us heal."

RESPONSE:
Today I will accept the purposes of God in the martyrdom of His saints and pray for courage and healing among the members of the families left behind.

PRAYER:
Thank You, Lord, for the way you are using the Hovsepian family in ministry back to their original homeland and region. May their efforts greatly expand Your kingdom.

January 20

FIX YOUR EYES ON JESUS

...fixing our eyes on Jesus, the pioneer and perfecter of faith. For the joy set before him he endured the cross, scorning its shame, and sat down at the right hand of the throne of God. Consider him who endured such opposition from sinners, so that you will not grow weary and lose heart
Hebrews 12:2-3

The letter to the Hebrews was written to first century Jewish background believers who were being severely persecuted. Some were even considering giving up their faith in Jesus. The unknown author pens what many Bible scholars feel was originally a sermon about the superiority of Jesus over anyone else and everything else.

He slowly builds his case to culminate in the great faith chapter. In this chapter, he also points out that some great men and women of faith lived to see the fruit of their faith while many others—also men and women of faith—died prematurely because of persecution. Now in chapter twelve, the author makes what I think is his critical statement or main point of the letter.

How do we walk by faith? We walk by faith by **keeping our eyes fixed on Jesus**! Not fixed on our problems or difficult environment of opposition. Jesus was the pioneer and perfecter of faith. He endured opposition to the point of crucifixion. So we follow His example and we will also patiently endure because of the joy we know that is yet to come.

In a communist country, a Christian girl named Viorica was beaten harshly in school because she had invited her schoolmates to church. She fainted during the beating, and an ambulance had to take her to hospital. Two days passed before she regained consciousness. When she did, the doctor at her bedside said, "You poor girl, at last you've opened your eyes. All this time I've been thinking of the cruelty of the director who beat you like this. My heart has been bitter with hatred. I wish I could take revenge on him."

Viorica smiled. "There is no need to hate him," she replied. Jesus taught us to love everyone. Just before I opened my eyes, I saw Him and talked to Him. He asked me whether it still hurts. And He told me that in heaven I will receive a very beautiful crown, which is reserved only for those who have suffered for Him. He told me to pray for those who mistreated me, and to love them, because our influence will help them to give their lives to God and so become His children."

From the mouths of children! **Keep your eyes fixed on Jesus!**

RESPONSE:
Today I will take my eyes off my surroundings, my problems, my fears and my suffering. I will keep them fixed on Jesus my Lord.

PRAYER:
Lord Jesus, help me keep my focus on You and in so doing bring glory and honor to You.

January 21

ENDURE HARDSHIP AS DISCIPLINE

Endure hardship as discipline; God is treating you as his children. For what children are not disciplined by their father?...No discipline seems pleasant at the time, but painful. Later on, however, it produces a harvest of righteousness and peace for those who have been trained by it.
Hebrews 12: 7-11

As we see in Hebrews chapter twelve, once we "keep our eyes fixed on Jesus," we will be aware of how we should then live. Now he teaches us about the value of hardships and discipline that does not seem helpful but in the end produces a harvest of righteousness and peace.

Alexander was on his first research trip to Cuba for Open Doors. He asked a Cuban pastor what his needs were. He expected the response to itemize the many material needs that the churches in Cuba obviously lacked.

"The first thing we need is your prayers," he replied, "to know the Body of Christ is with us." Then he went on to list their tremendous need for Bibles, teaching aids, Sunday school materials and printing supplies. Then he concluded with the statement that they could use anything and everything.

"If you send us just a bar of soap, we'll be grateful," he confessed. "We'll praise God for it!"

Alexander says, "I felt a big lump in my throat as I thought of all the Bibles, literature and freedoms I enjoyed. Yet even with all my blessings, my testimony was not as strong. So I struggled to articulate my feelings. 'Pastor,' I said, 'I can only begin to sense and imagine the difficulties you have encountered.'"

The pastor's eyes became misty and he softly responded, "Oh yes brother, we have been through the most difficult years. Yet we don't fear persecution. As a matter of fact, we welcome it because it purifies us!"

Freddie Sun spent years in prison in China because of his Christian faith. Prison was literally a trial of fire for him. He worked in a factory making tee-joints from pig iron. Every day he loaded and unloaded the furnace which fired up to 2700 degrees Fahrenheit. In the midst of this hell on earth, God spoke to him. "I have put you in this high-temperature furnace. Don't worry—you won't melt. But your impurities will be removed so you can become a useful tee-joint!"

RESPONSE:
Today I will receive God's discipline with the awareness that it is refining me to be more like Jesus.

PRAYER:
Lord help me to accept hardship as Your discipline for my life. I look forward to the harvest of righteousness and peace.

January 22

LIVE IN PEACE AND HOLINESS

Make every effort to live in peace with everyone and to be holy; without holiness no one will see the Lord.
Hebrews 12:14

As we see in Hebrews chapter twelve, once we "keep our eyes fixed on Jesus," we will be aware of how we should then live. Now the writer teaches us about the value of peace and holiness. It is difficult to live in peace with others until you have made your peace with God.

Every morning, during weekends, 10-year-old Abdul James goes around from house to house in his small village in Zamboanga City. He sells *pandesal*, typical breakfast bread among Filipinos. As he makes his rounds, other kids bully him because he is a Christian from the Sama tribe.

"I just ignore them, because I want to be a peacemaker for *Isa* (Christ)," James said.

James and 33 other children attended the first-ever Open Doors' Kids' Peace Camp. It was perfect timing for James, because the camp was all about being a *peacemaker* for Jesus Christ.

Historically, the Sama tribal people have been most open to the gospel. Open Doors' work in the Southern Philippines began with believers among this group about a decade ago. But among their fellow Muslim tribes, the Sama people are regarded as low-class citizens, and for that, they are discriminated against. So, peacemaking is an important characteristic and skill that Open Doors would like to impress on the tender hearts of the Sama children. It is never too early to start sowing seeds of peace.

Quarrels within families were the top cause of trauma among the campers. This is especially true for children having only one Christian parent at home. Another source of quarrels was tribal differences. In this first Kids' Peace Camp, children from two tribal groups came together in one place, and nobody seemed to mind.

"They (the children) played, ate, talked, swam, took a bath, and slept together! For them, they are brothers and sisters; they are one in

Christ," reported a worker.

More than setting aside differences, the best demonstration of peacemaking is self-sacrifice. Jesus did it for us; the children at the Kids' Peace Camp did it for others.

Jomark Manias is 11 years old. He shared that he used to quarrel a lot with his younger brothers. During the camp, he and the others were treated to a meal at a popular local fast food restaurant. They ate burgers, fries, and ice cream. But Jomark did not eat his burger. Later, his parents shared that when young Jomark got home from the camp, he gave his burger to his younger brothers.

Sometimes, children understand what it means to be a peacemaker for Christ better than adults do.

RESPONSE:
Today I will live at peace with others and reveal God's holiness in my life.

PRAYER:
Pray for more believers of Muslim background to find peace with God and others.

January 23

THE ROOT OF BITTERNESS

See to it that no one falls short of the grace of God and that no bitter root grows up to cause trouble and defile many.
Hebrews 12:15

As we see in Hebrews chapter twelve, once we "keep our eyes fixed on Jesus," we will be aware of how we should then live. The writer now turns to the issue of a growing root of bitterness which defiles and causes trouble and disunity.

A group of believers in rural Hubei Province in China came to Christ as a result of listening to Christian radio programs. When a local woman was healed of appendicitis after prayer, two whole families converted to the way of Jesus enlarging their group to twenty. Five years later a Brother Chen arrived in the village on a sunny spring day. One believer shares this report:

Some said Brother Chen was "sent straight from God to our company." He said so too. Looking back over a year later, I think he was Satan's man. But who knows, I may be harsh in my judgment.

I remember that night so clearly. We were all gathered in my father's house. The gas lamp flickered strange shapes against the whitewashed walls, on which we had stenciled "JESUS IS THE WAY, THE TRUTH, AND THE LIFE."

I remember Brother Chen saying, "Jesus needs our gold to build our mansion in heaven…the more gold we give him now, the bigger your mansion will be."

Well, we were poor. And because we were poor, the idea of having a golden mansion in the afterlife was very tempting to us. We handed over all we owned: family heirlooms, money, some expensive textiles from a distant ancestor. One in our group even gave his motorcycle, which he had saved for years to buy. Anyway, after all the "gold" had been collected, Brother Chen said he had to go and "open the gate for us." He left, on the donated motorcycle.

He took most of our savings. He hasn't been back.

Now the fellowship is ruined. Some of our group believes he is coming back, and was indeed sent by God to help us know Jesus better. Others of us believe he was a deceiver. It has split my family. My father thinks Chen was a good man. The rest of the family thinks differently, but we dare not disagree with my father openly.

We still can't read the Bible very well. We really don't know that much about Jesus, to be honest. We know he has saved us, and healed a family member. But we know little else. Brother Chen's deceit has made me bitter.

RESPONSE:
Today I will not allow Satan to grow a root of bitterness in my life or in my fellowship.

PRAYER:
Lord, help new believers around the world to recognize Satan's deceitful tactics and the bitter root that will keep them in bondage.

January 24

BROTHERLY LOVE

Keep on loving one another as brothers and sisters.
Hebrews 13:1

As we see in Hebrews chapter twelve, once we "keep our eyes fixed on Jesus," we will be aware of how we should then live. The writer now turns to the issue of brotherly love and he uses the verb form of repeated action. Keep on loving, over and over. Jesus Himself said that this would be the sign to the world of true discipleship—love for one another.

In China a house church network leader was being pursued by the Public Security Bureau (PSB) due to his active ministry. He had to be on the run and couldn't go home because the PSB were waiting for him at his house.

His wife went through much emotional suffering since she didn't know where her husband was. Other believers were afraid to come to the meeting held at the house and even other co-workers didn't come near due to fear. The wife had no money and eventually ran out of food. That was the hardest time in her life.

In spite of the PSB officers standing outside, an elderly Christian lady approached the house and boldly entered. The wife was surprised and asked the elderly woman why she was willing to take the risk. The lady said she wasn't afraid because she knew the woman's husband was serving the Lord and she was also serving the same Lord. The old lady prepared some noodles for young wife and her child. The young wife was really impressed with this love. Also the old lady told her that many outside were praying for them so this also brought tremendous strength and encouragement as they continued to suffer isolation.

Another house church leader in China spent time in prison. He wrote to his fellowship, "It is because of your prayers that I could go through the most difficult times while in prison. My mother, who also prayed for me every day, knew that there were many brothers and sisters who did the same for her son and that she was not alone. She too, would like to express her thanks to those who prayed for me.

"Following my release, I spent two weeks with my whole family. My daughter shared that she thought I was a bad person because she had seen the policeman arrest me right before her eyes. She was very angry with me until the day she received a card from a fellow Christian. In the card were the words, 'Your father is a hero for he has suffered for Christ.' Immediately all her anger dissipated and she became very proud of having a father who is a hero and willing to suffer for Christ."

RESPONSE:
Today I will make an extra effort to show love to all Christian brothers and sisters.

PRAYER:
Help me, Lord, to make love for the brethren a daily repeated action, for Your glory!

January 25

HOSPITALITY TO ANGELS

Do not forget to show hospitality to strangers, for by so doing some people have shown hospitality to angels without knowing it.
Hebrews 13:2

As we see in Hebrews chapter twelve, once we "keep our eyes fixed on Jesus," we will be aware of how we should then live. The writer now turns to the issue of entertaining strangers. After reminding us to keep on loving each other, he now shares that love should also be extended to the strangers in our midst. They could possibly even be angels. I'm sure the Jewish background believers hearing or reading this letter would immediately hearken back to Father Abraham when three strangers passed by one day. He extended full hospitality to them only to discover they were heavenly beings on a special mission.

Aunty Alice was the wife of Pastor Allen Yuan in China, known for her gracious hospitality to everyone who entered her door right until her death in the summer of 2010. Pastor Allen was imprisoned for twenty-one years and eight months for refusing to join the government controlled Three Self Patriotic Movement—the official Protestant Church under the communist regime.

Alice had five children and her mother-in-law to care for during those many years of her husband's absence. She was also branded a "counter-revolutionary" and thus could also secure a hard-labor job moving construction rubble from one site to another by heavy push wagons. This still did not generate enough resources to provide for the all the family's needs.

One night her mother-in-law informed her, "Alice, there is no rice left to feed the children tomorrow morning!" Alice was angry and complained to the Lord that He had promised to care for her. She opened her Bible and her eyes fell on the Matthew Scripture when Jesus says that if God cares for the birds, will He not also care for you? Her heart was rebuked. She asked forgiveness from the Lord and went to sleep peacefully.

The next morning before six o'clock there was a knock on the door. Alice slipped on her house coat and shuffled to the door. There stood a stranger with a big box in her hands. As was her custom, Alice invited her in. She stoked up the fire in the central heating oven and put the kettle on for tea. But the stranger just walked to the table, set down the box and began to leave.

Alice said, "Wait a minute. What's your name?" The lady replied, "I have no name. Just thank God for that box!" And the stranger disappeared.

With trembling hands Alice opened the box to find rice, meat and vegetables. Also in it was an envelope with more money than two month's salary. She knew it was truly an angelic visit.

RESPONSE:
Today I will be open to entertaining strangers realizing that God may be in the relationship.

PRAYER:
Thank You Lord for the way You work. Help me be an active participant in Your plans.

January 26

REMEMBER THOSE IN PRISON

Continue to remember those in prison as if you were together with them in prison...
Hebrews 13:3a

As we see in Hebrews chapter twelve, once we "keep our eyes fixed on Jesus," we will be aware of how we should then live. The writer now turns to the issue of remembering brothers and sisters in prison.

Matta Boush, an outspoken evangelist in South Sudan was arrested on political charges under questionable circumstances. He was given a sentence of thirty years at a local military prison. Many people around the world prayed for him, and for his family at home.

He asked prison authorities for permission to hold prayer meetings. At first they declined, saying, "We already have a mosque; you should go there." But Boush persisted and eventually the authorities relented. For the first prayer meeting, only six people showed up. In a few weeks, more people were going to the prayer meeting than the mosque.

A few years later, he was transferred to another city prison. As he had in the first prison, he asked for, and received permission to conduct prayer meetings. Again he was told to limit his work to non-Muslims, yet as he continued to minister to non-Muslims, they, in turn would talk to Muslims. The result was that during his five years of ministry in that prison, he helped lead between 150 and 200 people to Christ.

Transferred again to another prison, he was able to help build a prison chapel there. After several months, prison officials told him that he did not really belong in prison, so he was given the freedom to leave the prison by day and return by night. Boush was glad to get out and meet with friends he had in Khartoum, but soon he realized that he could not effectively witness to his fellow prisoners if he had freedoms they were denied. He told the prison officials he would no longer go out. He knew it was not God's time.

Later, he was offered private air-cooled sleeping quarters (summer

51

temperatures exceed 40 degrees Celsius). But Bousch's most productive time for witnessing was at night, so he declined the offer. He saw fruit for denying his own comfort to do what he felt God was calling him to do. In ten months, 200 more people came to the Lord in the prison.

Without warning, he was one day released early and returned to his family. Matta Boush's enemies had hoped to steal his life from him by throwing him into prison, but God had given him a true "life" sentence: to share the hope of eternal life that comes through Jesus Christ.

RESPONSE:
Today I will keep my eyes fixed on Jesus remembering to identify with my brothers and sisters in prison for their faith.

PRAYER:
Lord, meet the needs today of Christians around the world in prison for their faith in You. Help them to glorify You in their situation. Bless their family members waiting patiently at home.

January 27

THOSE WHO ARE MISTREATED

Continue to remember those...who are mistreated as if you yourselves were suffering.
Hebrew 13:3b

As we see in Hebrews chapter twelve, once we "keep our eyes fixed on Jesus," we will be aware of how we should then live. The writer now turns to the issue of remembering those who are mistreated. And again he adds an empathic and personalized application. Remember them as if you yourself were the one suffering!

Dr. Jan Pit often shared the poignant story of a young Christian in Egypt he met named Timothy. Through the Christian radio broadcasts of Trans World Radio Timothy was introduced to Jesus whom he received into his heart and began to follow.

But when he shared his new faith with his Muslim family, they reacted so strongly that he was told to leave home and never come back. After several years of living with other Christians, he decided to try and make contact with his family again. On his mother's birthday, he bought some flowers and walked to his family's home. When he knocked on the door, his mother opened it.

"Happy birthday, Mother!" Timothy said. "I brought you these flowers because I love you!"

Timothy's mother turned to him with a stern look and said, "I don't know who you are!" And she slammed the door.

Timothy said to Jan with tears streaming down his face, "I don't have a family any more. Will you be my family?"

Today you can be a surrogate family for Christians treated this way. You can also remember to pray for Christians like fifteen-year-old Shirin who has gone through a difficult time of persecution.

When Shirin became a believer he also met with much opposition from his relatives. They shouted at him, threatened him and finally gave him a choice: Jesus or the family.

He chose Jesus and then left his home. He was living on the streets; alone, hungry and very poor. A local Christian saw him, had pity on him and took him into his house.

Shirin loves God with all his heart! His mother and father are in prison now for being drug addicts, but he is witnessing to many about God's great love which has been revealed to him.

RESPONSE:
Today I will remember those believers who are mistreated and do everything possible to assist them in the way I would want assistance if I was in their shoes.

PRAYER:
Lord grant me empathy and a giving heart for those being severely persecuted today.

⚜ January 28 ⚜

SATAN'S CHANGING TACTICS

...We declare God's wisdom, a mystery that has been hidden and that God destined for our glory before time began. None of the rulers of this age understood it, for if they had, they would not have crucified the Lord of glory.
1 Corinthians 2:7-8

Today's devotional comes from our founder and friend, Brother Andrew:

Have you ever noticed the strategy Satan used throughout Old Testament history? His attacks were aimed at preventing the birth of the Messiah at Bethlehem, but, once Jesus was born, Satan's tactics changed somewhat. In some instances, he tried to kill Jesus before the Lord could reach the cross. At other times, Satan engineered numerous attempts to discredit Him—to cause Him to stumble or to sin.

But Satan met defeat at the cross. He failed to understand God's strategy, and his final blunder actually forced events so that Jesus, though innocent, was condemned to die. The Apostle Paul noted that Satan did not understand this in 1 Corinthians 2:8.

Since that time, Satan's tactics have changed. He's still concerned about preventing the Word—the Word that was with God and is God (John 1:1)—from reaching people who are under Satan's dominion. His attack is now two-pronged.

First Satan concentrates on the life and name of Jesus which each and every believer bears as the Lord's representative. I believe it is important for Christians undergoing persecution to realize the attack they are under is actually directed not at them, but at the life of Jesus in them, a life which they have power to transmit to others.

Satan will make every effort to discredit you, to frighten you and to silence your witness in order that the new life in you stops with you. Sometimes Satan overreaches himself, just as he did at the cross, and sends a believer to a martyr's grave but that life lives on in other believers who continue to bear witness more gloriously and triumphantly than ever.

That the church not only survives, but grows under such persecution has been demonstrated beautifully by the church in China. After missionaries were forced to leave in 1950, and all ties were cut with the body of Christ, believers were put through the horrible experience of Mao's Cultural Revolution. Christians were killed or imprisoned, Bibles burned, and the remaining believers scattered all over China. The attack was clearly on the life and name of Jesus as manifested in believer's lives.

As these sufferers scattered, they took the life of Jesus with them, and just as was the case with the early believers in Jerusalem, *"Those who were scattered went about preaching the Word"* (Acts 8:4). Now we see the harvest in China as millions of Christians are identified, meeting together for fellowship and worship in remote provinces…

I want others to have the one who makes me happy—Jesus.

RESPONSE:
Today I will be aware of Satan's attempts to silence my witness for Jesus and resist him!

PRAYER:
Thank You, Lord, for the way You bring good from the evil tactics of the enemy of our soul. Help me stand strong against his attack on the life and name of Jesus in me.

January 29

SATAN'S ATTACK ON THE BIBLE

For you have been born again, not of perishable seed, but of imperishable, through the living and enduring word of God. For, "All people are like grass, and all their glory is like the flowers of the field; the grass withers and the flowers fall, but the word of the Lord endures forever."
1 Peter 1:23-25a

Brother Andrew continues his teaching on Satan's strategic attacks:

The second prong of Satan's attack is on the written word of God. He has historically tried to prevent Christians from having access to the Bible.

Satan understands the power of the Word of God. At the temptation of Jesus, he even made a sly attempt to use Scripture (actually misapplying it) to deflect Jesus from His true mission (Luke 4:1-3). Twisting Scripture is still a favorite tactic of Satan, and we believers need to know the Word so we can respond, just as Jesus did, with a well-applied "It is written…"

Peter recognized the significant role the Word has in our salvation. In his epistle to Christians passing through "fiery trials" he gives the words of encouragement in today's Scripture above.

Now you can understand my life's passion to distribute the Bible, even in places where its importation or distribution is prohibited. Because I've gone around the world preaching that message, many people assume that I must have been the first "God's smuggler." Nothing could be further from the truth.

I personally believe that the first Bible smuggler probably was Timothy, the man Paul looked upon as his son in the gospel. This young man of delicate health, but of great spirituality and loyalty, was converted in Paul's first campaign at Lystra.

At the end of his life, when Paul was in prison in Rome, he looked to Timothy for comfort. In a letter to him, Paul asked his friend to bring his books to the prison the next time he visited.

In 2 Timothy 4:13 it becomes clear Paul was requesting that scrolls of Old Testament Scriptures be brought to him for further study. But how could Timothy get them into Rome and into the jail when, by that time, Christians has already become an outlawed sect? The only possible way would have been to smuggle them in with other items.

Billy Graham, in his book *Hoofbeats*, suggests that John the apostle had to write his Revelation secretly, while closely guarded by the Romans. The parchment manuscript pages would have been smuggled off the island of Patmos and Christian volunteers copy them for the churches...

This world is an enemy-occupied territory filled with souls to whom Christ holds rightful claim. Under Christ's command, we invade countries by any means that will help us to get in with the Word of God...

Today I want others to have what makes me grow spiritually—the Bible.

RESPONSE:
Today I will make every effort to ensure that the Bible is available to everyone to read and practice.

PRAYER:
Pray for many believers around the world still waiting for their first personal Bible.

January 30

COMMANDOS FOR JESUS

Jesus Christ is the same yesterday and today and forever.
Hebrews 13:8

Brother Andrew continues his teaching on Satan's strategic attacks:

Our methods of taking the Bible into places where it is not available nor permitted is actually very close to the New Testament concept of transmitting the Word of God. In our Western nations, we enjoy the rare privilege of seeing people come to us for the message. We even wait for them to come and we put up special buildings for them to come to. Then we open the doors and welcome them with a smile.

Such methods make me feel that we've responded very wrongly to Jesus' announced intention to make us "fishers of men." We have made a beautiful net of our church buildings and have set it up on the shore waiting for the fish to jump in of their own accord!

Our pattern of waiting for people to come to us is exactly the reverse of the Great Commission. Because we have done it this way for so long we have even begun to question the original way that God intended for it to be. What a topsy-turvy world we live in!

We must have the courage, the Holy Spirit boldness, to live a life that is more revolutionary than that of any non-Christian faith. The Lord will give us the courage to work like commandos if we want Him to, but we must go and carry out His commission.

The command has been given by the risen Lord and the call is clear: prepare for spiritual battle! Let's go in Jesus' name and do it! We can do it because ever since He first issued the orders, Jesus has given to every generation the ability, the strength, the manpower, and the opportunity to do it.

Although every generation has failed in some way, the first generation almost accomplished it. Almost! In our generation we don't need to fail. We can fulfill the commission because Jesus Christ is the same yesterday, today and forever. He who holds all authority in heaven and on earth has authorized us to advance on His enemy everywhere, including across every "closed" border. He still endues us with the power of the Holy Spirit that we might be witnesses to the uttermost parts of the earth.

"Awake and strengthen what remains" (Revelation 3:2). That is the watchword of our ministry to fellow-believers in China, Africa, Latin America and the Middle East. What constrains us is the love of Christ; for love, the Word of God tells us, is the fulfillment of all divine commands. I want others to have the one who makes me happy—Jesus. I want others to have what makes me grow spiritually—the Bible.

The God of miracles will bring it to pass!

RESPONSE:
Today I commit to going—not waiting—to carry out Jesus' commission and be a fisher of men in the power of His Holy Spirit.

PRAYER:
Lord, give me the boldness to advance against our enemy everywhere—even in so-called "closed" countries.

✠ January 31 ⚔

*But thanks be to God! He gives us the victory through
our Lord Jesus Christ.*

1 Corinthians 15:57

The five-year-old soccer goalie of Team One was an outstanding
athlete, but he was no match for three or four on Team Two who were
also very good and they began to score on him. The goalie gave it
everything he had, recklessly throwing his body in front of incoming
balls, trying valiantly to stop them.

After the third goal was scored against him, he could see it was
no use; he couldn't stop them. He didn't quit, but he became quietly
desperate. Futility was written all over him.

After the fourth goal, the little boy needed help so badly, and there
was no help to be had. He retrieved the ball from the net and handed
it to the referee. Then he fell to his knees and cried the tears of the
helpless and broken-hearted.

His father ran onto the field and said, "Scotty, I'm so proud of you.
You were great out there. I want everybody to know that you are my
son."

"Daddy," the boy sobbed, "I couldn't stop them. I tried, Daddy, I
tried and tried, and they scored on me."

"Scotty, it doesn't matter how many times they scored on you.
You're my son, and I'm proud of you. I want you to go back out there
and finish the game. I know you want to quit, but you can't. And,
son, you're going to get scored on again, but it doesn't matter. Go on,
now." The little guy ran back on to the field and they scored two more
times. But it was okay.

I get scored on every day. I try so hard. I recklessly throw my body
in every direction. I fume with rage. I struggle with temptation and
sin with every ounce of my being - and Satan laughs. And he scores
again, and the tears come, and I go to my knees - sinful, convicted,
helpless. And my Father rushes right out on the field—right in front of
the whole jeering, laughing world—and he picks me up, and he hugs
me and he says:

"Son, I'm so proud of you. You were great out there. I want

everybody to know that you are my son. And because I control the outcome of this game, I declare you - The Winner!"

RESPONSE:
Today I will rejoice in my Father's love and support. I will not give up as the battle rages.

PRAYER:
Thank You Lord for Your love and for declaring me a winner!

February 1

SATAN'S TACTIC OF GOSSIP

He who does what is sinful is of the devil, because the devil has been sinning from the beginning. The reason the Son of God appeared was to destroy the devil's work.
1 John 3:8

China's house church leaders representing more than ten million members met some years ago for a conference to discuss the main problems facing their churches. They ranked their top three problems, and came up with strategies to solve them. At the top of the list was gossip. Leader after leader told stories of how their ministries had been compromised by this subtle sin. One house church leader from Henan Province shared the following experience:

"I went into an area to lead Bible studies for coworkers and they wouldn't let me into the house where we were to hold the seminar. I asked them through the closed door what the problem was, but they wouldn't tell me. They just told me to go away. It was winter and I went a little ways outside the town, knowing I must start a fire to sleep beside or I would freeze to death. I wondered what on earth could have made those brothers and sisters turn me away on such a cold night without a word of explanation.

"But a brother took pity on me and brought me secretly to his home. I eventually pried the truth out of him. The leaders in the area had received an anonymous letter denouncing me as a 'lover of many women.' Try as hard as I might, I could not get them to listen to me or let me see the letter. Later in another part of the country, I learned the letter had been sent by a brother I had disciplined for moral laxity, and he had sent it out of spite.

"I went to him and he repented. He sent another letter, but because the first one was unsigned, they didn't believe him. Both of us offered to go there, but we weren't welcomed. The testimony of the church was ruined. I still have to explain myself wherever I go. It's a victory for the devil.

"I went with the offending brother out to the countryside and told him to pluck a chicken. We walked along while he did; the wind blew the feathers far over the fields. When he was finished, he asked, 'What now?' I told him, 'Pick up every feather, and put it back on the chicken.' He said, 'That's impossible.' I replied, 'You are right. It is impossible, just as the damage your words have done cannot be repaired.' "

The house church leaders pledged to be more loving, and to hold more face-to-face meetings with each other to minimize the sin of gossip in the future.

RESPONSE:
Today I will thwart Satan's temptations to offend others by committing the sin of gossip.

PRAYER:
Lord, enable me to stand strong today in the face of all that Satan tries to throw at me.

February 2

⚜ SATAN'S TACTIC OF PRIDE ⚜

God opposes the proud but gives grace to the humble.
1 Peter 5:5

We each have to come to terms with Satan's deadliest tactic, which the Bible calls *pride*. Ever since the Garden of Eden, Satan has promulgated The Great Lie: ***"You will be like God"*** (Genesis 3:5b). We all must learn to overcome pride, which was Satan's own initial sin and which is his pervasive and repetitive tactic against us.

In Proverbs 6:17, ***"haughty eyes"*** are first on the list of the seven things that are an "abomination" to God. Proverbs 27:2 adds, ***"Let another praise you, and not your own mouth."*** Christ spoke of pride in Luke 18:14 when He instructs, ***"Everyone who exalts himself will be humbled, and he who humbles himself will be exalted."*** Over and over again, we are reminded in the Bible of God's utter disdain for a prideful spirit.

Why does God have so much to say about this issue? Because, ultimately, a prideful person is saying, "I don't need God. I can do it on my own." As our Creator and Sustainer, God has the perfect plan laid out before us. Attempting to "go it alone" will only lead us down a path of self-destruction. No one knows that better than God—He has seen pride destroy the lives of His creations throughout time.

In the Old Testament we see an example of this in the life of King Nebuchadnezzar (Daniel 4:28-37) until he acknowledged the Most High God. We also see it in the life of King Belshazzar, who saw the handwriting on the wall and received judgment because of his pride (Daniel 5: 22-31).

In the New Testament, the Pharisees, filled with self-righteousness, denied the work of Christ, even as He stood before them. The Apostle Paul warned the Corinthians to ***"not take pride in one man over against another"*** (1 Corinthians 4:6). Peter repeats the warning about pride from Proverbs 3:34.

Pride is so devastating because of its deceptiveness. C. S. Lewis said, "A proud man is always looking down on things and people;

65

and, of course, as long as you're looking down, you can't see something that's above you." We may easily point out pride in the life of someone else, completely oblivious to the stranglehold that pride may have in our own lives. Pride causes us to focus solely on being "better" than someone else. Don't compare yourself to others; compare yourself to Christ. Remember where you came from, and recall what God has saved you from.

When all else fails, God may allow adversity into our lives. Nothing gets our attention better than going through a difficult time. He allows these experiences in order to filter out pride, causing us to return our focus on Him. As much as our prideful spirit may disagree, we cannot live a fulfilling life without God. Simply put, when God is out, pride is in!

RESPONSE:
Today I will keep my eyes fixed on Jesus and steer clear of pride's deceptiveness.

PRAYER:
Lord, I need Your help to keep focused on You and avoid pride's stranglehold.

February 3

SATAN'S TACTIC OF GUILT

If we confess our sins, he is faithful and just and will forgive us our sins and purify us from all unrighteousness.
1 John 1:9

Satan's internal tactics against us fall into two broad categories: **deceit** and **intimidation**. He continually accuses us in our own hearts to bring feelings of guilt and failure into our lives. True guilt is that which comes from disobeying God. One reason that this approach is so effective in crushing the witness of a saint is because it is partially true. We all have failed the Lord. None of us has triumphed in power over every circumstance as we could and should have done. So when Satan accuses us, we know in our hearts that there is much truth in his accusations.

But God has provided us with a way to cleanse ourselves of this sin and the guilt that accompanies it. When we realize we have failed the Lord, we confess it and He forgives and cleanses us. Once we have confessed it, the sin is gone, and our feelings of guilt are relieved.

David's experience shows us God's method of dealing with sin: conviction, acknowledgment, confession, seeking forgiveness, receiving forgiveness, praise and joyful service (Psalm 51; Psalm 32:3,4; 2 Samuel 12:1-13). Once sin is dealt with in this manner, true guilt will disappear.

The revolutionary army told a young Christian in Chad, Africa that he must submit to old animistic tribal rituals. They wanted to destroy Christianity and stimulate patriotism and loyalty by reviving the ancient pagan customs. The leaders of the churches of the area agreed together that Christians must refuse to participate in the animistic rituals.

When the young man refused and was beaten, he stood firm in his faith. But when the authorities stripped him naked and beat him in front of his mother, sisters and other young ladies, his courage failed and he permitted them to perform the pagan rituals.

Then he felt terrible. He had failed the Lord. His guilt was heavy. Satan tried to convince him that the Lord could never again accept him. But he knew the Scriptural promises of God, and he confessed his sin. The Lord forgave him and restored his joy.

He began to publicly witness to his neighbors and he was arrested. The authorities demanded that he denounce Christ or be buried alive. This time, his faith was strong and he refused to deny Christ. He was beaten and thrown into prison to await execution, but his faith grew stronger and the Lord delivered him. The oppressive government was overthrown and he was released.

RESPONSE:
Today I will confess my sin and receive God's forgiveness from the guilt so that Satan cannot use this tactic against me.

PRAYER:
Pray that this simple and straight-forward process of relieving guilt through confession of sin will be the experience of every believer so Satan loses one more tactic today.

February 4

SHUN FEAR AND COURAGEOUSLY PRESS ON

But even if you should suffer for what is right, you are blessed. "Do not fear their threats; do not be frightened."
1 Peter 3:14

One of the major tactics of Satan is to use difficult situations to create **fear** in us and thus immobilize our witness. For example, during the 9/11 attack in USA, Heather Mercer and Dayna Curry were being held in a prison in Afghanistan. In an interview with *Christianity Today* magazine on the tenth anniversary of 9/11, Heather Mercer said, "There is not a day that goes by that I don't think about it. God sent me to prison to set me free. I don't think I realized how much fear I actually had in my life until I had to confront some of my deepest, darkest fears. When I first set out to go to Afghanistan, I knew it might cost me my life to reach Muslims with the love of Jesus. Then I had this opportunity to face that fear of, 'What would I do if someone tried to kill me for sharing the gospel?' God made Himself known in such a profound way that now, what do I have to fear?"[3]

In Papua New Guinea (PNG), Wycliffe's Sue Ambrose was out for a walk on February 4th, 2009. She was talking to the Lord about people, issues and life. As she continued her walk, she read memory verses from three Gospels that say, *"Whoever desires to save his life will lose it, but whoever loses his life for my sake will find it."*

The slapping sound of bare feet running on packed earth causes her to turn around to see a crazed PNG man charge her with a large machete-like knife raised murderously above his head. After a quick altercation and feeling as though she was dying, Sue was rushed to the medical clinic where friends and co-workers were shocked to see her in such grave condition: many abrasions; a damaged hand; a puncture wound near the sternum just below the diaphragm and lungs; and the knife still stuck fast in her hip.

3   http://www.christianitytoday.com/ct/2011/septemberweb-only/heather-mercer-interview.html

Sue was remarkably calm through the process and felt no pain. Once stabilized, she was transferred to medical facilities in Australia. While in hospital, God gave Sue a clear vision of an angel, "A big warrior kind of guy that was eight or ten feet tall with his sword raised, saying, 'No, that is enough! I am not going to let you kill her.'" Sue says, "That really opened my eyes to the whole spiritual realm; that this man was part of Satan's attacks on us, on the training centre and on the work of SIL."

Two and a half weeks after being air-lifted out of the country, Sue returned to her ministry in PNG. The Wycliffe magazine, *Word Alive* reported: That seemingly simple act proves to be a strong counterstrike to the enemy—a living sermon calling others to shun fear and courageously press on in their respective callings. "I don't think that I ever considered not going back," says Sue. "God has given us the strength to return and it has spoken volumes to people." Sue models an attitude that we all must grasp, the article concluded. Let fear not rule![4]

RESPONSE:
Today I will not allow the enemy to use the tactic of fear against me.

PRAYER:
Thank You, Lord, for the wonderful examples of fearlessness shown by Your people today.

4   Craig Pulsifer, "Let Fear Not Rule," *Word Alive* (Wycliffe Bible Translators, Fall 2011), pp. 33-37.

February 5

FREEDOM IN CHRIST

It is for freedom that Christ has set us free. Stand firm,
then, and do not let yourselves be burdened again
by a yoke of slavery.
Galatians 5:1

Claiming one's freedom in Christ is central to the faith and fighting fear. For example, in China when authorities threaten house church leaders with the confiscation of their property, they reply, "If you want this farm, you need to talk to Jesus, as I have given it to Him. But if you do take it, I am free to trust God for my daily bread."

When Chinese Christians are threatened with torture, they claim they are "free to trust God for healing."

When they are imprisoned, they proclaim that they are then "free to share their faith with other prisoners."

When Chinese believers are told they will be killed, they state that then they are "free to be with Jesus."

The country of Bulgaria is plagued by a prevailing spirit of fear. Even many Christians suffer from it. It's a country that was occupied by the Turks for five centuries (1396-1878) followed by several wars. After 1946, it was ruled with an iron hand by the Communists. This long story of repression and sufferings passed on for generations from the parents to the children has left durable marks in their spirits which results in a deep anguish. It acts like a spiritual yoke and creates, as a consequence, the fear of taking any initiative. In families, this anguish has been passed on through generations like a legacy. It has become a vicious circle from which it is difficult to escape. A popular Bulgarian proverb says, "Fear has big eyes!"

Our co-workers were thus surprised when they delivered Bibles to Bulgarian Pastor Simeon Popov. He appeared radiant and serene. The absence of anguish could be explained as much by the action of the Holy Spirit, who releases us from yokes, as by the influence of his study time in Germany. According to the pastor, he not only studied theology, but he also learned to claim his freedom in Christ.

71

So this draws me to a significant conclusion and principle: **If you are a Christian, filled with the Holy Spirit, and have lost your fear of death, you are unstoppable until God calls you home to heaven!**

RESPONSE:
Today I will claim my freedom in Christ and live in the power He gives me.

PRAYER:
Thank You Lord for freedom from fear that comes only from You.

February 6

CONQUERING THE FEAR OF DEATH

I have been crucified with Christ and I no longer live,
but Christ lives in me. The life I live in the body, I live by
faith in the Son of God, who loved me and gave himself
for me.
Galatians 2:20

Fear of dying is the number one universal fear for human beings. Virtually every fear has a relationship to death and a connection to dying. For example, why are we afraid of flying? The plane may crash and we may die. Here are seven scriptural principles that enable us to conquer our fear of death:

1. God is in control. Read Psalm 91. (Mark 4:35-41; Phil 4:6-7)
2. Focus on fearing God and dying to self. (Acts 5:29; Galatians 2:20)
3. We are strangers and pilgrims on this earth. (Hebrews 10:32+)
4. God always brings good from evil. (Genesis 50:20)
5. The enemy can only harm our body, not our soul. (Matthew 10:28)
6. Absent from the body is to be present with the Lord. (2 Corinthians 5:8; 2 Timothy 2:11-12)
7. There is a crown of life for the faithful to death. (Revelation 2:10)

Co-workers had just finished an SSTS seminar on the island of Timor when a young pastor suddenly jumped up and proclaimed before all his colleagues "Now I am ready to die for Jesus!" These were no idle words. Every single pastor attending the seminar was directly or indirectly impacted by the massacres on the island of Ambon. Many of their churches had been burned and several had lost loved ones in the attacks on Christians.

As the meeting concluded, our colleague saw that young pastor making his way towards him. "Your being here has inspired me to go out and share the gospel in other areas," he announced.

"I am happy to hear that brother. Where has the Lord called you to?" he enquired.

"To Ambon!"

"My brother, are you sure. This is like signing your own death certificate. You know that most Christians are fleeing the massacre and you want to return?"

His response was simple and without pretense. "If I don't go back to tell the people about Jesus, who will do it? I am willing to give my life for Jesus!"

RESPONSE:
Today I will live prepared to die, and die prepared to live!

PRAYER:
When I fear you, Lord, I fear nothing else—even death. Today I pray for those who do not fear You and thus fear everything else—especially death.

February 7

⚜ BE NOT AFRAID ⚜

I sought the Lord and he answered me; He delivered me from all my fears.
Psalm 34:4

The one positive fear that the Bible endorses is the fear of God – loving, obedient worship! Wise Solomon said fearing God is the beginning of wisdom. It was Oswald Chambers who added, "The remarkable thing about fearing God is that, when you fear God, you fear nothing else; whereas, if you do not fear God, you fear everything else."

In Eritrea, Helen Berhane was frequently tortured during her almost three years in the shipping container prison. In spite of that she had no fear. Once when interrogated for teaching the Bible to the guards outside her cell, she replied:

"I am always looking for opportunities to talk about my faith and to spread the news about Jesus. I am not ashamed of the gospel and I will talk to anyone and to everyone. Jesus does not just want me to tell the prisoners about him, he wants me to tell the guards too. Even if the president were to visit the prison, I would tell him about the gospel.

"I am not afraid of you. You can do what you want to me, but ultimately all you can do is kill my body, you cannot touch my soul. You cannot even kill me unless it is God's will that I should die."[5]

Her persecutors had no answer and returned her to her shipping container.

Karim from Algeria lived with fear all his life in spite of his great accomplishments. He says:

By the time I was 28 years old, I had achieved everything a man could desire. But my heart was crying out, "What is the meaning of life."

---

5   Helen Berhane, *Song of the Nightingale* (Colorado Springs: Authentic Media, 2009), p. 75.

So I prayed a simple prayer to God…and I said, "You, my God who created me…today I make you responsible for the outcome of my life. I will give you 15 days, and if in that time you don't change my life, I will kill myself and you will be responsible."

At exactly midnight I woke up sweating. I was afraid.

A man grabbed me by the left shoulder. He said to me, "Karim, do not fear…I am here…The Karim from this morning is dead. You are a new Karim now."

And as he finished speaking, I realized it was Jesus.

I was overwhelmed by a peace I cannot describe. It was a new birth for me.

God is with us and His promises are stronger than fear!

RESPONSE:
Today I will live in the fear of God so that I will not fear anything or anyone else.

PRAYER:
Pray that all Christians in fearful situations today will have the attitude of trust in the Lord and not fear for their lives.

February 8

DOUBT AND FEAR

But as for me, I keep watch for the Lord, I wait in hope for God my Savior; my God will hear me. Do not gloat over me my enemy! Though I have fallen, I will rise. Though I sit in darkness, the Lord will be my light. Because I have sinned against him, I will bear the Lord's wrath, until he pleads my case and establishes my right. He will bring me out into the light; I will see his justice.

Micah 7:7-9

Chinese Pastor Wang Ming-dao was under tremendous pressure after his first arrest in the mid-1950's. He was promised release from prison and return to his pulpit if he would just "preach for the government." In his mind this would be lying and he was certain he could not live a hypocritical life.

Pastor Wang was firm in his resolve, until he heard that his beloved wife, Debra, had also been arrested and was in grave danger. He heard that she was not eating properly and was growing critically weak because of the poor food she was receiving in prison. She would not survive if something were not done. This news so disturbed him that he broke and agreed with his persecutors that he would preach "a lie" and join the government-controlled church.

His plan was to get his wife to safety with her mother and then he would commit suicide. He reportedly wandered the streets murmuring "I am Peter...I am Peter..." and his heart sickness began to affect his body.

When the authorities realized that he would not compromise himself by preaching in the government-controlled church, Pastor Wang and wife, Debra, were re-arrested. She received a fifteen-year sentence and he life imprisonment.

Early in this second imprisonment, God brought these verses from Micah 7:7-9 to his mind, which he had memorized at the age of twenty-one.

Wang Ming-dao was no longer afraid—for himself or his wife. He

77

was finally released in 1980 at eighty years of age—very frail, nearly blind and all-but-deaf. He had served over twenty-three years in prison. His wife Debra had been released three years earlier for health reasons. For the remaining eleven years of his life he was a great encouragement to the church in China as well as the many foreign visitors he and Debra entertained.

RESPONSE:
Today I will not give in to Satan's tactics of doubt and fear. I will concentrate on the greater cost to Jesus of my redemption.

PRAYER:
Thank you Lord for the reminder that persecuted Christians are not super-heroes but they show us how our failure must turn into repentance and renewal with deeper dependence on You and not into self-condemnation.

February 9

THE MEANING OF CRISIS

For God did not give us a spirit of timidity, but a spirit of power, of love and of self-discipline.
2 Timothy 1:7

Satan delights in causing "panic attacks" in a crisis situation. The Chinese have an interesting lesson in the two characters chosen for their word **"crisis"**. One character is **danger** and the other is **opportunity**. The inference is that in every crisis experience, both elements are present. So a crisis is a dangerous situation presenting an opportunity. When you focus on just the danger, you become paralyzed by fear. Focusing on the opportunity, however, enables you to fly with wings of faith. It is we, ourselves, who choose on which of the two we will focus.

Similar reasons for our personal fears also keep us from being the voice of God in a fallen world on behalf of His church. There is a time for Christians to speak out forcefully against the injustices and sinfulness of our own society and culture. This is especially true in situations where we can help our brothers and sisters who suffer. But fear can keep us tongue-tied. As the church, we must learn to speak out and not be cowed by fear.

As mentioned before, Pastor Simeon Popov was a recognized authority figure among the evangelical Christians of Bulgaria. Although his church was officially registered, the police were constantly watching his activities because he didn't agree with the restrictions imposed by the authorities, in particular those concerning evangelizing.

One day at a secret river baptism early in the morning, the group was all ready in their white gowns when Simeon saw some "shadows" moving behind the bushes. He realized immediately that they were agents of the secret police spying on them. One of them, who was awkwardly hidden, had a camera.

Without hesitating, Simeon called to him, "Hey, you. Come a bit closer!" The man sheepishly approached. "Since you have a camera, why don't you take a picture of our group?" The police officer was so surprised that he just did it without asking questions. Then the ceremony of baptism took place as planned! A few days later, the secret police agent was even fair enough to give the photograph to Simeon who kept it and made copies.

Remember, when we are fearful, we can claim the promise of Scripture: *"For God did not give us a spirit of timidity, but a spirit of power, of love and of self-discipline"* (2 Timothy 1:7).

RESPONSE:
Today I will not walk in fear but in the power of God's Holy Spirit.

PRAYER:
Pray for boldness for pastors today in countries where Satan tries to bind them with fear.

February 10

BOLD WITNESS NOT IN VAIN

Therefore, my dear brothers, stand firm. Let nothing move you. Always give yourselves fully to the work of the Lord, because you know that your labor in the Lord is not in vain.

1 Corinthians 15:58

Lung Singh was a spirit worshipper and opium addict for forty-five years in the little Southeast Asian country of Laos. When he turned to Christ, he became a powerhouse for the Lord. Dr. Jan Pit shares about the day he baptized Lung Singh:

"I'll never forget how, after coming up out of the waters, he began singing, 'I have decided to follow Jesus,' Then he pointed to the ripples spreading out in the water and said, 'Brother Jan, there goes my old life. All the old things have passed away. It's gone. Everything now is new.'

"Still soaking wet, he clambered onto the bank on the side of the famous Mekong River and knelt down. 'Devil,' he shouted. 'I've been your servant for 45 years. Now I belong to Christ. Now I only serve him.'

"I've never met a man so on fire for the Lord. After I left the country in 1973, Lung Singh continued his courageous ministry. He was constantly warned by the Pathet Lao Communists to stop his preaching, but he refused.

"'I cannot do that. Jesus saved me. He did everything for me. I can't be quiet!'"

Years later he was executed but not before impacting for good the kingdom of heaven.

Sister Wu is a leader in a house church in China. One day her home was suddenly raided by the police. She had Christian literature from abroad and it was confiscated. Sister Wu was arrested and taken to the police station. The police were cruel and abusive towards her. She was questioned overnight not only by the police but also by the head of the Religious Affairs Bureau (RAB) of the city. She bravely responded to

81

their questions.

Just a few days after her release, the chief of the RAB's brother was severely injured in an automobile accident and taken to the hospital. By the time Sister Wu knew about it, she went to visit this RAB chief's brother and mother. She led them to the Lord while they were in the hospital.

Later, on another occasion, Sister Wu was holding a Christian training class in a small room of a restaurant. One of the employees decided to report the meeting to the PSB hoping to make some money because it was an illegal meeting. The matter was reported all the way to the top of the RAB, but the chief of the RAB, upon discovering that it was Sister Wu conducting the meeting, said "Oh, don't bother her. She's okay." Sister Wu's boldness was rewarded.

RESPONSE:
Today I will live in the strength of Christ and fearlessly refuse to give in to my enemy, Satan's attempts to shut down my verbal and outgoing witness.

PRAYER:
Pray for boldness for all believers to share the gospel openly.

February 11

FEAR GOD, FEAR NOTHING ELSE

There is no fear in love. But perfect love drives out fear, because fear has to do with punishment. The one who fears is not made perfect in love.

1 John 4:18

The Apostle John repeatedly teaches that loving God (other Scripture writers refer to it as "fearing" God) is the antidote to fear. Fear is a tactic of Satan which all believers must face. Those under severe persecution often face this challenge early.

Behbaha, an Iranian secret believer from Muslim background (MBB), shares that her aunt went to a house church and she accompanied her. But she was afraid. She knew that the government controlled the church and that scared her.

"At that time I worked in a job that was state controlled. Every time they gave us questionnaires we should fill out, one of the questions is about religion. Of course you have to fill in, *'Muslim,'* but I could not do that anymore…"

In the house church she attended with her aunt she learned about the Bible and what Jesus taught in a very practical way. Taking a discipleship training course was a great blessing for Behbaha. She says, "I was able to understand the Bible, I saw the good Lord of the Bible, saw His love—and that changed my life." After six years of searching she gave her life to Jesus.

The good thing is that her family does not have any problems with her changing and going to church. "Neighbors are the problem", she states. "The government tells on radio and TV that if you know a person who is not dedicated to the government or to Islam you should go to the police and tell them when you suspect someone of being a Christian."

After she became a Christian she left her job. "Much too dangerous," she comments. "I am not able anymore to fill out that form [because of the religion question]. Now I am working part time with some small companies, who are not working with these forms asking about faith."

She does not know if she is observed by the secret police, because of her former job. Behbaha is not aware of being watched. "But I have to be careful, they are able to kill me," she says with conviction. "Sometimes people are killed; sometimes they have to leave the country. Maybe, if they catch me, I will be killed, but this week of training took away my fear."

After taking the training seminar she wants to teach the course to others—especially church people. Behbaha also wants to pass on the training to her family and friends. "I want to share and show love. My dream after this training is to have house groups with my family members, friends and colleagues to teach them. But…your life should be a good testimony to everyone and Jesus must increase in your life. I am working on that."

RESPONSE:
Today I will focus on fearing God so that I will not fear anything or anyone else.

PRAYER:
Pray new believers around the world involved in discipleship training will learn not to fear.

February 12

REFUSING TO COMPROMISE

Do not be afraid of those who kill the body but cannot kill the soul. Rather, be afraid of the One who can destroy both soul and body in hell.

Matthew 10:28

When do you compromise and when do you refuse to? On the one hand, Jesus instructed us to make friends with our enemy before any court case can develop; and on the other, he teaches us to be true to the principles of the kingdom of God.

The history of Christian persecution is filled with inspiring stories featuring people of principle—those individuals who are immortalized for refusing to compromise their beliefs. John Bunyan was one of those.

In 1660, England's experiment as a republic came to an abrupt end with the return to monarchist rule under Charles II. With this change, religious freedom also ended and Anglicanism was once again designated as the official state religion. It became illegal to conduct church services outside of the Church of England and unlicensed individuals were forbidden from addressing a religious gathering.

With these new laws, John Bunyan was arrested for preaching without a license. His growing popularity, though, prompted the judge to seek some sort of a compromise. Promising Bunyan immediate release if he only promised not to preach again, the judge's leniency was met with the reply, **"If you release me today, I shall preach tomorrow!"**

Three times in his life Bunyan was arrested, convicted and jailed for preaching without a license. In the end, he spent over twelve years in prison. At any time during those years he could have secured his freedom by simply promising not to preach. But Bunyan knew God's calling on his life and so he adamantly refused to compromise his convictions.

Those prison years were certainly not wasted. It was during this time that Bunyan wrote the book *Pilgrim's Progress*. Its immediate success and ongoing popularity has made it a Christian classic, the second most read book in English literature next to the Bible.

Today Christians around the world still languish in prison because they will not compromise their faith and give in to government suggestions for release. Christians in Laos are accused of following an "American" religion and would be released from prison and left in peace if they would sign a document recanting their commitment to Christ. Most refuse.

Christians in "shipping container" prisons in Eritrea would be released if they also signed such a document but prefer to suffer indefinitely for the cause of Christ than deny Him.

Compromise is not always bad, but when it comes to issues of faith, we are expected to stand for Christ and His kingdom principles.

RESPONSE:
Today I will stand strong and true to my convictions and faith in Jesus and His kingdom principles.

PRAYER:
Pray for those Christians in prison today mentioned above, that they will not give in to Satan's temptations to deny their faith.

February 13

I WILL REJOICE IN THE LORD

Though the fig tree does not bud and there are no grapes
on the vines, though the olive crop fails and the fields
produce no food, though there are no sheep in the pen
and no cattle in the stalls, yet I will rejoice in the LORD,
I will be joyful in God my Savior.
Habakkuk 3: 17-18

Cuba is an island full of color, warmth and smells, yet it is also run down and dilapidated. This island seems to be open, but it is subject to many restrictions. Almost all Cubans experience shortages of literally everything.

Christians can be found throughout Cuba, and shortages are extreme for them. There is a chronic shortage of Bibles and Christian literature. "Every month, we have baptism services and we often have tens and sometimes dozens of new Christians being baptized," reported a female pastor. "Due to the shortage of Bibles, we do not give people a Bible when they convert. They first have the possibility to enter a 'Christianity course' before being baptized. Once people have finished the course and have been baptized, they receive a Bible. This way we have more certainty that the Bible will really be used."

Christian leadership is lacking in Cuba. "There is a shortage of good, solid Christian leadership in the churches. We don't have the knowledge and could really use good study material on biblical leadership," stated a Cuban pastor.

Christians lack places to worship together. One pastor in Cuba said, "We don't have our own building and our houses are too small to meet in. Every Sunday we use all the means of transport that we can find to go out into the countryside. There we're less conspicuous and we can hold an open-air service. But if it's raining or too windy, it has to be called off. That's a pity, because we like meeting together so much."

When a pastor was asked what his greatest wish is, he replied, "To conquer the city for Jesus Christ!" This is the dream of many Cuban Christians, who show their resiliency in the midst of restrictions.

Are there too few Bibles? Then they simply share Bibles with each other and copy out Bible texts. Is it prohibited to proclaim God's Word outside your church building? Then they make sure that the music and the words of the psalms and hymns are heard through the open windows of the building. When the police drive them away while evangelizing on the street, then they carry on somewhere else tomorrow. The Scripture above is sung as a favorite hymn.

Cuban Christians see the restrictions as a challenge. They have the courage to dream. They stand up for their faith. In this way, the Word is heard and the church in Cuba is growing.

RESPONSE:
Today I will follow the example of Cuban Christians and rejoice in Jesus and serve Him faithfully even when the necessities and comforts of life are absent.

PRAYER:
Lord, I want to be so dependent on You that I can sing the closing song of Habakkuk too.

February 14

PRACTICAL LOVE

Dear children, let us not love with words or tongue but with actions and in truth.
1 John 3:18

In his book, *The Upside Down Church*, Pastor Greg Laurie says, "The first Christians didn't out-argue pagans—they outlived them... Christianity made no attempts to conquer paganism and dead Judaism by reacting blow by blow. Instead, the Christians of the first century outthought, outprayed and outlived the unbelievers.

"Their weapons were positive not negative. As far as we know, they did not hold protests or conduct boycotts. They did not put on campaigns to try to unseat the emperor. Instead, they prayed and preached and proclaimed the message of Christ, put to death on the cross, risen from the dead, and ready to change lives. And they backed up their message with actions: giving, loving."[6]

A co-worker shares a significant event he witnessed among Christian children in Egypt:

A crowd of smiling faces awaited us as we entered the small stuffy room. The ages of the children ranged from eight to eleven years and they were seemingly oblivious and unaware of the circumstances surrounding their village—poverty, problems and persecution. To be a Christian, let alone a Christian child, was not an easy life.

It was Saturday evening and the excitement that filled the air overwhelmed any feeling of self-pity and despair that might have existed. Between thirty and forty young boys, each equipped with a large maize bag, excitedly awaited orders.

As we entered the room the youth leader saw the frowns on our faces and answered our questions even before we could ask. "Yes, it's Saturday evening," he started explaining, "and tonight the children will once again 'invade' our little village. They will go to

---

6 Greg Laurie, *The Upside Down Church* (Wheaton: Tyndale Publishers, 1999), p. 46.

every house in every street. They will ask the inhabitants whether they have enough bread to eat or not. If there is more than enough bread in the house they will ask the families to place any extra bread in the bag for those who do not have enough bread.

"The children will continue until all the bags are filled to the top. Then the fun part of the evening starts. They will then go back to all the homes where there was not enough bread to eat and distribute so that every family in our village will have enough bread to eat for the next week.

"They do not have the means to provide it themselves, but regardless of their own needs, they have become instruments of love to eradicate all hunger in our village."

RESPONSE:
I will live this day showing love to those in need in the most practical ways.

PRAYER:
Lord, bless those Egyptian Christian children who love others and demonstrate it in a practical way.

February 15

SUFFERING CAN PURIFY MY FAITH

*In this you greatly rejoice, though now for a little while
you may have had to suffer grief in all kinds of trials.
These have come so that your faith—of greater worth
than gold, which perishes even though refined by fire—
may be proved genuine and may result in praise, glory
and honor when Jesus Christ is revealed.*
1 Peter 1:6-7

Believers in North Korea's underground church recite five
principles, along with the Lord's Prayer, at their secret gatherings. The
special place of purifying suffering in the spiritual life of this church
is striking:

1. Our persecution and suffering are our joy and honor.
2. We want to accept ridicule, scorn and disadvantages with joy in
   Jesus' name.
3. As Christians, we want to wipe others' tears away and comfort
   the suffering.
4. We want to be ready to risk our life because of our love for our
   neighbor, so that they also become Christians.
5. We want to live our lives according to the standards set in God's
   Word.

Christian singer, Helen Berhane was arrested for sharing her faith
in her home country of Eritrea. She spent almost three years in prison,
much of this time in a metal shipping container. Because she would
not deny her faith or stop sharing her faith, she was beaten so severely
she could not walk. During her time in the containers she wrote
new Christian songs and spent her time encouraging other Christian
prisoners, as well as witnessing to the prison guards.

After her release, she resettled in Europe and has written her
prison memoirs in a small book titled, *Song of the Nightingale*. In
the introduction when describing her feelings inside the shipping
container prison, she writes:

Sometimes I cannot believe that this is my life—these four metal walls, all of us corralled like cattle, the pain, the hunger, the fear. All because of my belief in a God who is risen, who charges me to share my faith with those who do not yet know him. A God who I am forbidden to worship. I think back to a question I have been asked many times over my months in prison: "Is your faith worth this, Helen?" As the guards continue on their rounds, I whisper the answer: "Yes."[7]

RESPONSE:
Today I will accept suffering as something that can prove and purify my faith.

PRAYER:
Lord, thank You for those trials and challenges that help me be more like You. You are worth it all and more!

---

7 Helen Berhane, *Song of the Nightingale* (Colorado Springs: Authentic Media, 2009), p. xiii.

February 16

SUFFERING BURNS AWAY PRIDE

To keep me from becoming conceited because of these surpassingly great revelations, there was given me a thorn in my flesh, a messenger of Satan, to torment me. Three times I pleaded with the Lord to take it away from me. But he said to me, "My grace is sufficient for you, for my power is made perfect in weakness." Therefore I will boast all the more gladly about my weaknesses, so that Christ's power may rest on me. That is why, for Christ's sake, I delight in weaknesses, in insults, in hardships, in persecutions, in difficulties. For when I am weak, then I am strong.

2 Corinthians 12:7-10

Suffering burns away pride, as it did in Paul's life. When Paul prayed three times for the removal of his "thorn in the flesh," he saw that it was God's will for him, and he accepted it.

Many Christians are defeated at this point because they are not sure that they are in the will of God, so they are not sure if the suffering is really His will for them. Without going aside into a Bible study on knowing the will of God, we can just present this thought. Our great God *"works for the good of those who love him..."* (Romans 8:28). If we consciously submit to His will, He will give His divine direction. Our suffering and persecution can be placed in His hands by a simple act of our will. No believer needs to suffer alone and in doubt. Commit it all to the Lord (Proverbs 16:3).

In an unscheduled visit to Lat Village in Vietnam, a co-worker had the joy of visiting Father Tranh, the leader of the local church. Realizing the isolation and loneliness of this leader the group with our co-worker immediately asked how they could pray for him.

Not having an abundance of fellowship, he started sharing his hardships and needs. He confirmed the persecution and discrimination against the tribal people as already expressed by all the leaders they had met in Saigon. He shared the hardship of ministering to his people

93

and the difficulties of restriction both by the police as well as the dense forest that limited his movements.

Father Thanh had 6,000 members in his congregation and found it an overwhelming task to be the only leader. "How do you do it brother?" the group asked. "How many people assist you in this enormous task?"

"**I am only me!**" he responded and immediately went on to conclude his answer, "**but even though I am limited, the Holy Spirit is unlimited.**"

RESPONSE:
Today I will recognize that God may send suffering into my life to burn away my pride.

PRAYER:
Pray for Persecuted Church leaders around the world today—especially Father Thanh.

February 17

SUFFERING CAN MAKE OUR LIVES MORE HOLY

Our fathers disciplined us for a little while as they thought best; but God disciplines us for our good, that we may share in his holiness.

Hebrews 12:10

Christmas is a time of peace and joy for those who are fortunate enough to celebrate the birth of their Saviour in freedom. For Marko and his two fellow believers it was the fifteenth Christmas that they had to celebrate behind the bars of a prison cell in a Muslim country.

The next day some colleagues felt they had to visit Marko and his friends as an encouragement and confirm to them once again the love of Immanuel—God with us.

Even though they often heard the saying that a prison cell in the Middle East is the closest to hell that you will experience on earth, nothing prepared them for the sense of hopelessness that they experienced in that waiting room of despair.

As the prisoners entered, it was not difficult to recognize Marko and his two friends. Beaming eyes and smiling faces immediately assured them Marko and friends knew they had not been separated from the love of God.

Tears flowed freely as they shared how lonely they were on Christmas day and how joyful they were to know that they were not forgotten.

"It was so difficult yesterday." Marko spoke softly. "Apart from being Christian prisoners in a Muslim prison, it was also a fast day of Ramadan. We were not allowed out of our cells and we were not allowed to talk to anyone. Fortunately, a week ago the three of us got hold of pieces of a cake and we hid them underneath our cushions especially for Christmas day. Yesterday, when the fast was broken, we simply walked to one another, held the slices of cake together and said "Merry Christmas!"

The visiting hour flew past and soon it was time to say goodbye.

Before being marched back to his prison cell, we looked at Marko and asked him a final question. "What are you going to do when you get to your cell and are once again all alone?

Marko smiled and answered, **"I will simply spread the wings of my spirit and fly to Jesus."**

RESPONSE:
Today I will seek to understand the biblical principle that suffering makes our lives more holy.

PRAYER:
Lord, help me, like Marko, to keep my eyes fixed on You regardless of my circumstances.

February 18

LIVING CHRIST IN THE FAMILY

All your sons will be taught by the Lord, and great will be your children's peace.
Isaiah 54:13

A frail old man went to live with his son, daughter-in-law, and four-year-old grandson. The old man's hands trembled, his eyesight was blurred, and his step faltered. The family ate together at the table. But the elderly grandfather's shaky hands and failing sight made eating difficult. Peas rolled off his spoon onto the floor. When he grasped the glass, milk spilled on the tablecloth.

The son and daughter-in-law became irritated with the mess. "We must do something about Grandfather," said the son. "I've had enough of his spilled milk, noisy eating, and food on the floor." So the husband and wife set a small table in the corner. There, Grandfather ate alone while the rest of the family enjoyed dinner.

Since Grandfather had broken a dish or two, his food was served in a wooden bowl. When the family glanced in Grandfather's direction, sometimes he had a tear in his eye as he sat alone. Still, the only words the couple had for him were sharp admonitions when he dropped a fork or spilled food.

The four-year-old watched it all in silence. One evening before supper, the father noticed his son playing with wood scraps on the floor. He asked the child sweetly, "What are you making?"

Just as sweetly, the boy responded, "Oh, I am making a little bowl for you and Mama to eat your food in when I grow up." The four-year-old smiled and went back to work.

The words so struck the parents that they were speechless. Then tears started to stream down their cheeks. Though no word was spoken, both knew what must be done.

That evening, the husband took Grandfather's hand and gently led him back to the family table. For the remainder of his days he ate every meal with the family. And for some reason, neither husband nor wife seemed to care any longer when a fork was dropped, milk spilled, or the tablecloth soiled.

Children are remarkably perceptive. Their eyes ever observe, their ears ever listen, and their minds ever process the messages they absorb. If they see us patiently provide a happy, godly home atmosphere, they will imitate that attitude for the rest of their lives.

The wise parent realizes that every day the building blocks are being laid for their children's future.

RESPONSE:
Today I will purpose to live a life that exemplifies to everyone the love of Jesus...especially in my home.

PRAYER:
Help me, Lord, to be a positive Christ-like impact on members of the younger generation.

February 19

SUFFERING CAN CONTRIBUTE TO THE SPIRITUAL STRENGTH OF OTHERS

Because of my chains, most of the brothers in the Lord have been encouraged to speak the word of God more courageously and fearlessly.

Philippians 1:14

A pastor imprisoned for his faith in Eritrea recently wrote to his wife:

God, by His holy will, has prolonged my prison sentence to five years and four month. I very much long for the day that I will be reunited with you my dear wife, our children and God's people in the church.

My dear, listen to me—not only as a wife, but also as a Christian woman who has come to understand who God is and how deep and mysterious His ways are. Yes! I love you, I love the children, and I would love to be free in order to serve God. **But, in here, God has made me not only a sufferer for His Name's sake in a prison of this world over which Christ has won victory, but also a prisoner of His indescribable love and grace. I am testing and experiencing the love and care of our Lord every day.**

When they first brought me to this prison, I had thoughts which were contrary to what the Bible says. I thought the devil had prevailed over the church and over me. I thought the work of the gospel in Eritrea was over. But it did not take one day for the Lord to show me that He is a sovereign God and that He is in control of all things—even here in prison.

The moment I entered my cell, one of the prisoners called me and said, "Pastor, come over here. Everyone in this cell is [unsaved]. You are very much needed here." So, on the same day I was put in prison, I carried on my spiritual work.

My dear, the longer I stay in here, the more I love my Saviour and tell the people here about His goodness. His grace is enabling me to overcome the coldness and the longing that I feel for you and for our children. Sometimes I ask myself, Am I out of my mind? Am I a fool? Well, isn't that what the Apostle Paul said, "Whether I am of sound mind or out of my mind, I am Christ's!"

My most respected wife, I love you more than I can say. Please help the children understand that I am here as a prisoner of Christ for the greater cause of the gospel.

RESPONSE:
Today I will live in the awareness that God is in control of all that happens in my life. My suffering can contribute to the spiritual strength of others.

PRAYER:
Please pray for the wives and families of pastors imprisoned for their faith. Pray that they will be strengthened and an encouragement to others, despite their own pain.

February 20

SUFFERING ACCOMPLISHES UNKNOWN PURPOSES

Now we see but a poor reflection as in a mirror; then we shall see face to face. Now I know in part; then I shall know fully, even as I am fully known.

1 Corinthians 13:12

The Bible makes it clear that Christians will suffer. Some pastors have the idea that teaching this fact will drive away new believers. Note that when Paul traveled throughout Asia Minor, he told the new believers; *"We must go through many hardships to enter the kingdom of God"* (Acts 14:22). He was preparing them for the future as well as explaining their present situation. We should prepare for the same. Paul showed us an example of this when he prayed three times for the removal of his *"thorn in the flesh."* Then he saw that it was God's will for him, and he accepted it. (2 Corinthians 12:7-10)

When suffering Christians are not sure they are in the will of God they will be unsure if their suffering is really God's will. However, our great God *"works for the good of those who love him..."* (Romans 8:28). If we consciously submit to His will, He will give His divine direction. Our suffering and persecution can be placed in His hands by an act of our will. No believer needs to suffer alone and in doubt. Commit it all to the Lord (Proverbs 16:3).

As a young Muslim boy, twelve years of age, Abdul, experienced a tragedy that would change his life forever. Abdul drowned and was dead for more than an hour.

During his death he had a vision of angels coming to fetch him and then bringing him to a closed door. A man met him at the door and asked him where he was going. Abdul answered that he was on his way to heaven. The man answered that he would not be allowed in because Abdul still had a lot of work to do on earth. He woke up on his bed to find a pastor praying for him.

This happened twenty years ago and ever since, Abdul's life has been changed. Even though Abdul only completed fifth grade in school, he is currently the pastor of a small church in a very poor village on the island of Mindanao in the Philippine Islands.

In his own words Abdul says, "I don't understand God's purposes in my suffering, but I now know the Lord."

Abdul has a ministry in healing and is a source of great encouragement in his village.

RESPONSE:
Today I will accept that suffering accomplishes purposes unknown to us now.

PRAYER:
Pray for Christians who are suffering today and cannot accept this as God's will. Praise God that someday we will understand all things fully.

February 21

SUFFERING BRINGS A GREATER HARVEST OF SOULS

On that day a great persecution broke out against the church at Jerusalem, and all except the apostles were scattered throughout Judea and Samaria...Those who had been scattered preached the word wherever they went.

Acts 8:1, 4

Again and again we see that in many countries, right before persecution comes, the church grows rapidly. This happened in northern Korea one hundred years ago just before the Japanese occupation and persecution.

It is helpful to remember this theme from the book of Acts: **persecution does not necessarily cause church growth but church growth appears to cause persecution!**

Church leaders among the many house church networks in China (the fastest growing church in the world) repeatedly share that suffering for Jesus often brings about a greater harvest of souls.

Sariman was a young student preparing himself to serve the Lord among the thirty million Sundanese of Indonesia, the largest unreached people group in the world. During a violent attack on the Bible school, Sariman was killed and many other students were wounded. Sariman bravely assisted his friends although he could have saved himself. Before his death he was tortured and other students testified how Sariman was slaughtered. He was hit with a bar of wood and iron, then hacked, stabbed and his mouth was cut from the left cheek to the right cheek.

Upon hearing yet another testimony of martyrdom, many questions arise. "Why this tragedy, Lord? How long will you allow this to continue? This is such a terrible loss for this wonderful ministry. What is the sense in all of this?"

Then the dean of the Bible school completes the testimony and indirectly answers our questions: **"The victory in this tragedy is** that only ten days after the murder of Sariman we had ten new applicants to study at the Bible school. Today, six months after the incident, we have ninety-eight new students who are willing to go where Sariman would have gone. The blood of the martyrs is indeed seed."

Paul clearly warns the church in Galatia (Galatians 5:1) to stand firm in the midst of freedom. Freedom is not a time to relax. Freedom often creates a new kind of slavery. There is a price tag attached to freedom and we need to count the cost. It is time to open our hearts to the valuable lessons that we can learn from those that follow Christ in restricted countries—even to their death.

RESPONSE:
Today I will accept the biblical teaching and the many church growth examples that suffering often brings about a greater harvest of souls.

PRAYER:
Lord, we pray today for Your fast-growing suffering churches around the world. May they be encouraged as they see many more souls added to Your kingdom.

February 22

WALK IN UNITY

"I in them and you in me. May they be brought to
complete unity to let the world know that you sent me and
have loved them even as you have loved me."
John 17:23

Persecution, pressure and suffering also bring about a unity that honors God. Burma is the model to which I was first exposed. Missionaries were all expelled in 1966. My first visit was in the early 1970's. The church was a small minority in a dominant Buddhist society with a secular socialist government. On Sunday morning, I was asked to speak and break bread with the Brethren believers, in the afternoon share with the Baptists and in the evening speak at the Pentecostal Church. No one asked me my denomination. I was simply a "Brother in Christ" and represented an evangelical radio organization, Far East Broadcasting Company (FEBC).

I found this unity so refreshing. And praise the Lord I have discovered it in other parts of our world, most often outside of North America. The closest geographic location is on the island of Cuba. What a joy to be with Baptist and Pentecostal pastors together who regularly spend hours on their knees before God with one another. How refreshing to attend youth evangelism meetings with a variety of denominations represented in the audience and speakers. Is there any wonder why revival continues to sweep through the island to this day?

Ugandan pastor, Kefa Sempangi, shares that under the intense persecution of Idi Amin, the Holy Spirit united the hearts of Uganda's church leaders. The emphasis became loving one another and rejecting the earlier focus on differences and mass evangelism. He writes:

Most of us had in various ways tried to be evangelists in our own rights. In the mission command we had heard as young converts, the emphasis had been on go, not love. It was the ministry, not the brethren, that was most important. As a result we had come to love our sermons more than the people to whom we preached. We had come to love the faceless converts of mass evangelism more than our brothers and sisters in Christ.

Now as the Holy Spirit began to unite our hearts we saw that before the Great Commission, came the commandment: love one another. We were to confess and reject our disagreements. In the past we had majored on our differences—Anglicans did not say hello to Baptists and, when a Pentecostal met a Roman Catholic, he did not feel he was meeting a brother. But now we heard God's call to live broken lives before one another. We were not to build our fellowship on the foundation of baptism, tongues or liturgy. We were to build on the reconciling blood of Jesus Christ."[8]

RESPONSE:
Today I will rejoice in God's plan and God's will: that His children walk together in unity.

PRAYER:
Lord, may my love for brothers and sisters today, and the resulting unity, show the world that You sent Jesus.

8   F. Kefa Sempangi with Barbara R. Thompson. *A Distant Grief* (Glendale, CA: Regal Books, 1979), pp. 42-43.

February 23

TEARS OF SUFFERING

Record my misery; list my tears on your scroll—
are they not in your record?
Psalm 56:8

Somewhere in this world a persecuted Christian might be crying right at this moment. It might seem that their tears are in vain and simply drop to the ground. But ages ago King David was convinced that God was interested in his tears. In the passage noted above, alternate translations for listing tears on a "scroll" include putting tears in a "bottle" or "wineskin."

Today in the Middle East it is not uncommon to see a collection of oddly-shaped bottles, labeled only as "sprinklers." But in ancient Middle Eastern times these bottles were known as "tear-catchers." When a husband went off to war, his wife would collect her tears for him in a bottle. On his return she would hand him the bottle as proof of her love. In times of death or serious trouble, family members would bring their tear-catchers and collect tears from all the people present. Sometimes the tears would be stored in a small round jar with a lid. These tear bottles represented the sorrows of the family; tears serving as a message in a bottle. In those days each person was buried with his or her tear bottle; archaeologists have found many of these bottles in ancient tombs.

In the days of King David of Israel the bottle was more likely made of animal skin. David was a man who went through a lot of suffering and persecution. David had no doubts: his tears were not shed in vain, but were collected by God. The words in Psalm 56 could also be those of our persecuted brothers and sisters. They serve as a reminder for us to "treasure" their tears.

The words of David are still true today. People try to trample on our brothers and sisters; want to harm them; spy on their movements. David put his trust clearly in the Lord. In verses 3 and 4 he says, *"When I am afraid, I put my trust in you. In God, whose word I praise—in God I trust and am not afraid. What can mere mortals do to me?"*

Watching the moving DVD documentary, *A Cry from Iran*, you will be brought to tears as you see and hear the story of Iranian Pastor Haik who was martyred for his faith in the mid-1990's. He worked tirelessly for the release from prison of Christian brother Mehdi Dibaj who was sentenced to death for apostasy. Miraculously Mehdi was released. At Pastor Haik's funeral, a teary-eyed Mehdi Dibaj said, "I was the one who should have died, not Haik." Six months later he too was martyred.

Recently our office for the Middle East received an Iranian "tear-catcher" as a present. The bottle helps us to remember the tears of the Iranian Christians, but with them all of the Christians around the world who are being persecuted. It speaks about grief, about tears, about suffering; but also about faith and confidence in the Lord.

Let us remember their tears, knowing that as one member suffers, all members suffer. And let us rejoice that someday God will wipe away all tears from their eyes and our eyes.

RESPONSE:
Today I will remember those of my extended Christian family around the world who are suffering and shedding tears.

PRAYER:
Pray for Persecuted Church believers today who may be shedding sorrowful tears of grief.

February 24

FAITHFUL TO THE END

This calls for patient endurance on the part of the people of God who keep his commands and remain faithful to Jesus.
Revelation 14:12

Patient endurance is an oft repeated theme throughout the New Testament. But it seems to be one theme we don't talk about or preach about much. Yet it is a constant challenge for members of the Persecuted Church.

Since 1975, Bengali pastors in Bangladesh have faced increasing persecution for preaching the gospel. Some are beaten, imprisoned or even killed. As a result, their wives and children often face isolation. They are verbally and physically abused, and they face extraordinary challenge to remain free from bitterness.

Pastor Mir wanted to take the gospel to a place in Bangladesh that had not heard about Jesus. So he brought his wife Anjali and their children to a Muslim community that had never seen a Christian before. The community thought that Christians must look different somehow. Christians seemed so foreign to them. So they came to see what Christians looked like and introduced themselves.

Over the next several years, people began opening their hearts to the message of Jesus. But, not everyone responded so positively. Some in the village pressured the Mirs to leave. Nonetheless, they stood strong in their faith. Then one night, Anjali heard a loud noise. Someone was shot. Her husband had been walking to the market when two men caught him, shot him in the mouth and he fell on the ground. Then they took a dagger and stabbed him in the critical points of his body.

After a long while, Mrs. Mir heard that the man who had been shot was her husband. Though she longed to go to him, she knew her two small children required her care. So she could not leave her home. She was thinking, *He's going to die, and I have two boys. What am I going to do? How am I going to raise my two boys?*

When Pastor Mir told onlookers he was dying, some fellow

109

believers defied the threat of his attackers, and took him to a hospital. Miraculously, he survived. After years of extensive medical treatment, he is preaching again, but his injuries continue to plague him. His wife still worries over her children's safety—and faces the challenge of helping them understand why their father was attacked.

Despite persecution, Pastor and Mrs. Mir are committed to staying in their village for the sake of their new Christian brothers and sisters. Anjali says, "If we leave, then there will be no church and the people who have just put their faith in Jesus, may fall away."

The real cry of their heart is wanting to be faithful to Jesus to the end.

RESPONSE:
Today I will keep Jesus' commands and practice patient endurance.

PRAYER:
Ask God to enable workers in areas of persecution to endure patiently the challenges they face for the sake of Jesus and His church.

February 25

OVERCOMERS

They overcame him by the blood of the Lamb and by the word of their testimony; they did not love their lives so much as to shrink from death.

Revelation 12:11

The only original disciple of Jesus spared from martyrdom was the Apostle John who experienced persecution in different ways. While exiled on the island of Patmos he was given the revelation of Jesus which he wrote down for the churches of his day—and ultimately for us too. He describes our enemy Satan and the cosmic spiritual battle he wages against us as disciples of Jesus. John also points out that Satan is especially angry as he realizes his time is short.

The letter of Revelation is written in a chiasm form (often used structure in ancient literature) which uses the central section as the focus and climax of the writing or teaching. In Revelation, chapter twelve is the central section and verse eleven is the central and focused idea. John reveals in this climactic message that our enemy, Satan, will ultimately be overcome and defeated. We accomplish this victory as disciples of Jesus in three ways:

- by the blood of the lamb
- by the word of our testimony
- by willingness to sacrifice our own physical life

Darrell Johnson in his excellent book, *Discipleship on the Edge*, writes:

There is only one way to "overcome": the way Jesus did, as a Lamb, as pictured in Revelation 5. Thus 12:11, the central verse of the whole book—"they [disciples of Jesus]overcame him [the dragon] because of the blood of the Lamb and because of the word of their testimony, and they did not love their life even to death."

The structure itself declares the message that since Jesus overcomes evil not by being a Lion who hurts others, but by being a Lamb who absorbs hurt, so too we overcome evil in the world, not by inflicting more hurt, but by absorbing the hurt, even if it costs us our lives. The structure itself declares the mystery that in losing our lives we actually win, "overcome," just as Jesus did.[9]

Over the next three days we'll look more closely at each of these three elements of our victory over Satan.

RESPONSE:
Today I will rejoice in the guarantee that I can be a victor over Satan, my enemy.

PRAYER:
Lord, may I be willing to absorb hurt, even as Jesus did, in order to overcome evil in the world.

9 Darrell W. Johnson, *Discipleship On The Edge: An Expository Journey Through the Book of Revelation* (Vancouver BC: Regent College Publishing, 2004), pp. 395-396.

February 26

THE BLOOD OF THE LAMB

They overcame him by the blood of the Lamb *and by the word of their testimony; they did not love their lives so much as to shrink from death.*
Revelation 12:11

On the cross Jesus conquered forever the worst that sin and evil could do to Him–death! He met the full assault of evil and overcame it by the shedding of His blood and the power of His resurrection. Those who have entrusted their lives to Him also share in that victory over evil and death.

In the context of this verse, Satan is noted to be the "accuser" of the brethren. He knows we are sinners and is constantly accusing us of it. But that is not the whole story. It is through the sacrifice of Jesus on the cross (the blood of the lamb) that sin is forgiven. When we receive by faith what Christ has done, our sins are wiped out. We are cleansed by faith in Christ's blood. His saving grace and a willingness to receive us as sinners saved by grace is the key to this principle, not our feelings of worthiness.

We overcome him—our enemy—by confessing we are sinners and then confessing the cleansing of that sin through the sacrificial blood of the Lamb. **And when we are forgiven there is then nothing of which we can possibly be accused by Satan.** There is no possible accusation he can make against one who is completely forgiven! Thus we overcome him first, by the blood of the Lamb.

Romans 8:33-34 in the J. B. Phillips version reads, *"Who is in a position to condemn? Only Christ and Christ died for us, Christ rose for us, Christ reigns in power for us, Christ prays for us!"* So Satan, you are defeated and impotent! Get out of here!

Charles Wesley wrote about this in one of his beloved hymns:

No condemnation now I dread;
Jesus, and all in Him is mine!
Alive in Him, my living Head,

And clothed in righteousness divine,
Bold I approach the eternal throne,
And claim the crown, through Christ my own.

RESPONSE:
Today I will overcome my enemy, Satan, by faith in the shed blood of Jesus, the Lamb of God.

PRAYER:
Thank You Lord for providing all I need to be an overcomer.

114

February 27

THE WORD OF THEIR TESTIMONY

They overcame him by the blood of the Lamb and by the word of their testimony; they did not love their lives so much as to shrink from death.

Revelation 12:11

Overcoming believers also declare Christ's love and forgiveness aloud to themselves, to Satan, and to the world. It is the second way we become *"more than conquerors"* (Romans 8:37).

Daniel was called by the Lord to the north of Vietnam where he soon found himself in the midst of a revival. People were coming to know the Lord and Daniel immediately started a training program to equip these new believers. He also witnessed the power of God as people were healed and many were delivered from their addiction to opium. The inevitable soon happened and Daniel was sent to prison, his "training school," for three years. With a smile that illuminated the room, Daniel shared his experiences in prison:

"After my arrest I was put in solitary confinement and chained to the ground for six months. This was a very hard time for me. The cell was small, there were no lights in the cell and I only had one bowl of rice and salt a day. A piece of bamboo was stuck over my crossed legs and chained to the ground. Being chained to the ground for such a long time also resulted in my body swelling and creating a lot of pain. I felt totally deserted. I asked the Lord to take my life. It was too much for me.

"I prayed a lot but thankfully the Lord did not do what I asked.

"One night in my prison cell, chained to the ground, I saw a vision of the Lord. He did not speak a word. He just placed his hand on me and I felt how new strength filled my body. I cried and repented before the Lord. Then I knew the Lord was saying to me that He would not allow me to leave this world defeated, that when He takes me "home" it will be victoriously.

"The next day the police came and took me to another cell with other prisoners. Today I can see why God allowed this difficult time.

I could share the gospel with many people in prison. After three years in prison there is a church in every area where I spent time in a prison and more than 200 inmates came to know the Lord while I was in prison. Three other prisoners who came to know the Lord also started churches in prison. When I was released from prison, I found my church in the village had grown to 500 people."

As Daniel concluded his testimony co-workers could positively see the grace and love of the Lord in this humble man. He looked at them and summed up a life of sacrifice with the following words. "I know that God has a good plan—He sent me to prison to preach the gospel and to become a strong warrior for Him."

RESPONSE:
I will overcome today by speaking out the word of my testimony to myself, to Satan and to the world.

PRAYER:
Lord, even though I am not in prison, I can be a faithful overcomer today by sharing your love with others I meet through the word of my testimony.

February 28

WILLING TO GIVE THEIR LIVES

They overcame him by the blood of the Lamb and by the word of their testimony; they did not love their lives so much as to shrink from death.
Revelation 12:11

Within overcomers is the ultimate secret of victory that destroys any consideration for reputation, safety, comfort or freedom. They make themselves a willing self-offering patterned on Christ's own life—a repeated message in the Gospels. Not just martyrdom, but loyalty to Jesus ahead of comfort, safety and security.

In March 2007, a co-worker had the joy of training a group of Arab Christians who were preparing for an outreach to various Muslim countries in North Africa. His teaching focused on bringing glory to God and also on a biblical understanding of opposition, persecution, hardship and possible martyrdom. The students ended the week with a declaration, as they stood up one by one, committing themselves to live to the glory of God. They declared to live a life to be forgotten so that Christ can be remembered.

A month later two outreach teams from the school travelled to Sudan. One team was sent to the Juba Mountains in partnership with a local church. The team was staying in a village and went out to a rural area to show the *JESUS* Film. While they were travelling in a truck back to the village at about 10:30 pm, they were ambushed by armed gunmen. The truck driver drove away as quickly as possible, but a number of Sudanese and Egyptians on the truck were wounded in the shooting. Three Sudanese and one Egyptian were killed.

They first drove franticly to the nearest town looking for a clinic to tend to the wounded and the dead. With no facilities or medicine there, they then had to drive a further five hours to the nearest hospital for help. The darkness and hopelessness turned the journey into an eternity. The questions, the fear and yet the serenity of it all made it seem surreal. When they finally reached the hospital it was too late for Daniel, one of the wounded Egyptians. Daniel died in the arms of one of the leaders. His last words to his faithful friend reflected the words of his commitment to his beloved Saviour: "Tell my father that I died for the glory of Jesus."

Two years later, our co-worker trained another group who were again on their way to Sudan. The group committed themselves to go back to the very region of the traumatic event, not **despite** the tragedy but **because** of the tragedy.

Our co-worker concluded, "I realized anew that the battle is real but also that victory only belongs to those who participate. So often I hear Christians say 'we are more than conquerors!' You can only say that if you are part of the battle."

When martyrs meet torture and death without fear, they demonstrate power over Satan's attempts to try and control us by fear. Evil is defeated because it cannot ultimately win. Then you are an overcomer!

RESPONSE:
Today I recommit myself to live a life to be forgotten so that Christ can be remembered.

PRAYER:
Jesus I adore You; lay my life before You; how I love You.

February 29

ABC'S OF VICTORY

Commit your way to the LORD; trust in him and he will do this: He will make your righteous reward shine like the dawn, your vindication like the noonday sun.

Psalm 37:5-6

A lthough things are not perfect
B ecause of trial or pain
C ontinue in thanksgiving.
D o not begin to blame,
E ven when the times are hard.
F ierce winds are bound to blow.
G od is forever able.
H old on to what you know;
I magine life without His love,
J oy would cease to be.
K eep thanking Him for all the things
L ove imparts to thee.
M ove out of "Camp Complaining."
N o weapon that is known,
O n earth can yield the power
P raise can do alone.
Q uit looking at the future;
R edeem the time at hand;
S tart every day with worship.
T o "thank" is a command
U ntil we see Him coming
V ictorious in the sky.
W e'll run the race with gratitude;
X alting God most high.
Y es, there'll be good times and yes some will be bad, but...
Z ion waits in glory...where none are ever sad![10]

---

10 Author unknown.

RESPONSE:
I am too blessed to be stressed!

PRAYER:
Thank You, Lord, for the encouragement I receive from following Your ways.

March 1

JESUS THE OVERCOMER

But he was pierced for our transgressions, he was crushed for our iniquities; the punishment that brought us peace was upon him, and by his wounds we are healed.
Isaiah 53:5

Dr. Felix Ruh, a Jewish doctor in Paris, had a granddaughter who died of black diphtheria. Vowing to find out what had killed her, he locked himself in his laboratory for days and emerged with a fierce determination to prove, with his colleague, Louis Pasteur, the germ theory. The medical association had disapproved of Pasteur and had succeeded in getting him exiled, but he hid in the forest near Paris and erected a laboratory for his forbidden research.

Twenty beautiful horses were led out into the forest to the improvised laboratory. Scientists, doctors, and nurses came to watch the experiment. Ruh opened a steel vault and took out a large pail filled with black diphtheria germs, which he had cultured carefully for months. There were enough germs in that pail to kill everyone in France.

The scientist went to each horse and swabbed its nostrils, tongue, throat, and eyes with the deadly germs. Every horse except one developed a terrific fever and died. Most of the doctors and scientists wearied of the experiment and did not remain for what they thought would be the death of the remaining horse.

For several more days this final horse lingered, lying pathetically on the ground. While Ruh, Pasteur, and several others were sleeping on cots in the stables, the orderly on duty had been instructed to awaken the scientists should there be any change in the animal's temperature during the night. About two a.m., the temperature showed a half degree decrease, and the orderly wakened Dr. Ruh. By morning the thermometer had dropped two more degrees. By night the fever was entirely gone, and the horse was able to stand, eat, and drink.

Then Dr. Ruh took a sledgehammer and struck that beautiful horse a deathblow between the eyes. The scientists drew blood from the veins of this animal that had developed the black diphtheria but had overcome it. They drove as fast as they could to the Paris municipal hospital and forced their way past the superintendent and the guards. They went into the ward where three hundred babies lay, segregated to die from black diphtheria. With the blood of the horse, they inoculated every one of the babies. All but three lived and recovered completely.

The blood of an overcomer saved them. The blood of an Overcomer has also spiritually saved many people. He too had to die to bring life to others.

RESPONSE:
Today I will repeatedly praise Jesus for the blood He shed as an Overcomer for my sin.

PRAYER:
Thank you, Lord, for sacrificing Yourself, an Overcomer, so that I might have abundant and eternal life.

March 2

THE WAY OF THE CROSS

I want to know Christ and the power of his resurrection and the fellowship of sharing in his sufferings, becoming like him in his death...
Philippians 3:10

Members of the Persecuted Church around the world have long understood the true significance of the cross of Christ. Pastor Allen Yuan in China, who spent almost twenty-two years in prison for his faith away from his large family, often talks about his sufferings over those years. But he invariably concludes with the statement, **"They are nothing compared with the Cross!"**

The best known and loved pastor in China was Watchman Nee who was martyred in the early 1970's. One of his elderly co-workers said recently, "If we call ourselves Christians—people following Christ— we should know what road we are taking. Christ went the way of the Cross. We should be prepared to do likewise."

A Canadian Christian aid worker was overwhelmed at the enormous need among the believers of southern Sudan. He recalls some children in a village wearing nothing but hand carved bone crosses fashioned in necklaces around their necks. He pointed to the cross on one emaciated child and questioned her with hand motions. She smiled broadly, took off the necklace and handed it to him.

His thoughtful analysis is this: "That little act symbolizes the state of the Persecuted Church in Sudan. With absolutely nothing in the way of material possessions, they still have the cross of Jesus Christ. They are prepared to share its hope - even though it means death."

Indian missionary and martyr, Sadhu Sundar Singh, wrote in his diary, "It is easy to die for Christ. It is hard to live for him. Dying takes only an hour or two but to live for Christ means to die daily [to self]."

A thirty-two-year-old pastor works in upper Egypt, an area of intense persecution for Christians. He runs a day care centre, a medical clinic, a literacy training program as well as caring for the families of those in prison. He has been beaten twice by Muslim extremists and threatened daily with death. He knows they are trying to kill him...but he continues to daily bear his cross.

A leading pastor in Egypt shared about a parishioner who tearfully came for counselling. Young people she had trained at her work were recently promoted to be her supervisors. She was passed over solely because she was a Christian. The pastor concluded, **"That's the cross we must bear here in Egypt!"**

The essence of these examples is that instead of exercising and asserting my will, I learn to co-operate with God's wishes and comply with His will.

RESPONSE:
Today I will walk the way of the cross with Jesus and comply with His will.

PRAYER:
Pray for believers under severe persecution who today will take up their cross to follow Jesus.

March 3

FOLLOW IN HIS FOOTSTEPS

To this you were called, because Christ suffered for you, leaving you an example, that you should follow in his steps.
I Peter 2:21

In the old Museum of Atheism and Religion in Leningrad (now St. Petersburg) during the cold war era, visitors upon entry were first subjected to a major display of pro-evolution propaganda. Second was the world religions section dominated by displays of the sordid history of Christianity such as the Inquisition and the Crusades.

Towering over that display area was a huge crucifix. The museum guides would explain it this way: "Christians love to suffer. Ever since their leader, Jesus Christ was crucified on a cross like this, they have had a persecution complex!"

While we are definitely not called upon to have a persecution complex, we as Christians are repeatedly reminded in Scripture that our lot is indeed to follow in the footsteps of our Lord and Master.

When Jesus gave His last major teaching session to his disciples, he included a serious prediction about the reactions of the world. In what we now call the Upper Room Discourse (John 15-17), Jesus told his closest followers—probably as they were walking along (see John 14:31b)—that they were to remain [abide] in Him as a branch in the vineyard is connected to the main stalk.

He then reiterated his command that they were to love each other as He had loved them and was willing to lay down His life for them—the highest form of love. Little did they understand that prediction. Yet it would be fulfilled the very next day.

Then he contrasts that love of the brethren with the reaction of hatred from the world: *"If the world hates you, keep in mind that it hated me first...for they do not know the one who sent me"* (John 15: 18-21). A little further down in the discourse, He says, *"...in fact, a time is coming when anyone who kills you will think he is offering a service to God"* (John 16:2b).

125

Jesus was indicating that as He suffered, so would His disciples. Every human being endures some suffering in his lifetime. It may be the physical suffering of sickness or injury. It may be the inner suffering caused by the death of a loved one, rejection by friends, or simply loneliness. Whatever the cause may be, we all seek to avoid it as much as possible. The Scriptures make it very plain that Christians are subject to all the causes of suffering common to men, plus the added persecution that comes with taking a clear stand for Christ.

RESPONSE:
Today I will walk in the suffering footsteps of Jesus, my Lord and Saviour; no complaints.

PRAYER:
Lord, give me grace to accept the responses of the world as Jesus did. As I abide in You, may I also show Your love to everyone.

March 4

CHOOSE TO FOLLOW JESUS

Then he called the crowd to him along with his disciples and said: "Whoever wants to be my disciple must deny themselves and take up their cross and follow me."
Mark 8:34

They stood out like lighthouse beacons. We spotted them while walking through the tables of artisan wares in old Havana. Two oil painting portraits side-by-side propped in front of the table. Portraits of two famous revolutionaries: Che Guevarra and Jesus Christ.

The Cuban people are well acquainted with Che. The Argentina-born socialist revolutionary joined Fidel Castro in the Cuban revolution of 1959. Fidel made him Minister of the Interior for the first five years. Then Che disappeared only to surface in Bolivia where he was captured and executed. Cuba has made him out to be a martyr for the revolution. His face and sayings are even more wide-spread in the country than Fidel's.

Jesus is also becoming well-known in Cuba due to revival that has swept the island since the late 1980's.

These two portraits depict the major choices for most people today. One revolutionary says, "Follow me and I will make you a liberator of men—teach them how to fight!" The other says, "Follow me and I will make you fishers of men—teach them how to really live!"

One revolutionary says, "Follow me and USE your life for the sake of the revolution!" The other says, "Follow me and LOSE your life for my sake and the gospel's (and you will find it)!"

The one says "Follow me and we will build a utopia on earth!" Jesus says, "Follow me and we will build the Kingdom of God on earth (and the world will be a better place)!"

Those who have chosen to follow Jesus in Cuba are making a significant impact for the Lord. I met a twenty-three-year-old Cuban young lady who is a committed follower of Jesus. She ministers to four churches in the mountains where no male graduate from the seminary is willing to serve. The one mountain-top church we visited with her required forty-seven crossings of the winding mountain river in climbing the eight kilometres distance. In rainy season the mud is up to her knees.

I asked her what the last message was she had shared with believers. She replied, "Take up your cross and follow me!"

We also saw a young male evangelist en route to a meeting point which would take him seven hours to walk. That's commitment!

Today Jesus is also calling you and me to truly follow Him. It may mean leaving behind our favourite time-waster and our comfort zones. But Jesus promises his personal presence and his abundant blessing. It's an adventure like no other. If you listen carefully, you can hear his voice right where you are this moment. He's saying, **"Follow me!"**

RESPONSE:
Today I choose to follow Jesus, regardless of the cost.

PRAYER:
Lord, may Your call on my life ever draw me closer to You and Your kingdom.

March 5

WORTH FOLLOWING

Even though I walk through the valley of the shadow of death, I will fear no evil, for you are with me; your rod and your staff, they comfort me.

Psalm 23:4

The first thing most Christians think of when they hear or read the word, "persecution" is torture. And indeed torture is what many persecuted believers experience. Helen Berhane was kept in Eritrean shipping container prisons for almost three years because she would not deny her faith. She was beaten so severely she could not even walk. Other times Helen was chained for hours outside in the severe heat of the sunshine.

One tine after a full day of being chained outside, she was handcuffed and thrown into an old rusty shipping container full of holes. She lay on the icy floor in her thin dress. With no blanket, she soon began shivering. Her whole body ached from the cold and the beating she had received. She feared she might die from the freezing cold so she composed this song and sang it repeatedly throughout the chilly night:

I love you, that's why I draw myself closer to you

I know that it's worth following you.

I am not only ready for prison, but I trust you until death.

Even in a closed space or in a pit I will not surrender to evil spirits,

Not even if I am bound or I am chained and I am suffering from cold,

I will sing and I am not going to tire of singing, nor give up.

My heart is burning with your love,

And my heart declares I will never stop respecting you or lifting you up.

I will sing again and again,

I will sing a melody for you,

My soul is pleased to sing for you.[11]

RESPONSE:
I will praise the Lord today and every day—regardless of my circumstances.

PRAYER:
Pray for all Christians who today are persecuted by being tortured. Pray they will respond as Helen did.

11 Helen Berhane, *Song of the Nightingale* (Colorado Springs: Authentic Media, 2009), p. 52.

March 6

DRAWN TO JESUS

"No one can come to me unless the Father who sent me draws them, and I will raise them up at the last day…"
John 6:44

Throughout the Muslim world, Jesus ("the man in white") has appeared to seekers in special ways—often in dreams and visions. For example, Achmed is forty-two, married and has four daughters. A year ago, the Lord Jesus appeared to him in a dream. Coming from an Egyptian fundamentalist family, Achmed was a committed Muslim. The dream caused his Islamic faith to waver. As a secret believer, he has gone into hiding in Cairo. He describes his dream:

In the field, there were hundreds, perhaps even thousands of people. They were all dressed in white and were looking up to heaven expectantly. They didn't pay any attention to me. Suddenly a dazzling light shone on the crowd. Out of the light, the Lord Jesus stepped forward. He hovered over the people and blessed them. Then he pointed at me.

At that moment, I woke up. I was completely confused. I knew Isa (Jesus) only from the Koran. I knew that he was a man who had performed miracles, a prophet. Never had I thought that he would reveal himself to me. I was shaking all over my body and woke up my wife. "What's the matter?" she asked. I could only say, "They're right. They're following the right way. They're right…" I couldn't go back to sleep. I had to know more about this man.

The easiest way was to turn on the television and look for Christian satellite stations. Achmed also read the Bible and watched the JESUS film. He had bought this on impulse a year before at a book fair in Cairo. He spoke to a Christian neighbour, who took him to a church in Cairo. He says, "I started to attend the services in secret and took part in a Bible study group. The love of the Christians touched me. The members of our Bible study group are like family to me." Achmed had been supernaturally drawn to Jesus.

RESPONSE:
I thank God today that I have also been drawn to Jesus, and He will raise me up!

PRAYER:
Pray that God will continue to draw many, many Muslims to Jesus around the globe.

March 7

THE SUPREMACY OF JESUS CHRIST

"What is mankind that you are mindful of them, the son of man that you care for him? You made him a little lower than the angels; you crowned him with glory and honor and put everything under his feet." In putting everything under him, God left nothing that is not subject to him. Yet at present we do not see everything subject to him.

Hebrews 2:6-8

Today we hear from co-worker, Jan Vermeer:

The inspired writer of the book of Hebrews says that everything was put in subjection under Jesus Christ (2:8). Does His supremacy actually show in the country of North Korea full of idols, hunger and death camps?

The North Korean church consists of 200,000 to 400,000 members. Fiercely persecuted, all of them hide their beliefs from the authorities. The church is truly an underground church, divided into thousands of small networks and cell groups. Most Christians hardly know other Christians outside their families. In case of an arrest, not many other Christians are in danger. The most visible proof of their faith is the possession of a Bible, which is illegal and punishable by death. Probably nowhere else in the world are so many copies of God's Word literally hidden underground!

But the church is definitely growing. Many Christians keep their faith secret and are surviving. Open Doors is able to support almost 60,000 Christians with Bibles, books, training, food, clothes and medicines. Yet it is the individual tragedies that make it difficult to see with spiritual eyes that Jesus Christ is supreme even in North Korea.

For example, a middle aged man was arrested after the police found a Bible in his home. He is being terribly beaten in prison, as we learn from released prisoners who witnessed it. "His face is deformed. He told us he is certain he will die."

How can Christ be supreme if one of his disciples is tortured so severely? I've known this man for a long time," says a Christian friend

133

of the prisoner. "When he came to faith, he made the decision that one day he would die for Christ. Every Christian in North Korea has made that choice. Every Christian in my country has the spirit of martyrdom in him. If you lose that spirit for one second, you cannot carry the burden of being a follower of Jesus. My friend knew that one day he could get caught and on that day he had to be steadfast in the faith and loyal to Jesus. I am convinced he can take the suffering because he constantly reminds himself of the joy that is set before him."

The suffering North Korean Christians reveal Christ's supremacy because they look at the reward: Jesus Christ Himself. He is our Treasure. He calls us to Himself, to suffer outside the gate and bear the reproach He endured (Hebrews 13:12-14). The kingdom of the Kim's is limited in size and time. The Kingdom of our Lord is eternal and will come with power!

RESPONSE:
I will rejoice in the supremacy of Jesus Christ, my Lord, over everything and everyone.

PRAYER:
Lord, I too rejoice in the joy set before me with You. Keep me steadfast, faithful and loyal.

March 8

STOP MAKING GOD "SAFE"

"Do not suppose that I have come to bring peace to the earth. I did not come to bring peace, but a sword."
Matthew 10:34

Open Doors colleague, Ron Boyd-MacMillan, shares the following insight from his teaching, "Why I Need to Encounter the Persecuted Church."

Don't let them make God safe!" These words of send-off for me at the Bombay airport were from an Indian Christian evangelist. He had a low opinion of Western churches. After visiting them he confided, "They have managed to turned a dangerous God into a safe one… instead of a God that burns with fury against hypocrisy, idolatry and injustice, they have a God that turns a blind eye to all our faults, just keeps on loving us with a disinterested air, and seems not to care whether we stand out for him or not."

The persecuted never let us forget that knowing God should bring chaos, not safety, because God's gospel is so subversive. The life of the Indian evangelist proves this point. He used to work as a river guide in the Hindu holy city of Varanasi. It was his job to row tourists around the river especially at sunrise so they could take pictures of the morning sun shining on the giant rows of temple steps, called *ghats* that hugged the river bank. His employer insisted he provide sexual services for the tourists who hired the boat, and he soon became a male prostitute.

A few years later he received the gospel as a result of a chance encounter with a tourist. After becoming a Christian he said, "I felt relief that I did not have to behave that way again. Suddenly a whole new set of choices opened up for me. But I was apprehensive too— the choices that pleased God would not please anyone else." His employer had him beaten by thugs. But he refused to return to work as a prostitute. He was sacked and immediately had to leave town.

At first he went back to his family, but they were not happy to see him. His mother wailed, "We sold you so you could look after us in our old age, and now you are following a bad god who has made you refuse to provide for us."

He became convicted that he must return to Varanasi and work to free all the other sex slaves. He began setting up a bank so that low paid workers could borrow at reasonable rates of interest, and not have to go to loan sharks that kept them in financial slavery. He said, "Jesus Christ had given me freedom, and now I had to fight for the freedom of other people just like me. I had to. Jesus makes us pure and sacred, and it is not right that his children should be bought and sold and used like cattle."

He has survived two assassination attempts. His wife had acid thrown over her by thugs employed by the leaders of the prostitution rackets. This man is driven by a love for a God that is determined to set his children free.

God has been made far too safe when we can attend churches and never be roused to do something about the challenge of the poor, the needy, the persecuted. God wants us to stand up and out against sin. He promised us that following Him would get us into a fight. The fight will come to us if only we realize how subversive His gospel really is. Let the persecuted help.

RESPONSE:
Today I will stand up and stand out for God and His righteousness…not look for a safe life.

PRAYER:
Lord, bless all, like the Indian evangelist, who stand up for You today in a spiritual fight.

March 9

GOD KNOWS WHAT IT IS LIKE TO LOSE A CHILD

But God demonstrates his own love for us in this:
While we were still sinners, Christ died for us.

Romans 5:8

Young Nam left his family behind in North Korea to search for money and food in China. Christians there helped him but on the way back he bumped into a North Korean patrol, and he was arrested on the spot. A prison official let Young Nam go after taking away all his money. Young Nam fled again to China, only to be arrested by Chinese policemen. And now he was back in the same prison with the same official who took a bat which was wrapped in newspaper. After Young Nam had taken the beating, the guards dragged him back to an overcrowded cell.

He convinced the prison official that he was not going to betray him and was released a second time. If he wanted to survive, the only option was to go back to China and stay there. He was able to secure a job working in the kitchen of a Beijing restaurant.

There he met Eun Kyung who also came to work in the kitchen. Her husband had died in North Korea. Her sweet daughter died in her arms and her son was put in an orphanage. She and a bunch of other women were locked up in a house and sold into marriage to Chinese men.

Eun Kyung protested. "I have just lost my husband. Don't force me to marry someone!" The human traffickers listened to her and placed her on a Chinese farm, where she had to work for room and board, but the family treated her very well. She ultimately came to Beijing and met Young Nam.

There was chemistry between them. They took some secret Bible study classes together and they married, also in secret of course. After a while, the situation in Beijing became too tense for North Korean refugees, and the restaurant boss arranged false passports and put Young Nam and Eun Kyung on a plane to another country.

Now, Young Nam and Eun Kyung live in small apartment far away from their home country. There is little that reminds them of their painful past, unless it's the eyes of their baby. Inevitably the eyes look similar to the eyes of the child she left behind in that wretched country with its love-wrecking system. Eun Kyung holds her few-months-old son tightly. The child is tense. Eun Kyung doesn't seem to notice. She will protect this precious child with her life.

After their escape from China, Young Nam and Eun Kyung really got to know God by studying the Bible with a local pastor. They realized it was God who protected them. "God saved us, brought us together and gave us another child. We are very grateful for his love."

Young Nam and Eun Kyung look to their son. For them, the child is a symbol of God's hope and love. They know that God will not undo the past. However, God promises us that all tears will be wiped from our faces. That's possible because the Son of God, out of love, let Himself be crucified. God Himself carried our pain. He knows what it is like to lose a child.

They conclude, "No matter what happened to us, we trust in God. We know that He is love."

RESPONSE:
Today I will forget the past, rejoice in God's love and be thankful for all His gifts of life.

PRAYER:
Thank You God that You can feel the pain of those who have lost a child. May Your love envelop them today and wipe the tears from their faces.

March 10

VISIONS OF JESUS - MESSIAH

Then those who were in the boat worshiped him, saying,
"Truly you are the Son of God."
Matthew 14:33

Some of Jesus' disciples took time to come to a place where they recognized this very human being they followed was also God. Interestingly, in Matthew's account of their journey with Jesus, it was the calming of the terrible storm that finally convinced them.

Jesus later told His disciples that people who have not seen His miracles and still believe are even more blessed. But still today, many people need a supernatural revelation to trust Him.

Throughout the Muslim world come reports of people having dreams and visions of Jesus. In this way, He becomes real to them and further reading of Scripture confirms His status as Messiah and Savior.

Hedayat is an Iranian youth who had always been a good Muslim and practiced the rituals required by his faith, but he had never considered the message of the Quran to be very positive. An Armenian Christian friend of Hedayat sometimes shared a little with Hedayat about the Christian faith of his family. He didn't say too much, because he did not want to get in trouble for it. But one day he gave Hedayat a movie, warning him to watch it when he was alone.

Watching the movie did not convince Hedayat of the Christian faith, nor his dream afterwards. He says, "I had prayed the prayer at the end of the video, and then I had this dream. I saw a man in my house, standing before me. I saw marks in his wrists and feet, and I just knew this must be Jesus, but I could not respond."

Hedayat recalls after that, he had felt very confused and did not want to accept any of this. He realized that especially his older brother might become furious if he accepted the Christian faith. So he decided to block any thoughts about this and cut the relationship with his Armenian friend.

Although the Armenian tried to get in touch many times, Hedayat always refused. Four years later the Armenian believer mustered up courage and went to the electronics shop where Hedayat worked. Walking up to his old friend, he shoved a small present over the counter.

"I will never forget you and will always pray for you," the Christian said. Then he turned around and left the shop, leaving Hedayat astonished.

"From the size of the package, I thought it was a pocket-diary. But it turned out to be a New Testament," Hedayat remembers. "At the moment I unpacked it, I felt anger coming up, because he was chasing me with his Christianity! I put it away, but in the evening I became curious and wondered if I could discover if the Bible indeed was corrupted, as I was told."

So Hedayat started reading Matthew, Mark, and Luke. After a few months, Hedayat contacted his Armenian friend at the phone number that was on a little note in the Bible. The Word of God had convinced him that there was no Mehdi coming, as Iranian Shias believe, but that it was Jesus the Messiah he should be expecting. Through his friend, he was soon welcomed into a house church and discipled.

RESPONSE:
Today I will thank God for His Son revealed through His Word which is enough for me.

PRAYER:
Pray for many more who see Jesus in dreams and visions to come to a place of acceptance.

March 11

JESUS IS WORTH IT ALL

For you know the grace of our Lord Jesus Christ, that though he was rich, yet for your sake he became poor, so that you through his poverty might become rich.
2 Corinthians 8:9

In Eritrea today, thousands of Christians are imprisoned for their faith without formal charges. Recently three prisoners who had escaped the prison setting were interviewed in safety. Their interpreter said, "They have really suffered. They did nothing wrong. But just for their faith they have spent years in prison. They were locked up in containers, tied up in the helicopter position, denied food. Why? Because they worship Christ. Because they say they are born-again. Because it is wrong to be an evangelical Christians."

The three men, Peter, Paul and John met in prison after being arrested for their Christian activity involvement. They worked hard. They farmed, mined, did building work on government projects—always in the sun. No shade or rest in very high degree heat.

They say, "The prisons are very dirty. There is no washing, no cleaning. And the food is very little—just bread many times, sometimes even no food. This makes many prisoners sick. They did not allow us to see a doctor. Many people died. It is very sad. Also, they beat us very much, for no reason. Some had broken hands, legs, even chest bones and most of the time no doctor to attend to our injuries. Some died from their injuries. We think some also died because they lost hope. Their hearts just gave up! We saw some die like this."

They were repeatedly asked to deny their faith and sign an official document. One said, "The police threatened to arrest our other family members also if we refused to recant and sign the document. But we refused because we do not want to leave Jesus and become Marxist."

They say they encouraged each other not to give up. Finally, one evening they broke out of the line and jumped over the fence surrounding the prison. One said, "The fence was made up of plants with big thorns. We jumped over them and ran. When the prison guards started shooting, we went in different directions. We heard bullets flying over our heads but none hit us."

The Lord proved faithful and all three men separately and safely crossed the border after walking for days. How happy they were when they were miraculously reunited at a camp. They however could not stay at that refugee camp as they were informed that they could still be arrested and repatriated. And through the help that God provided using Christian brethren, they moved on to a safer place where they are awaiting God's opening of doors to resettle at a more secure place.

One of them spoke for the others in saying, "When I reached here, I looked back, and saw that I had lost my freedom. But I also see now that I had lost time. I could not continue with school, I could not get skills training. I do not know how to do office work. I can't even see myself marrying and having my own family. I am almost forty years now and I have to start from nothing." Then he smiled and concluded, "But I still have Jesus. And He is worth it all."

RESPONSE:
Today I will appreciate what I have in Christ and know that He is worth every deprivation.

PRAYER:
Pray for the many still in prison today in Eritrea. Pray they will also be strong in faith.

March 12

PRISONER OF JESUS CHRIST

*I, Paul, the prisoner of Christ Jesus
for the sake of you Gentiles...*
Ephesians 3:1

Prison! Even the word sends shivers down the back and the thought is immediately pushed to the back of our minds. Yet we in the Western world often have no idea just how horrible conditions are in prisons in non-Western countries.

For most people anywhere in the world, imprisonment is simply the biggest shock of their life. One of the most famous prisoners, Aleksandr Solzhenitsyn, was almost poetic in his description in his book *The Gulag Archipelago*. "Arrest [and imprisonment] is an instantaneous, shattering thrust, expulsion, somersault from one state to another."

Prison is extremely challenging for those, like Aleksandr, who find themselves there unjustly or for only spiritual reasons. It is rigorous even for those who acknowledge their guilt and must pay the price. But a strong faith in God and trust in God's ultimate goodness and purposes enables Christian prisoners to emerge with victorious testimonies. And like the Apostle Paul they can say they were "prisoners of Jesus Christ."

For example, Pastor Steven in Vietnam is a courageous leader of the unofficial church. He had a ticket to the USA in 1975 but chose to stay and suffer with his people. He is passionate about the gospel and says, "I always have my suitcase packed by the front door, ready for prison again."

He spent seven and a half years in a tiny cell after being arrested for "illegal Christian activity." He was tortured for sharing Christ with other prisoners, but his faith impacted thousands. One Vietnamese pastor says, "Before 1975, we were only allowed to preach in prisons on Tuesdays, but now there are brothers witnessing there seven days a week!"

An Open Doors-Africa co-worker named Solomon was assigned to find out if there were many Christians in prison or labor camps in Mozambique during the communist regime there. While researching, he was arrested himself. "In prison, all my possessions, including my Bible were taken from me. Then I was subjected to a cross-examination for six hours, after which I was thrown into a cell, exhausted. I had to sleep on a concrete floor without even a blanket.

"Knowing that my heavenly father would never forsake me, I directed all my attention to my fellow-prisoners. Although I still had to sleep on the floor and was harassed by malaria, bugs and gnawing hunger, I tried to talk about my faith as much as possible…

"I had the opportunity to preach to my companions. I prayed for the sick and the Lord heard my prayers and healed them. That was of great support to them and during my stay in prison, I led fifteen people to the Lord.

"Unexpectedly, I found out that there were more Christians in prison. Now it became clear to me why I had to be arrested. In the first place, to bring the message of salvation to the lost ones in prison. And secondly, to strengthen my fellow Christians.

RESPONSE:
Today I accept the fact I can be a witness for Jesus anywhere and everywhere He leads.

PRAYER:
Pray for Christians in prison (Hebrews 13:3) and pray they will be used of God while there.

144

March 13

WHY PERSECUTION AND MARTYRDOM?

...in fact, the time is coming when anyone who kills you will think they are offering a service to God.
John 16:2b

Today we begin a two-part look at the testimony of a terrorist persecutor named Maulana who ultimately gave his life to Christ and became a Christian missionary:

I was born in a Muslim family in a small town of Demak, central Java, Indonesia. My family was very strict in following Islamic Sharia laws. As a Muslim, I read a lot of the Koran, Hadits, the sayings of the prophet Mohammed, and all the other books that help me be a devoted Muslim.

I started to learn about a famous international Muslim named Ayatollah Komeini from Iran. I welcome Ayatollah Khomeini's ideas and his call to revolution to all Muslims because it will be very nice to have Islamic Sharia law applied in our society. That would arrange all ways of life in this country according to the truth of the Koran. I don't like the West because their lifestyle has affected the Eastern lifestyle, young people dress like those in the West, which is so far from Islamic propriety. I hate that.

And this has also caused me to hate tourists who come to Indonesia. They bring Western lifestyle and can't be a role model for us in Islam. I see Christians as hindering Sharia teaching in Indonesia. Indonesia must be cleansed from the cross. It's a must! Sharia must happen in civil society. The Christians worship Jesus, who is merely a man. For us this is sin, and we must stop this movement through churches.

The Indonesian government is committed to freedom of religion, as stated in our national constitution. But for Muslims this is not good. It will not bring any good to the country's future. Because we do not get support from the government, we take law into our own hands. We attack churches; we shoot pastors while they are preaching to cause fear. We do it because the government does not back us up, so we do it by ourselves. We do not fear death because we were encouraged by Ayatollah Ruholla Khomeini to spill our blood to the last drop to make this happen.

Remember the bombing in Bali? That was a combined expression of our frustration and our goal. Calling us terrorists is a big mistake, because we're just Muslim God lovers.

The government supports Eastern Indonesia and the islands to be Christian, and is actually hindering us from teaching or implementing Sharia law there. So we devised secret plans to bring about Sharia law in Eastern Indonesia. I was one of the first 5,000 soldiers sent from east Java on a ship to the island of Ambon. En route from Surabaya to Ambon, we hijacked the ship in Solo. We searched the ship and checked each passenger's identity. Anyone with a Christian ID was either killed or thrown into the ocean. And together our group took over the ship and headed for Ambon Island to eliminate the church of Jesus Christ.

Tomorrow the change that comes to Maulana's life when he meets Jesus.

RESPONSE:
Today I understand that it is Jesus in me which prompts persecution and martyrdom.

PRAYER:
Pray for Christians in conflict zones like Indonesia who risk their lives living for Jesus.

March 14

PEACE THAT OVERCOMES FEAR

Peace I leave with you; my peace I give you.
I do not give to you as the world gives. Do not let your
hearts be troubled and do not be afraid.
John 14:27

Yesterday we shared the first part of the life story of Maulana the Islamic terrorist persecutor from Indonesia. Here is part two of his dramatic conversion story:

The first brigade of jihad conquered all of Ambon Island. Our focused activity was how to close churches. From the persecution, the Christian people do not fight back. When I see children with no parents running around the church, I feel guilty.

As time passes, my heart becomes softer, then love enters my heart. There's a change in my heart that I become sensitive and start to love them slowly. The love becomes thick. One night, I was fasting and praying, I said, "God, you're the one who create my heart, show me your righteousness." In the middle of my heart-crying, I saw a man appear to me. There was fresh blood spattered on the bottom of his white robe, He greeted me with *"Salaam Al I Kum,"* (Peace be with you!) I tried to figure out who I had seen in my vision. It could be the angel of Gabriel, or Mohammed, or could be Nabi Isa, maybe He is Jesus.

To earn income, I became a distributor of an Islamic magazine in Solo, and then went to a small town called Desa Mangu. One day I was distributing magazines, and an old man called to me. He said, "Maulana, come here. I was waiting for you." It was Friday at lunch time. He asked me to eat rice and noodle sarimi together with him. Then he prayed in the name of Jesus before eating. I was shocked!

After lunch, he brought me to a room, and he picked up a large Bible and opened it to John 14:27. It said, "I am leaving you with a gift, peace of mind and heart. And the peace I give is a gift the world cannot give. So don't be troubled or afraid." The mystery of the voice is Isa (Jesus). I confess that Jesus is God! Jesus is great!

And I cry, and I received Him, Isa, as the Lord of the people of Ambon whom I've persecuted.

Now that I believe Jesus is Savior, there is a miracle that happens in my life. What I received from God is an assignment, instead of regrets. My first Christmas morning as a Christian, I was walking with courage and joy on my way to church. But all of a sudden there's a group of young people standing in front of me. One of them knew me and asked, "Where are you going?"

I said, "To church." They said, "Stop! You're not going there!" Then punches from all directions come to my body. When I was there in the hospital, I prayed like Stephen prayed. "God, forgive them for they know not what they were doing." Spiritual strength from within!

That is powerful and gives me strength to be brave and give testimony. I deliver to the people that this government is under His authority. God's authority works in every believer so that we have the freedom to speak. The authority is from the Lord. God's authority is in every believer, so you don't need to be afraid.

RESPONSE:
Today I will be thankful and submit to the peace Jesus gives that overcomes troubles and fear.

PRAYER:
Pray that many more terrorists will have an encounter with Jesus and become His follower.

March 15

TO THE GARDEN AND THE CROSS

When he had finished praying, Jesus left with his disciples and crossed the Kidron Valley. On the other side there was a garden, and he and his disciples went into it.

John 18:1

Today's devotional comes from a Chinese house church pastor who was arrested and held for three weeks just prior to this talk. He says:

When we suffer for Christ, what actually happens? I mean, what really goes on spiritually within us when we are going through suffering?

I ask the question because a young sister was listening to me recently recount my experience of being in jail for three weeks last year. She said, "You talked of having constant diarrhea, of being kicked and punched painfully, and you even feared that God was punishing you…yet you talked also of feeling joy and experiencing peace." She said to me, "I don't understand how these things go together."

My reply to her, and I give it also as an instruction to you all (for you will all suffer at some point for His Name), is that when we suffer, three spiritual experiences happen to us all at once: angelic strengthening, superhuman forgiveness, and human incomprehension. These three things appear contradictory, but if you suffer, you will find they come together as they did in the life of Christ.

An old Christian used to say to me, "When they lead you away to jail, tell yourself you are merely going with Christ to the Garden of Gethsemane, and to the Cross." To the Garden, and to the Cross. I liked that. I tested it. It's true…

So that is why suffering Christians appear to speak out of "both sides of their mouth." On the one hand we talk of joy and endurance. On the other hand, there is anger at God, pain and a feeling of spiritual desertion. They sit together, because there is always a war of different feelings and emotions.

149

Although we are angelically strengthened and the recipients of superhuman forgiveness, we also experience a sense of spiritual abandonment as a result of our human incomprehension.

But the greatest thing of all is to walk the way of Christ. That is the privilege of suffering: to suffer a little as our Lord Jesus suffered. As He identified with us by suffering pain, so some are called to identify even more closely with Him by going into the Garden, and onto the Cross.

Never fear, my friends, when you are arrested. You will receive strength. You will also be bewildered. Think of Christ, and follow him into the Garden, and onto the Cross.

For the next three days we will listen to his contrasting explanation of the Garden and the Cross: angelic strengthening; superhuman forgiveness; and human incomprehension.

RESPONSE:
Today I will walk with Jesus whether into the Garden or onto the Cross.

PRAYER:
Thank You Lord, that You strengthen Your people in preparation for suffering and even during it.

March 16

ANGELIC STRENGTHENING: THE GARDEN

An angel from heaven appeared to him
and strengthened him.
Luke 22:43

Today's devotional comes from a Chinese house church pastor who was arrested and held for three weeks just prior to this talk. He says his experience was going with Christ to the Garden and to the Cross. Today he explains The Garden:

My arrest was totally unexpected. There was no warning. I was teaching a seminar in one of our church groups in northeast China, when in the middle of the afternoon, six policemen burst in and the next thing I knew I was punched in the stomach and lying on the floor. One of the policemen put his foot hard on my neck and I couldn't move. I was then allowed to get up. Someone rammed me in the kidneys with a baton and I fell again, gasping from the pain. The pain was sharp and severe all the way to the police station, and I couldn't take anything but the shallowest breaths. It turned out my digestion was ruined for months.

Although it was unexpected, there was a strange way in which I had been prepared for it. The night before, I was praying at midnight for the seminar. I had a list of all the participants, and was praying for each one. The more I prayed, the more discouraged I became. These men and women were too young, or too uneducated, or too wounded. I just felt that they were not good enough to be leaders in our movement. I slumped and sighed and felt very depressed. Also, I was having a bad stomach ache. For weeks my stomach was sore and nausea had been my constant companion.

Then all of a sudden I felt a depression on the sofa, like someone had entered the room and sat down beside me. I opened my eyes. There was no one there, but the depression on the sofa remained. Then I felt a large hand on my back. It was hot and pressed into my lower spine, straightening me up. I felt strong again and my nausea disappeared. Then a soft voice said, *"I am strengthening you for the fight. Do not worry about these young people. I am the strength of God, sent by Jesus to look after them and you. I will help you because He loves you."*

That was an angel. I am convinced of that. Just as the Scripture says of Jesus in the Garden of Gethsemane, ***"Then an angel from heaven appeared to him and gave him strength"*** (Luke 22:43), so it was for me. Angels appear to give us strength. And so all the time I was being taken to the police station in a cramped van, I was repeating the words of the angel to me, *"I will help you because He loves you."*

So I want to make this clear to you all. Whenever you face the challenge of suffering for Christ, you will be angelically strengthened beforehand. You need to keep praying, because that's when the angel comes. But if you pray, you will be ready, because an angel will be there to strengthen you to bear anything.

RESPONSE:
Today I will continue to pray and trust God for His angelic strengthening.

PRAYER:
Thank You, God, for Your angelic host who come to strengthen in our greatest point of need.

152

March 17

SUPERHUMAN FORGIVENESS: THE CROSS

Jesus said, "Father, forgive them, for they do not know what they are doing."
Luke 23:34

Today's devotional again comes from a Chinese house church pastor who was arrested and held for three weeks just prior to this talk. He says his experience was going with Christ to the Garden and to the Cross. Today he explains The Cross:

This is what amazed me the most. Whenever I was beaten up (and that was quite often during those three weeks), I would first feel searing pain, and then another feeling would flood in, almost wiping the pain away. Do you know what that feeling was? Pity. Pity for the man who was beating me.

I kept seeing my interrogator as a man gone wrong. I felt sorry for his mother, who would be so ashamed of him. I wondered what kind of father he must have had, to turn him into such a monster. I felt sad to be in the presence of one of God's creatures that could treat another human so badly with so little concern.

Then I would get amazed at myself. Through the pain I would think, "I should be angry, but I'm not, all I want is for this man to be saved." I had three ribs and a wrist broken, two teeth knocked out, my kidneys were malfunctioning, and yet all I could wish for was for the man beating me to find Christ and forgiveness.

Now I agree with that young sister. It sounds very strange. It doesn't even ring true. It's more human to be angry, or to be afraid. But I can only say this was not myself making me feel that way, but Christ within me. It was superhuman. It was Divine. And to this day, it serves as the greatest assurance I have that I am saved.

Again, this is also the way of Christ. In Luke 23:34, He says from the Cross itself, in the midst of excruciating pain, "Father forgive them, for they do not know what they are doing." I tell you, it gives you such a thrill to know that you feel as Christ felt. That's why suffering is counted such a joy, such a privilege. It confirms to the

153

sufferers that they are Christ's, and He lives in them. We don't have to trust a word that this is so. We feel it in our very breastbones.

RESPONSE:
Today I will forgive those who are causing me grief as Jesus would and did on the cross.

PRAYER:
God, fill me with Your superhuman forgiveness so that I may walk today as Jesus did in forgiving those harming Him. Help me also feel pity and compassion for those who so easily treat others badly.

March 18

HUMAN INCOMPREHENSION: THE CROSS

And at three in the afternoon Jesus cried out in a loud voice, "Eloi, Eloi, lema sabachthani?" (which means "My God, my God, why have you forsaken me?").
Mark 15:34

Today's devotional again comes from a Chinese house church pastor who was arrested and held for three weeks just prior to this talk. He says his experience was going with Christ to the Garden and to the Cross. Today he continues and explains another aspect of The Cross:

But it is not all triumph. I know some pastors who said they just smiled all the time from the moment they were arrested, and felt unutterable joy the whole time. I suppose that is possible. After all, Shadrach, Meshach and Abednego seemed to be very calm throughout their ordeal. But we must not make that the test of true spirituality. The Psalmists are full of despair and questioning as they go through hard times. So were Jeremiah and Job and Habakkuk. And most sobering of all, our Lord Himself was heard to cry from the Cross, *"My God, my God, why have you forsaken me?"* (Mark 15:34)

This is the dark side of the experience. What makes suffering hardest to bear are the questions, the voices that well up within each of us, that are full of doubts, despair and depression. And I believe this is okay. As humans we were not meant to suffer. We were made to be part of a perfect world, with no sorrow or sighing, an Eden where everyone was righteous and fulfilled. So when we suffer, there is a sense in which our bodies and spirits witness saying, *"This is unnatural, this is not why we were created."*

In my own case, I wondered whether God had turned His back on me, or was punishing me for past sins. Yes, I know that sounds odd after all I have just said about feeling the power of God within to forgive my persecutor, and having the angel strengthen me. But you forget these things in the dark watches of the night, sleeping sandwiched between two prisoners and being cursed by everyone because you need to rise and go to the toilet, and so everyone must wake up and shift their position. It was the nights that were worst.

But most of these doubts were not weaknesses as such; they were attempts to comprehend the incomprehensible. Where is God here? What's He up to? How can this possibly extend His kingdom? How is His glory served by one of my sisters being raped by an interrogator? The fact is, when we suffer, there is so much that we cannot understand. I read somewhere that "because we are human, we yearn to understand, but because we are human, we cannot understand."

Suffering puts us in our place. It humbles us to realize that we are not really in charge of our lives. This is a hard realization. God is in charge, and His purposes can be hard to discern at times. He takes even the sin of the world, and turns it to good account. We often do not see how He does this, but we believe it. Accepting it in faith is never easy when you are suffering.

RESPONSE:
Today I will not try to understand the incomprehensible. I will accept God's goodness in everything by faith.

PRAYER:
Pray for Christian prisoners going through great pain today that they may know His touch.

156

March 19

A PRIVILEGE TO DIE FOR CHRIST

For to me, to live is Christ and to die is gain.
Philippians 1:21

The Apostle Paul was convinced that whether he was alive or dead, Christ is gain. This enabled him to minister amid severe hardship and persecution. It also helped him face the potential of premature death without fear and concern. When Christ is everything, life and death are left in His hands.

Bad news interrupted the Standing Strong Through the Storm (SSTS) training for pastors in a rural town of Colombia clouding the happy spirit felt in that meeting.

A letter was received from Pastor Manuel who explained that he was prevented from attending the workshop. Guerrilla leaders found out about the event. They told him that because of his insistence on preaching the gospel, they would not let him travel out of the village.

The amazing thing is that in spite of the continuous threats against Pastor Manuel, the guerrillas have not been able to carry them out against him. On repeated occasions, the army has come just in time to save him from some guerrilla attack.

While participants were grieving from this news about Pastor Manuel, another pastor, Hermes, told about two attempts against his own life by the same subversive band the previous month. Immediately participants expressed their desire to continue their ministry in places where the gospel is prohibited.

However, seven days later, the guerrillas brought together all the leaders that participated in the SSTS workshop and told them, "We are tired of the Christian's disobedience. We do not want to kill anybody; the only thing we want is that you stop telling the people about the Bible. We will have to execute you. Tell Pastor Hermes that we will take drastic measures against him since we know that he is the one who encourages you…"

Pastor Hermes reported that instead of frightening the believers, this difficult situation generated a more intense plan of spiritual and

157

ministerial action. The leaders want Open Doors seminars to come to places where it is impossible to preach.

How are they going to do it? Pastor Hermes said that a network of prayer was established during the time they were together. He believes the only way is through personalized training, or delivering a booklet and training to only one person at a time. For now it is the only way to use this tool to strengthen the believers. The training will take longer, but it is very dangerous to meet and to preach in houses because the guerrillas have cleverly infiltrated the area.

He concluded, "Materials from *Standing Strong Through the Storm* have been the driving force for us to continue preaching…Others also are striving to follow Christ and we have to do the same to prevent our church believers from losing their fervor.

"Besides prayer and fasting, we have to take action…God has protected us up to this moment, and if one day we die for preaching Christ, it will be a privilege."

RESPONSE:
Today I will live in such a way that Christ is honored and glorified. If it takes all my strength or even my death, I will sacrifice all for Him and consider it a privilege.

PRAYER:
Pray for strength and endurance for pastors in rural Colombia facing death threats daily.

March 20

THE MARTYRS HYMN

Here is a trustworthy saying: If we died with him, we will also live with him; if we endure, we will also reign with him. If we disown him, he will also disown us; if we are faithless, he remains faithful, for he cannot disown himself.

2 Timothy 2:11-13

Paul is writing his last letter before execution addressed to his spiritual son, Timothy. New Testament scholars are convinced that Paul is quoting here an ancient Christian worship chorus or "hymn." It is assessed to be one of the songs Christians sang as they were walking into the arena to face certain death. Paul himself may have sung this hymn when he was executed in Rome.

There is plenty of historical evidence that people of the pagan world were amazed at the courage and joy — often expressed in music — Christians exhibited when facing their death. Early church father, Tertullian was reportedly converted soon after first observing this exhibition of abnormal joyfulness. He later made the oft-quoted statement that "the blood of the martyrs is seed!"

The first couplet is powerful because it is in the Greek aorist tense which indicates a specific moment in the past. When Christ calls us, we die to sin and to ourselves. Therefore, the song begins, "We have already died with Him and we will therefore live with Him!" It goes on to proclaim that when we endure, we'll reign with Him; if we deny Him, He will deny or disown us; but when we are faithless, He always remains faithful because it is a characteristic of His unchanging nature.

Korean Elder Kwan-Joon Park was called an "Elijah of Korea" or sometimes a "Daniel of modern times." He died as a martyr for his faith in Christ and his opposition to the Japanese colonial rule during the Second World War when Korea was occupied by the Japanese Imperialists. The latter enforced Shinto worship on the Korean people.

On March 24, 1939, Elder Park went to Japan to protest against inhuman colonial policies of Japan. He walked into the 74th Imperial Diet of Japan. When the opening pronouncement of the lower house was made, he stood up from his seat in the visitor's balcony and shouted, "This is a great mission of God, Jehovah's great message!" Then he threw leaflets to the floor below exposing cruel abuse of Korean Christians by Japan and warning them of God's imminent judgment and destruction of Japan as a result of her wrong doing and tyranny. They also explained the resistance against Japanese imposition of Shinto shrine worship upon Korean Christians.

Elder Park was arrested and sentenced to six years in Japanese prison. While serving his sentence he was martyred at the age of seventy. We don't know if he sang. But one line from his last poem written during his imprisonment expresses well his firm resolution to die willingly for Jesus Christ: "Since Jesus died for me, I will die for Jesus!"

RESPONSE:
Today I will resolve to live courageously even if it means facing death for Jesus who died for me. I will express my joy in living and dying for Him in every way – including singing!

PRAYER:
Lord, help me to be joyful even in the face of death knowing that You are always faithful.

March 21

RELATIONAL ASPECT OF COMMITMENT

Then he said to them all: "Whoever wants to be my disciple must deny themselves and take up their cross daily and follow me.
Luke 9:23

The relational aspect of commitment is found in the phrase, *"Whoever wants to be my disciple…"* There is a desire on our part that causes us to want to come to Jesus to be His follower. It is a relationship that you seek to establish with Him. But what is the origin of this relationship? We do not have anything in us that is good enough to be offered to God. It is God Himself who has committed Himself to us. It is He who has taken the initiative that makes it possible for me to respond in commitment to Him.

We see God's commitment in His creation. He made humankind in His image. And we see His true commitment when we messed up in the fall of humankind. Thus began God's plan for salvation, the redemption story that culminated in the coming of Jesus Christ. God's commitment to us is one of total love. This caused Him to not even spare His only Son from the cruelty of the cross to redeem us from the curse of sin.

In addition, when Jesus was on earth, it was He who took the initiative. In fact, when there were some who wanted to volunteer their services prior to their understanding of the true nature of discipleship and the commitment that is required of them, they were discouraged from doing so:

When Jesus saw the crowd around him, he gave orders to cross to the other side of the lake. Then a teacher of the law came to him and said, "Teacher, I will follow you wherever you go."

Jesus replied, "Foxes have holes and birds of the air have nests, but the Son of Man has no place to lay his head." Another disciple said to him, "Lord, first let me go and bury my father." But Jesus told him, "Follow me, and let the dead bury their own dead."
(Matthew 8:18–22)

This is the relational aspect of commitment; one in which we desire to follow Jesus because God first committed Himself to us and calls us to follow Him. We who have experienced His love and grace desire to respond to Him.

RESPONSE:
Today I commit to a relationship with Jesus in being a true learner and follower.

PRAYER:
Lord, I respond to Your love and grace today and desire to become a fully devoted disciple.

March 22

ENTRUSTING ASPECT OF COMMITMENT

Then he said to them all: "Whoever wants to be my disciple must deny themselves and take up their cross daily and follow me.
Luke 9:23

On the basis of certain facts, a relationship has been established between two parties. Now there must be actual evidence to prove that one has made that commitment. This is the aspect of entrusting oneself to that second party. In our Luke text, we see two phrases that reflect this **entrusting aspect of commitment**, *"deny yourself"* and *"take up your cross daily"*.

Deny Yourself:

The commitment we have made costs something. The word "deny" literally means "say no to oneself" or "renounce self—leave self behind." The biblical concept of commitment calls the follower of Jesus to "deny oneself" not self-denial. This is not to deny something, but a more complete and total denial of oneself in which one no longer seeks for what pleases self.

This is in direct contrast to the normal way of life where everyone is out for himself or herself. The basic sinful nature of the world, whether communist, capitalist or revolutionary is the same. It desires the promotion of self at the expense of someone else.

Jesus says his followers will be known as those who deny themselves.

Take Up Your Cross Daily:

The second part is even more extreme. Commitment also calls for the taking up of the cross. In commitment to Jesus, you deny yourself even to the point of willingness to go to your own execution! We only commit ourselves to the point of willingness to die when we understand that the present life ends up in death anyway and the One who has promised us forgiveness and eternal life can really deliver.

In Jesus Christ, the believer has found real life. Therefore the denying of self and the way of the cross are only logical steps for him or her to take.

A young man who had recently become a Christian was returning home to a country where the punishment for conversion to Christ was death. He was asked whether or not he was afraid to go back. He replied, *"I have already died in Christ!"*

Jim Elliott, a missionary who was martyred in Ecuador, said, *"He is no fool who gives what he cannot keep to gain what he cannot lose."*

RESPONSE:
Today I will commit to entrust myself to Jesus by denying self and taking up my cross.

PRAYER:
Lord, I entrust myself to You and purpose to live the rest of my life to the fullest in ways that only You decide.

March 23

COMMISSIONING ASPECT OF COMMITMENT

Then he said to them all: "Whoever wants to be my disciple must deny themselves and take up their cross daily and follow me.
Luke 9:23

The personal and trusting relationship between God and His followers now leads the believer to the **commissioning aspect of commitment**—a task that is characteristic of being His true followers—*"and follow me."* This commitment is not to a task but to a person. To be a follower of Jesus is to be a disciple of Jesus. A disciple is one who follows the teaching of another; one who is like another; one who models after another.

What is the task to which he has called us? The task is none other than the words of what we call "The Great Commission":

Then Jesus came to them and said, "All authority in heaven and on earth has been given to me. Therefore go and make disciples of all nations, baptizing them in the name of the Father and of the Son and of the Holy Spirit, and teaching them to obey everything I have commanded you. And surely I am with you always, to the very end of the age." (Matthew 28:18–20)

The Christian's task is nothing short of being a servant of Jesus Christ proclaiming the message of Jesus Christ and helping others become followers of Jesus. Our primary responsibility is neither overthrowing governments nor opposing ideologies but a proactive one of making disciples of all nations.

In the course of our obedience to God's authority, we may come in conflict with the existing government. We have been called to be good citizens and history has proven that Christians are generally law-abiding and hard working. But when conflicts come, the Christian is ready to choose his commitment to Christ over his or her commitment to local authorities (Acts 4:19–20).

RESPONSE:
Today I complete my commitment to follow Jesus in sharing His love with others.

PRAYER:
As a true disciple, I give myself, Lord, to the task of world evangelization starting where You place me today.

March 24

THE ROAD TO CALVARY

They took palm branches and went out to meet him,
shouting, "Hosanna! Blessed is he who comes in the
name of the Lord! Blessed is the king of Israel!"
John 12:13

There were two crowds who greeted Jesus on that first Palm
Sunday. The first crowd were Passover celebrators who came out from
Jerusalem to meet Jesus as he approached from Bethany (John 12:12).
The second crowd was made up of those accompanying Him from
Bethany who had witnessed the recent miraculous resurrection of
Lazarus (John 12:17). Both crowds loudly proclaimed praises to Jesus
as he rode into town on a donkey on the road leading Him to Calvary.

John's account of this day also indicates there were two types of
responses to Jesus as he rode into Jerusalem. One outspoken group
"continued to spread the word" about Jesus causing many people
to look for Him. It even caused the Pharisees to say, "Look how the
whole world has gone after him" (John 12: 19).

A second group believed in Jesus but would not publicly confess
their faith because of fear of losing their status in the local synagogue.
They loved praise from men more than praise from God, John
concluded (John 12:42-43).

Palm Sunday is thus a challenge to us about how outspoken or not
we are about King Jesus. Do we continue to loudly proclaim Him as
our King or are we so fearful of consequences that we hold back and
hesitate, losing every opportunity to make Him known.

A pastor friend of Rev. Joseph Tson in Romania was told by an
interrogating officer, "We know that Mr. Tson would love to be a
martyr, but we are not so foolish as to fulfill his wish."

Pastor Tson said:

Now that I had placed my life on the altar and decided I was
ready to die for the gospel, they were telling me they would not
kill me. I could go wherever I wanted in the country and preach
whatever I wanted knowing I was safe.

As long as I tried to save my life, I was losing it. Now that I was willing to lose it, I found it...

Jesus taught us long ago: with Him, the road down leads upward. With Him, the path of suffering ends in victory. The road to Calvary does not stop until resurrection.

RESPONSE:
Today I commit to joining the group of disciples who "continue to spread the word."

PRAYER:
Lord, help me walk the Calvary road with You right through to resurrection!

March 25

COME AND DIE

Very truly I tell you, unless a kernel of wheat falls to the
ground and dies, it remains only a single seed.
But if it dies, it produces many seeds.
John 12:24

When our children were young, we would often sing before dinner
the chorus, "Come and dine the master calleth, come and dine..." One
day our youngest, Melinda, our adopted Filipina asked, "Daddy, why
does Jesus say we have to come and die?" The family laughed at this
question concluding that we really needed to work on our singing
diction.

But as I study Jesus' teaching, I've come to realize that Melinda
was singing correctly all the time. Because Jesus also indicates that
discipleship means there is a cross to bear. All too often the cross
becomes for us just an historic symbol. One day a North American
minister was showing a foreign visitor his newly built church
building. Outside, a spotlight illuminated a huge cross on the steeple.
The pastor boasted, "That cross alone cost us $10,000."

The visitor looked at him quizzically and replied, "Where I come
from, Christians can get them for free!"

A Canadian Christian aid worker was overwhelmed at the enormous
need among the believers of southern Sudan. He recalls some children
in a village wearing nothing but hand carved bone crosses fashioned
in necklaces around their necks. He pointed to the cross on one
emaciated child and questioned her with hand motions. She smiled
broadly, took off the necklace and handed it to him.

His thoughtful analysis is this: "That little act symbolizes the state
of the Persecuted Church in Sudan. With absolutely nothing in the
way of material possessions, they still have the cross of Jesus Christ.
They are prepared to share its hope - even though it means death."

To Jesus the cross meant the willing denial of self for the sake of
others. Seeking to save your life, you'll lose it while losing your life
for Jesus will save it.

169

Dietrich Bonhoeffer, the German theologian who gave up his life taking a stand against Hitler wrote, "When Christ calls a man, he bids him come and die." That's what it means to lose our life in order to save it. Jesus himself was our example being willing to go to the cross on behalf of others—even a lost world.

RESPONSE:
Today I will deny myself, take up my cross and follow Jesus.

PRAYER:
Lord, I respond to Your call to "come and die to myself" in order to find real life in You.

March 26

TAKE UP YOUR CROSS

Anyone who loves their life will lose it, while anyone who hates their life in this world will keep it for eternal life.
John 12:25

A tentmaker missionary in Morocco struggled with the issue of dying for Christ. He shares these words:

Is faith in Christ worth dying for? I quickly saw that if it wasn't, I had no business presenting the gospel to Muslims. You see, when a Muslim receives Christ, he faces certain persecution and possible death. How can I ask a Muslim to receive Christ as Lord if I have doubts in my own heart. If Christ isn't worth dying for, He isn't worth living for. On the other hand, if Christ is worth living and dying for, then we have a gospel that is of infinite value to Muslims...

Ahmed came to see me one day, honestly sharing his fears with me about following Christ. He asked, "What if I go to prison?" This kind of question had always intimidated me; I wasn't sure that I could ask someone to be willing to go to prison when I myself had never gone. Yet now I realised that it was Jesus who was calling him to take up his cross and follow, not me. This was between Ahmed and the Lord.

A thirty-two-year-old pastor works in upper Egypt, an area of intense persecution for Christians. He runs a day care centre, a medical clinic, a literacy training program as well as caring for the families of those in prison. He has been beaten twice by Muslim extremists and threatened daily with death. He knows they are trying to kill him...but he continues to daily bear his cross.

A leading pastor in Egypt shared about a parishioner who tearfully came for counselling. Young people she had trained at her work were recently promoted to be her supervisors. She was passed over solely because she was a Christian. The pastor concluded, "That's the cross we must bear here in Egypt!"

The essence of these examples is that instead of exercising and asserting my will, I learn to cooperate with God's wishes and comply with His will.

RESPONSE:
Today I give my will over to God and comply with His will for me.

PRAYER:
Lord, I want to cooperate with Your wishes and desires. Help me bear my cross for You.

March 27

FOLLOW ME

Whoever serves me must follow me; and where I am,
my servant also will be. My Father will honor the one
who serves me.
John 12:26

I'll never forget my first visit to the house church of Pastor Samuel Lamb in Quangzhou, China with my wife Dianne. That night we were introduced to his twenty-four-year-old assistant pastor. We soon learned that she had no danwei or work-unit. This was how all people in China were identified and registered. Even some shopping required a danwei.

When asked, "Isn't it risky for you to work full-time in a house church and not have a danwei?" she simply replied, "It's the way of the cross!"

One of our Canadian couriers to Cuba asked a leading pastor who received many needed Spanish Bibles from us, "We're placing you at risk, aren't we?" He answered with his hand on his heart, "Risk? What risk? I took a risk when I accepted the Lord Jesus Christ as my Saviour and became a minister. And if they want to shoot me, so much the better. I'll go into glory sooner."

Rinaldo Hernandez is a Methodist pastor in Cuba. His father spent five years in prison for political subversion and wanted the family to escape to Miami. But Rinaldo decided that staying in Cuba was a cross he must bear:

"I remember my father told me that I would pay a high price for that decision," he says. His price was to come later when his seminary education was disrupted by assignment to compulsive military service in a work camp. There conditions were primitive and most of the men were hardened criminals.

He and seven other Christians met secretly at night in the sugar cane fields to pray, read the Bible and encourage one another. "I became a pastor in that work camp, not in seminary," he concludes.

A Chinese Christian brother from the north-west province of Xinjiang was released after serving twenty years in prison. He shared this poem written by his wife just before her death in prison:

> As a real disciple I have dedicated my life hoeing the fields energetically,
>
> Begging for food shamelessly,
>
> Wearing worn-out clothes as if they were formal dresses
>
> Freezing to death at the windy station yet uttering not a word of complaint.
>
> Only if the gospel would be widely spread
>
> Am I willing to be hung upside down on the cross...with no regret.

The late Jamie Buckingham made this memorable statement: "The risk-free life is a victory-free life. It means life-long surrender to the mediocre and that is the worst of all possible defeats."[12]

RESPONSE:
I will not surrender to the defeat of mediocrity but follow Jesus whatever the risk.

PRAYER:
Lord, help me to truly follow You – even to the cross!

---

12 Jamie Buckingham, "Best Quotes," *Charisma* (August, 1995), p. 51.

March 28

TAKE THIS CUP

"Father, if you are willing, take this cup from me; yet not my will, but yours be done."
Luke 22:42

On hearing the news of the violent assassination of Christian government minister, Shahbaz Bhatti, Maaria from Pakistan wrote these words in her "Secret Believers" blog:

Another man laid to rest, not like men who die for a better tomorrow or men who die for the restoration of a nation, or men who die for a noble cause. I am writing of a line of men and women who have entered Christ's rest because they chose to believe in Him above the laws of the land and the laws of Islam. They chose to stand up for Christ...

Mr. Bhatti's name has been added to that list. Every time I try to sleep, images of his car, the blood, the bullet holes, the sound of what it must have been like, the stench of what must have filled the air come to me along with the voice of a woman hidden away in a prison. A woman whose persecution started this spate of hatred and anger—Aasia Bibi, my sister—in solitary confinement, afraid, alone and waiting for the day she is hung for a crime she did not commit.

For every bullet that was sprayed, whether it hit him and spilt his blood or not, I offer the Al Quaida, forgiveness. I cannot speak yet for my aching people. I will give them time to get there. But I know there are Maarias who forgive the Al Quaida for taking away a man who loved Jesus and loved the church and loved Pakistan. For every bullet, I remember the nails on the cross and ask the Lord to *"Forgive them for they know not what they do."* They have been brain washed. They are not born for this. God allows them into the world for great things. I ask that you forgive them too.

For every drop of blood spilt, forgive them. Jesus hung on the cross and his blood was spilt for us. For every drop of blood, I urge you my Christian family around the world, to remember the sips of wine from the cup that Jesus passed among his disciples in the upper room…Then remember those of us for whom the words of Christ are so real today, *"Lord…take this cup from me."* I am sure there were nights when Mr. Bhatti spoke into the darkness to God and asked Him to deliver him from this. But God gave him the courage to carry on. He did not bend to the demand to give up and walk away.

RESPONSE:
Today I will pray for courage to honor Jesus and forgive those who snuff out His light.

PRAYER:
Lord, grant Your courage, peace and forgiving spirit to all who grieve injustices today.

March 29

LIVING FOR JESUS

"And I, when I am lifted up from the earth, will draw all people to myself." He said this to show the kind of death he was going to die.
John 12:32-33

Manuel was an effective evangelist among the mountain Quechua people in Peru. He felt called by the Lord to take Bibles and share the gospel with the anti-government guerilla soldiers who camped in hiding in the mountains. For the many illiterates he took the New Testament on cassette. It was a bold and risky ministry.

One day some Shining Path guerrillas with their big AK-47 guns intercepted him on the trail and ordered him to stop going to the mountains; stop handing out Bibles, cassettes and other Christian materials; and stop preaching about Jesus. They threatened his life if he did not desist.

Some months later Manuel did not return home when expected. A search party discovered his dead body at the side of the trail. It was more than just a cadaver. His feet, hands and tongue had been cut off. And with a knife they had carved on his torso a message in Spanish, "We told you to stop!" The chopped body parts completed the message, "stop visiting the villages; stop distributing Bibles; stop preaching about Jesus!"

There was a memorial service for Manuel attended by many believers. Hundreds of people came from the mountains to honor his memory. Our Open Doors co-worker reported that there were more people standing outside the rural church than sitting inside the crowded sanctuary.

An evangelist preached the memorial service message and challenged young people to come forward and take Manuel's place. Ten young people made the commitment and knelt at the front altar.

An elder standing at the side asked in a loud voice, "But young people. What if the same thing happens to you as happened to Manuel?"

One of the youths at the front cried out, "If we die, a hundred will spring up and take our place!"

Living for Jesus is actually harder than dying for Jesus. It means I must die to myself every day!

RESPONSE:
Since Jesus gave His life for me, what more can I give Him than my own life. And until that day of physical death, I will die to myself daily.

PRAYER:
Thank You Jesus, for giving Your life blood for me. I give You my life in service today and every day until You call me to be with You in Your heavenly home.

March 30

WOUNDS FOR CHRIST

The apostles left the Sanhedrin, rejoicing because they had been counted worthy of suffering disgrace for the Name.

Acts 5:41

Today's devotional comes from Ron Boyd-MacMillan's excellent volume *Faith That Endures*:

The Biblical scholar William Barclay famously described a New Testament Christian as having three remarkable characteristics: "One, they were absurdly happy; two, they were filled with an irrational love for everyone; and three, they were always in trouble!"

Persecuted Christians are constantly in trouble. As a Palestinian pastor put it, "If you speak truth to power, power always reacts." An encounter with the persecuted reveals the incendiary nature of this gospel we follow, and if our witness does not provoke some sort of explosive reaction, we have to check whether our gospel powder is damp or dry. We should be in trouble for Jesus! If we aren't, something is wrong...

Persecuted Christians are not tempted into the illusion that the world is actually a friendly place that does not mind our identifying with Christ. The world for them is unmasked in its hostility to Christ.

Once when visiting Czechoslovakia in the 1980's, I delivered a Bible to an elderly pastor. He had not seen a Bible in years. He smelled it, kissed it with trembling lips, cradled it, and then with great reverence, opened it. Then he turned to me and said, "Let me tell you of my wounds." And he poured out his trials for God, which included seven beatings by the secret police and the awful seduction of his daughter by a government agent who then fooled her into betraying him. Then he turned to me, his eyes boring into my soul, and asked, "What wounds have you for the Master?" I was embarrassed to have so few to share.

The questions of the Persecuted Church are simple: Are you in trouble for Jesus? Where are your wounds? If you don't have any, maybe you've forgotten you're in a fight at all. Whatever culture we are in, we are always being subtly coerced into spending our money, or time, on what is not of Christ. Persecution afflicts us all if we stand up for Christ. The world, the flesh, and the devil will never reach an accommodation with Christ. Like it or not, we are caught up in cosmic warfare. The gospel has landed us in it. We will all be scarred by the battle. We will all experience persecution. The difference is only one of degree and type.[13]

RESPONSE:
Today I will evaluate my life and assess what are my wounds for Christ. I will then rejoice in suffering for Jesus.

PRAYER:
Lord, I submit to Your Lordship over my life and accept whatever wounds You will enable me to bear for Your sake and the gospel's.

13 Ronald Boyd-MacMillan, *Faith That Endures* (Grand Rapids: Fleming Revell, 2006), pp. 322-323.

March 31

CHRIST IS RISEN INDEED

***But Christ has indeed been raised from the dead, the
firstfruits of those who have fallen asleep.***
1 Corinthians 15:20

Brother Andrew shares today's devotional:

At the time of the cruel persecution in the Soviet Union under
Stalin, public meetings were regularly held in order to ridicule
religion, the church and the priests. On one occasion the inhabitants
of a town were summoned to the main square. From a platform on the
square, a fluent 'scholarly' atheist, who seemed to have many proofs
against the Bible, God and the clergy addressed the public.

The crowd had listened silently. But when the local priest was called
to the front to answer this brilliant oration, an uneasy muttering rippled
through the crowd. The man went and stood close to the microphone and
everyone held his breath. The tension could be cut with a knife, and you
could hear a pin drop. What would his answer be?

We shall never know what went on in the heart of this man - his
fear, his prayer - but at last his voice could be heard, resounding
through the loudspeakers, not only to the crowd, but also to a large
part of the city: *"Khristos voskrese!"* ***Christ is risen!***

For one split second there was silence. A shudder went through the
crowd and then, as a blazing testimony to the priest and to the atheist
opponent, the cry broke out, unanimous and powerful: *"Voistinu
voskrese!"* ***The Lord is risen indeed!***

That was a bad day for atheistic propaganda in Russia. It was also a
bad day for the religious leaders in Jerusalem, nearly 2,000 years ago,
because they had to bribe the soldiers with much money to get them to
tell lies (Matthew 28:12-13). It was also a bad day for the guards who
"became like dead men" (Matthew 28:4).

But it was a bad day especially for the devil because if he had
known this, he "would not have crucified the Lord of Glory"
(1 Corinthians 2:8).

The one who believes in the Cross and the Resurrection takes the side of those who are persecuted. Or, to put it another way, whoever identifies with the Persecuted Church stands in the power of the Resurrection - a target of misguided and corrupt people, but nevertheless together with the mighty Conqueror. The Lamb conquers and we conquer too...in Him. Hallelujah!

RESPONSE:
Today I rejoice in the glorious truth of the resurrection of Jesus Christ our Lord.

PRAYER:
Lord, may the Persecuted Church around the world resound today with a vocal outburst of assurance that Jesus is alive.

April 1

WHEN LIFE STINKS, OUR PERSPECTIVE SHRINKS

The LORD said, "I have indeed seen the misery of my people in Egypt. I have heard them crying out because of their slave drivers, and I am concerned about their suffering. So I have come down to rescue them from the hand of the Egyptians and to bring them up out of that land into a good and spacious land..."
Exodus 3:7-8

God's chosen people were enslaved in miserable bondage and were crying out to Him in their suffering. God speaks to Moses about it at the burning bush and reveals His sustaining care for His people.

First of all, they were in Egypt **because** God cared for them. He rescued the Israeli nation from death by famine during the time of Joseph who himself was rescued from injustice and suffering to bring a solution to the coming famine crisis. This saved both the Israeli and the Egyptian nations. But a Pharaoh came along in time who did not know about Joseph and chose to persecute the growing Israeli population because of his fear of them.

In this situation they were not forgotten by the God of their fathers. Though, for wise reason, He delayed to appear in their behalf for several hundred years, yet He was not indifferent to their sufferings. Every tear they shed was preserved and every groan they uttered was recorded as testimony against their oppressors. Only God sees the beginning from the end. We are time-bound creatures and as problems arise, our perspective becomes diminished. African-American preachers articulate it this way: "When life stinks, our perspective shrinks!"

Years earlier God spoke to Father Abram in his sleep: *"Know for certain that for four hundred years your descendants will be strangers in a country not their own and that they will be enslaved and mistreated there...In the fourth generation your descendants will come back here, for the sin of the Amorites has not yet reached*

183

its full measure" (Genesis 15:13, 16). In this situation God reveals His plan to Abram ahead of time and explains the "why." He does not always do this, but from this example we learn we can trust His Father-heart.

So today we pray for Persecuted Church members who are suffering severely from Satan's tactics of deceit and intimidation: loss of family members (Nigeria), economic deprivation (India), incarceration in metal shipping containers (Eritrea), lack of personal peace (Pakistan), fear of discovery (Middle East). As we pray, we can rest in the fact that they (and we) are part of God's wise and caring plan, no matter how inscrutable that plan may appear to human eyes. There is hope because He hears the cry; He sees the misery; He is concerned about the suffering. When it seems dark and hopeless, the persecuted testify "God is good—all the time!"

RESPONSE:
I will live in the light of God's loving care and view my problems from His perspective.

PRAYER:
Pray that persecuted believers will trust God and not suffer from shrunken perspectives.

April 2

GOD AS DELIVERER

"And now the cry of the Israelites has reached me, and I have seen the way the Egyptians are oppressing them. So now, go. I am sending you to Pharaoh to bring my people the Israelites out of Egypt."
Exodus 3: 9-10

Moses may have been delighted to hear that the God of Abraham, Isaac and Jacob was a God with a heart for His people's suffering. Delighted too that this God with such a father's heart then rises from His throne—not commanding armies of angels to relieve the suffering of His people—and comes down in His own person to deliver them from the hands of the Egyptians.

But Moses is totally taken back by the command, "I am sending YOU, Moses, to Pharaoh in order to bring the Israelis out of Egypt." Moses reaction is one of self-deprecation and insecurity. He poses innumerable questions and obstacles. God promises to go with him and give Moses the exact words to say. God is able to deliver. And often He will ask YOU to be His agent.

In Iran, Pastor Haik Hovsepian (martyred in 1994) recorded many messages. It has been possible to distribute thousands of his tapes. One of the people who recently got hold of a tape is a Quran reciter. He has a very powerful voice and many times he has been invited to recite the Quran in different mosques in Iran. He also passionately recited about the life of the dead Imams (Muhammad's descendants) in mourning ceremonies in order to make people cry. He used to be a very religious person himself.

When he got hold of a sermon of Haik, he realized that through religion he cannot be saved. He was in captivity of some immoral sins such as alcohol abuse and adultery. When he heard about the difference between religion and salvation of Jesus, the Spirit of God spoke to his heart. Every time he listened to this tape, he felt even more convinced that he needed the salvation of Jesus, until he finally gave his life to the Lord. By then he was not only liberated from the captivity of his sins, but also from the captivity of the religion with which he was identifying. He is now using his voice to sing for the Lord and shares about Jesus wherever he goes.

As he was a well-known person among Muslim religious leaders and other people, one evening the secret police knocked at his door. Two weeks later, they released him from prison on bail until his trial date. He had to borrow half of the money from his relatives as his savings were not enough. Since he lost his job as a Quran reciter, he does not have any source of income, so it is difficult for him to live and to pay the money back to his family. He is trusting God to totally deliver him. Praise God for the steadfast faith of this brother in following Jesus.

RESPONSE:
Today I will trust God for deliverance from every challenge and temptation I face.

PRAYER:
Thank You Lord for this precious deliverance record of Your power and goodness. I am available to act as Your agent in this world of suffering.

April 3

THE MYSTERY OF REDEMPTION AND RESCUE

For he has rescued us from the dominion of darkness and brought us into the kingdom of the Son he loves...
Colossians 1:13

The imagery of God's intervention in the suffering of the Israeli's in Egypt recorded in Exodus 3:7-8 has captured the imaginations of many oppressed people. For example, African-American believers see a strong parallel between American slavery and the bondage of the Jews in Egypt and God's personal and powerful exodus rescue of His people.

New Testament writers saw a powerful parallel with our sinful, lost, human condition and God's redemption through the sending of His only Son who "pitched his tent" among us and purchased our salvation with His shed blood. For example, in Colossians 1:13, the Apostle Paul states it clearly. We have been *"rescued from"* Satan's dark domain and *"brought into"* the kingdom of God's Son.

The Exodus passage also brings great hope to persecuted Christians today. God has feelings. He cares. He sees. He hears. He knows. He's concerned. And in His time, He rescues! The mystery of this rescuing action is God's timing. Galatians 4:4 tells us it was when *"the time had fully come"* that God sent His Son to redeem us. We saw two days ago that the Israelis waited hundreds of years for deliverance from oppression in Egypt and entrance to the promised land while *"the sins of the Amorites reached full measure"* (Genesis 15:16). God alone sees the end from the beginning. We wait for His timing in His promise of coming down to rescue us.

Iranian Christian leader, Mehdi Dibaj, spent over nine years in prison for his faith as a believer from Muslim background. He was emotionally prepared to die a martyr's death. His day was indeed to come. In late 1993, he was tried on charges of apostasy (from Islam) after being a Christian for over forty years. He made his own defence and used his written statement to share his commitment to Jesus Christ. In early 1994, he was sentenced to execution. There was a great international outcry when the news of Mehdi Dibaj's scheduled execution was publicized. Suddenly on January 16, 1994, the Teheran government released Mehdi Dibaj from prison and denied it had sentenced him to death for converting from Islam to Christianity over forty years earlier.

It was a great day of rejoicing for the believers in Iran. When Mehdi Dibaj first met with them, their immediate response was to burst into song, "*In the name of Jesus, we have the victory!*" Even *TIME* magazine reported the release under the title "Answered Prayers." Yet in God's perfect timing, this man who had experienced God's rescue multiple times, was martyred by vigilantes after six months of freedom from prison.

RESPONSE:
Today I will acknowledge God's timing is best for me as I await His rescue.

PRAYER:
Thank You Lord for my deliverance from the kingdom of darkness to Your kingdom of light through Your Son, Jesus.

April 4

GOD IS GOOD – ALL THE TIME

*...But this happened that we might not rely on ourselves
but on God, who raises the dead.*
2 Corinthians 1:9b

Over the past three days, we have seen that we need to watch and listen diligently for God's eternal story of deliverance. God is at work behind life's miseries and mysteries.

Today I want to share with you a personal testimony from our Standing Strong Through the Storm (SSTS) seminars of this wonderful principle at work.

In 2004, Jim Cunningham and I were invited by our Central Asia Director to hold SSTS seminars in several countries of that needy region where persecution is often severe for the many believers from Muslim background. The first two seminars in one country went extremely well due to young interpreters (we sometimes refer to such as "interrupters") who were very fluent. Before we finished mentioning a Scriptural reference, they would be immediately quoting it in Russian (the colonial language of the area frequently used).

The third and final seminar was to be held in a neighboring country. After significant travel challenges to arrive at the location, we were greeted by our host with the news that there was no one to translate us into the local language, so they had hired Svetlana (not her real name) who reportedly was fluent in English and Russian. They could easily understand the latter.

The three-day seminar took place at a Christian camp ground very suitable for such training and where accommodations were excellent and private. Many of the forty assembled believers had not met before, so the three days were filled with great fellowship, music and worship.

But the seminar itself was a disaster! Svetlana was not a believer and not familiar with the Bible. Secondly, her English vocabulary was extremely limited. She did not understand even simple words like "grace" and "forgiveness." We spent three frustrating days trying to explain biblical terms and principles to her and despairing that the group understood anything we had come to share. I left that event considering it had been a waste of time and effort.

In December 2010, Jim and I were back in the region working with SSTS trainers from all the five or so countries of the area. A young man approached us and said, "You don't know me, but you know my mother, Svetlana. She was your interpreter in my country six years ago."

I smiled sardonically. How could I ever forget Svetlana! But he continued with an almost unbelievable tale. After the SSTS seminar, his mother began reading her Russian Bible and ultimately gave her life to Jesus. Then she led her whole family to faith in Him. And now her son, standing before us, was selected to be here for training as an SSTS teacher in that particular country where I had thought our efforts were such a waste! God is good—all the time!

RESPONSE:
Today I will serve God knowing that He is at work behind all life's miseries and mysteries.

PRAYER:
Lord, today I will rely on Your strength and power to accomplish Your good purposes.

April 5

RELGIOUS LIBERTY

So if the Son sets you free, you will be free indeed.
John 8:36

Ron Boyd MacMillan is a perceptive communicator. He writes for the next two days:

As my plane touched down after a trip to the Middle East, I breathed a big sigh of relief. I was back where I did not have to watch my back, be careful what I said, or where I went. Whew. I was back in a country that had religious freedom. I prayed to God, "Thank you for the men and women who fought to bring me this freedom. Thank God they won."

Then two incidents happened one after the other that made me think again.

I was at an art exhibition and looking at a painting entitled, *Man startled on a horse*. I sought out the artist and said, "Was that the Apostle Paul on the Damascus road you were depicting?" I thought he would be pleased I had figured it out.

But he looked horrified, and glancing around he hissed, "For goodness sake keep quiet. Do you want me to get labeled as a religious artist? I'd never sell another painting if that happened."

Then I was talking to a priest in charge of a large church in my city. His church had just received a large sum of money from the state for the refurbishment of a church hall. Then he said, "Well, we had to sign an agreement that the church would be available for everyone of any religion, and that we would not try to convert anyone. But we were happy to do that. We just want to be a community resource."

Suddenly I became aware that I had to fight for religious liberty in my own country. I had thought that because certain toleration laws were in place, I was safe.

But no, it was clear from the artist that to admit one's Christian faith in a public context was professional suicide.

How did my society suddenly get so prejudiced?

And look at the priest blithely giving up his right to evangelize,

191

without a thought to the long-term cost. Who was asking him to refrain from evangelizing? And how could he be so unaware of the freedom he just signed away?

RESPONSE:
Today I will not assume that freedom is automatic. I will stand up for the truth of God's Word and be truly free.

PRAYER:
Lord, may I never take the free expression of my faith for granted. Help me to understand the challenges that representing Your truth will bring.

April 6

RELIGIOUS FREEDOM

"If the world hates you, keep in mind that it hated me first. If you belonged to the world, it would love you as its own. As it is, you do not belong to the world, but I have chosen you out of the world. That is why the world hates you. Remember what I told you: 'A servant is not greater than his master.' If they persecuted me, they will persecute you also. If they obeyed my teaching, they will obey yours also. They will treat you this way because of my name, for they do not know the one who sent me.
John 15:18-21

Ron Boyd-MacMillian concludes his two-part analysis of religious freedom in our country:

It was a persecuted Christian in the Middle East who gave me the eyes to see that religious freedom always needs protecting, wherever one is.

"Freedom is fragile," she said. "Religious freedom is not about having the right laws to protect belief—that's a myth put out by the human rights community. No, religious freedom is protected not by laws, but by a climate of respect and openness that ensures the laws are correctly applied. A toleration law, for example, can be used for or against Christians. Christians always have to fight to ensure the climate is tolerant."

She added, "I don't care what country or state you live in, you also live in a culture that hates Christ. That's your fight, and every Christian on the earth has the same fight, whether you belong to a so-called Christian society or not."

She was right. A climate of prejudice against Christians has crept up by stealth in Western cultures, even in apparently Christian ones. We are in a battle in our own backyard. Thank you, Persecuted Church, for awakening me to the fight!

As Ron writes, we are in a battle even at home. It doesn't take much insight—or even imagination—to assess the direction of the moral slide in our free societies, especially in the Western world. Biblical values are disappearing and secular philosophies with a pseudo-biblical aura are fast taking their place.

As I've travelled and spoken in Western countries, it is not uncommon to have folk share with me how they lost their employment because of their faith. They had not been obnoxious nor spending company time witnessing. They had simply expressed their support for biblical principles that were being violated. Jesus warns in our Scripture today that this treatment is because of His name. Let's make sure that it is not because we refuse to be His salt and light.

RESPONSE:
Today I will walk with my eyes open to the reality of anti-Christian prejudice. And I will retaliate with the only weapon Jesus authorized: love for all others—even my perceived enemies.

PRAYER:
Lord, I know that because of Your life in me I am bound to generate negative reactions. Help me to respond in a truly loving manner as You exemplified and be Your salt and light in a darkening world.

April 7

FEAR OF DEATH

"Don't be afraid of those who want to kill your body; they cannot touch your soul. Fear only God, who can destroy both soul and body in hell.
Matthew 10:28

Satan uses and plays on one of the basic elements and instincts of our nature—fear. It is natural for finite man to fear—especially the fear of the unknown, the fear of being hurt and the fear of death. There is nothing more Satan would like than to see us paralyzed with fear just like King Saul when facing the Philistines and Goliath.

Why do we allow fear to be so controlling? On the one hand, we have past experiences that we don't want to relive and on the other hand, we are very hesitant about what might lay ahead. But often the events and situations creating most fear in people have no basis in reality.

All fear is based on perception. Thus fear has been described in the English language as an acronym for "**F**alse **E**vidence **A**ppearing **R**eal." If we could consciously remember this, it would help us to allay many fears. But that false evidence sometimes is so convincing! However, we must always realize that dread and fear—like other tactics of the enemy—are based on a lie. This is why throughout the Scriptures we are repeatedly commanded—366 times—to *"fear not."* It is intensely liberating for our witness when we personally overcome the fear of death. This allows us to focus on Christ and His kingdom.

Living as a Christian under Romania's dictatorship posed extreme difficulties and dangers. Even though Rev. Joseph Tson had counted the cost and served the Lord and His flock faithfully, he feared the day that he would be called in by security. He knew the possibility of facing death was inevitable.

The day that Joseph feared arrived. Security officers arrived at his home one day and took him to their headquarters. He was instructed to sit on a chair and a gun was put to his head. "The choice is easy," came the commander's voice. "Deny Jesus or we pull the trigger."

This was indeed the moment that Joseph feared all through his ministry. But suddenly the Spirit of the Lord filled his whole being. "If you kill me today you will do me a great favor. All my sermons that were recorded will be in great demand because I will be a martyr for Christ. You will help me greatly to share my messages. You will also help me to go to my Lord quickly!" Joseph fearlessly replied.

The officer dropped the gun. "You Christians are crazy," he shouted and then commanded the officers to take Joseph back home.

Joseph's life was spared but in a sense he lost it that day. "Never again did I fear what man can do to me. Never again did I fear to lose my life," Joseph concluded.

RESPONSE:
Today I will not allow Satan's favorite tactic of fear and intimidation to conquer me in any way.

PRAYER:
Lord, enable me to overcome the fear of physical death as I realize that I am already dead to myself in You. May this be true today too for believers in conflict zones of our world.

April 8

PEACE IN THE FACE OF FEAR

You will keep in perfect peace those whose minds are steadfast, because they trust in you.
Isaiah 26:3

Twenty-nine-year-old Maryam Rostampour and thirty-two-year old Marzieh Amirizadeh spent 259 days in Tehran's notorious Evin prison in 2009 in Iran. They had to overcome the fear of life imprisonment and the possibility of execution because they loved and followed Jesus Christ. They had to remain strong through weeks in solitary confinement, and endless hours of interrogation by Iranian officials and religious leaders. They had to endure months of harsh living conditions and debilitating sickness. In their first interview (with Sam Yeghnazar of Elam Ministries), they shared what life was like in prison and how they survived.

When asked about the worst part of the prison experience, Marzieh wept as she explained:

"One of the worst was the execution of two of my fellow prisoners. I had never experienced such a thing. One of those killed was my roommate. We had spent a lot of time together. And one day they took her to be executed. For a week I was in shock that killing a human being was so easy…After these executions the spirit of sorrow and death hung over the prison. There was deadly silence everywhere. We all felt this. There was nothing we could do. Everyone was under pressure. The sadness was overwhelming. We stared at each other but had no power to speak. This was the worst experience. It was horrifying and tangible."

When asked if she feared execution, Marzieh responded:
"I never thought about execution, I thought we might be sentenced to life imprisonment because that is the punishment for women convicted of apostasy. I just thought this was something we would have to bear.

"Before prison we talked about execution, but when we got to prison and experienced the fear of it—our way of talking changed. The very first night that we were arrested, when they threatened us, we were really frightened. We never imagined we would be so frightened; we had talked about these things before. But the atmosphere there and what happened to us frightened us beyond our expectations. We were confined to a dark and dirty room and paralyzed with fear. We could see the fear in each other's faces. We prayed and what calmed us was the presence of God and the peace that He gave us.

"It is easy to say that I give my life for the Lord and I will do anything for Him, even die. I always thought it would be a privilege to give my life for the Lord. You say these things. I know for sure that if this would happen to us we would rejoice ultimately. But human fears gripped us. The power the Lord gave us helped us to overcome these fears, just as when we prayed in the police station, God banished our fear and renewed our strength."

RESPONSE:
Today I acknowledge that God can grant His peace in every trying situation I face.

PRAYER:
Thank You Lord for the promise of Your presence, Your peace and renewing strength.

April 9

GOD'S PROMISES ARE STRONGER THAN FEAR

Whoever dwells in the shelter of the Most High will rest in the shadow of the Almighty. I will say of the LORD, "He is my refuge and my fortress, my God, in whom I trust."
Psalm 91:1-2

"Two days ago the police raided our house. They took away all the Bibles and Christian books that we had in the house," says Lazar, a church leader in Uzbekistan. The roots of communism seem not to have withered yet. Uzbek Christians are balancing between fear of surveillance, intimidation and imprisonment and faith in God's promises.

The penalty which Lazar may receive for possession of the "illegal books" he had in his house is a prison sentence of fifteen days or a hefty fine.

"I would prefer a prison sentence," says Lazar. He knows comparable cases when fines equivalent to over a year's salary were imposed. Leila, his wife seems bewildered by her husband's response. "I don't want you to go to prison," she responds.

Lazar counters, "The Pharisees persecuted Jesus, but still He went on with His work. The evening after the raid, I read Psalm 91. *God is my refuge and my strength. I can hide in Him.* I don't want to allow myself to be governed by fear, because that doesn't help you at all. After my arrest, one of the neighbours telephoned me. 'Lazar,' he said, 'we've packed our things and we're ready to leave for Moscow. Should we go?'"

Lazar can understand this, but he resolutely teaches his church members to take a different approach. "We must oppose people who are sowing fear. God's promises are stronger," he emphasises. "We have difficulties, but we believe that God is with us and that His promises are stronger than fear."

Still this fear may suddenly take a grip on you if you're in the middle of a situation of direct persecution. A few days later Lazar suddenly says, "I'm leaving the city tonight. My lawyer has advised us to take a break. It may be the case that another raid is conducted on our home. We can't cope with this now and so we're leaving. Please pray for me and my family."

In the space of a few days Lazar struggles with the horribly hard hand of the regime and with the values of his faith. He's balancing between fear and faith. Pray that the fear which the government is trying to sow shall not take root in his heart.

A few weeks later, Lazar reports that he and his family are back at home. But the problems are not over. Legal proceedings have been taken against him and he has been threatened with death by the authorities.

RESPONSE:
Today I will boldly affirm that God is with me and His promises are stronger than fear!

PRAYER:
Pray for Christians like Lazar and Leila who are on the teeter-totter between fear and faith. Pray that Satan's tactic of fear will not take root in their hearts.

April 10

TROUBLE CANNOT SEPARATE US FROM THE LOVE OF CHRIST

Who shall separate us from the love of Christ?
Shall trouble…?
Romans 8:35a

The question asked is a personal one. Not "what" can separate us but "who"? The inference is our enemy, Satan, who tries every tactic he can garner to make us think we can be separated from Christ's love. Today we look at his tactic of "trouble."

Chinese Brother Mak spent years in prison and tells of the trouble he experienced from his captors and what he learned from it:

At first they would punch and kick me. There was a certain guard who slapped my face over a hundred times, until his hand hurt. Then I said to him, "Praise the Lord! I will pray for your hand."

The most painful experience was when they raised me with my hands turned backwards, and using handcuffs, attached my hands to two bars on an iron gate. Then they moved the iron gate back and forth from left to right, pulling my whole torso. It felt as if my entire body would rip apart. The area where my hands were cuffed especially hurt. The iron from the handcuffs seemed to enter my very joints, preventing the blood in my palms from circulating normally.

During this time, I experienced just how much the Lord loves me. Because He does love me, He calls me to suffer, and to experience more of His love. He also makes me realize how minute and temporal peoples' suffering is, compared to a future eternity with the Lord. This is God's teaching. He is teaching me how to walk the way of the cross.

If I don't suffer, how can I learn to serve? My suffering is for my benefit. Suffering leads me to face death. Only in this way can I die with Christ, and then be buried and resurrected with Him. Living is a struggle. This is the only way to reach heaven and experience victory. Thanks be to God! Jesus Christ has already triumphed over everything.

RESPONSE:
I will live this day in the awareness that troubles can never separate me from Christ's love.

PRAYER:
Lord, may all Christian prisoners today gain the insights of Your love like Brother Mak.

April 11

HARDSHIP CANNOT SEPARATE US FROM THE LOVE OF CHRIST

Who shall separate us from the love of Christ? Shall...hardship...?

Romans 8:35b

The question asked is a personal one. Not "what" can separate us but "who"? The inference is our enemy, Satan, who tries every tactic he can garner to make us think we can be separated from Christ's love. Today we look at his tactic of "hardship."

Sixteen-year-old Lakech had always known a stable home in her small Ethiopian village of Moche. Her childhood as one of eight children was not carefree. But it was uncomplicated. Her father, a godly man, worked hard to provide the needs of his large family. They did not have an abundance, but they survived. While Lakech was growing up, her father and mother came to Christ. They laboured hard and devoted themselves to bringing up their eight children in a God-fearing way. But two years ago, her father was framed by some enemies and charged with stealing trees.

The legal battle started with a hearing a few days later, dragging on for a year when the court found Lakech's father guilty and sentenced him to a year's imprisonment. He found himself sharing a cell with about fifty criminals, and his family was left in turmoil.

At home, mother was not coping well. Neighbors were mocking the children, claiming their father would be jailed for seven more years. "I started noticing that it was hard for my mother to put food on the table," explained Lakech. "I could not watch my mother battle on her own. I wanted to finish school, but it was impossible for me to just carry on," admitted the timid young teenager. "My mother needed help."

Despite her age and innate shyness, Lakech left school and found a full-time job as a house servant some distance from her home town. For long periods of time, Lakech stayed away from home working, sending all her earnings home to her mother. Following her example,

Lakech's second oldest brother, also in his teens, quit school and took over the farming on their small land.

Then the local church began to help support the family, and Open Doors was alerted to the difficult struggle to just feed the family. The ministry was able to come alongside the entire family, helping supply their food, and then paying school fees so Lakech could return home and resume her studies with her brother.

Soon afterwards, to the family's great joy, father was pardoned because of good behavior and released after serving nearly half of his sentence. He was overjoyed and declared, "I was saying to myself, by the time I finish serving the sentence, I will find my family scattered and needy. But it was different. They lacked nothing and everything was covered.

"I was also thinking no one will be with us," Lakech's mother shared. "But we now are in joy. I am happy to be relieved from my worries and above all to have my husband beside me. The Lord has blessed me with these two successes; both my daughter and husband have come home."

RESPONSE:
I will live this day aware that hardships can never separate me from Christ's love.

PRAYER:
Lord we rejoice in Your goodness and in Your provision for every real need.

April 12

PERSECUTION CANNOT SEPARATE US FROM THE LOVE OF CHRIST

Who shall separate us from the love of Christ?
Shall...persecution...?
Romans 8:35c

The question asked is a personal one. Not "what" can separate us but "who"? The inference is our enemy, Satan, who tries every tactic he can garner to make us think we can be separated from Christ's love. Today we look at his tactic of "persecution."

Heart-pounding terror—that's what most Cambodians felt when Pol Pot seized power in 1975. Setan Lee was a young teen-aged medical student when the Khmer Rouge communist forces took over control of Cambodia. Their horrors and atrocities against their own citizens brought the label "Killing Fields" to the era. Setan was in the most vulnerable class as an educated young person. By God's grace alone he survived the ensuing persecution, starvation and hardships. But as the young man gained strength, hatred for the Khmer Rouge gripped his heart. He plotted how he would get revenge, especially on the guard named Er. "She was the lady who I hated and I wanted to kill," he said.

When the Vietnamese invaded Cambodia in 1978, many prisoners fled the slave camps. Setan was one of thousands who began the dangerous journey to freedom in Thailand. He walked to the border and en route a preacher led him to faith in Jesus. He was later amazed to find all his family alive, except for his brother, who had been killed by the Khmer Rouge. Together, the family went to a Thai refugee camp, where Setan Lee became a young preacher.

One day, while preaching in a camp of 35,000 refugees on this text in Romans 8:35, an eerie feeling swept over him. As he looked over the many faces in the crowd, he spotted the guard Er in the crowd. "I prayed and asked the Lord to take control of me," he said.

"First, I wanted to kill her," he added, "but then something told me to have compassion and mercy toward her." Lee told Er, "I forgive you for what you have done to me and my friends. I want you to believe in Jesus. He forgave me for what I wanted to do to you. So, in return, I forgive you. And it's not me, but God."

Although Lee prayed for Er, he never saw her again. He feared the Khmer Rouge's grip on her life pulled her back into the jungle, yet he knew the Lord of the Universe had helped him forgive her for the persecution she had inflicted on him for years.

When I heard Setan share his amazing story, he concluded, "I realized through it all, that persecution could not separate me from the love of Christ."

RESPONSE:
I will live this day aware that persecution can never separate me from Christ's love.

PRAYER:
Thank You Lord for the wonderful lessons we learn from the persecuted who know that it cannot separate them from You. May I know this assurance today no matter what I face.

April 13

FAMINE CANNOT SEPARATE US FROM THE LOVE OF CHRIST

Who shall separate us from the love of Christ?
Shall...famine...?
Romans 8:35d

The question asked is a personal one. Not "what" can separate us but "who"? The inference is our enemy, Satan, who tries every tactic he can garner to make us think we can be separated from Christ's love. Today we look at his tactic of "famine."

Wilson Chen from Vietnam spent five years in one of those harsh and primitive re-education camps. He was forced to spend long hours of hard backbreaking work clearing jungles for farmland, cutting trees for lumber and farming the fields. He had looked forward to a successful secular career and also to marrying his lovely girlfriend. In his final year in camp, he received the crushing news that his girlfriend had given up hope, married another and escaped from Vietnam.

The camp food was barely enough to keep him alive. "The constant brutality attacked our minds and spirits; the malnutrition attacked our bodies," he recalls. The constant hunger drove them to eat anything. He would search the ground with other prisoners for rats, toads, worms, snakes, insects and birds to supplement their diet and keep them alive and to simply ease the feeling of constant hunger.

Wilson remembers companions who went insane from the pressure of hunger. Others committed suicide. Many died from diseases caused by the malnutrition.

Every night they were subjected to mental torture and political indoctrination. Always in their minds were thoughts of escape. But Wilson Chen says, "It was hope in the Lord Jesus that kept me alive. I fed this hope by secretly reading the Scriptures..." In that camp situation, Wilson promised the Lord that he would serve him if he ever received the opportunity. The Holy Spirit whispered to him, "You have opportunities right here!" Very soon three fellow-prisoners came to know the Lord.

Camp experiences helped him reflect on the significance of the sufferings of Jesus. In that context he found refreshment and exhilaration in his own weakness. And he says, "...Jesus gave me peace in the midst of tribulation."

RESPONSE:
I will live this day aware that famines can never separate me from Christ's love.

PRAYER:
Thank you Lord that You give peace in the midst of tribulations.

April 14

NAKEDNESS CANNOT SEPARATE US FROM THE LOVE OF CHRIST

Who shall separate us from the love of Christ?
Shall...nakedness...?

Romans 8:35e

The question asked is a personal one. Not "what" can separate us but "who"? The inference is our enemy, Satan, who tries every tactic he can garner to make us think we can be separated from Christ's love. Today we look at his tactic of "nakedness."

In the northeast part of China there was a severe flood. Most of the homes were ruined and peoples' belongings were totally destroyed. There was a couple who were not Christians. The wife was paralyzed from the waist down. They lost everything in the flood so the husband bought some poison pills and was going to give them to his wife and then also take them himself so they could both commit suicide.

They had no place to live so they could only lie on the ground at the train station. They were ragged and filthy with nowhere to bathe and without food. A Christian walked by, saw and smelled them, and asked them what happened. He then invited them to his home. The Christian even carried the crippled wife on his back. This Christian had his wife bathe and clothe the crippled wife. He bathed and clothed the husband. Then they gave them food and shared the gospel with them and this couple committed their lives to Jesus.

The husband of the couple said that they could see from the lives of their hosts that God is real and is a God of love.

The whole church helped this couple to build a house and it also later became a house church meeting place.

RESPONSE:

I will live this day aware that nakedness can never separate me from Christ's love.

PRAYER:

Lord give me eyes of love to help those who need You and also need a practical example of Your love for them.

April 15

DANGER CANNOT SEPARATE US FROM THE LOVE OF CHRIST

Who shall separate us from the love of Christ?
Shall...danger...?
Romans 8:35f

The question asked is a personal one. Not "what" can separate us but "who"? The inference is our enemy, Satan, who tries every tactic he can garner to make us think we can be separated from Christ's love. Today we look at his tactic of "danger."

Dr. Paul Negrut pastored the largest Baptist Church in Europe which is located in Oradea, Romania. He served the church faithfully under the cruel Ceaucescu regime and often suffered personal mistreatment.

He shared with our Open Doors leaders that the most difficult time he remembers was a night he returned home rejoicing after a very successful evangelistic crusade. But when he walked in the house, he saw his wife weeping and his nine-year-old daughter was trembling. Through her tears his wife shared that when their daughter was coming home from school that day, the Securitate (Romanian secret police) tried to rape her to destroy her and the family.

Paul said, "That night I was in a great struggle. For the first time I was thinking to emigrate from Romania. I asked the Lord, 'Should I leave the blessing of suffering or should I endure to see my girl like that?'

"I talked to my wife and after prayer, we chose to stay. Two days later they tried to rape our daughter again. And two days later they tried to rape my wife. But every time God was protecting them in a miraculous way."

Today Dr. Paul Negrut is the pastor of Emmanuel Baptist Church in Oradea and the Chancellor of Emmanuel Baptist University.
Dr. Negrut weathered the days of communism in Romania and rose to great influence when the Iron Curtain came down. He was offered a job with the new democratic government in a free Romania, but turned it down believing that serving the Lord was a higher calling.

Emmanuel University and the Emmanuel Baptist Church in Oradea are known throughout Europe. The university trains people from all over Romania and many other parts of the world.

RESPONSE:
I will live this day in the awareness that danger can never separate me from Christ's love.

PRAYER:
Help me remember, Lord, that You are there in the midst of all my troubles.

April 16

THE SWORD CANNOT SEPARATE US FROM THE LOVE OF CHRIST

Who shall separate us from the love of Christ?
Shall...sword...?

Romans 8:35g

The question asked is a personal one. Not "what" can separate us but "who"? The inference is our enemy, Satan, who tries every tactic he can garner to make us think we can be separated from Christ's love. Today we look at his tactic of "sword" or violence.

Sister Pasqualita spoke at the "Mexico, I Love You" Congress. She had suffered severe ostracism in her small town in the very southern part of Mexico because she had become an evangelical. Other Christians had already been forcibly driven from the town.

One night a group of her persecutors surrounded her grass-roofed home setting it on fire. As she opened the door, someone fired a gun at her. A co-worker shares her story in his own words:

"When she was sharing her testimony she was crying. She said, 'I thank the Lord that only twenty-one ammunition bits touched me.' She had been shot all over her body and even in the neck. She was still able to run and fell into a hole where her persecutors couldn't see her in the dark. She was losing blood quickly but some other townsfolk who appreciated her testimony somehow took her out through the mob to another nearby town's clinic. She survived but three other family members in the house were murdered.

"She complained to the Lord saying, 'Lord, why now that I've given you my life and my family am I suffering this way?' The Lord reminded her of a song that she used to sing very often, 'I have decided to follow Jesus, no turning back.'

"She continued, 'Then I understood that when I decided to follow Jesus, it was in the midst of any situation, any persecution. My life now belonged to Him. I gained strength in that song. I am preaching again and I am encouraging the rest of the believers that when we decide to follow Jesus there is no turning back.'"

Today Pasqualita continues to be a strong Christian leader and teacher in her community and she still loves to sing, "I have decided to follow Jesus, no turning back."

RESPONSE:
I will live this day in the awareness that physical weapons and violence can never separate me from Christ's love.

PRAYER:
Lord, help me to react to any threats of intimidating weapons with complete confidence in Your love.

April 17

THE ARMOR OF GOD

Therefore put on the full armor of God, so that when the day of evil comes, you may be able to stand your ground, and after you have done everything, to stand.
Ephesians 6:13

In the valley stood a ten-foot-tall giant, bellowing out threats against God's people and mocking their God. "Send one man out to fight me," he roared. "If I win, you will serve us. If he wins, we will be your slaves."

If the physical presence of Goliath wasn't daunting enough, the stakes for Israel were. It would be an all-or-nothing fight for the future of the people. On top of that, he mocked God. The fight would be a showdown between the giant's pagan gods and the God of Israel.

Courageous David decided to face the monster. King Saul, looking at David's physical disadvantage, insisted the young man take his armor. But David knew the spiritual battle was more crucial than the physical battle. Faith in God, not superior weaponry, would be his salvation. David stepped out in the name of God, and the giant fell.

Most of us are so focused on our physical circumstances that we fail to see the basic spiritual challenges before us. We spend our energies trying to make ends meet. We exhaust ourselves by constant activity. We are so distracted and frightened by what we see that we miss our chance to slay the giant. Instead, we find *his* foot on *our* neck.

Christian attempts to live victoriously in Christ when in a hostile environment could become frightening if we did not believe that God provides for us in every trial. The sovereign God of eternity knew every kind of attack the enemy would use before time began. And He has provided His spiritual armor—His Word, prayer and the Holy Spirit—so that we might be victorious when these attacks come against us. God has equipped you as a servant of Jesus Christ with these spiritual weapons, the resources you need to defeat the enemy and gain great victories for His kingdom.

Paul instructed Christian converts to put on the impenetrable armor of God—coverings God provides—so that we can stand **victorious** in every situation we face as we move forward confidently in the work God has called us to do. He also understood it to be a protective covering for the mind and spirit, ensuring that injuries to the body will not embitter or destroy the soul.

RESPONSE:
Today I will take advantage of all the spiritual armor God provides for me to stand strong.

PRAYER:
Help me Lord to not try and fight spiritual battles in my own strength but with the resources You freely provide.

April 18

THE BELT OF TRUTH

Stand firm then, with the belt of truth buckled around your waist...

Ephesians 6:14a

The Roman soldier's wide leather belt held the various garments and pieces of armor securely in place. Loose armor was not only uncomfortable, but also unsafe. The belt also held the scabbards for swords and daggers. It was foundational to keeping everything balanced and in place.

Truth secures everything in our spiritual life. We can't know what is truly right or wrong apart from truth. In this spiritual warfare we wage, we "put on" Christ, Who Himself is the "truth" (John 14:6). This is our positional application of the belt. Putting on Christ Himself who is the truth enables us to talk, walk and "fight" proclaiming Christ, the truth.

On another application level, buckling the belt of truth around your waist is more than just seeking truth to find out facts. The servant-soldier of Christ who puts on the armor of God must be willing to overcome his own prejudices to find out the truth. He must struggle against his pride, which clings to his preconceived ideas and makes him unwilling to re-examine them and change his opinions.

Second, to wear the belt of truth means binding one's whole nature together with inner integrity. The belt of truth refers to the knowledge of one's own inherent wickedness, weaknesses and propensity to sin (Matthew 15:19; 7:4). King David said, *"Surely you desire truth in the inner parts; You teach me wisdom in the inmost place."*(Psalm 51:6). This is why a servant of Christ must review the basics of having a humble spirit, mourning to God, seeking His meekness and hungering for righteousness.

Truth directly opposes Satan, the father of lies. His first challenge to Eve was to even question God's truthfulness. When we know and walk in God's truth, it sets us free (John 8:32).

Wuillie Marcelino Ruiz, an attorney and an evangelical Christian, was wrongly accused of and sentenced to twenty years at the maximum-security Castro prison in Lima, Peru for the crime of "terrorist collaboration" by a special faceless court. Growing up in a close-knit family, his mother's death during the first year of his imprisonment was a cruel blow for him.

During a visit by an Open Doors team, Wuillie said, "Not everything inside the prison is sadness. Many of our fellow inmates are receiving Jesus Christ as the deliverer of their souls... God is touching the hearts of the authorities in Peru; here in the prison we are not treated so harshly anymore. As the Scriptures tell us, we are not confined because the truth makes us free."

Jesus is the Truth. Truth is on your side. Truth will win over the enemy's lies. Fill your heart with truth and stand by it. Put on the belt of truth!

RESPONSE:
Today I put on the belt of truth so I can stand strong against Satan's lies.

PRAYER:
Lord, help me fill my heart with truth today for it will set me free. May innocent Christian prisoners know that freedom also.

April 19

THE BREASTPLATE OF RIGHTEOUSNESS

Stand firm then...with the breastplate
of righteousness in place.

Ephesians 6:14b

The soldier's breastplate of the Roman times was to protect his vital organs. It was usually made of hardened slabs of leather or pounded bronze or a combination of both. The soldier's rank and his country's seal were affixed to it. It covered the soldier's chest and stomach but not his back. So it was designed to face the enemy, not for retreat from the enemy.

Because we are waging a war against an invisible enemy, we must always be armed. Our breastplate is made not of heavy metal but is molded by the Spirit of the living God to fit us properly in our inner being. Our righteousness is not a metal front, but given by Christ to show to everyone in all our day-to-day relationships and circumstances.

Our enemy will point out your failures and shortcomings. He will try to convince you that you are unworthy to be a child of God. He is right. But your relationship with God is based on Jesus' uprightness before God, not yours. Your sins have been wiped out. When God sees you, he sees Jesus. Stand tall before the enemy...in your breastplate of righteousness.

Mikail Khorev, a very effective evangelist in Russia, spent many years in prison for his continued public ministry. On one occasion his family was refused visiting rights and sent home. When the prison guard was taunting him about it, he replied:

"I would like to tell you that my God is fulfilling his plans through you and will use you for our blessing. I love my family very much and being together with them means a lot to me, but if it brings more honor to the Lord for us to part rather than be together, then why should I insist on seeing them? If his name is glorified more through my being in prison than through my being at liberty, then I tell you that there is no greater joy for me than to die on this prison bunk as a prisoner, as my father did and as many of my brothers in the faith have done."

Mikhail is also quoted as saying, "I have to admit to you that prison is a very useful school for our education and for the testing of the genuineness of our faith...I'm grateful to the Lord for this school and for his leading."

RESPONSE:
Today I put on the breastplate of righteousness...protected under the blood of Jesus Christ.

PRAYER:
Lord, may my breastplate of righteousness guard my heart from evil so I will remain pure and holy in the face of trials.

April 20

THE SANDALS OF PEACE

*...and with your feet fitted with the readiness that comes
from the gospel of peace.*
Ephesians 6:15

The cry for peace is as old as the dawn of history and as fresh as the morning newspaper. Several centuries before Christ, the prophet Isaiah said, *"How beautiful on the mountains are the feet of those who bring good news, who proclaim peace...."* (Isaiah 52:7)

When the Hebrew prophets foretold the coming of a divine deliverer, they said one of his names would be *"Prince of Peace."* When the Savior was born, the note struck by the angelic chorus in the nativity story of the shepherds was *"...and on earth peace to men on whom his favor rests."* (Luke 2:14)

Therefore, it is not surprising that when describing the armor of God, Paul included the element of peace. As God's peacemakers, our sandals enable us to march into circumstances to bring peace, not destruction. Christ calls people who have made their peace with God to fight for fellowship, not against it (Hebrews 12:2-3). So we must be ready to go where God sends us with the message of peace, forgiveness and hope. We may be called to march right to the gates of hell—which He promised would not hold us back (Matthew 16:18). It is in this sense that we can be considered "waging" peace.

Your life thus centers on the good news of the kingdom. Everything else comes second. Know how to share the good news. Understand what it has done in your life. See how it can help others. Ask God to give you opportunities to share with others. Be alert for the opportunities. Be prepared to take advantage of them...standing strong in your sandals of peace.

Brother Alagaw in Ethiopia started an aggressive gospel ministry in his region. People accepted the Lord through his preaching. The people of the traditional church colluded with the Muslim fundamentalists to fight Alagaw and his followers. They said, "These people will destroy our country, nation and religions if we do not stop them immediately."

Alagaw and his followers organized their first evangelistic meeting at the local stadium. They hired sound systems for this big occasion. Early in the morning they started with their outreach. At about 10:00 a.m. a big crowd approached the stadium. Without saying a word, they destroyed the sound system and a lot of other property. Some believers went to the local police station, but the police refused to help. During the attack, a pregnant woman lost her baby.

After this incident other forms of harassment followed. During church services stones were thrown on the roof of the church building. Faceless people burned down their church building. However, the Lord has blessed their ministry and their peaceful responses with one hundred and twenty new believers.

RESPONSE:
Today I put on the sandals of peace and stand firm in the good news of the gospel.

PRAYER:
Lord, may Your peace shine through me today and be a light to all I encounter.

April 21

THE SHIELD OF FAITH

In addition to all this, take up the shield of faith, with which you can extinguish all the flaming arrows of the evil one.

Ephesians 6:16

The Roman shield was the defensive piece of armor that was almost always used together with the sword. It was used to ward off a blow from the opponent while making your own sword-thrust. Likened to a shield, our faith in God is that piece of spiritual armor that enables us to withstand attacks by the enemy that are too much for the mind and body. The shield of faith has a three-fold duty

1. It is a saving faith that is the inward confidence in God.
2. It is a serving faith that inspires our servant hood.
3. It is a sanctifying faith that lays hold of the power of God for our daily lives.

When you come under enemy fire, take shelter behind your faith in God. Do not be deceived by circumstances and events. Walk by faith, not by sight. Be confident that God has secured victory. Stake your life on His faithfulness. Trust Him to deliver you as you wear the shield of faith.

A colleague tells the story of Gabriel in violence plagued Colombia. His calling is to share the gospel with guerrilla soldiers hiding in the mountains. As he approaches a camp site with his bag of Spanish Bibles, a perimeter guard often steps out and sticks his AK-47 in Gabriel's stomach.

"What are you doing here?"

"I've come to tell you about the love of Jesus which you can read about in these books."

"We don't want your books. Get lost or I'll kill you!"

It's at this point that Gabriel's faith rises. Pushing the barrel of the gun aside he casually answers, "No you won't! You can't kill me until God says you can kill me," and he boldly walks ahead into the camp where he distributes Bibles and preaches the gospel to those who will listen. He is still on the trail and has not been killed yet. He is convinced the day will come when his life will be taken. But his faith is solidly grounded in the assurance that it will only happen in God's will. Meanwhile he is a powerful witness to the truth of the gospel because of his faith.

RESPONSE:
Today I take the shield of faith so I will not be vulnerable to spiritual defeat.

PRAYER:
Lord, help me be strong in faith, ready for Satan's fiery darts of doubt, denial and deceit. Give me bold faith like Gabriel's.

April 22

THE HELMET OF SALVATION

Take the helmet of salvation…
Ephesians 6:17a

In describing the Christian's helmet, Paul wrote in 1 Thessalonians 5:8, "…and the hope of salvation as a helmet." The best armor you can give a soldier is the kind that cannot be destroyed by the enemy. Paul, knowing the eternal nature of God's salvation, exhorts the servant-soldier to put on—that is, believe in—the hope of life beyond this world. Soldiers without fear of death? What a mighty force!

God also provides the helmet to protect our minds. When the enemy tries to infiltrate our thinking with doubts about our salvation, the helmet becomes our protection.

You are God's own child. He Himself redeemed you from slavery. He does not want the enemy to overcome you. You are secure in your relationship with God. The power within you is greater than the power in your enemy. Give no place to doubt. Take your stand for God in confidence wearing you helmet of salvation.

Teshome comes from northern Ethiopia and grew up in the traditional Orthodox Church. In Sunday school he was taught that the evangelical Christians eat the meat of dogs and cats when they celebrate Holy Communion. Their Sunday school teachers made a mistake by asking them to read the Gospels and so Teshome discovered the truth about Jesus Christ. He went to evangelical Christians to hear more about Jesus.

He found that his Sunday school teachers, priests and bishops were teaching him lies. He accepted Christ. After this he was chased away by his family, community and congregation.

Brother Teshome and new friends went to live with Christians who received them in their homes. It was during their stay with these Christians that they heard about a well-established evangelical church. They contacted its leadership and joined after getting a positive reply. Presently they have sixty members in their region. Brother Teshome's vision is to go back to his people and witness to them.

RESPONSE:
Today I put on the helmet of salvation so Satan will not have a stronghold on my thoughts.

PRAYER:
Lord, I rejoice in my salvation and ask You to help me keep my mind focused on You.

April 22/14

Padre,

Te quiero decir que todavía extraño mucho a mi papá. A veces me sorprendo porque ya no está al querer llamarte por teléfono.

Gracias porque el está contigo!

Qué alegría es saber con certeza que eso!

Te amo Padre y te doy gracias por mi esposo tan comprometido y por mi hijo. Gracias x tan buen juego de baseball.

April 23

THE SWORD OF THE SPIRIT

...and the sword of the Spirit, which is the word of God.
Ephesians 6:17b

Scripture is God's Word to us. Get to know it. It is the source of truth, assurance and comfort. Learn its lessons. Let God use it to speak to your heart. Look to it to cut through the enemy's lies and spiritual deception, and to reveal the truth. Use it to persuade others about God's love and forgiveness.

When God's Spirit impresses us with a verse or a passage of Scripture to use in our battle against the enemy in a particular conflict, we are able to defeat our enemy. The Bible calls this taking the *sword of the Spirit*.

Jesus defeated Satan the three times he was tempted in the wilderness by using the sword of the Spirit. (see Matthew 4).

Ruth's world changed when she chanced to find a Bible. She was fifteen when she was rummaging through her Muslim family's library. She found it hidden behind the other books. She says, "I quickly read a few pages and the message immediately touched my heart, even though I understood practically nothing of it. Secretly I began to read the Bible regularly in my room. I knew that I had to do more with this. I wanted to get to know Jesus better."

She adds, "I don't remember how it happened, but my family realized that I was showing too much interest in Christianity. My whole family was against me, especially my mother."

"You're a Muslim," she said. "Why are you throwing your life away? Why aren't you like other girls? You'll soon be going to university and then you're going to marry a respected Muslim!"

Ruth's voice falters and for a moment, she doesn't say anything. "I suffered a lot," she continues. "But still I kept reading the Bible in secret. The Lord Jesus keeps drawing me closer to Him."

RESPONSE:
Today I take the sword of the Spirit so I can expose the tempting words of Satan.

PRAYER:
Lord may the two-edged sword of Your Word be ready in my hands today and in the hands of those reading it for the first time.

April 24

ALL KINDS OF PRAYER

And pray in the Spirit on all occasions with all kinds
of prayers and requests. With this in mind, be alert and
always keep on praying for all the Lord's people.
Ephesians 6:18

Prayer is mentioned in the context of the wardrobe of the Christian warrior but not as a specific weapon of war or a piece of armor. That's because prayer is the key to consistent victory in our warfare. Therefore, prayer is one of the most important things we can do when fighting the enemy.

David's battle with Goliath was not won when the stone flew from the sling. It was won in David's close relationship with the Living God. Our battles are won or lost in the way we walk with God. Prayer is talking with God and letting Him talk with you. Prayer is taking a stand against the spiritual forces of darkness that influence events and circumstances in the world.

Prayer is asserting God's victory before we walk into battle. But prayer is more than kneeling before God. Prayer is as much an attitude as it is an act. Prayer is keeping your heart open to His leadership. Prayer is the constant communion with God needed to face the challenge of completing Jesus' mission.

A Bible courier recounts: "We walked up to the customs with our suitcases full of Bibles. We know that at that moment there are as many as a hundred people praying for us. And can you feel it! We felt peace and joy as we push our trolley of suitcases towards the customs desk. I am absolutely certain that we were surrounded by angels. It sounds strange, but I just know.

'Excuse me, ladies, do you have anything to declare?' says the custom agent. At that moment, a good friend rushes up to the officer. They greet each other profusely. The customs man no longer sees us. We walk on, and a moment later we are standing with all our suitcases, which have not been opened, waiting for a taxi.

"I feel small and think, 'Who am I? I only walk past the customs with my suitcases and I don't even have to answer any questions. That's all that God asks of me. And it's He who does the rest— incredibly!'"

RESPONSE:
Today I commit myself to being a person of prayer as I put on the whole armor of God.

PRAYER:
Pray today with all kinds of prayers for all of God's people. A great challenge and a great opportunity!

April 25

STANDING AGAINST THE DEVIL

Put on the full armor of God so that you can take your stand against the devil's schemes.
Ephesians 6:11

The Bible clearly says to use the full armor. We usually feel we are doing okay if we have most of the pieces of armor in place. Yet, if even one piece is missing, we have a weak spot where Satan can injure us, causing us to lose ground rather than standing firm. (1 Peter 5:8-9)

The New Living Translation in Ephesians 6:11 puts it this way: *"Put on all of God's armor so that you will be able to stand firm against all strategies and tricks of the Devil."* It further says in verse 13, *"Use every piece of God's armor to resist the enemy in the time of evil, so that after the battle you will still be standing firm."*

RESPONSE:
Today I will put on the *full* armor of God to stand strong against Satan's darts of doubt, denial and deceit.

PRAYER: "The Warrior's Prayer"

Heavenly Father, Your warrior prepares for battle.

Today I claim victory over Satan by putting on the whole armor of God!

I put on the Belt of Truth.

May I stand firm in the truth of your Word so I will not be a victim of Satan's lies.

I put on the Breastplate of Righteousness.

May it guard my heart from evil so I will remain pure and holy, protected under the blood of Jesus Christ.

I put on the Sandals of Peace.

231

May I go out and proclaim the good news of the gospel so your peace will shine through me and be a light to all I encounter.

I take the Shield of Faith.

May I be ready to deflect Satan's fiery darts of doubt, denial and deceit so I will not be vulnerable to spiritual defeat.

I put on the Helmet of Salvation.

May I keep my mind focused on you so Satan will not have a stronghold on my thoughts.

I take the Sword of the Spirit.

May the two-edged sword of your Word be ready in my hands so I can use it to take authority over the enemy.

By faith, your warrior has put on the whole armor of God.

I am prepared to live this day in spiritual victory.

Amen.[14]

---

14 Author unknown.

April 26

GOD USES PROBLEMS AND PERSECUTION TO DIRECT YOU

"Sometimes it takes a painful situation to make us change our ways"
Proverbs 20:30 TEV

Here is one of five ways God uses problems and persecution in your life: God uses problems and persecution to **DIRECT** you.

Idris Nalos was an African animist converted to the Christian faith in southern Sudan. Soon after his conversion he became an evangelist. He went out preaching in the remotest places. Within a few years, he planted three churches. Soon considered as dangerous because of his activities, he was arrested by the Islamic authorities and put in prison. There he suffered torture to make him to deny his Christian faith. Beaten for hours every day, he was also totally deprived of sleep.

About to collapse, Idris prayed, "Lord, prevent me from being like Peter. I am about to give up, help me." And God answered in giving Idris a vision where he saw all those to whom he had preached the gospel and who, in turn, proclaimed the good news to other people.

"I saw those who were saved," he said. In this vision, he realized that even if his life was taken, others had already taken up the baton. From this moment, Idris was no longer afraid for his life. After three weeks of ceaseless torment, his torturers released him without explanation.

To avoid another arrest he immigrated to Khartoum in the north, where he founded three new churches in a fundamentalist Muslim territory. He had learned how to trust and wasn't afraid anymore. God showed him where to go and what to do.

Sometimes God must light a fire under us to get us moving. Problems and pressures often point us in a new direction and motivate us to change. Is God trying to get your attention?

RESPONSE:
God is at work in my life—even when I do not recognize it or understand it. It is much easier and more profitable when I cooperate with Him. This is the way to victory!

PRAYER:
Lord, point me in the direction of Your will. May I not need problems and persecution for You to get my attention.

April 27

GOD USES PROBLEMS AND PERSECUTION TO INSPECT YOU

"When you have many kinds of troubles, you should be full of joy, because you know that these troubles test your faith, and this will give you patience."
James 1:2-3 NCV

Here is another of five ways God uses problems and persecution in your life: God uses problems and persecution to **INSPECT** you.

An African Christian businessman shares this testimony:

Born in a rich family I was living for earning big money. My businesses were very profitable. All over town people knew me. When God revealed to me the insignificance of money and richness, I accepted Christ after a long struggle. He changed my life. No longer was I running after money but I started sharing what God had done in my life.

After some time, suddenly the police came to our house. Officers carrying guns took me to their office to interrogate me, asking me all kinds of questions, treating me as if I was a criminal. The next day the same thing happened. A lot of soldiers entered my home and stood in every room making my children cry. For over a period of six months they threatened me. Day after day they asked me and threatened me to stop sharing the good news, the gospel of Jesus Christ. Every time I responded saying: "No, I am not going to stop sharing about the life I received through Jesus Christ"

After six months they stopped. One man of the security forces told me, "The reason we could not do anything to you is because we couldn't find any lie in your life."

A year later, I saw on television the whole group of security men that had intimidated my family and me. They were shivering with fear in front of a judge. The government had changed and those people had to appear before the court because of things they had done. It was as if God told me, "This is what happens with those that oppose you, when you share My words."

People are like tea bags...if you want to know what's inside them, just drop them into hot water! Has God ever tested your faith with a problem? What do problems reveal about you?

RESPONSE:
God is at work in my life—even when I do not recognize it or understand it. It is much easier and more profitable when I cooperate with Him. This is the way to victory!

PRAYER:
God may I be found faithful to You through every test.

April 28

GOD USES PROBLEMS AND PERSECUTION TO CORRECT YOU

"...It was the best thing that could have happened to me, for it taught me to pay attention to your laws."
Psalm 119:71-72 LB

Here is another of five ways God uses problems and persecution in your life: God uses problems and persecution to **CORRECT** you.

Some lessons we learn only through pain and failure. It is likely that as a child your parents told you not to touch a hot stove. But you probably learned by being burned. Sometimes we only learn the value of something—health, money, a relationship—by losing it.

John 17 clearly teaches that He does not desire to have His church in the comforts of a problem-free society. He desires for His church to be faithful in the midst of trials and testing.

During a recent visit to Indonesia, some co-workers had the joy of participating in an Open Doors Standing Strong Through The Storm (SSTS) seminar held in an area of intense conflict. The constant presence of armed soldiers outside the building confirmed that this seminar was far more than just a theology course—this was reality! More than seven hundred churches were already burned to the ground and the church was facing a severe onslaught.

On the second day of teaching, one pastor suddenly jumped up and with all his heart cried out: **"My brother, please don't teach us just to survive, teach us to be faithful."**

In understanding God's purposes for the church it is vital to understand His requirements for us to remain faithful within these purposes. Faithfulness is not a request it is the duty of every believer. **"Teach us to be faithful in the midst of our circumstances"** should be a far greater priority in our prayers than that of making our society a safer place. Perseverance is far more important than transformation or preservation.

William Barclay said the following about praying for our circumstances. "When we pray for ourselves and others, we should not ask for the release from any task or situation, but strength to complete it and endure it. Prayer should be for power and seldom for release: not release but conquest must be the keynote of the church."

RESPONSE:
God is at work in my life—even when I do not recognize it or understand it. It is much easier and more profitable when I cooperate with Him. This is the way to victory!

PRAYER:
Lord, teach us to be faithful in the midst of our circumstances.

April 29

GOD USES PROBLEMS AND PERSECUTION TO PROTECT YOU

"You intended to harm me, but God intended it for good to accomplish what is now being done, the saving of many lives."
Genesis 50:20

Here is another of five ways God uses problems and persecution in your life: God uses problems and persecution to **PROTECT** you.

A problem can be a blessing in disguise if it prevents you from being harmed by something more serious. Last year a friend was fired for refusing to do something unethical that his boss had asked him to do. His unemployment was a problem—but it saved him from being convicted and sent to prison a year later when management's actions were eventually discovered.

Eritrean Christian singer, Helen Berhane, testifies that God helped her at every turn during her almost three years of imprisonment in the infamous shipping containers. She saw God repeatedly turn evil plans into good:

> One day they [the guards] brought two girls to my container. Their names were Rahel and Elsa. They were both in the army before they were arrested. They were supposed to spy on me and report back, because the authorities could not understand how, despite their treatment of me, I was still defiant. However, things backfired because the girls really liked me. Very soon we had become good friends and they even told me, "We were supposed to spy on you. But we like you, and so we won't!"
>
> ...Since the girls were not spying as they had been told to, Rahel was released, but they left Elsa in the container with me for a while. Rahel left all her spare clothes for me. This was a blessing, as for a long time I had not been allowed any more clothes, even when the old ones were worn out. **I felt that this was God's provision for me, like the ravens he sent to Elijah. It was my experience that no matter what hardship I was in, God always sent someone to**

help me. So, although these girls were sent to spy on me, God used them to bless me.[15] (emphasis mine)

RESPONSE:
God is at work in my life—even when I do not recognize it or understand it. It is much easier and more profitable when I cooperate with Him. This is the way to victory!

PRAYER:
God help me to trust You to bring good from the challenges, difficulties and persecutions I might be subjected to today.

15 Helen Berhane, *The Song of the Nightingale* (Colorado Springs: Authentic Media, 2009), pp. 57-58.

April 30

GOD USES PROBLEMS AND PERSECUTION TO PERFECT YOU

"We can rejoice when we run into problems...
they help us learn to be patient. And patience develops
strength of character in us and helps us trust God more
each time we use it until finally our hope and faith
are strong and steady."
Romans 5:3-4 LB

Here is the final of five ways God uses problems and persecution in your life: God uses problems and persecution to **PERFECT** you.

Problems, when responded to correctly, are character builders. God is far more interested in your character than your comfort. Your relationship to God and your character are the only two things you are going to take with you into eternity.

Christian singer, Helen Berhane, wrote a song of victory while in the terrible conditions of an Eritrean shipping container cell for almost three years:

Christianity costs you your life
But at the end, its outcome is victory

The beating of the Hebrews with the whip was awful
The waves of the sea and the mighty wind
Crushed by the stone, suffering by day and night;
Paul's faithfulness was tested by a sword.

Christianity costs you your life
But at the end, its outcome is victory

The journey of Ruth was a hope where there was no hope;
A sacrifice was paid even for a despised tribe.

Although there was nothing promised for Ruth
By faith she made her way toward Nazareth
And she entered into Jesus' genealogy.

Christianity costs you your life
But at the end, its outcome is victory[16]

RESPONSE:
God is at work in my life—even when I do not recognize it or understand it. It is much easier and more profitable when I cooperate with Him. This is the way to victory!

PRAYER:
Thanks be to God who gives us the victory!

30/Abril/2014

Padre, por favor
cuida de Javier
y ayúdalo a
salir victorioso
de las tentaciones.

Hoy recibimos las llaves de
Emerson! Gracias Padre
por tu provisión, ayúdanos
a siempre poner esta
casa a tu servicio.
En el nombre del
Señor Jesús, te
lo pido.

---

16 Ibid, p.106.

242

May 1

SPIRITUAL WARFARE TACTICS

For our struggle is not against flesh and blood, but against the rulers, against the authorities, against the powers of this dark world and against the spiritual forces of evil in the heavenly realms.

Ephesians 6:12

A Filipino pastor, who is a former Muslim, lives on the island of Mindanao in the southern Philippines. He was a notorious gang leader and spent years in prison for robbery and murder. But there in prison he met Jesus Christ.

After his release, he was so effective in leading Muslims to Jesus back home in Mindanao that Muslim extremists in his area kidnapped his fourteen-year-old daughter. They would only return her, he was told, if he stopped preaching about Jesus and returned to Islam.

He and his wife prayed intensely about this and felt they could not give in to this blackmail. He continued to preach faithfully for three years with no definite news about his little girl.

He concludes, "Despite the terrible things they have done to my daughter, I fear no one but God alone! Pray for my daughter and that I will continue to preach Christ."

Three years later, he received a letter from his daughter. She shared with her parents that she had been sold into prostitution in neighbouring East Malaysia. But God had helped her escape. She was then taken in by a sympathetic Malaysian family and hidden for her safety. And then she fell in love with a young man and married him. She and her parents planned to visit together in a safe place.

Spiritual warfare is the cosmic conflict that rages between the kingdom of God and the kingdom of Satan. Remember we are not talking about two equal kingdoms battling-it-out for victory. Satan is only a created being. Christ has all authority and power. Satan's power was broken at the cross. The Apostle Paul records for us in Colossians 2:15, *And having disarmed the powers and authorities, he made a public spectacle of them, triumphing over them by the cross*. So the only power Satan has today is the power to deceive the people of the world - to blind them from seeing the glory of God (2 Corinthians 4:3-4).

Satan's primary strategy is to divide and conquer. His key tactics include accusation, deception, and the interruption of our relationships with the Father and with each other. He is actively leading mankind to defile the land, which is God's, in order to keep humanity in darkness. This is one reason unity in the Body of Christ is so critical for the fulfillment of the Great Commission.

Why would someone lost in the chaos of the world want to be part of a fellowship of people that is disorderly, dysfunctional, and even destructive? The church of Jesus Christ must be ruled by love. We must be a refuge, a place of safety!

RESPONSE:
I will be alert to Satan's spiritual warfare tactics today without getting distracted from the Lord's primary ministry directions.

PRAYER:
Pray for witnessing brothers and sisters on the frontlines who experience Satan's greatest fury.

May 2

SPIRITUAL WEAPONS

The weapons we fight with are not the weapons of the world. On the contrary, they have divine power to demolish strongholds.
2 Corinthians 10:4

Helen Berhane was imprisoned for almost three years in the shipping container prisons in Eritrea. She shares how a Muslim man with epilepsy was also imprisoned. She says in her testimonial book titled *Song of the Nightingale*:

I noticed that he wore two charms on his belt. I pointed at them, "Where did you get those charms from?"

"I saw a witch doctor, before I was arrested, about my fits. He said that they would make me better, but I should never take them off."

"Jemal," I said, 'those charms cannot heal you. Only prayer to God can do that."

As I spoke he began to have a fit, and so I prayed for him. I did this often until, miraculously, he agreed to take the charms off. I took them away and burnt them, but whatever was in them smelled awful, and the guards demanded to know what I had been doing, which gave me the opportunity to explain to them that only prayer can heal a person, not charms from a witch doctor.

Jemal's health improved and his fits became less frequent. I was delighted but he was worried.

"Helen, if they know that I am feeling better they will keep me here, and I want to be released."

"If you continue to trust in God, no one can keep you from going home, not if God wills that you should be released."

I was very pleased when he was released shortly afterwards.[17]

---

17 Berhane, p. 31.

RESPONSE:
Today I will live in the awareness that the spiritual battle rages all around me and I can be used to counter Satan's bondage over people.

PRAYER:
Lord, you have given me the spiritual weapons with which to demolish the strongholds of the spiritual battle that I find myself against today. Help me not to depend on the weapons of the world.

May 3

FIVE EXTERNAL TACTICS

Then the chief priests and the elders of the people
assembled in the palace of the high priest, whose name
was Caiaphas, and they plotted to arrest Jesus in some sly
way and kill him.
Matthew 26:3-4

In the New Testament we see Satan using five external tactics against the church: rulers, priests, merchants, mobs and families—and of course, these often occurred in combinations. The followers of Jesus tend to unite the enemies of Jesus, so that quite unlikely alliances can be created. Jesus himself saw this when the Pharisees and the Herodians—two groups that never spoke to each other—got together to plot his assassination after he healed a man with a withered hand on the Sabbath (Mark 3:6).

It is surprising to some that the rulers are not the biggest persecutors of Christians in the New Testament. That dubious honor falls to the Jewish priestly caste. But there is no doubt that strong opposition came from the rulers. Pontius Pilate was complicit in the death of Jesus; Herod Agrippa killed the apostle James in Jerusalem (Acts 12:2); and of course Nero initiated a terrible persecution against the Christians of Rome in AD 64—the community most think Mark's Gospel was written to encourage.

Though it was Pilate's order, it was really the Jewish high priest who pushed Pilate into giving the order for the crucifixion when he was inclined to let Jesus go (see John 18:31), and tried to accomplish this by arranging a crowd clemency scene. All throughout his ministry, Jesus' bitterest enemies were the priests. And so it proved for the early church. The first flogging of Christians was administered under the auspices of the Sanhedrin (Acts 5:40), and the first martyrdom of a Christian (Stephen) was carried out by enraged clerics (Acts 7:54-59). And so it continued also for Paul, the main character of the early church, ironically a former Pharisee and a witness to the stoning of Stephen.

247

But it is a sad fact that the class threatened most by radical Christian faith is the clerical class, whether of one's own religious persuasion or of a rival one. This is not to say all clerics are persecutors. Many Pharisees became followers of Jesus, and some, like Nicodemus and Simon, were the very model of courtesy and open-mindedness. Nevertheless, in the history of the church, other "believers" have perpetrated most violence on Christians.

RESPONSE:
Satan uses external as well as internal tactics to attack the advance of the Kingdom of God.

PRAYER:
Lord, help me show love to other "believers" who do not hear Your voice but are used as tools of the enemy.

May 4

MERCHANTS AND MOBS

But the Jews were jealous; so they rounded up some bad characters from the marketplace, formed a mob and started a riot in the city. They rushed to Jason's house in search of Paul and Silas in order to bring them out to the crowd.

Acts 17:5

The next two groups of external tactics Satan used in the New Testament are merchants and mobs. Merchants or businessmen represent the economic establishment and are often opposed to Christians purely because Christians are a threat to their business.

The two clearest examples of opposition from businessmen in Scripture are when Paul visits Philippi and later Ephesus (Acts 16 and 19). In Philippi, Paul and Silas ended up in jail because of the actions of the owners of a demon possessed slave girl who was healed. Seeing their source of income disappearing because of her conversion, her owners pressed a false case against Paul, and had him jailed for "disturbing the peace." But the Scripture makes clear their economic motive, *"when her owners saw that their hope of making money was gone..."* (Acts 16:19).

Then when Paul gets to Ephesus the impact of his preaching is so great it causes the former members of the Artemis cult to hold a bonfire of their trinkets and shrines. A shop steward called Demetrius, on behalf of the silversmiths of the town, figures anything that reduces the appeal of the temple of Artemis is going to be bad for business. He stirs up a riot and Paul has to hurry out of the city.

Mobs play a major role in persecution, often when an elite group cannot induce the government to do their dirty work for them. Mobs are easily manipulated. They can be believers swayed by the heady rhetoric of clerics, or ruffians ready to commit grievous bodily harm for the sake of money and excitement.

Christians in Pakistan and Indonesia face the constant threat of annihilation of their property by mobs. A news agency journalist said,

249

"I am amazed at how quickly a mob can get going in Pakistan. It just takes three phrases from a mullah at Friday prayers, and five minutes later thousands are streaming out into the streets bent on inflicting injury or even killing Christians."

RESPONSE:
Our enemy, Satan, uses every tactic possible to come against those in the kingdom of God.

PRAYER:
Pray for Christians in areas noted above that they will be protected from Satan's arrows.

May 5

FAMILY PERSECUTION

"...I have come to set a man against his father, and a daughter against her mother, and a daughter-in-law against her mother-in-law, and one's foes will be members of one's own household."
Matthew 10:35-36

Anyone who has become a Christian in a family of unbelievers can testify to the hundreds of ways persecution can be experienced. Jesus warned us up front about this in chilling language. It was Jesus who experienced this from his own family, being chided and misunderstood (Luke 2:48), and his "own people did not accept him" (John 1:11).

Most families in the world are not nuclear in nature, but extended, so an entire web of kinship relations are fouled up by the action of becoming a Christian. It can be very difficult to make one's way in the world accordingly. We could even say it is one's family culture that rejects the Christian witness. One reason for this is over-familiarity. Jesus generalizes from his experience of rejection in Nazareth saying, *"Truly I tell you, no prophet is accepted in the prophet's hometown"* (Matthew 13:57).

This goes right back to the dawn of human history. The first recorded act of violence was due to family persecution—Cain murdering his brother Abel out of religious jealousy. King David bemoans the betrayal of a close friend in Psalm 41:9, *"Even my bosom friend in whom I trusted, who ate of my bread, has lifted his heel against me."* Jeremiah is dismayed to find members of his own family involved in an assassination plot against him; *"...even your kinsfolk and your own family, even they have dealt treacherously with you; they are in full cry after you"* (Jeremiah 12:6).

In China today, if a student converts to Christianity it is the parents that insist he or she give up her faith, for fear of an inferior work placement bringing dishonor to the family. In many Buddhist societies, like Burma, to become a Christian is tantamount to saying

"I am no longer Burmese."

It is family misunderstanding that is often hardest to bear. After all, we long for the love of those who have nurtured us. To have that love relationship ruptured ranks as one of the greatest traumas a human being can face.

In Pakistan, a father was asked why he murdered his daughter. He answered simply, "I didn't murder my daughter. When she became a Christian, she was no longer my daughter." He will never be charged for his crime.

RESPONSE:
Today I will treasure my family and watch for Satan's subtle attacks against it.

PRAYER:
Pray for those experiencing Satan's deadly tactic of persecution from family members.

May 6

NATIONALISM

There is neither Jew nor Greek, slave nor free, male nor female, for you are all one in Christ Jesus.
Galatians 3:28

Satan has inspired rulers to try to force Christians to return to their former folk religions or the pagan gods of their ancestors—all in the name of patriotism or nationalism. *Religious nationalism* is where a particular territory or culture is staked out exclusively in religious terms.

Leaders say, "Only Hindus are allowed to stay in India." Or, "You are a true Sri Lankan only if you are a Buddhist." In such cases where religious nationalism reigns, Christians either must accept second-class citizen status, face daily discrimination, or leave.

Research done by Open Doors indicates that to establish a "religious state" the religious nationalists require four elements: *a villain, a lie, a mob,* and *a vacuum*. They need a "villain" who can unite the people with a powerful message; a "lie" (Christians are intolerant); a "mob" to create chaos (media support helps); and a "vacuum" (absence of moderates in power to control the nation).

Some in India and Nepal argue that their country is Hindu hence other religions are foreign and imperialistic. State assistance is denied to those who convert to non-Hindu religions.

At one point, the Mongolian State Intelligence Bureau described Christianity as a "foreign religion." And today, Mongolia's new laws imply that Christianity is "against Mongolian customs."

In Mexico, a mayor of a community in the southern state of Chiapas has tried to justify the ongoing persecution of evangelicals with the claim that they "attack...our culture and traditions." In reality, tens of thousands of Christians have been expelled from their homes for not joining in the syncretistic community spiritual activities.

Christians in an area of Swaziland were told by their chief that each Christian would be fined a cow for not attending the annual cultural ceremonies at the king's royal cattle kraal. The chief announced that he had compiled a list of all his subjects who deliberately avoided two yearly ceremonies: the *umhlanga* (reed dance) and the *incwala* (first fruit). Pastors of churches accused of preaching against Swazi culture are among those fined. Pastors in the area plan to challenge the chief's fines in a court of law.

Christians must avoid the mistake of identifying religion with nation, and nation with religion—even in the West. To do so severely hinders the growth of the Body of Christ where there is ***"neither Jew nor Greek."***

RESPONSE:
I will not make the mistake of identifying religion with nation... and pray for those who do.

PRAYER:
Pray for Christians who struggle to survive in the midst of religious nationalism and extreme patriotism.

May 7

RELIGIOUS INTOLERANCE

Make every effort to live in peace with all men...
Hebrews 12:14a

Other religious groups are one of the most threatening tactics Satan uses against the church of Jesus Christ. In the book of Acts we see over and over that the primary opposition to the spread of the gospel in the early church was from religious groups. Again we must never view these groups as the enemy. We know who our real enemy is. In some parts of the world, the small percentage of extremists among Hindus, Buddhists and Muslims have encouraged mob violence and other forms of persecution against Christians. Our attitude toward them should be as Brother Andrew's acronym for **ISLAM** suggests: **I S**incerely **L**ove **A**ll **M**uslims.

The tactic that our enemy uses in these major religions of the world is the same. It comes from his character of deceiving and lying. Some people are able to perceive elements of truth within the major religions of the world, but their essential teachings are deceivingly false.

Wherever possible, missionaries of cults and other religions do whatever possible to encourage Christians—usually those who are Christian in name only—to convert to their religion. Unfortunately, in countries such as Egypt, a significant number do convert to a cult or to some other religion. The lure to convert can be marriage, money, employment, social acceptance, and any other similar attraction.

Hardini was born to a devout Muslim family in Indonesia where everyone must go to the mosque every day to pray. Her father had strict rules for everyone in the family. One rule was that Hardini should never associate with Christians. Despite Hardini's devotion to Islam, her heart was heavy and she longed for inner peace. A Christian with a great sense of joy and peace befriended Hardini.

Hardini had the courage to tell her new friend about her spiritual hunger, and the friend offered to pray for her in the name of Jesus.

After the Christian girl prayed, peace filled Hardini's heart and her life radically changed.

When Hardini's family discovered she had become a Christian, they spent hours and hours trying to entice her with force to recant her new faith. Hardini remained steadfast. Finally her parents made a painful decision—they totally disowned their daughter. That left Hardini with the choices of either recanting her faith or fleeing from her home and family. She chose to flee.

RESPONSE:
Today I will pray for believers like Hardini who experience religious intolerance.

PRAYER:
Lord, help me to sincerely love all Muslims and people of other faith systems.

May 8

TRAINING CHILDREN

...do not exasperate your children; instead bring them up in the training and instruction of the Lord.
Ephesians 6:4

A Chinese Bible Woman shares the following situation that helped train her and her children in righteousness while her husband was in labor camp:

One day I said to my children, "The Lord has told me that today I will go to prison for Him. Father is also in prison so please behave. Love each other and don't forget to bring food for your mom!"

During that time there were so many prisoners that the government could not provide for all of them so family members provided their food.

The children cried when they heard this. Daniel replied, "But mom, we have only five catties of rice left. How can we have rice and also send you some? When it's all gone, we'll die!"

I told the children, "The Lord can turn nothing into something!" and I reminded them of the story of Elijah and the widow. They had a simple child-like faith and believed that God could provide for their need. So they concluded, "Even though our rice is not enough, we will cook for you too!"

After talking with the children, The Public Security Bureau police came to the door and arrested me. Daniel followed me to the prison to find out which cell I would be in. The younger two children knelt in prayer. As I was taken away, my heart was wrenched as I heard their little voices trailing off.

I was in prison on that occasion for thirty days. All the while Daniel faithfully sent rice for me. When I returned home I asked, "Is there any rice left?"

Daniel's response was, "Mom, our rice container is overflowing!" It really was. Those five catties had inexplicably grown to about forty catties and were literally overflowing the container.

I said, "Praise the Lord! Now we can continue to cook for the other inmates and feed them as well." The Lord's grace is beyond measure.

RESPONSE:
In fulfilling the functions of the church in each Christian home, we have the great responsibility to train and instruct our children in faith and righteousness.

PRAYER:
Lord, help me model today Your love, faith and righteousness before the little ones I am in a position to influence.

May 9

TEACH YOUR CHILDREN THE COST

As they were walking along the road, a man said to him, "I will follow you wherever you go." Jesus replied, "Foxes have dens and birds have nests, but the Son of Man has no place to lay his head." He said to another man, "Follow me." But he replied, "Lord, first let me go and bury my father." Jesus said to him, "Let the dead bury their own dead, but you go and proclaim the kingdom of God."

Luke 9:57-60

One of the costs of following Jesus is the impact on our children. If we, as parents, try to shelter our children from the cross then we are guilty of the third temptation of Christ. Our children need to understand that there will not be a victorious life in Christ without following the footsteps to the cross. Not around the cross, as we often desire, but through the cross.

A co-worker once asked a Christian in Vietnam how he introduces the gospel in the villages where people have never heard about God. Without hesitating he answered "Oh very easily. I simply say, **'I have good news for you but it might cost you your life, would you like me to continue?'** People want to hear good news and most of the time they eagerly ask me to tell them. But the introduction is always that there will be a cost involved because for us in Vietnam, being a Christian means a life of self-denial. When they are persecuted and imprisoned they are not surprised. They expect it."

The co-worker went on to say, "It sometimes amazes me how we find it suitable to counsel our children regarding the costs involved in buying a new bicycle or starting a new hobby but we never sit down and discuss the cost of following Jesus. We need to train our children in no uncertain terms that being ridiculed at school, being rejected and facing mockery, is part and parcel of being a Christian. It comes in as a package and you cannot have the one without the other. We need to train our children to sacrifice; we need to train our children to count the cost; we need to train our children that they do not belong to themselves.

"Our lives are often based on our expectations. If we are confronted with the unexpected, we seldom know how to react. If we neglect to teach and expose our children to the reality of the cross, difficulties will come as a surprise.

"But, once again, if we as parents cannot testify through our lives by being examples of living sacrifices, our teachings will be futile. When was the last time you were ridiculed for the name of Jesus? When was the last time you sacrificed your time and money to work among the lost? When was the last time you sacrificed anything to visit the Persecuted Church?"

RESPONSE:
Today I will be an example to my children and teach them the cost in following Jesus.

PRAYER:
Lord, help me to be willing to sacrifice everything to follow You and to be an example.

May 10

WITHOUT WOMEN THERE WOULD BE NO CHURCH

Many women were there, watching from a distance.
They had followed Jesus from Galilee
to care for his needs.
Matthew 27:55

The New Testament records the fact that many women were among the larger body of disciples that followed and served Jesus Christ. Unfortunately, we only know the names and stories of a few. They were more loyal to Jesus at the time of his crucifixion than his male disciples.

Despite the patriarchal society of that day, four women—two of them Gentile foreigners—were named in the genealogy of Jesus in Matthew's Gospel chapter one.

It is significant that Jesus included women in his teaching putting them on equality with men. The same ethical and moral standards were demanded from both genders and the same way of salvation was offered for both.

Throughout the Bible, women filled significant roles—from leadership like Deborah to unique motherhood like Mary. The same has been true of those in the Persecuted Church.

A pastor in Cuba once told me, "Lenin said that without women there would be no revolution. I say that without women there would be no church!"

In China, the group of Christians who have had a major role in the revival and church growth are referred to locally as "Bible Women." Chairman Mao once said, "Women hold up half the sky." But it is estimated that about seventy per cent of the active Christian workers and church leaders in China today are women.

For example, Chinese Bible Woman, Ding Xianggao, has an incredible testimony. She is a young itinerant evangelist in China. Very much aware of the cost, she says, "In my country there are many brothers and sisters who suffer for Christ. Some of my co-workers have spent thirty years in prison for the sake of the gospel."

Two of her associates were actually martyred. Because she is a hunted woman, she often sleeps in caves and fields to avoid capture.

Her commitment is expressed this way: "Jesus died for me. The least I should do is die for Him. To suffer and go to prison for Him is my honor, and I look forward to it." She ended up in a large prison with over eight hundred inmates involved in prostitution, murder and kidnapping. But Ding believed God had placed her there for a reason. After three years she was released from prison. But not before seventy-eight people had made a personal commitment to Christ.

Sister Chan was sent to prison for six months for public preaching in central China, a prison with six thousand other women. During her time there, she led eight hundred women to faith in Jesus.

God uses everyone who is available in establishing His kingdom on earth.

RESPONSE:
Today I will not assume that I am not useable by God. I will make myself available to Him.

PRAYER:
Pray for the ministry of Christian women around the world— especially those who serve our Lord in difficult assignments or places.

May 11

BLESSINGS FOR PARENTS AND CHILDREN

He will turn the hearts of the parents to their children,
and the hearts of the children to their parents...
Malachi 4:6a

ManFu's parents are key leaders in a house church network—his father serves as a regional pastor in one of the largest cities in China, and his mother is a Bible teacher. They travel constantly, preaching and teaching at a different congregation almost every weekend. Their little pre-school daughter goes along, but it's not a stable environment for ManFu, their teenage son, to keep up with his studies. So they enrolled him in a boarding school in his father's home village, so he could spend weekends with his grandfather.

They pledged to telephone him every Saturday night, but for itinerant pastors in China, Saturday nights are busy, demanding times. ManFu's parents would sometimes get so caught up with ministry that they missed their weekly call to their son—sometimes three in a row.

And even then, they often cut off what he was telling them with a hurried barrage of questions which felt critical and unloving to their son. Although their questions were rooted in concern for his welfare, to ManFu each conversation felt like an interrogation, and he began to wish they would stop calling. His parents became frantic as to how they could effectively reach out to him.

Brother Samuel, an Open Doors trainer, suggested they begin by writing a letter to their son, pouring out their hopes and love and prayers for him. "Share about the struggles you have and how much you long for him to be by your side. Help him to see all that is in your heart. Kneel before the Lord and pray before you begin this letter. Don't mention the past. Whenever your son thinks of you, he will take the letter out and read it and know his parents are praying for him."

Accepting their mentor's assignment, they went home to write to their first-born, hundreds of miles away. Unknown to the parents, their letter never arrived. But by the time they found out, they told Samuel, it didn't matter anymore. Their phone conversations had been transformed week after week, as the parents focused on sharing their love and prayers for ManFu. Although the letter itself was lost, its contents had been written in their hearts—and ManFu felt their love.

When ManFu's summer school vacation approached, Samuel advised the anxious parents to set aside special family times to do things together. "It doesn't matter where you go – to the park or for walks – but you must take a family photograph," he advised. "Then take one photograph and write on the back of it for your son to take back to school with him. Whenever he looks at it, he will be reminded of his parents and that you love him."

When Samuel shared this testimony with pastors in other regions, many admitted that they also had strained relationships with their children. Confused how to resolve the guilt they were experiencing, they had simply given up—until they heard how God worked in ManFu's family.

"It's amazing to see parents being set free and healed from their feelings of guilt, to see them turn to God and experience His love," Samuel said. "And this in turn blessed their children."

RESPONSE:
Today I will work on communications with family members to assure them of my love.

PRAYER:
Pray for mentors like Samuel who strengthen pastors and their families in China's unregistered church through balanced, holistic ministry.

May 12

THE EXAMPLE OF MOTHERS

*Just as a nursing mother cares for her children,
so we cared for you. Because we loved you so much,
we were delighted to share with you not only the gospel
of God but our lives as well.*

1 Thessalonians 2:7b-8

Corrie ten Boom, a close friend of Brother Andrew's in Holland, was well-known for her statement: **"When God has a task to be done, he calls a man. When He has a DIFFICULT task to be done, he calls a woman!"**

Motherhood is often one of those difficult tasks for women. I can remember how difficult it was for my own mother in the 1950's to raise a family with four active, hungry boys on a total budget of twenty-five dollars a week. Yet she was such an example to us of sacrifice, commitment, and faithfulness. We knew she would give everything she had for us and our father.

The Apostle Paul reminded the Thessalonian church that the apostles could have become a burden to them but instead they treated the new growing church gently, like a mother caring for her little children, willing to give everything—even their lives.

Today mothers in the Persecuted Church continue to reflect the example of Jesus in sacrifice, commitment and faithfulness. I think of the wife of Santiago, a dynamic church pastor in one of Colombia's deeply troubled areas. Santiago's life is threatened because has an intense love for God's people, and a deeply ingrained sense of justice. His strength comes from the Lord. But his second source of strength is his wife, Deborah, who stands by him no matter what.

Recently, she opened up her heart to a small group of visitors. "I feel a profound emptiness and fear that can only be mitigated by the Lord. Although many people claim that the war here has dwindled, I cannot agree because I still see what the people here go through. Just yesterday four people were murdered in our town, two of them very close to our church."

At that point, the tears flooding Deborah's eyes reveal one of the deepest fears of her heart. "I beg my Lord not to take Santiago away from us, as it would be an extremely painful blow. I remember having the doors locked, believing that at any moment they would come looking for Santiago to kill him. Every time he left for church, my children also waited for someone to arrive bearing the horrible news that he had been murdered. The children beg him, 'Daddy, please quit the church. We know that people in the area are speaking badly of you, and you know that several other pastors have been murdered.'"

Deborah continues, "God changed our plans to leave. It is not His will that we run away, and our brothers and sisters would not allow us to do so either." Then she pleads, "I request your prayers for the Lord to heal the wounds of my heart, to remove the fear, so that I can continue fighting. But, more importantly, that I will know how to pray according to His will." Deborah's deep devotion to her husband and children is obvious. She is also their tower of strength.

RESPONSE:
Today I will honor mother and encourage other mothers I see struggling with life's issues.

PRAYER:
Father, bless Deborah today—and others like her—with courage, strength and faithfulness.

May 13

WOMEN WHO FEAR GOD

Charm is deceptive, and beauty is fleeting; but a woman who fears the LORD is to be praised. Honor her for all that her hands have done, and let her works bring her praise at the city gate.

Proverbs 31:30-31

Evangelism is an important function of the church everywhere. But in communist Vietnam, followers of Christ cannot openly share their faith. Those who do are often threatened or imprisoned. In response, Open Doors developed several programs to help. One was a women's discipleship program based on one-on-one relationships. It is called Priscilla Training.

A Vietnamese woman named Han says, "When I was young I went to church. We were a godly family. But I found the church very dull, very boring. The Bible did not speak to me. I knew some of the stories. And I listened to our pastor each week.

"One night when we were all asleep the police came and took our pastor away. They think if they take him away the church will die. They want all churches to die. They kept him in prison for five years. It's natural this happens. I live in a communist country.

"When the communists tried to kill my church, it challenged my heart. I knew I had to be strong. Before, I was just a church member. Now I have to become a serious follower of Jesus.

"I started reading my Bible every day, and it became fresh to me. It spoke to my heart. It was very, very good feeling, and I liked it. It was good for my life. I wanted others to have God in their lives too.

"Attending a secret house church is a risk. But it is a greater risk going to a training class. And I decided to take that risk. I went far away to receive Priscilla Bible and leadership training. I felt God calling me to be in ministry. I want to teach other women what I have learned. My first disciple was named Tuyen."

Tuyen says, "My friend introduced me to a godly lady. Her name is Han. She taught me how to study better, know God better, and be a true disciple of Jesus. I reach out to people and tell them all the good news I have in my heart, and the good hope I have in me today.

"A neighbor told me that a lady, a new follower of Jesus, wants to learn more about him. She will be my first disciple. I will teach her what I've learned from Han.

God has equipped thousands of women through the Priscilla Training in Vietnam and all members of the church are thus able to help fulfill the function of evangelism.

In June 2011, Vietnam's Evangelical Church celebrated its centenary. The government allowed the missionaries to Vietnam (who were still living and able to travel) to return for the celebrations. When they left in 1975, there were estimated to be 160,000 evangelical Christians in the country. In 2011 they found the church had grown to over 1.4 million. That's nearly 900 per cent growth! During the centenary celebrations, Open Doors was officially given an award from the leaders of the Evangelical Church for help in training given through the difficult years.

RESPONSE:
Today I will honor women who fear God and share their faith with others in need of help.

PRAYER:
Pray for more women in Vietnam to be able to effectively share their faith and train others.

May 14

PRAYER: TURNING PERIODS INTO COMMAS

Then some Jews came from Antioch and Iconium and won the crowd over. They stoned Paul and dragged him outside the city, thinking he was dead. But after the disciples had gathered around him, he got up and went back into the city.

Acts 14:19-20a

This passage of Scripture has always amazed me. It is one I wish Luke, the writer of the book of Acts, would have given us more graphic details. For example, what did the disciples do when they gathered around Paul left for dead on the ground? But Luke assumes we know the obvious answer.

Open Doors' author and co-worker, Anneke Companjen uses these concluding paragraphs in her first book, *Hidden Sorrow, Lasting Joy*:

My husband, Johan, likes to speak on Acts 14 when he challenges Christians around the world to care for the Persecuted Church.

In that chapter we read how the authorities won the crowd over and stoned Paul. They dragged him out of the city, thinking he was dead.

"Period!" Johan tells his audience. "The devil wanted to put a period here. Paul was finished as far as the enemy was concerned. But God had other plans. The story continues, *'But after the disciples had gathered around him, he got up and went back into the city'* (Acts 14:20). Something happened that turned the devils period into God's comma. What made the difference? The disciples' prayer."

God loves to change the devils periods into commas, and he's still doing it today.

It is my heart's desire that he will use you and me to make a difference in the lives of Christians who are persecuted for their faith around the world. We can reach out to them, each in our own church and community and in our own way, through awareness, through action, and most of all, through prayer.[18]

RESPONSE:

Today I will not underestimate the power of prayer for persecuted brothers and sisters around the world. I will pray asking God to turn the devil's periods into His commas.

PRAYER:

Pray for persecuted Christians today whether they are experiencing pain or pressure, guilt or relief, sorrow or joy, faith or denial, isolation or fellowship, prison or freedom, hope or despair, forgiveness or bitterness.

18 Anneke Companjen, *Hidden Sorrow, Lasting Joy* (Wheaton: Tyndale House Publishers, 2001), pp. 216-217.

May 15

SINGING PRAISES

After consulting the people, Jehoshaphat appointed men to sing to the LORD and to praise him for the splendor of his holiness as they went out at the head of the army, saying: "Give thanks to the LORD, for his love endures forever." As they began to sing and praise, the LORD set ambushes against the men of Ammon and Moab and Mount Seir who were invading Judah, and they were defeated.

2 Chronicles 20:21-22

The overflow of singing praises amid great difficulties has tremendous spiritual power for helping to win the spiritual battle. Paul and Silas set the biblical pattern in the prison in Philippi. Pastor Jack Hayford enjoys sharing the story as told by his favourite black preacher. Paul and Silas' prison cell singing was heard all the way to the throne room of God. He began to tap his toe to the music. Since heaven is His throne and the earth is His footstool, that foot-tapping created an earthquake!!!

Ivan Antonov shares how he survived twenty-four years in Russian prison camps for preaching:

I would sing hymns. I was really glad that I knew so many. I had memorized about one hundred seventy hymns, and in order not to forget them, I reviewed several every day. So over a time, I sang through all of them. I want to emphasize to my young friends that you should worship God with songs and poems and memorize them. They will come in handy...I sang hymns every morning and at night before going to bed...In those quiet [morning] hours, I would go outside in the fresh air and sing hymns of praise to God and pray. Then I went in for breakfast with everyone else.[19]

China's notable pastor Wang Ming-dao shared upon his release from prison that he frequently sang praises to God to buoy his spirits.

---

19 Ivan Antonov, "Survival 101: How to prepare for imprisonment," *Prisoner Bulletin* (1989), p.13.

The songs that meant the most to him were "All The Way My Saviour Leads Me" and "Safe In The Arms Of Jesus."

His contemporary, Allen Yuan shared with me two songs which he repeatedly sang aloud throughout his nearly twenty-two years in prison. One was "The Old Rugged Cross" and the other "Psalm Twenty-Seven" from the Chinese Psalter. It was always an emotional highlight to hear him sing these songs.

RESPONSE:
Today I will sing praises to the Lord my God.

PRAYER:
Lord, help me to rejoice and sing praises to You, especially when I feel the challenges of spiritual warfare.

May 16

SYNCRETISM

For although they knew God, they neither glorified him as God nor gave thanks to him, but their thinking became futile and their foolish hearts were darkened. Although they claimed to be wise, they became fools...
Romans 1:21-22

Satan has led many quasi-religious groups to unite around a mixture of religious teachings and then brand honest Christian believers as *bigots* for clinging to salvation in Christ alone. An outgrowth of the postmodern era in which we live is that many people no longer believe in absolute truth. A natural extension of this lack of absolutes is the widely held view that there is good in every religion and all roads lead to heaven. Individuals can then pick and choose the elements they wish from whatever faith and mix them all together. This is true syncretism. Chuck Colson refers to its impact on our faith as "salad-bar Christianity!"

Satan is delighted when people believe and expound on his lies. He does not want anyone to know the truth and come to a personal relationship with Jesus who is **the** truth, **the** way and **the** life (John14:6). Jesus is the **only** way.

One man reportedly traveled the world to find one name for God that would be universal and bring all people together. Instantly the word *love* came to his mind. He later wrote, "Give God the universal name of Love and we will create a golden cord to tie together the truths of all the religions of the world." But *love* is not God's name. It is His nature. And God expressed it most fully when He sent His Son to die for our sins (John 3:16). Only when we accept Christ's sacrifice for us will we know the love of the one true God that can bind people together.

A few years ago, an inter-faith group of 10,000 people met at the Vatican in Rome. The group included the Pope, the Dalai Lama and Muslim Imam W. D. Mohammed. An outspoken Hindu woman was quoted as saying, "It was refreshing to note that the idea that all religions have universal truths, and are merely different paths to the same goal was accepted as a given from the outset by all delegates without a single dissenting voice."

The same delegates also endorsed a general condemnation of "aggressive" proselytizing. This is the prevailing thinking of our day and age. Satan will do all he can to cause this thinking to even invade the church and individual Christian thinking and action.

The end result of syncretism in free societies will be anti-conversion laws and a prohibition of Christian witnessing. The euphemism for this law will probably be called "religious freedom."

RESPONSE:
Today I will guard carefully against the deceptions of Satan leading to syncretism.

PRAYER:
Lord, help me to fix my eyes on You and Your Word today so that I will not stumble.

May 17

MATERIALISM

For the love of money is a root of all kinds of evil.
Some people, eager for money, have wandered from the
faith and pierced themselves with many griefs.
1 Timothy 6:10

Satan subtly promotes the attitude that says money, property, possessions, physical comforts, as well as worldly fame and honor are the most important things in life. While God created all things and is the source of all we have, He does not condone our allowing things and money to usurp His first place in our lives. The prosperity that He so freely gives us, and wants us to have, is indeed a blessing until it takes the place of God.

Materialism is thus the attitude that says money, property, possessions, physical comforts, as well as worldly fame and honor, are the most important things in life. Not to say, "There is no God," but to say, "I don't have any need for God!"

For Christians, materialism is much like the frog in a pan of water that is slowly being heated. He boils to death because he does not realize the danger quickly enough to jump out of the pot before it is too late.

A church leader from the country of Romania, which was once a communist-dominated land and is now free, commented, "In my experience, 95% of the believers who face the test of external persecution pass it, while 95% of those who face the test of prosperity fail it!"

Satan is ecstatic when he succeeds in luring us into this trap. This is the dark side to money and possessions that many Christians are either unaware of, or unwilling to face. As a result, the spiritual vitality of many has been sapped and the church as a whole has been weakened spiritually. Like fire, money is a good servant but a destructive master.

If the church is to survive this challenge, there is an urgent need to be aware of the true nature of materialism. Unfortunately, it has become such a vital part of our culture that Christians are often unaware of its control.

By the standard of the people around Jesus, many of today's so called poor are very rich as well as almost all those in free societies. In Jesus' day, a rich person was one who had more food than needed for the day and who had more than one set of clothing.

Are you a rich person? Go to **www.globalrichlist.com**

RESPONSE:
Today I will not be a frog in the boiling water. I will be alert to Satan's attack on the materialism front.

PRAYER:
Thank You Lord for all the material blessings I have received from You. Help me to use them for Your glory and Your kingdom.

May 18

SERVING TWO MASTERS

"No one can serve two masters. Either he will hate the one and love the other, or he will be devoted to the one and despise the other. You cannot serve both God and Money."
Matthew 6:24

Riches are dangerous because their seductive power often causes people to reject Christ and His kingdom. The rich young ruler who turned sadly away after being told that he had to part with his riches to inherit salvation prompted Jesus' statement, *"How hard it is for the rich to enter the kingdom of God."* (Luke 18:24; Mark 10:23; Matthew 19:23)

A desire for riches can cause people to do almost anything—even to the extent of selling their souls. The result, Scripture warns, is anguish now and damnation later (1 Timothy 6:9-10). An abundance of possessions can easily lead us to forget that God is the Source of all good. The people of Israel were warned of this before they entered the Promised Land (Deuteronomy 8:11-17).

The pursuit of wealth often results in wars. James 4:1-2 says this clearly and it is amply confirmed from world history. Instead of fostering more compassion toward the poor, riches often harden the hearts of the wealthy. Rich persons are often unconcerned about the poor at their doorstep. (Luke 16:19-31; Isaiah 5:8-10; Amos 6:4-7; James 5:1-5)

Money is not neutral; it is a power with a life of its own. It is a power that is even demonic in character. When Jesus uses the Aramaic term *mammon*, translated as *money* in the NIV, (Matthew 6:24) to refer to wealth, He is giving it a personal and spiritual character as a rival god. Mammon is a power that seeks to dominate us.

Hence, money is an active agent. It is a law unto itself—capable of inspiring devotion. It is tremendously instructive to stand back and observe the frantic scramble of people for money. And this does not occur just among the poor and starving. Even the super-rich still seek

it furiously. The middle class continue to buy more houses,
more cars and purchase more clothes than they need. If money
only a medium of exchange, it would make no sense at all to a
such prestige to it. We value people in relation to their income.
give people status and honor in relation to how much money they
or appear to have.

**We can have all the Christian externals and yet be complete
materialists in our hearts.**

RESPONSE:
**I choose to serve God, so I will not give money any place of
prominence in my life or in my heart.**

PRAYER:
**Lord, I need Your help today to stay focused on You and not on all
the "things" around me.**

May 19

FIGHTING MATERIALISM

Jesus looked at him and said, "How hard it is for the rich to enter the kingdom of God!"
Luke 18:24

How is the god Mammon conquered? The Bible offers a perspective from which to view all of life's economic decisions. The Holy Spirit is with us; Jesus is our present teacher. The following are some suggestions:

- *Get in touch with our feelings about money.* Get in touch with our fear, insecurity, guilt, pride or envy. We are afraid to be short of money. And our fears, though irrational, are real. We need to face up to these feelings before we can apply God's promises to our financial situation.
- *Stop denying our wealth.* Instead of seeing the small picture of our situation, let us become world citizens, looking at ourselves in relation to all humanity.
- *Create an atmosphere in which confession is possible.* Much of our preaching about money has been either to condemn it or to praise it but not to help each other relate to it. Many of us feel isolated and alone. How much better if we could confess our fears and temptations.
- *Discover one other person who will struggle with you through the money maze.* Together covenant to help each other detect when the seductive power of money is beginning to win. This needs to be done in a spirit of love and graciousness but also rebuking and prodding.
- *Discover ways to get in touch with the poor.* One of the damaging results of affluence is allowing us to distance ourselves from the poor so that we no longer see their pain.
- *Give with glad and generous hearts.* Giving has a way of rooting out the tough old miser within us. The very act of letting go of money, or some other treasure, destroys the sin of greed.

279

Chinese house church leaders met together to discuss their problems. They concluded that their number two problem (after gossip) was money and the lure of materialism. There are two main sources of this. One is the rising standard of living in the coastal areas, which is tempting good teachers into commerce, depriving the church of much-needed leaders. The other is the kind, but often indiscriminate, giving of some wealthier Christians and missions to house church networks.

RESPONSE:
Today I commit to living a simple life style and not give in to materialism.

PRAYER:
Lord, I want to follow You all the way. And I want to be obedient as You direct and instruct.

May 20

TAKING AWAY THE CROSS

Jesus turned and said to Peter, "Get behind me, Satan!
You are a stumbling block to me; you do not have in mind
the concerns of God, but merely human concerns."
Matthew 16:23

A Western co-worker was visiting the Chinese city of Dandong which borders North Korea. He shares his challenging experience at a local house church meeting:

It was the first time I had ever been called "Satan!" But no one could fault the careful exegesis as this fiery Korean preacher bellowed to the 200-member house church.

"The third temptation of Jesus," he declared, "was when the devil offered him the kingdom without the cross. The devil was basically saying, 'Don't go off and make all those sacrifices, touch all those lepers, spend nights in agony praying, and end up being tortured by soldiers and dying a horrible death. Just take it all now…from my hand!'" He went on, "The church often has the same temptation. The devil offers us power without suffering. And…I've got to say this even though our Western friend is here…this is a temptation one part of the church tempts another part of the church with. We have to call that part of the church 'Satan,' just as Jesus had to call Peter 'Satan' when he made the same suggestion later in his ministry."

Good rip-roaring stuff, and thoroughly biblical. But I was intrigued as to why this pastor had singled out the Western church as the tempter. He was happy to explain over a meal.

"I hosted five pastors from North America last year. All Koreans. They came with reading material. Good stuff as far as it went, and they were supplying a sort of formula for church growth. But could one of them even bring himself to mention suffering? No! And when I heard those Korean pastors preach, it was also absent."

He leaned forward and whispered, "When these pastors preach to the Persecuted Church, and mention everything but suffering, they are taking away the cross from the Christian life. That's why I have to say that they are bringing a satanic suggestion. Anyone who says you can follow Christ but not carry your cross is no better than the old deceiver himself. Jesus said so. He said it to Satan, and he said it to Peter. And I'm going to say it to anyone else who dares to think they can be a witness for Christ from anywhere else but on a cross."

RESPONSE:
Today I will focus on the things of God realizing they will always require me to carry my cross.

PRAYER:
Lord, I will no longer try and eliminate the way of the cross from my Christian living. May I never again attempt to substitute power for suffering.

May 21

PERSECUTION CAN HAPPEN HERE!

I write to you, young men, because you are strong,
and the word of God lives in you,
and you have overcome the evil one.
1 John 2:14b

Colleague Ron Boyd-MacMillan recounts an interesting experience in China:

There's a house church in Beijing I like to take my friends to visit. The members are all young professionals, about twenty of them, and they meet in a huge, darkened, open-plan office at midnight once a week. It's totally illegal. Some of them are quite high ranking members of the communist party. If their faith is discovered, it would end their careers...or worse.

At the beginning of each meeting, the leader goes round and asks each member this question – the most challenging question I've ever heard in church: **What are your wounds for Christ this week?**

On one occasion I had brought two pastor friends, and the same question—through translation—was put to each of them. They replied, "Oh, we are not wounded or persecuted, you see, we live in Britain, where we have religious freedom, and we are so grateful for that!"

This reply was greeted with uncomprehending silence by the Chinese house church. Then a young woman spoke up, and without a trace of irony asked, "You mean, they don't let the devil into Britain?"

The house church leader patiently explained to the visitors the biblical understanding of persecution. "In the Bible, to be persecuted means to be pursued by the enemies of Christ. When we become a Christian, his enemies become our enemies, and we are pitched into a battle with the world and the devil, and this fight will draw wounds. So it doesn't matter whether you are in Beijing or Birmingham, the fight is the same, only the degree and type of suffering may differ. You're going to get pursued...that's persecution."

"But we thought persecution was legal discrimination, or being put into jail for one's faith" replied the pastors. The house church leader answered, "That's the extreme tip of it. Look, we may not sit on the same thorn, but we all sit on the same branch."

Still the pastors did not look convinced. Another Chinese member said, "If you don't have wounds for Christ, how do you know you are alive in Christ? Wounds bring joy, because then you know you are making a difference."

This struck a chord with the visitors. As preachers, they knew that nothing communicates like joy. That's why Persecuted Churches are growing churches—they are alive in Christ, and they know it because they have wounds! So find the source of resistance to the gospel in your local area, and when you apply the gospel, watch the fight begin.

RESPONSE:
Today I will accept negative reactions as a sign that I am making a difference in my community.

PRAYER:
Lord, may I also experience the joy resulting from doing right and opposing evil in my sphere of influence.

May 22

OVERCOME EVIL WITH GOOD

Do not be overcome by evil, but overcome evil with good.
Romans 12:21

Colleague Ron Boyd-MacMillan shares part two of his experience in China:

The Chinese house church pastor put it this way, "Confront the defining evil in your area or your society–that will bring persecution. For us, the evil is obvious; for you, it may be more subtle." You won't necessarily be persecuted if you speak out against evil. You won't necessarily be persecuted if you write an article about the evil. You won't necessarily be persecuted if you organize a prayer meeting to pray against it. But you will be persecuted if you become a **threat** to the evil.

One pastor went back to his church in an inner city area of London. He asked the question, what's the defining evil of this area? He became convicted that the youth gangs were the defining evil in the area, especially as they were going on killing sprees and starting to become drug pushers.

He began prayer meetings, and outreaches to the gangs. He even became a chaplain to a particularly violent gang. After a while, he saw fruit, but he also got a visit from a local gun runner,

"Leave the kids alone, or else" he said, "You're bad for business."

One night, six months later, a bullet came through the window as the church baptized five converted gang leaders. The reaction of the pastor could have come from the mouth of the Chinese house church leader. He said, **"It was a beautiful bullet...because now we knew we were making a difference."**

That pastor had joined the Persecuted Church, and led his congregation into a greater awareness of worldwide Christian persecution. They wanted to know about their brothers and sisters in Eritrea, China, North Korea and Iran not just because the Christians there needed their prayers and their money, but because they were one in the same battle. Christians in the West need the insights and prayers of suffering Christians around the world to fight their own battles better.

The other pastor returned to his church in a very upscale, business district. After praying with his elders, they came up with the defining evil or idol of the area, which they called "The Lie—get rich; be free." This was the besetting idol, they felt, and began to model an downsizing lifestyle in the community that reversed consumerist expectations.

The pastor confesses, "I'm facing almost weekly votes of confidence from my elders because they don't think I am teaching people enough about how to be successful." But he also says, "I feel so much better, because I'm not such a hypocrite in the pulpit anymore."

RESPONSE:
Today I will respond to the defining evil around me and overcome it with good.

PRAYER:
Lord, I need Your power and strength to effectively overcome the evil I experience. Help me stand strong in my opposition to the evil one.

May 23

NEVER SHAKEN

*Truly he is my rock and my salvation; he is my fortress,
I will never be shaken.*
Psalm 62:2

In December 1999, a Muslim mob attacked the Doulos Bible
School on the outskirts of Jakarta, Indonesia. One of the main aims
of this Bible School is to evangelize among the 30-million-strong
Sundanese, the largest unreached people group in the world, who live
in West Java. One student died and forty-four other students were
wounded. About eighty percent of the buildings were destroyed.
Domingus is a young student who was injured. He shares his personal
story of the events that fatal evening:

That night I was asleep in bed so I didn't know what was
happening. Suddenly a friend woke me up and shouted that we
were being attacked. The building was already burning and I did
not know where to run to. I knew if I ran to the main gate I would
be killed. I ran to the back of the campus where my friend lived. I
prayed "Lord, if I die, I know I will go to heaven."

Suddenly the crowds arrived and they shouted to kill me. They
grabbed me and blindfolded me. The Lord spoke to me "Don't be
afraid, I will be with you." They hit me with a big stick and I lost
consciousness. I felt my spirit leave my body. Through a sequence
of events I was brought to a place where people were singing and
worshipping God. I saw a very bright light and I closed my eyes and
bowed down. A voice said "Your time has not come yet, it is time to
go back!"

I regained consciousness and realized where I was. I tried to look
at my watch but I discovered my neck was very badly cut. I saw all
the blood. I prayed that the Lord would send someone to take me to
hospital. I thanked the Lord that I could be persecuted for the gospel
and that through this I could meet Him.

When the police arrived they asked, "Where did you find this
corpse?" They took me to hospital. I tried to open my eyes and I still

287

saw the angels around me. The doctors said I would be paralyzed but as you can see I am not.

Upon the conclusion of his testimony, Domingus was asked the obvious question: "What now? They will come back to finish the job and kill you. What do you want to do with your life Domingus?" He replied with great conviction, "I just want to serve Jesus."

RESPONSE:
Today I reaffirm my faith in God as my only protector who does not allow me to be shaken.

PRAYER:
Thank You Lord, that only in You can I find safety and protection. You have promised that You will always be with me.

May 24

ANSWER TO VIOLENCE

When they kept on questioning him, he straightened up and said to them, "Let any one of you who is without sin be the first to throw a stone at her."

John 8:7

"Get dressed and come along, we have a traitor we are going to necklace. We have a tire, a bottle of petrol and matches." The group of angry youths at the door did not even give their South African youth leader, Julia, a chance to protest.

Julia's parents were Christians who tried to raise her in the ways of the Lord. She rebelled at an early age and mixed with bad friends, abused drink and drugs, and married a man who deserted her. As a single parent she did her utmost to find a job, but work and food were scarce.

Julia joined a political party and participated in every gathering in her neighborhood. Violence, she thought, is the only solution to the country's and her own problems. She was soon chosen as leader of a large group of young people who made their presence known in the streets.

Nevertheless, Julia's problems were not solved. Every day was one long struggle to keep body and soul together, to find employment and to care for her child. One day, things became too much. She realized that no person could help. "Lord," she prayed in the dark, "if You truly are there, as my parents maintain You are, You must help me now."

The Lord answered her prayer. He laid His hand on this young woman and changed her life. She would never again be alone without her Heavenly Father who cares for her by her side. After her repentance she spent much time pondering and praying about her political aspirations and how she would handle her youth group.

That morning with the youths at her door, Julia got dressed and accompanied them to the man they wanted to execute by necklacing. Julia says, "I did not say anything. All that I could do was to pray and ask the Lord, 'What must I do now?'

"Fortunately it wasn't long before I got an answer from the Lord. I scraped all my courage together, looked at my comrades and said, 'If there is one of you who has never made a mistake, who is not a "sell-out," let him fasten the tire around the man's neck, let him set it alight.'

"Not a single one of the young people had an answer. One by one they silently parted and left me with the man who was to have been executed. I asked him to help me to carry away the tire and the rest of the things. I never saw him again.

"I must admit, I was quite afraid that the young people would return to burn down my house. However, God is great and wonderful because nothing happened. I am still their leader."

RESPONSE:
Today I will be bold to live like Jesus when facing difficult situations.

PRAYER:
Pray for young people caught in Satan's lie that violence is the solution to their problems.

May 25

DEAD ALREADY – AND HIDDEN IN CHRIST

For you died, and your life is now hidden with Christ in God.

Colossians 3:3

Kefa Sempangi was pastor of the large Redeemed Church of Uganda. Easter Sunday 1973 was his first serious brush with death at the hands of Idi Amin's goons. After an all-day worship service he went exhausted to the vestry to change clothes—too exhausted to notice the five strangers (government secret police goons) following him into the room:

They stood between me and the door, pointing their rifles at my face. For a long moment no one said anything. Then the tallest man, obviously the leader, spoke. "We are going to kill you," he said. "If you have something to say, say it before you die." He spoke quietly but his face was twisted with hatred.

I could only stare at him. For a sickening moment I felt the full weight of his rage. We had never met before but his deepest desire was to tear me to pieces. My mouth felt heavy and my limbs began to shake. Everything left my control. They will not need to kill me, I thought to myself. I am just going to fall over dead and I will never see my family again.

From far away I heard a voice, and I was astonished to realize that it was my own. "I do not need to plead my own cause," I heard myself saying. "I am a dead man already. My life is dead and hidden in Christ. It is your lives that are in danger, you are dead in your sins. I will pray to God that after you have killed me, He will spare you from eternal destruction."

The tall one took a step towards me and then stopped. In an instant, his face was changed. His hatred had turned to curiosity. He lowered his gun and motioned to the others to do the same. They stared at him in amazement but they took their guns from my face.

Then the tall one spoke again. "Will you pray for us now?" he asked. I thought my ears were playing a trick. I looked at him and

291

then at the others. My mind was completely paralyzed. "Father in heaven," I prayed, "You who have forgiven men in the past, forgive these men also. Do not let them perish in their sins but bring them into yourself."[20]

RESPONSE:
Realizing I am dead in Christ brings boldness to proclaim truth even in fearful situations.

PRAYER:
Lord, help me to trust You in times of fear and challenge and allow Your Spirit to take control of every situation.

---

20 F. Kefa Sempangi, *A Distant Grief,* Glendale, CA: G/L Publications, 1979, pp.119-120.

May 26

COURAGE FROM JESUS

I am the vine; you are the branches. If a man remains in me and I in him, he will bear much fruit; apart from me you can do nothing.

John 15:5

Yesterday we read the testimony of Kefa Sampangi in Uganda when he was threatened with death by Idi Amin's goon squad. The story continues:

"Father in heaven," I prayed, "you who have forgiven men in the past, forgive these men also. Do not let them perish in their sins but bring them into yourself."

It was a simple prayer, prayed in deep fear. But God looked beyond my fears and when I lifted my head, the men standing in front of me were not the same men who had followed me into the vestry. Something had changed in their faces.

It was the tall one who spoke first. His voice was bold but there was no contempt in his words, "You have helped us," he said, "and we will help you. We will speak to the rest of our company and they will leave you alone. Do not fear for your life. It is in our hands and you will be protected."

I was too astonished to reply. The tall one only motioned for the others to leave. He himself stepped to the doorway and then he turned to speak one last time. "I saw widows and orphans in your congregation," he said. "I saw them singing and giving praise. Why are they happy when death is so near?"

It was still difficult to speak but I answered him. "Because they are loved by God. He has given them life, and will give life to those they loved, because they died in Him."

His question seemed strange to me, but he did not stay to explain. He only shook his head in perplexity and walked out the door. I stared at the open door of the vestry for several moments and then sat down on a nearby straw mat chair. My knees were no longer strong and I could feel my whole body tremble. I could not think clearly. Less than ten minutes before, I had considered myself a dead man. Even though I was surrounded by 7,000 people there was no human being to whom I could appeal. I could not ask the elders to pray, I could not appeal to the mercy of the Nubian killers. My mouth had frozen and I had no clever words to speak. In that moment, with death so near, it was not my sermon that gave me courage, or an idea from Scripture. It was Jesus Christ, the living Lord.[21]

RESPONSE:
Today I will walk in the power of the living Lord and not in my own strength or courage.

PRAYER:
Lord, help me realize that You are my sufficiency. Without You, I can do nothing.

21 F. Kefa Sempangi, *A Distant Grief,* Glendale, CA: G/L Publications, 1979, pp.120-121.

May 27

DEFEATING THE ENEMY'S ATTACKS

You, dear children, are from God and have overcome them, because the one who is in you is greater than the one who is in the world.

1 John 4:4

Ung Sophal established eight house churches in Phnom Penh, Cambodia and the surrounding provinces. He and his wife lost their third and youngest child during the Pol Pot genocide. After many close calls, he was separated from his wife and children and sent to work in the fields. During these very difficult times, he still was able to lead sixty-five people to Jesus and even water baptize them. God miraculously spared his life on numerous occasions.

When the Vietnamese invaded Cambodia in 1979, Ung Sophal was able to return to Phnom Penh. It was now a ghost town. With a handful of other Christians, he started a house church, which grew from five members to six hundred in eight months.

That Christmas he invited some Christians to his home for a fellowship — including some Christian Westerners working for aid organizations. Two weeks later he was arrested for this "illegal" activity and accused of holding a political meeting with CIA participation.

He was interrogated for days and beaten severely. When the interrogation proved profitless, he was left in prison for five months chained hand and foot. He lost seventy-five pounds and was very sick but he heard the Lord instruct him to fast and be silent for three days.

The authorities became alarmed at the end of his fast and took him to the hospital thinking he was dying. There he constantly heard the sounds of other people being tortured with electricity and being beaten and kicked. "Even without the beatings it was very hard," he said, "I had a taste of hell, but God protected me."

Ung Sophal was successfully treated by a Cuban doctor who was also a Christian (God has his people everywhere). One night when the electricity went out because of a tropical storm, the doctor helped Ung escape. Later he fled with his wife and children to Thailand and spent ten years ministering to other Cambodian exiles — the last five years as a widower.

In 1990, as restrictions against Christianity began to be eased in Cambodia, Ung made his first visit back to his homeland to encourage and teach the church. Word of his return spread quickly and three hundred people came to see him. He is eager for the task ahead. "I want to build my people," he said. "God has a great work yet to do in Cambodia."

RESPONSE:
Today I will stand strong in Jesus' strength no matter what Satan throws at me or against me.

PRAYER:
Lord, thank You for encouraging testimonies of faithful people like Ung Sophal. Continue to grow Your church in Cambodia, I pray.

May 28

STRATEGIC LEVEL SPIRITUAL WARFARE

Then he [angel] continued, "Do not be afraid, Daniel. Since the first day that you set your mind to gain understanding and to humble yourself before your God, your words were heard, and I have come in response to them. But the prince of the Persian kingdom resisted me twenty-one days. Then Michael, one of the chief princes, came to help me, because I was detained there with the king of Persia.
Daniel 10:12-13

There is considerable interest and teaching today about "territorial spirits," that is, spiritual warfare waged against high-ranking principalities and powers assigned to a locale. The Scripture passage here indicates that a particular evil spirit was assigned to Daniel's human government or territory. But what we lack biblically is any example of or injunction to engage these spirits directly or by name. Daniel only prayed to his God who sovereignly directs angels to war against the territorial rulers. The Apostle Paul taught that demonic emissaries who attack the church and hinder its mission can be overcome only through reliance on the power of God.

That same power of God is much needed in the world today. For example, witchcraft is being used as a strategic weapon by traditional Indian authorities in western Colombia in an attempt to weaken and even stamp out the faith of indigenous Christians. Sorcerers or witchdoctors, called te walas by the indigenous peoples, have started sending messengers to sit in the back during church services, rather than going directly themselves. When the pastors invite listeners to receive Christ, these messengers say, "No, we have just come to listen." But while Christians are praying, the *te walas* sprinkle the cursed waters around the church.

If their incantations bring no results, the *te walas* themselves come to the church, surrounding it with occult rites to cause the believers to lose their desire to pray and read the Bible. In some recent night-time visits by these traditional "healers," the witchdoctors made pacts with animal blood as well as sprinkled their cursed waters on the church.

A seventeen-year-old girl in one church was induced to participate in these practices, despite having Christian parents. She actually made a pact of witchcraft, her pastor said, to give over one of her relatives to Satan. Discouraged, her parents cannot understand how this could happen in their home, where she learned to know and love God. Church leaders and the pastor have united with this family to intercede for urgently for this young girl's deliverance. The pastor admitted that he feared that more such cases are happening that have yet to be discovered. They need our prayers.

RESPONSE:
Today I'll not underestimate the power of God to defeat all that Satan throws against me.

PRAYER:
Lord, may Your mighty power overcome the evil united against Your church in Colombia.

May 29

COMPROMISED BY DECEIT

...but each person is tempted when they are dragged away by their own evil desire and enticed.
Then, after desire has conceived, it gives birth to sin; and sin, when it is full-grown, gives birth to death.
James 1:14-15

One of the touristic highlights of visiting China is to walk on the Great Wall. Six thousand kilometers of wall with ten thousand strategically placed towers stretch across the north of China, reportedly the only man-made object observable from space. Construction of various sections began back in 770 B.C. when rival feudal kingdoms built walls around their territories to keep out invading nomadic tribes from the north. These were eventually joined into one wall. The wall averages eight to ten meters in height and five meters wide.

When you walk on the wall, two history lessons make the visit somewhat somber. First, the wall was built at great cost. Prisoners of war, convicts, soldiers, civilians and farmers provided the labor. Some estimates say "millions died for this cause". Their bodies were buried in the very foundations of the wall or used to make up its thickness. You walk on top of a cemetery.

The second lesson is that the wall was reportedly breached by Mongol soldiers disguised as peasants pretending to be gathering firewood and leaving behind pieces of fruit when they left the area. The guards decided to go out and retrieve the tempting fruit. This was repeated over time. Eventually the guards were compromised and overpowered and the Mongol army streamed through that tower thereby breaching the Great Wall. So after all the effort to build such an amazing structure for protection, it was rendered useless through simple deceit.

One of Satan's favorite tactics against believers is deceit. Earlier I shared about Brother Chen, a cultic preacher in China who talked about heaven being a city of gold. He said, "Jesus needs your gold to build your mansion in heaven and the more gold you give him now, the bigger your mansion will be." He left the group to open the gate of heaven for them on a donated motorcycle. He took most of their savings and he hasn't been back.

In the mid-1990's, a more insidious persecution threat came to Christians in China in the form of a deceptive cult known as "Eastern Lightning." Its members try to destroy the church through infiltration, deception, entrapment and even physical violence. Attractive young women are sent out to sexually entice and blackmail male Christian leaders and missionaries. Those who cannot be attracted by deceit are kidnapped and even mutilated.

Tony Lambert recounts in his book, *China's Christian Millions*, how a charismatic preacher in rural Henan province convinced gullible peasants to sell everything they had and wait all evening for Jesus to appear out of a local river. When the peasants waded into the river, they were all swept away and drowned. Satan's deceit can be as deadly as physical violence.

RESPONSE:
Be aware today of Satan's subtle tactics of deceit and intimidation.

PRAYER:
Pray for new house church believers in China who are easily deceived by false prophets.

May 30

WHICH ARE YOU?

I can do all this through him who gives me strength.
Philippians 4:13

A young woman went to her mother and told her how things were so hard for her. She did not know how she was going to make it and wanted to give up. She was tired of fighting and struggling. It seemed as one problem was solved a new one arose.

Her mother took her to the kitchen. She filled three pots with water. In the first, she placed carrots, in the second she placed eggs and the last she placed ground coffee beans. She let them sit and boil without saying a word. In about twenty minutes she turned off the burners. She fished the carrots out and placed them in a bowl. She pulled the eggs out and placed them in a bowl. Then she ladled the coffee out and placed it in a bowl.

Turning to her daughter, she asked, "Tell me what you see?"

"Carrots, eggs, and coffee," she replied.

She brought her closer and asked her to feel the carrots. She did and noted that they were soft. She then asked her to take an egg and break it. After pulling off the shell, she observed the hard-boiled egg. Finally, she asked her to sip the coffee. The daughter tasted its rich aroma.

The daughter then asked. "What does it mean, mother?"

Her mother explained that each of these objects had faced the same adversity—boiling water—but each reacted differently. The carrot went in strong, hard and unrelenting. After being subjected to the boiling water, it softened and became weak. The egg had been fragile. Its thin outer shell had protected its liquid interior. But, after sitting through the boiling water, its inside became hardened. The ground coffee beans were unique, however. After they were in the boiling water they had changed the water.

"Which are you?" she asked her daughter. "When adversity knocks on your door, how do you respond? Are you a carrot that seems strong, but with pain and adversity, do you wilt and become soft and lose your strength? Or are you an egg that starts with a malleable heart, but changes with the heat? Do you have a fluid spirit, but after a loved-one's death, a relationship breakup, a financial hardship or some other trial, have you become hardened and stiff? Does your shell look the same, but on the inside you are bitter and tough with a stiff spirit and a hardened heart? Or are you like a coffee bean? The bean actually changes the hot water, the very circumstance that brings the pain. When the water gets hot, it releases the fragrance and flavor. If I am like the bean, when things are at their worst, I get better and change the situation around me through Christ-likeness.

When the hour is the darkest and trials are their greatest do you elevate to another level? How do you handle adversity?

RESPONSE:
Christians are like carrots, eggs or coffee beans. They don't know how strong their response is until they get into hot water. Which are you?

PRAYER:
Lord, help me realize that every experience You gives me, every person You put in my path, is the perfect preparation only You can see.

May 31

ONE WITH THEM

If one part suffers, every part suffers with it; if one part is honored, every part rejoices with it.
1 Corinthians 12:26

For Marina Shestakov and her three daughters, the imprisonment of their husband and father, Dmitry, was a time of great loss. But four years of loss soon became four years of gain, as Marina and the girls discovered they had a new family—a family without boundaries. Christians from around the world came alongside them reminding them of God's love through their prayers, letters of support and offers of practical help.

In 2007, Pastor Dmitry Shestakov was sentenced to four years in a labor camp. He was leading a church in the east of Uzbekistan and had been watched by the security services for some time. In an attempt to blacken his name, he was falsely accused of many things, such as the excessive use of drugs and alcohol.

Marina will never forget the moment Dmitry was arrested. "It was a huge shock," she says. "Suddenly I was left alone. Quickly many things changed in our family. The girls (Sasha, Masha and Vera) were at an age when they were discovering all sorts of things, and sometimes they did not take notice of what I told them. Once Dmitry was gone, that changed. Gradually we became a close-knit team. That was good, but at the same time hard. They missed a part of their childhood."

After Dmitry's arrest, division arose in the church that he led. Some of the Christians were afraid and fled. However, God also brought good out of the situation. "Often in Central Asian cultures, when the pastor is removed, the whole church falls apart," explains Marina. "Although some families left, new leaders arose as well. I'm thankful to everyone who took over Dmitry's work," she adds.

When Dmitry's arrest became known outside Uzbekistan, several organisations launched aid campaigns for the Shestakovs. Open Doors started a writing campaign and encouraged its supporters to send cards and letters to encourage the Shestakov family. This support was vital for Marina and the girls.

"All the cards were a great encouragement for me," shares Marina. "I thought it was so wonderful that people sent cards which were intended especially for one of us: for Dmitry or for me, or for one of the girls.

"I gained most strength from the Bible verses. The promises of God that He was watching over me, that He was holding me in His hand: those promises that people had written on the cards helped me to get through."

RESPONSE:
Today I will thank God for the oneness of His body around the world and the encouragement we can be to one another.

PRAYER:
Pray for the Shestakov family—and others like them—as they struggle to resume their lives after the pressures of isolation and separation.

June 1

WHERE IS YOUR HOUSE?

"Do not store up for yourselves treasures on earth, where moths and vermin destroy, and where thieves break in and steal. But store up for yourselves treasures in heaven, where moths and vermin do not destroy, and where thieves do not break in and steal. For where your treasure is, there your heart will be also.
Matthew 6:19-21

This Scripture is best illustrated by the testimony of a nameless (for security) Arab Christian woman:

"My grandfather was born in one village, grew up, got married and died in the same village. I was born in one city, and by the age of ten, I already had lived in three different countries and moved five times because my parents were looking for better job opportunities. After marriage, and by the age of thirty-five, I had already moved fifteen times mainly because of three different war situations in my home country!

Is there some kind of prize for people moving so often? Some of the changes were done willingly but for most of them, I had no choice! I lived in stone houses, brick houses and even in a prefabricated one (with thin walls like cardboard) and that was at a time when Beirut was being bombarded! I have to admit that I had fears not because of the bombardment but because of not being able to find a place we could afford to pay rent!

One day, I was so worried that I couldn't sleep; so, I sat down to figure out how I would overcome this fear. I thought to myself, *What is the worst thing that can happen to me? If I cannot afford to sleep in a building, I will go and sleep under a tree; no one would charge me money for doing that and no one has died because of sleeping under a tree!*

Then, I looked back into the past years and saw how God had taken good care of me, helping me not only to survive during wartime, but also to be productive and render services to my community. If, by faith I am God's child, according to His promises in the Bible, He will continue to take care of me. So, having these thoughts, I began singing, **"You are my hiding place, You always fill my heart with songs of deliverance, Whenever I am afraid, I will trust in you!"** That was it, my fears were gone! I still do not own my own place to live, but I carry the same song in my heart and in my laptop, to listen to whenever I change the places I sleep!

I discovered that the best thing to do is not to get attached to material things or even people, because they will be there for some time and will be gone soon. The best thing is to get my heart attached to God, because He will go with me everywhere, will provide for me what I need and in the end take me to live in the heavenly city where my eternal house is! So, where is your house?"

RESPONSE:
Today I will seriously evaluate where my "treasure" and "house" are because that's where Jesus says my heart will also be.

PRAYER:
Help me Father to accumulate treasures in heaven and not on earth.

June 2

OPEN DOORS OF OPPORTUNITY

But I will stay on at Ephesus until Pentecost, because a great door for effective work has opened to me, and there are many who oppose me.

1 Corinthians 16:8-9

The Apostle Paul was always focused on opportunity. Yet he was a realist who knew the opposition he faced from the enemy of our souls. He expresses here an interest in visiting the Corinthian Church for a significant period of time. But it would not be until after Pentecost because of great open doors for effective work in spite of much opposition. In doing kingdom work we should always expect opposition but that should not blind us to the great opportunities.

A young pastor in the southern Philippines who attended a Standing Strong Through the Storm (SSTS) seminar, shares his personal experiences with this principle:

"The SSTS taught me a lot of things. First, it taught me to stand firm in the Lord during tough times. Second, it taught me to establish my relationship with God and not to focus on difficulties. Third, it taught me to lead my whole family to serve and obey God even though hardship and persecution come. And also it taught me to continue on with the ministry, even if others abandon us.

"My wife and I were newlyweds and fresh graduates of a Bible school when God called us to start a work among the Muslims. We were afraid of them and did not know how to minister to them. Open Doors gave us books on how to love the Muslims. In one community we started literacy classes among the children.

"But the more we grew in our desire to obey God, the more our faith was tested. In 2004, I was diagnosed with stage-four pancreatic cancer. But my sickness did not stop the Lord in accomplishing His purpose for our lives. In 2008, He led us to permanently settle in a place where most Christians dared not go. As we obeyed God, we experienced His great power—that same year, my doctor told me that I was cancer free!

"The Lord also paved the way for us to reach one Muslim tribe through an adult literacy project. We built relationships with our students and eventually shared the gospel with them. We seized every opportunity to help them with their needs, more so with their relationship with Jesus Christ.

"I would say that the biggest test of our faith was not when I got sick, but when our sending church abandoned us and cut our support. I felt alone, but God sustained me and my family.

"The Lord is continuously opening more opportunities for us to minister to our Muslim brothers. Right now, with Open Doors' help, we are holding literacy classes among the three Muslim tribes in our area. We are also distributing the *JESUS* film when there is any opportunity to do so."

RESPONSE:
Today I will not allow opposition to blind me to the opportunities of service God provides.

PRAYER:
Lord give me strength to walk through open doors of effective work in the face of opposers.

June 3

HOPE IN THE FACE OF BAD NEWS

"As the heavens are higher than the earth, so are my ways higher than your ways and my thoughts than your thoughts."
Isaiah 55:9

Open Doors colleague, Ron Boyd-MacMillan, shares the following insight from his teaching, "Why I need to encounter the Persecuted Church."

Wouldn't it be wonderful to have an idea of what God is really up to in this world? One thing we can be very sure of—that the story of the world as we find it in history books and newspapers, is not to be confused with the real story of what God is doing **underneath**. But what is God's story as opposed to history? What's he really up to? Must the daily diet of wars, murder and mayhem in my newspaper always get me down. Can I ever be sure something is going on underneath? Well, we can't know perfectly as "his ways are so much higher than our ways" (Isaiah 55:9). But we are afforded glimpses. This glimpsing really excited the early Christians. You can hear the delight in Paul when he writes, "God's secret plan has now been revealed to us..." (Ephesians 1:9). The persecuted seem to get more glimpses than most.

I think of China. The headlines said in June of 1989 a terrible massacre took place. Five thousand young people were mown down by the Chinese army. The headlines all mourned the death of the pro-democracy movement. It was terrible, but what was God up to underneath? Out of that massacre came a remarkable turning to Christ among China's students for the first time in history! The headlines never saw it. It's not part of history. But "His story" went on.

I think of Afghanistan. When the Soviet Union invaded that country in 1980 the world was outraged. The headlines were all full of fierce denunciations of the action, and rightly so. But I remember meeting a missionary from Kabul who said, "Yes, what the Russians did was wrong, but the fact is it is now much easier under the Russians for

309

Christians to evangelize than it was before under the Islamic regime." Again, another more significant story, of God building his kingdom, was going on undetected by the world at large.

I think of Sudan. The headlines in the 1980's were full of a dreadful civil war which isolated the Dinka people from the outside world. It was terrible. There was untold suffering on vast scale. But underneath, God was bringing the 2 million Dinkas to himself. By 1993, 80% of them were Christians and this among a tribe that was historically very resistant to the gospel.

Notice that these are all stories from the persecuted. They seem to be better placed to notice the real story. And so I need to keep in touch with them because this glimpse delivers me from despair. In 1989 in China, there was not just a massacre, but a revival. In 1980 in Afghanistan, there was not just an occupation, but new missionary opportunities. In Sudan, there was not just a brutal war that killed millions, but a new kingdom of believers among an unreached people.

So every day when I open my newspaper, I remind myself of two things, thanks to the persecuted: the story I see is not to be confused with the *kingdom story*; and underneath even the saddest news, God is surely up to something good. There is hope because God is always at work.

RESPONSE:
Today when I read or hear the news, I will thank God that He is at work behind the scenes.

PRAYER:
Thank You Lord, for Your promise to bring good out of the terrible events of this world.

June 4

LIVING TO PLEASE GOD – WITHOUT FEAR

For I am the LORD your God who takes hold of your right hand and says to you, Do not fear; I will help you.
Isaiah 41:13

Today we share the testimony of overcoming fear from Sister Sarah in Bangladesh:

"I knew my husband since childhood. We grew up in same village and studied in same school. But his family was devoted to Islam; his father was a Muslim imam. Just imagine the disappointment when his family learned that he became a Christian! To leave Islam and marry me, a Christian girl, is to bring great shame to his family. It was like pouring more oil into the fire! His family plotted to kill him, but God save my husband from their hands.

"My in-laws blamed me and my parents for my husband's conversion. My parents received lots of threats, finally forcing my parents to move to another place. Those days were very painful for me but my husband and I always prayed, 'Lord help us stand firm in our faith.' God would speak to my heart through His Word that He held me by His right hand... that I didn't need to be afraid, because He was there to help (Isaiah 41:13).

"The first few years of my marriage were the toughest. We feared for our lives every night. During those years, we moved six times because of threat from my in-laws. After three years or so, my in-laws rejected my husband completely and they left him without inheritance. It was painful, but I also felt relieved, because that meant there would be fewer threats.

"When the tension lessened, I joined an organization that was working among disadvantaged women. I found joy in being with lots of people. I felt satisfaction in what I was doing, though it was for a secular company. Later on, however, it motivated me to pursue working with a Christian ministry. I began praying, 'Lord I want to serve You by serving Your people. Would You please open a door for me and equip me for Your work?'

"God was quick to answer! In 2008, my husband and I enrolled in a Bible school abroad through the support of Open Doors. Throughout those four years of seminary training, God taught me to develop inner beauty through faith, obedience, courage, and prayer. I became more confident in introducing Christ to others, more supportive of my husband as he fulfilled his calling and potential, and more conscious of helping my children grow up as God-fearing persons.

"This year, we returned to our home country Bangladesh. My husband got an opportunity to serve God and His people through a Christian organization. Please pray that God will help me encourage my husband so that he remains faithful in his calling, raise my kids in a godly way, and obey His command to make disciples."

RESPONSE:
Today I will thank God that He is with me and I do not need to fear anything or anyone!

PRAYER:
Pray that God's promises will sustain Sarah and her husband in living for God without fear in their new ministry.

June 5

THE BIBLE

Above all, you must understand that no prophecy of
Scripture came about by the prophet's own interpretation.
For prophecy never had its origin in the will of man,
but men spoke from God as they were carried along
by the Holy Spirit.
2 Peter 1:20-21

Daniel, a Chinese brother from Singapore, sat in the chair still shaking his head in unbelief. He had just returned from his first extensive visit to the People's Republic of China. Now in the freedom of his home city, he was trying to assimilate and communicate all the impressions and messages he had received.

"How would you summarize what you learned on your visit, Daniel?" I asked him. He continued to shake his head and smile. Finally he began to speak.

"Probably by my visit to one particular house church," he slowly replied. "It numbers several hundred believers who have had a lot of persecution over the past years. I asked them how they had been victorious and even grown in numbers during such terrible experiences. They quickly replied, telling me three things," he continued. "First, obedience to the Word of God; second, communication with God, that is, prayer. And third, love for the brothers and sisters."

This group memorized one chapter of the Bible every week. They began doing this because of a lack of Bibles, but continued doing so after they realized the blessing it brought to their lives.

The Bible is God's written revelation of Himself and His desire for a relationship with people. It is more than just a revelation of God's character. It is also a revelation of His intricate plan for the world. We could never have understood our great God if He had not chosen to reveal Himself.

His greatest revelation of Himself was when He came to live among us in a human body and was known as Jesus Christ. But even our knowledge of that revelation depends upon His written Word, the Bible.

Satan has conducted a massive propaganda campaign in the last century in an attempt to discredit the Bible. He would love to see Christians lose faith in the Word of God. In spite of his efforts, however, no one has ever been able to disprove its reliability. It remains the only absolute truth known to humankind.

The Bible is our God-given basis for faith, doctrine and practice. Many times Christians have knowingly departed from its teachings and suffered because of doing so. Many times when Christians depart from the Word, it is because they do not know or understand it.

The church can only be true to the revealed Word of God when its people know what it teaches. Study of God's Word is an essential part of the Christian life. When Christians doubt, ignore or fail to understand the teachings of Scripture and depart from its principles, they lose their spiritual power.

RESPONSE:
Today I will recommit to the daily study and application of God's Word, the Bible.

PRAYER:
Pray for believers in many parts of the world who still yearn for a copy of the Bible.

MEMORIZING GOD'S WORD

*All Scripture is God-breathed and is useful for teaching,
rebuking, correcting and training in righteousness,
so that the man of God may be thoroughly equipped
for every good work.*
2 Timothy 3:16-17

When China's best-known pastor, Wang Ming-dao, was finally released from prison, he stated, "In these past twenty years, I have not had a copy of the Bible. Happily between the ages of twenty-one to twenty-four, I spent my time at home doing the housework and studying the Scriptures. I memorized many passages. These passages in my heart came out one by one and strengthened me. Had it not been for those words of God, then not only I, but many others, would also have been defeated."

Pastor Lamb in southern China was in prison for many years at that same time. "I understood then why I had memorized so much of God's Word while in Bible school," he says. "I kept my sanity only by repeating Bible verses over and over."

The best way the church can prepare for trials and persecution is by seriously studying and learning the Word of God. Christians need an overview of the whole Bible. Understanding God's outline for mankind in the Bible aids in memorization as well.

What is the right attitude to bring to Bible study? Some read and study the Bible with the intent to get something from it to teach to others. But first, we should approach the Bible with the desire to see the goodness and loving-kindness of God and understand how *"wide and long and high and deep"* is His love for us (Ephesians 3:17-19). Let His love show you His supply for your own need and then you are better able to meet the needs of others.

Second, approach the Bible with humility. Study the Bible to discover what God has said. Bible study is meant not merely to inform but to transform.

In restricted countries where Bibles are in short supply, pastors are often in a quandary as to which of the many spiritually needy he should share these precious books with. Progress in Bible memorization is one method they can use for determining who will receive the available Bibles. One house church group in Vietnam decided to give them to the believers who were most determined to use them. The criterion used was memory work. So Bibles were shared only with those who recited flawlessly Psalm 119—all 176 verses!

Open Doors is committed to provide God's Word to those for whom it is not available. *"It is the power of God for the salvation of everyone who believes..."* (Romans 1:16)

RESPONSE:
Today I will memorize a new verse from God's Word, the Bible.

PRAYER:
Pray for the Christians in restricted countries where there is a shortage of God's Word.

June 7

THE WRITTEN WORD OF GOD

Now that you have purified yourselves by obeying the truth so that you have sincere love for your brothers, love one another deeply, from the heart. For you have been born again, not of perishable seed, but of imperishable, through the living and enduring word of God.
1 Peter 1:22-23

The Bible has always been an important resource to those who have not had access to it — especially those in prison. Christian singer, Helen Berhane shares how she smuggled a Bible into a shipping container prison in Eritrea and later was moved to another container which already held eighteen Christian women who had refused to give up their faith. She writes in her book, *Song of the Nightingale*, how the Word of God impacted her and the other women:

We were very overcrowded, but I was happy to join a Christian group again. Since I was the longest serving prisoner, I took charge. I wanted to help them as much as I could, because I knew they would be comforted by the thought that someone cared for them. I would fold the older ladies' blankets when they went out to the toilet in the morning, and I would stay behind to clean the container [of human waste].

Many of them were worried about their husbands and children, so I tried to keep them busy and establish a routine. I would start by preparing breakfast; at this point we got four bread rolls each, two in the morning and two in the evening, with weak lentil soup, and a cup of tea.

Then I would lead a Bible meditation and then I would sing. A month after I was first imprisoned I had managed to smuggle a Bible past the guards. I can't tell you exactly how I did it, as people still use this method and it is important that the authorities don't find out how it's done, but I can say it was a whole Bible split into five smaller sections. This made it easier for me to hide it. Previously I

317

had just read it alone, but now we did group readings every day. I also sang new songs to the group that I had written in prison.[22]

RESPONSE:
Today I will cherish my Bible and make sure that in my freedom I internalize it as much as those in prison for the faith.

PRAYER:
Pray that all Christian prisoners will somehow gain access to a Bible or the message of the Bible today for encouragement and hope.

22 Berhane, p.49.

June 8

INTERNALIZE GOD'S WORD

Do not let this Book of the Law depart from your mouth;
meditate on it day and night, so that you may be careful
to do everything written in it. Then you will be prosperous
and successful.
Joshua 1:8

A co-worker who was teaching Christian leaders in Vietnam shares this experience:

I immediately realized that not one of these pastors owned a Bible and that they were waiting to hear from Scripture. As I started sharing, one pastor raised his hand. "Excuse me brother, is that the Bible or is that you?"

"This is Scripture," I answered and immediately the leaders took out a notebook and eagerly started writing every word down. I then understood that this was the only way that they could collect Scripture verses. I wanted to cry.

As I continued the teaching, the same question came once again. "Excuse me brother, is that the Bible or is that you?"

"This time it's me," I answered and suddenly everybody put their "Bibles" down and took out a different notebook and once again wrote down every word I said. Then came lunch break and the leading pastor stood up. "We will now have a time to test our Bible knowledge," he announced.

I wondered how my Bible knowledge, with more than ten Bibles at my disposal, would measure up with these leaders who do not have their own copies. The leader asked the first question. "What does it say in Obadiah 2:4?"

I shrank in my chair. *Please don't look at me*, I thought. I know there is a book of Obadiah but I must confess it has been some time since I read it. The pastors started laughing and then one raised his hand.

"Obadiah only has one chapter, brother!" I felt so ashamed. How is it possible I did not know this and these believers without their own Bibles knew.

Then came the second question. "What does the Bible teach in Nahum 1:7?

An elderly pastor in the front row raised his hand like an eager school child. He then started quoting the Scripture: *"The Lord is good, a strength in the day of trouble. He cares for those who trust in him."*

"Well done brother," said the leader. "You may sit down now." But the elderly pastor was not finished yet. "Please," he asked, "may I continue?" After a nod, he quoted the whole book of Nahum faultlessly.

I was also later introduced to another believer who came to know the Lord only during recent years. His passion for the Word of God is displayed in the fact that he has already memorized seventy-eight chapters of the Bible.

RESPONSE:
Today, I will begin a program to internalize God's Word and hide it in my heart.

PRAYER:
Lord, give me a passion for Your Word like believers in Vietnam.

June 9

MEDITATE ON GOD'S WORD

I have hidden your word in my heart
that I might not sin against you.
Psalm 119:11

Over and over the Scriptures direct us to meditate on God's Word. This activity takes time and discipline but brings much spiritual benefit and reward. Meditation is focused thinking about a Bible verse or passage in order to discover how we can apply its truth to our own lives.

In applying Scripture, we need to ask three primary questions.

• What did it mean to the original hearers?

• What is the underlying timeless principle?

• Where or how should I practice that principle?

Here are six specific ways to meditate on a verse or passage:

• **Picture it.** Visualize the scene in your mind.

• **Pronounce it.** Say it aloud each time, emphasizing a different word.

• **Paraphrase it.** Rewrite the verse in your own words.

• **Personalize it.** Replace the pronouns or people with your own name.

• **Pray it.** Turn the verse into a prayer and say it back to God.

• **Probe it.** Ask the following questions:

- Is there any sin to confess?   Is there any promise to claim?

- Is there any attitude to change?   Is there any command to keep?

- Is there any example to follow?   Is there any prayer to pray?

- Is there any error to avoid?   Is there any truth to believe?

- Is there something for which to thank God?

When Laos was taken over by a communist government, the leading pastor, Rev. Sali was put into a prison camp for three years of "re-education." He referred to it later as his university experience. During that time he led five men to Christ in the camp. He had no Bible so

321

he discipled these new believers on Scriptures he had memorized and internalized. Later those men became leaders in the church.

RESPONSE:
Today I will learn to meditate on God's Word.

PRAYER:
Pray for Christians in prisons of the world where they do not have a Bible.

June 10

THE POWER OF GOD'S WORD

For the word of God is living and active. Sharper than any double-edged sword, it penetrates even to dividing soul and spirit, joints and marrow; it judges the thoughts and attitudes of the heart.

Hebrews 4:12

Jesus is our best example of dependence on the written Word of God. He quoted Scripture repeatedly. When Satan tempted Him in the wilderness, for example, He quoted Scripture in answer to each of Satan's demands (Matthew 4:1-11). Jesus based His teaching on the Old Testament Scriptures and referred to them frequently for historical examples. It can be said that Jesus authenticated almost every book in the Old Testament by quoting from it at least once as divine authority!

It is especially interesting to note how Jesus used the Scriptures after His death and resurrection. While walking with some followers on the road to Emmaus, He began *"with Moses and all the Prophets"* explaining *"...to them what was said in all the Scriptures concerning Himself"* (Luke 24:27).

The central place Scripture held for the early church is evident throughout the book of Acts. Scripture was used to explain the events of Pentecost (Acts 2:16-21), to identify Jesus as the Messiah (2:25-28), to determine their reaction to persecution (4:23-26), to state the church's position in the face of persecution (7:1-53), to preach Christ (8:29-35), and to determine how to accept Gentile believers (15:13-21).

There are literally hundreds of examples of New Testament Christians and the writers of the epistles using the Old Testament Scriptures to prove their positions. In fact, it is so basic to sound biblical teaching that it is still common in evangelical circles today. The Bible is our true source of divine knowledge.

Outside the city of Seoul, Korea stands the memorial to the martyrs of the Korean church. Interestingly, the first picture in the gallery is of a Welshman, R. J. Thomas. We learned about him earlier as he gave his life taking the Bible into northern Korea in 1866. The nephew of a scholar became a Christian by reading a Gospel portion plastered on the compound wall of the man who killed Thomas. The young man reportedly helped a Scottish missionary, John Ross, make the first translation of the New Testament into Korean in Shenyang, China a mere twenty-five years later. This led to the first group of Protestant believers in the country of Korea even before foreign missionaries arrived. The Word of God is powerful!

RESPONSE:
I will treasure God's powerful and living Word, today.

PRAYER:
Thank You Lord for the power of Your Word! May it impact North Korea anew in my generation.

June 11

COMMUNICATION WITH GOD

Devote yourselves to prayer, being watchful and thankful.
Colossians 4:2

Pastor Ha's church in Vietnam grew from twenty-nine to over 5,000 in just a few years during the communist regime in the late 1970's. When asked the secret of this phenomenal church growth, Pastor Ha replied, "I have a very simple theology. When you have problems, pray! When you have more problems, pray more!" Every morning this church had a well-attended prayer meeting at six a.m. And the church grew and grew. Although they were constantly living under pressure, there was one Scripture text chosen for the wall of their sanctuary, *"In everything give thanks."*

And yet after his years of imprisonment, Pastor Ha said, "When I had my freedom, I worked with prayer sometimes in the background. In prison, I discovered that prayer is everything. It's like a pilot using a checklist before he takes off. If he skips the first item, many lives might be in danger. **The first item on our checklist should always be prayer. If we skip it, the whole mission is in jeopardy.**"

Vietnamese Pastor Cuong also spent over six years in prison. He says this about prayer:

In my work I was so busy I had no time to pray. But in prison, I was thankful to God that He gave me time for prayer. I had about six hours of prayer every day. I had time to recall every member of my congregation to pray for them. Before that, although I served the church, I didn't have enough time to pray for them. **I learned about the real presence of God in prayer there. When you kneel down and pray wholeheartedly with the Lord, you feel His answer right there.**

All of the world's major religions emphasize prayer. The Buddhists repeat their prayers fervently, although they do not believe anyone is listening. The Hindus pray regularly, believing one of their many Hindu gods may be listening, but they do not really expect any response to their prayers. The Muslims pray five times a day.

They believe that Allah is listening, but he will not alter his plans to meet their needs.

Devout Buddhists, Hindus and Muslims consider Christianity a prayerless faith, because they rarely see Christians praying. Yet we believe—and know—we have a God who not only hears our prayers, but also will answer them in mighty power!

RESPONSE:
Today I recommit to spending time in communication—prayer—with my Lord.

PRAYER:
Pray that all Christians in prison will experience God's presence in a special way today.

June 12

TASK PRAYER

Elijah was a man just like us. He prayed earnestly that it would not rain, and it did not rain on the land for three and a half years.

James 5:17

Rev. Dr. David Cho who pastors the largest church in the world—a cell group based church—is also very strong on the significance of prayer. As a pastor of a growing Korean church, he felt he could not pray less than five hours a day.

He distinguishes between the type of prayer we usually think of—fellowship prayer—and what he calls "task" prayer. Both are important forms of prayer but task prayer is terrific labor and takes much energy. It is closest to intercessory prayer and is usually very focused prayer about an intense need.

Here are the characteristics of "task" prayer:
1. Have a clear goal – be very focused
2. Use simple words
3. Mobilize all the emotion in your heart
4. Be persistent (Luke 18:1-8)

Believers in China are very much involved in this type of prayer. Here is one description of believers who had gathered for a special meeting in a cave twenty-five feet below ground level. After a three-hour message:

They prayed with tears running down from their eyes, and the stream of tears intermingled with their 'noserun,' dripping down like transparent noodles, which they ignored. For their hearts were so turned to the face of Christ that they became totally oblivious of their own unkempt state. One sister prayed for over 45 minutes standing, pleading with the Lord to release her fellow-evangelist and her fiancé from prison. He had fasted for many days and refused to divulge any information on the churches' evangelistic activity.[23]

23 Ross Paterson, *Heart Cry For China* (Chichester, UK: Sovereign World, 1989), p.190.

RESPONSE:
When I have an intense need, I will practice task prayer.

PRAYER:
Lord, help me to have the faith, persistence and emotion of Elijah when I pray.

June 13

PRAY FOR PERSECUTORS

"But I tell you who hear me: Love your enemies, do good to those who hate you, bless those who curse you, pray for those who mistreat you."

Luke 6:27-28

In Luke chapter six, Jesus defines persecution with four verbs: hatred, exclusion, insult and rejection (Luke 6:22). But later in the chapter Jesus gives much more emphasis on how you and I are to respond to persecution that comes our way.

One of the great lessons from the Persecuted Church is praying for those who persecute you. This is a parallel principle with loving your enemies. Multiple examples can be shared how God has honored this principle of prayer:

Noskie was a former Imam in the southern part of the Philippines. He was a devout Muslim and one who generated respect from that little community in which he lived. Coming home from a fishing expedition one day, he was shocked to discover that his two daughters had converted to Christianity. He was well aware of the shame that this would bring to the whole community.

In his anger, he mercilessly beat them hoping that they would renounce their new faith. But the daughters remained faithful. They loved their father and knew that nothing was impossible with God so they started praying for their father's conversion.

Sometime later, while fishing, Noskie felt a sudden piercing pain in his stomach. As the pain intensified, his belly began to balloon. He writhed in unbearable pain. He prayed but nothing happened. In desperation he cried out to the God of his daughters, Jesus Christ, and was instantly healed.

Noskie emerged from the experience a new person. He submitted his heart and surrendered to the Lordship of Jesus Christ. Today he faithfully serves the Lord as a lay pastor. His daughters help in the ministry.

RESPONSE:
I am committed to respond to persecution with non-violence as Jesus taught.

PRAYER:
Lord, I realize today that when I pray for my enemy and love my enemy, he or she is no longer my enemy. Help me to always respond this way.

June 14

PERSISTENT PRAYER

As for me, far be it from me that I should sin against the LORD by failing to pray for you.
1 Samuel 12:23a

An important aspect of prayer is to pray patiently. God meets our needs *"at the proper time"* (Galatians 6:9). Too often Christians weary of praying, and give up. This is often justified on the basis that God's failure to answer means the request is not according to His will. Remember, God can:

Deliver - whatever we ask in His name;

Delay - to fit His perfect timing (only He sees the end from the beginning);

Deny - and say 'No' because we ask amiss or give a

Different and better answer.

Jesus urges us to be persistent in prayer (Luke 11:5-8). This does not mean that God does not want to meet our needs and that we need to try to persuade Him. It simply means that only God, who completely understands the whole situation, can know when and how to answer. Only when we have assurance in our hearts from the Lord, should we remove a matter from our prayer list.

Many times Christians lose heart in prayer because they do not recognize when the Lord does answer their prayers. Sometimes this is due to the fact that they did not pray specifically enough and sometimes because they have decided in advance how God must answer. Perhaps they think that only a great miracle can meet their need.

But the Lord may change the circumstances so that the need seems to be supplied "naturally." Mature believers will recognize that the events of everyday life also come from the Lord. Our daily bread and safety are miracles of God in this troubled world Let us not presume to tell God how to answer, and let us praise Him for His daily care.

RESPONSE:
Today I will acknowledge God gives His best to those who leave the choices to Him.

PRAYER:
Lord, help me to be patient and persistent...and leave the answers to my prayers in Your hands.

June 15

TEACH YOUR CHILDREN

These commandments that I give you today are to be on your hearts. Impress them on your children. Talk about them when you sit at home and when you walk along the road, when you lie down and when you get up.

Deuteronomy 6:6-7

An extraordinary life in Christ does not just depend on teachings, circumstances or comfort. In many countries in the world today there are severe restrictions and obstacles facing parents in instructing their children in the ways of the Lord. In communist countries like China and Vietnam it is officially against the law to share the gospel with anybody under the age of eighteen years, including your own children.

In the Middle East, Christian schools are non-existent and Christian children are forced to attend Muslim schools and receive instruction from the Koran and Muslim teachers. Yet, it seems as if Christian families in restricted areas are more Godly and committed to the Lord than their counterparts in the West, where opportunities abound and Christians live in abundance.

The lessons that we learn from the Persecuted Church are of far more value than seminars or devotionals can ever be—the lessons of true discipleship and wholesome living. Lessons that are neither theology nor speculation but teachings of life, reality and practice.

Gerhard Hamm was one of the thousands of faithful believers through whom God's light continued to shine in the Soviet Union during the years when communism reigned there.

He grew up in the Ural Mountains where his parents farmed. But then communism arose and in 1929 the "bandits" came, as Gerhard later often called the Bolsheviks. Because his father was a Christian and of German descent, he was arrested and exiled to Siberia. The farm was confiscated.

Mother Hamm and her twenty children also moved to Siberia. For a few years, the family was together. Then Gerhard's father was taken away from his family and never came back. None of the family knows where his grave is. All the churches were closed and atheistic propaganda was being disseminated all around

As a young boy Gerhard lost his father, his security, his home and his freedom—all because of the name of Jesus. Hunger and cold were his daily lot, an obvious reason for a young teenager to resent God and His commands. But despite the difficulties, ridicule and persecution, Mother Hamm prayed every day with her children, and they read the Bible together.

When Gerhard Hamm died in 1999 at the age of 76, he left a legacy of faithful children behind. All of his children and their spouses were devoted Christians. His grandchildren have all committed their lives to the Lord. All of Gerhard's nineteen brothers and sisters and their spouses and children followed the footsteps of Jesus and many are still involved in various ministries reaching all corners of the globe.

RESPONSE:
Today I will take seriously the challenge of teaching, training and discipling my children or young people with whom I have close relationship.

PRAYER:
Lord, help me to live a life of self-sacrifice so young people will see You and want to follow.

334

June 16

FATHERHOOD

For you know that we dealt with each of you as a father deals with his own children, encouraging, comforting and urging you to live lives worthy of God, who calls you into his kingdom and glory.

1 Thessalonians 2:11-12

The Apostle Paul is very specific here in defining a fatherly role and gives three special characteristics of a Christian father. We fathers tend to apply them in reverse order but Paul states them as:

a. Encouraging

Like children, we are often tempted to give up. When that happens, the real need is for someone to come along side who can identify with and encourage them to keep going. A Christian father is one who is always there to give an encouraging word when needed. And the need is often!

b. Comforting

This reference is to the kind of comfort that helps a child or another person carry a burden of grief or pain. Just by coming alongside in this concerned way, the burden is made lighter and the pain is lessened. We were not created to be alone, especially in grief. The Christian father and disciple maker is also always there for times of comfort giving.

c. Exhorting

This is the direction and assertiveness characteristic that should be evident in the father/disciple maker relationship. There are times when the father moves from the side to stand squarely in front and confront them with something that they need to face. The dangers in not exercising this responsibility are very great and should compel us to be diligent toward both our children and our brothers and sisters in Christ.

J.J. Andrews is an elderly Lutheran pastor friend in Rangoon, Burma—now Myanmar—with a great father's heart for ministry. Several years ago his daughter died of viral hepatitis. Two months later his wife passed away from a broken heart. Six months after that one of his sons suddenly died. He was crushed. He said, "I felt like Job, only no one visited me."

A young Filipino staff member of Open Doors heard about this situation. He made a special trip just to visit Brother J.J. and encourage him. J.J. said, "Thank you for coming in my darkest hour."

Some months later, I was visiting Brother J.J. in Rangoon. He had his young grand-children laughing and playing around his home. He smiled as he shared unforgettable lessons with me. The words I remember verbatim were, "God rewarded me for my perseverance and healed my broken heart!" The ministry of encouragement is straight from the heart of Father God.

RESPONSE:
Today I will commit to being an encourager, comforter and exhorter.

PRAYER:
Thank You Lord for Christian fathers who have modelled Your heart with their children.

June 17

HAS GOD FORGOTTEN HIS CHILDREN?

How long, LORD? Will you forget me forever? How long will you hide your face from me? How long must I wrestle with my thoughts and day after day have sorrow in my heart? How long will my enemy triumph over me?
Psalm 13:1-2

If any believers can identify with this cry of David, it is those in North Korea. Today we hear from our co-worker, Jan Vermeer:

Looking at the desperate condition of the scattered North Korean church is a test of faith. Was the church meant to be underground or to be a bold witness? Should the name of Jesus Christ be proclaimed or whispered in silence? And if Jesus is King, why doesn't He come to the rescue of his followers? Why do hundreds or even thousands perish in prisons or death camps each year?

An Open Doors contact in North Korea talks about their prayer meetings. "If you could attend one of those rare prayer meetings, your hearts would break," he says. "We cover the portraits of the leaders on the wall and then we kneel down in a circle. We pray for strength and endurance. We pray that God will keep our country. 'Father,' we say, 'The Israelites sinned and you made them wander in the wilderness for forty years. But for us, Lord, after more than fifty years we are still being punished. However, we have sinned and You are just. We bowed before the idols of Kim Il-Sung and before that to the idols of the Japanese. Forgive us. Please Father, restore the churches of past times in North Korea.'"

Feeling that sense of guilt in the North Korean believers is utterly painful. It makes you cry out with them the words of David, *"How long, oh Lord? Will you forget me forever?"* It's a heartfelt cry, but is it the truth? Has God forgotten His children in North Korea? For that answer we have to investigate the spiritual life of North Korean Christians.

The Open Doors contact adds, "If you do that, you'll find North Korean Christians are very mature. They know how to approach unbelievers and how to train new Christians, including their children once they are old enough. The Christians don't mind to be tested. In fact, they are determined to sacrifice themselves for the Kingdom of God. They see trials as purifying."

North Korean Christians know that when they pray earnestly, God will answer. The contact continues, "Whenever we do a project with Open Doors, first we fast for seven, sometimes ten days. Only when God tells us separately that we can continue with the project do we give the green light and carry out the project. Sometimes we have a very vivid dream in which God tells us what to do and sometimes we all just feel exactly the same about the project. Our believers are bolder and stronger than before, even though the persecution is also stronger."

Where people love and follow Jesus, there is always hope!

RESPONSE:
Today I bask in the sunshine of this hope. God does not ever forget His children!

PRAYER:
Pray today for isolated believers in North Korea who do not have the warmth of Christian fellowship and group prayer.

June 18

PROJECT PEARL

"Again, the kingdom of heaven is like a merchant looking for fine pearls. When he found one of great value, he went away and sold everything he had and bought it."
Matthew 13:45-46

One hundred-foot-long tugboat *Michael* lumbered along at the sleepy speed of three knots. It towed the semi-submersible barge, *Gabriella*, loaded with the million Chinese Bibles in 232 waterproof wrapped one-ton packages. By 9 p.m. on that historic night of June 18, 1981, *Michael* and its crew of twenty men weaved through a maze of anchored Chinese navy ships in the darkness near the port city of Shantou, southern China. Thousands of local Christians waited patiently in the darkness on the appointed beach.

The off-loaded floating packages were towed to shore by small rubber boats. Chinese believers came out in the water—some up to their neck. They pulled the blocks up onto the beach and cut them open with shears, handing the 45-pound cardboard boxes of Bibles to one another up the sand to the tree-line.

Two hours later, *Michael* and *Gabriella* and the crew left the scene with one million Bibles in the care of Chinese believers. They promised to circulate them across the entire country. In some cases, that process took as much as five years and many Chinese Christians paid dearly for it.

Over the past 30 years, Open Doors has received documented story after story—often from unusual places and situations—of the impact of those Bibles on the fast growing church in China. Project Pearl Bibles have been seen in virtually every province of the country.

A former colleague of mine from Singapore continues to minister in China. In the late 1990s, he met a large house church network of Christians in central China who still had no contact at all with foreigners from outside the country. They testified that it was the receiving of many Project Pearl Bibles that encouraged them and motivated them to share the gospel widely and thus grow to their current significant numbers.

One of those pocket-sized Bibles was received by a young Christian who had been praying for a Bible of his own for three years. After reading it through three times in three weeks, he felt God calling him to become one of the many itinerant evangelists preaching in China's countryside. After fifteen years of ministry, he pastored a network of house churches that grew to over 400,000 members. His network of churches continues to need more than 20,000 Bibles a month just for new believers.

RESPONSE:
I will appreciate the several Bibles I have and commit myself to learning and living from it.

PRAYER:
Pray for Christians today in a variety of situations who are still waiting for their first copy of God's Word.

Read the complete and detailed story of Project Pearl in **Night of a Million Miracles** *available from your Open Doors national office or on Amazon.com*

June 19

PROJECT PEARL WET BIBLES

*All creatures look to you to give them their food
at the proper time. When you give it to them,
they gather it up; when you open your hand,
they are satisfied with good things.*
Psalm 104:27-28

There are stories and reports of "wet" Bibles and "perfume" Bibles from Project Pearl that continue to be shared to this day. Four hours after we left the beach that night of delivery of the one million Chinese Bibles on June 18, 1981, a patrol of Chinese police came by and found some boxes of Bibles stashed under the trees. They had not yet been transferred to the storage areas. The police tried unsuccessfully to burn the Bibles and then in frustration threw them into the water. The next morning, fishermen plucked these floating volumes out of the sea and put them on the roofs of their homes to dry. Later they sold them to Christians in the area. I personally treasure a sample of one of these "wet" Bibles that was used by a Chinese believer for fifteen years. One of the leading house church network leaders in China acknowledges receiving "wet" Bibles from Project Pearl.

Chinese Sister Ling shares the poignant story of how she pleaded with God for a Bible as a young evangelist. She found believers without Bibles doing unusual things—like carrying extra oil around so they'd be ready like the five wise virgins.

At the time of Project Pearl, she heard of a woman who had received "wet" Bibles and dried them. When Ling asked her for a Bible, the woman required her to quote the Lord's Prayer without a single mistake to prove she was a believer. Ling memorized it from a handwritten copy of the Bible and passed the test. She received one "wet" Bible.

The woman apologized for being so overly careful but then explained, "After our brothers collected these Bibles from the shore, they began to distribute them about China. It was very dangerous and

341

some paid with their lives. Remembering their sacrifice, I treasure these Bibles even more." Ling went on to experience much suffering for her leadership role in the house church movement but now aware that suffering in the will of God has meaning and purpose.

RESPONSE:
Today I recommit to living the principles of God's Word and not be ashamed of publicly sharing them.

PRAYER:
Thank God for the number of Bibles you have and ask Him to provide for those still without even one copy.

June 20

PROJECT PEARL PERFUME BIBLES

They are more precious than gold, than much pure gold; they are sweeter than honey, than honey from the honeycomb.
Psalm 19:10

In 1977, Peter Xu became the leader of the Born-Again Movement—a large house church network today in China. Ten years ago he was visiting in the United States and shared a devotional at the Open Doors-USA office. When he saw a sample of a Project Pearl Bible on the shelf, he became very animated. Then a long story developed:

After Project Pearl Bibles were stored in depositories in southern China in the early 1980s, Peter Xu sent three men every month by train to the depository contacts to bring back about 1,000 Bibles per trip for his growing house church movement. One month the three men were discovered with their Bible load by the local police of the depository city. The police threw the 1,000 Project Pearl Bibles into the cesspool of the public latrine and the three men were interrogated and jailed for the weekend.

Monday they were released and commanded to return straight home and never return. Instead they waited inside the latrine until darkness fell. Then they climbed down into the filthy cesspool of human waste carefully retrieving each of the foul smelling books. They washed them off under the local water tap and carried them home. There they dried them out, sprayed them with perfume and circulated them through their network. Such was the hunger and importance of every copy of God's Word.

Project Pearl certainly had an impact on the future printing of Bibles inside China which continues today. Shortly after the project was completed, China's Three Self Patriotic Movement announced the first official printing of Bibles inside the country. Noted author and China watcher, David Aikman, wrote in his book, *Jesus in Beijing*, "[Project]

Pearl had a major long-term impact on the overall availability of Bibles in China."[24]

But more important are the personal evaluations from Chinese believers: "These gifts are more precious than gold!"

RESPONSE:
Today I will treasure God's Word as more valuable than any precious metal or gem.

PRAYER:
Thank You, Lord, that Your precious Word is being made available in countries where it is not valued by those in authority.

24 David Aikman, *Jesus in Beijing* (Washington, DC: Regnery, 2003), p. 270.

June 21

IN STEP WITH THE SPIRIT

Since we live by the Spirit, let us keep in step with the Spirit.

Galatians 5:25

Jesus said He would not leave us alone but would give us a Helper to be with us forever (John 14: 16-18). He taught us that the Holy Spirit would be our Counselor (John 14: 26). Jesus also called Him the Spirit of Truth (John 14:17).

Two sisters in southern China came to Christ in a house church meeting. Twenty months later a friend from Hong Kong visited them and asked what they had been doing since their conversion. "Starting home meetings," was their timid response.

"How many home meetings?"

"Only thirty," was their halting reply.

"How many attend your meetings?" was the next nonchalant question.

"Well, at the smallest one about two hundred and eighty!"

Now the questioner was totally involved and quickly continued, "How many attend your largest meeting?"

"Not even 5000, only about four thousand nine hundred!"

The Hong Kong Christian was flabbergasted. And in his excitement quickly asked, "How do you ladies—both new Christians—know what to do?"

They simply replied, **"We pray. And after we pray, the Holy Spirit tells us what to do!"**

It is also obvious that these two ladies were then obedient to the Holy Spirit's direction. The goal of all Christians should be to live so completely under the control of the Holy Spirit that it can be said we are walking in the Spirit (Galatians 5:25). As Paul reminded the Galatian Christians, they began their Christian lives by a miracle work of God, new birth in Jesus, and they could only expect to continue it by God's power. This fact is even more evident in a hostile environment.

RESPONSE:
The Holy Spirit wants to be my guide and counselor today. I will be obedient to His leading.

PRAYER:
Lord, help me to walk this day in the power of Your Holy Spirit. May I also keep in step!

June 22

THE HOLY SPIRIT

"If you then, though you are evil, know how to give good gifts to your children, how much more will your Father in heaven give the Holy Spirit to those who ask him!"
Luke 11:13

Imagine the Christian movement in your country suddenly cut off from all those who are now its leaders! In the period of confusion that immediately follows a takeover, some small groups of Christians may be able to move to a different locality and become underground churches, but they must leave their "institutional forms" behind.

But who would lead such groups? Who would provide leadership for "house" churches and "family" churches? God, through the Holy Spirit, would raise up and equip leaders for His church in such circumstances, as He always had in the past. The members of a home fellowship must be prepared to accept the leadership of the Spirit and of those through whom He chooses to minister.

When regular lay Christians actually begin to understand that they can pray directly to the Lord, when they can take a passage of Scripture, written or memorized, and understand it under the direction of the Holy Spirit, they are then on the road to surviving victoriously in whatever set of hostile circumstances that may come along. One exciting discovery will lead to another. These Christians will begin to let the Holy Spirit use them to touch the lives of others and minister to their needs. No authority on earth can destroy this kind of spiritual church!

In China, a Christian woman was in charge of security at a coal mine. The woman suddenly felt the Holy Spirit urging her to pull the alarm lever, even though there was no apparent reason to do so. Although everything seemed quiet and normal, she obeyed the prompting within her. The whole mine was evacuated as a result of the alarm sounding, but when all the men had assembled on the surface, it seemed as if a huge mistake had been made. Just moments later the ground beneath their feet shook and a large section of the mine collapsed from the earthquake.

Because of this sister's sensitivity and willingness to obey God's Holy Spirit, everyone's life had been saved. Additionally, however, 400 of the miners surrendered their lives to Christ after recognising that God had miraculously saved them from death.[25]

RESPONSE:
Today I will thank God for the gift of His Holy Spirit.

PRAYER:
Lord, use me today through Your Spirit to touch the lives of others and minister to their needs.

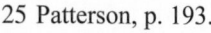

25 Patterson, p. 193.

June 23

STRENGTH FROM THE BIBLE

Your word is a lamp for my feet, a light on my path.
Psalm 119:105

In Eritrea, the government restricts the freedom of religion of faith groups. The only groupings permitted are the Eritrean Orthodox Church, Roman Catholic Church, Evangelical Lutheran Church and Islam. Everyone who is caught at a meeting of believers outside these four official religious groups, even in a private house, can be arrested, tortured and put under pressure to renounce his faith.

Thousands of Christians are being held at police stations, in containers, at military bases and in prisons. Even though many of them have been held for years, none of them has had a trial. In many cases, Christians are also beaten or abused in some other way.

Isaac is one of these prisoners. He heard about God's love from soldiers in the military unit in which he was fighting during the war with Ethiopia. On the basis of their testimony, he decided to become a Christian and was secretly slipped a Bible. He buried it in the sand and when he had the opportunity, he read the Word of God somewhere outside the army camp. He tried to do so as inconspicuously as possible, but one day he was discovered.

Almost from his first day as a Christian, he was persecuted. He was tortured and even left out in the burning sun, but he refused to renounce his faith. God's love and God's Word had become too important for him. In the end, he was locked up, just like other Christian prisoners in Eritrea. He has become a living legend, because he has held on to his faith.

A number of Christian prisoners, who are being held in containers, have been given Bibles in secret. They have divided them into portions, and in this way, each believer has a small part of the Bible. When the container is closed, it is too dark to read. But as soon as the doors are opened to let in some air or to hand out food, something amazing happens. The prisoners do not immediately run outside for fresh air or to eat. First they inconspicuously hold their portions of the

Bible to the light in order quickly to be able to read a few verses and to be strengthened by God's Word.

RESPONSE:
Today I will treasure my freedom to read and meditate on God's Word.

PRAYER:
Lord, I pray Your Spirit of Peace upon my brothers and sisters in prison today in Eritrea. May they be encouraged by Your Word!

June 24

HOLY SPIRIT CALLING

*But when he, the Spirit of truth, comes, he will guide you
into all the truth. He will not speak on his own;
he will speak only what he hears, and he will tell you
what is yet to come.*
John 16:13

Johnny Li of Nexus ministry shares today the story of his "calling"
by God's Holy Spirit:

"Your son asked me to come and visit you!" As I spoke these
words to the elderly man in front of me, I could see the utter
surprise and even confusion in his eyes. Suddenly the man grabbed
me and quickly jerked me inside the small room.

My mind began to retrace my steps and all the events that had led
to this: first meeting young Brother Wang in Hong Kong after his
daring escape from China; then the challenging request from my
pastor to take Bibles to the family of Brother Wang in China; then
the daring and dangerous expedition that led me here.

Mrs. Wang quickly excused herself and I spent the next hour
bringing greetings and love from Brother Wang as well as all the
other believers from our small church in Hong Kong. Curious about
the sudden disappearance of Mrs. Wang I enquired where she went.
"She is in the room next door praying for our safety", Brother
Wang's father replied.

After memorable fellowship, the final words of Brother Wang Sr.
pierced my heart. "You must come again", he pleaded.

I smiled politely but in my heart I knew I would not likely
return. The trip was much too risky and dangerous for my
liking. Being Chinese I knew that my destiny would be prison if I
were caught. "You must come again and bring more Bibles", old
Brother Wang pleaded as if he could read my troubled mind.

I gave the only correct answer I could think of. "I will pray about
it."

351

In a daze I walked to the train station and boarded the first train home to safety. My heart was torn because this was the country responsible for arresting my mother and causing me to grow up as an orphan. I decided I would not return!

Then I heard the unmistakable voice of the Holy Spirit, "Do you need a calling, Johnny?"

"Lord what do you mean", I asked? "You have seen the need. You have heard my voice. Why do you need a calling to respond?"

I knew I had no choice. The Lord had spoken. I knew this was the way for me.

This was thirty years ago and Johnny Li has been an immense blessing in assisting the fast-growing church in China. He's been responsible for producing the first Chinese Children's Bible in modern Chinese and has delivered thousands of Bibles and other Christian literature into China. Today he trains Chinese missionaries committed to take the gospel to the Muslim world.

RESPONSE:
Today I will listen to the Spirit's voice before making decisions and plans.

PRAYER:
Lord, help me to listen to Your Spirit's direction in my life since He will direct my steps.

June 25

EFFECTIVE PRAYER

*The prayer of a righteous person is powerful
and effective.*
James 5:16b

For fifteen years from 1981 to 1995, in one Chinese city there were many cases of murder, armed robbery, rape, gangs of thieves, local village local tyrants were rampant and small children were being kidnapped, taxis were being robbed and taxi drivers being killed. People's hearts were nervous. Traffic related disputes were increasing and society was not in a peaceful state. There were less than 3000 believers in the city.

At this time, the Holy Spirit moved Sister Zhou to the city. This Christian sister helped the church there for over one month. She received a burden while praying that the church should set up a prayer watch. So, the first prayer watch group was established. When it started, there were only 6 people. On Sundays these six people would all watch and pray simultaneously.

After almost six months of this kind of prayer, the national police cleaned up and eliminated the triad gangs and local village tyrants and brought about a change for a better environment in the city.

At the time when children were being kidnapped, old Sister Chang began to fast and pray. Every day she would pray saying, "O Father God, save and rescue these children. Send an old granny to look after them!" After a year's time, the problem of children being kidnapped was transformed.

One problem would be solved and then another problem would come up for prayer. The rate of deaths in that city due to traffic accidents was an average of one to two people per day. Many more than that were injured daily. They then decided to make the city's traffic safety to be a special prayer topic. They prayed and relied on God to solve the traffic problems.

From 1995 until now, small groups of prayer watches have expanded from one to three core groups. Each person prays at a designated time and the time for prayer rotates to another person in the group. It has now expanded into a large prayer network. Now the city is peaceful and safe. The work of the gospel is stable and steadily expanding. There are more than 30,000 Christians in the city attending meetings.

The people's attitudes and appearance all seem like they are renewed. Although there are many laid-off workers, they seem to be able to find enough work to still be able to feed their families. This truly is the effect of prayer. It is the work done by our Father for the city.

RESPONSE:
Today I will recommit myself to believe in the power of prayer and practice that belief.

PRAYER:
Pray for the problems in your city or community. Ask God for like-minded partners.

June 26

GOD ANSWERS PRAYER

If you remain in me and my words remain in you,
ask whatever you wish, and it will be done for you.
John 15:7

In the mid-1990's, my Canadian co-worker, PJ, and I were leading a ministry trip of Canadians and Americans to Iran. This was the first trip with a sizable group of Americans so there was a lot of excitement about it. And as expected, it took us right to the wire (two hours before our air flight) to secure their visitor visas.

As we finally relaxed on the long air flight, we realized we'd been so busy with travel details we'd had no time to shop for gifts for the brothers and sisters we'd be meeting. So on the airplane, we bought every box of chocolates that were on the duty-free carts.

On arrival in Iran, our women were all conservatively dressed in their black chadors allowing them to travel anywhere in the country and be accepted. It also enabled many discussions with other women on the street. Only their shoes gave them away as Westerners.

One of our tasks was to deliver some funds for widow support for the several Christian widows of martyred pastors in the country at that time. We channelled this through Sister Takoosh who was the widow of well-known Pastor Haik, the leader of the evangelicals in the entire country until his untimely murder.

We sent our group of chador-covered ladies to meet Takoosh at night at her home. They were received with the traditional great hospitality of the Persian culture and Christian community. They drank tea together and enjoyed wonderful fellowship in Jesus after sharing the financial and other gifts they brought.

Just before leaving, one of the Canadians remembered something. She reached into her large purse and pulled out a box of chocolates. She handed it to Sister Takoosh and said, "The two Pauls sent this as a gift for you."

Unexpectedly, Takoosh began to weep. She then wiped her tears and said, "I really love chocolate. And when I get any, I cut it into small pieces to make it last as long as possible. Just yesterday I ate my last piece. And I said to the Lord, 'I know this is a very selfish request, Lord, but would You please bring me some more chocolate!'"

God is concerned about even the small things in our lives. Talk to Him about them.

RESPONSE:
Today I will talk to God about every detail of my life and trust Him with the answers.

PRAYER:
Thank You, Lord, that You care about my every need. I will trust You to take care of every detail.

June 27

PRISON PRAYER MIRACLE

So Peter was kept in prison, but the church was earnestly praying to God for him.
Acts 12:5

Nadia was in a prison in the Middle East for some months because she was a believer from Muslim background. She told the prison officials that she would not give them any information about the people she knew or about her husband, only about herself. This led her to being placed in an isolation cell for four days. The cell was small and extremely cold. There was no toilet or washing facilities at all.

"At one point," Nadia reported, "I was feeling very cold and found the whole experience tough. Suddenly though, I felt warm air blowing in my face. So warm, in fact, that when I breathed in and the air hit my lungs I had to cough."

She had no idea where the warmth was coming from and at the same time she became very joyful. This sense of joy overwhelmed her so much that she began to dance in the cell. Yet, at the same time, she also felt confused. *How could she feel warm and joyful in a cold prison cell*, she asked herself?

"Then I heard a voice," said Nadia. She emphasized that it wasn't an internal voice but audible, "as if someone in the cell was saying, 'That is because people are praying for you. This is the Spirit of happiness that has come upon you. Receive it.'"

Later on, after her release, Nadia shared her amazing experience in the cell with her sister. Asking when it had happened, Nadia's sister mentioned the same exact day and time when thirty-two believers had met to pray for Nadia and another believer in prison. Two of the participants had been appointed to represent Nadia and the other Christian. The remaining thirty believers gathered around them to ask God to comfort them, to fill them with joy and send His Spirit of happiness upon them." They were deeply encouraged to hear Nadia's experience.

Pastor Gambo Boka from northern Nigeria was falsely accused and sentenced by the Islamic court to three years of imprisonment. When he was put in prison, together with five other falsely accused Christians, he said, "God has a purpose in all of this. My soul is at rest."

Though he lost weight and became weak, his faith became increasingly strong. He shared the gospel with many fellow prisoners, who were almost all Muslims. "I experience comfort in this terrible place." said Gambo. "I know that God's promises are true."

The Islamic court gave Pastor Gambo thirty days to appeal. While members of Pastor Gambo's church prayed, God performed a miracle. Gambo and the other five Christians were acquitted by an Islamic court because of a lack of evidence.

"This is God's grace," said one of the church members. "Our prayers have been heard and my faith has been strengthened. God's promises are so special!"

Pastor Gambo and the other five Christians left the court singing, thanking God for His intervention.

RESPONSE:
Today I will remember that God's promises are true and He still performs miracles.

PRAYER:
Pray earnestly today for Christians around the world in prison for their faith.

June 28

PRAY AS A WARRIOR

Epaphras, who is one of you and a servant of Christ Jesus, sends greetings. He is always wrestling in prayer for you, that you may stand firm in all the will of God, mature and fully assured. I vouch for him that he is working hard for you and for those at Laodicea and Hierapolis.
Colossians 4:12-13

Today's devotional comes from a Bible study prepared by a church leader in North Korea encouraging his fellow believers to "pray as a warrior." It is fascinating to see how our persecuted brothers and sisters in North Korea regard prayer. He begins in Colossians 4:12-13:

What can we learn from this?

That Epaphras wrestled in prayer. He prayed as a warrior. The word "wrestling" in the text means "battling, fighting." We, too, must pray as warriors. I must do so. In the past, I often went to the mountains and prayed all night…God uses this prayer to open doors. It is not for nothing that Paul tells us at the beginning of chapter four that we must be watchful and thankful and must keep praying. Then…God opens doors to proclaim the mystery of Christ.

What does "praying as a warrior" entail?

1. Discovering God's will - Just like Paul, we must take our strategies from the Lord God. Paul wrestled in prayer in order to discover the will of God. This meant that God was able to lead him…When we make plans, we must pray according to His will. The Spirit knows what Satan is intending. God will reveal it to us and warn us if there is any danger.

2. Concentrated prayer - We must pray in a concentrated way, and for a long time…while I was praying in a concentrated way, a sentence came to my mind: "I can do everything through Him who gives me strength." I did not know this text. When I spoke to a friend about it, he told me that it is in the Bible, in Philippians 4:13. There was much sin in my life. I had to pray long and often in order to break down the barriers between God and me. This, too, is praying as a warrior.

3. Prayer of sacrifice - The prayer of a warrior is also the prayer of sacrifice. Praying is the most important thing you do in a day. Whatever you do each day, begin everything with prayer. Prayer is the shortest way, not the longest! By sacrificing yourself and applying yourself to praying as a warrior, God will open the hearts of people and break through their thinking…this type of prayer helps us to conquer evil with good. This is why we pray that Kim Jong-Il will become a Christian. And even more, that he will combat the evil in our society.

Epaphras remained faithful to Jesus Christ until the end. He was a prayer warrior. In this, he followed our Lord Himself…How can we manage without this prayer?

RESPONSE:
Today I will pray as a warrior…especially remembering Christians in North Korea.

PRAYER:
Thank You, Lord, for the example of Epaphras in the hard work of wrestling in prayer.

June 29

THE DISCIPLINE OF FASTING

But when you fast, put oil on your head and wash your face, so that it will not be obvious to others that you are fasting, but only to your Father, who is unseen; and your Father, who sees what is done in secret, will reward you.

Matthew 6:17-18

Jesus assumes in this passage that His followers practice fasting. He says "when" you fast—not "if" you fast and then goes on to give these instructions. Fasting is a significant spiritual activity that goes along with intensive prayer times. To fast means to put God first. Fasting is an attitude of the heart in which we interrupt our normal life to pray for a specific matter or cause. It means to abstain from food—and for some, even drink—so that we can focus on God and be more sensitive to spiritual matters. Fasting is also perseverance in prayer until you have received an answer—be it yes, no, wait or something different. In essence, fasting means that we rend our hearts before God, confess our sins and turn to the Lord anew (Joel 2:12-13).

Fasting is biblical. Consider the following: Moses fasted twice for forty days (Exodus 34:28); Daniel fasted (partially) for twenty-one days (Daniel 10:3); Joel called for a day of fasting (Joel 1:14; 2:12); Ezra withdrew for a period of fasting and mourning (Ezra 10:6); Elijah fasted for forty days (1 Kings 19:8); Leaders of the church in Antioch fasted (Acts 13:2-3); Jesus fasted for forty days (Luke 4:2); Paul and Barnabas fasted (Acts 14:23; 27:33).

Captain Bill Tinsley was arrested on false charges under President Marcos in the Philippines following the completion of Project Pearl in 1981. As the days of his confinement passed, Bill fasted from eating. After a few days of fasting, his blood pressure rose very higher. A doctor visited him daily. Everything possible was done to get him to eat. He was accused of staging a hunger strike. Bill carefully explained to his captors many times, "My fasting is a spiritual exercise. If I want my God to take my part, I must become weak that He may become strong. President Marcos is a very powerful man. I cannot fight him. I must let God take my part." His explanation brought only a certain resignation by his jailers. They did not understand.

Each day during his captivity Bill went for a walk. A soldier always went along to guard against possible escape. On that tenth morning, after reading of Elijah's running a great distance while fasting, Bill jogged. The soldier that went along couldn't keep up and was forced to take shortcuts across the fields to stay with him.

"How can you be so strong without eating?" a colonel asked referring to the jogging incident that morning.

"It's the power of God," Bill told him sincerely. "And if you keep me here, you're going to see me grow stronger and stronger!" The eyes of all the men present grew large. They believed him and that prospect was not to their liking. It was with some reluctance Bill later walked out of his cell for the last time. He had experienced God's presence there. His captors, the same ones that had falsely arrested him, gave him a send-off as they would a dear friend.

RESPONSE:
Today I resolve to practice all the spiritual disciplines...including fasting.

PRAYER:
Help me, Lord, to practice fasting as a spiritual discipline without making it obvious.

June 30

MYSTERY

He made known to us the mystery of his will according to his good pleasure, which he purposed in Christ...
Ephesians 1:9

Human beings always want to know "why?" and "why not now?" But it's precisely because we are human we cannot know. That's why mystery is so important to understand. The entire book of Job is all about the "why" of suffering and in the end God invites Job to see a bigger picture than even his suffering.

Creation is a mistake if all you see is your suffering. But if you lift your eyes wider and let your gaze roam over the whole universe with God, you can also see that creation has even more beauty and grace.

So we are to value mystery because it enables us to feel God's love... love that was fully revealed in Christ.

Sometimes we get to see "why?" and "why not now?" (one of the good aspects of growing older). Often we don't because we are the players of life in the universe, not the playwright.

Christine Mallouhi in her excellent book, *Waging Peace on Islam*, makes this significant conclusion:

> The victorious and triumphant Christian life does not conjure up pictures of suffering and death and feelings of abandonment. But this was all part of God's victory in Christ. If this was the path the Master trod why should it be any different for the servants? Jesus cried out "why?" and "where are you?" to God when circumstances were crushing him. God is always greater than our understanding of him and there will always be mystery about him that causes us to fall down in awe and worship. This mystery, which we want to tidily categorise, keeps causing struggles in our life. Every time we get God tidied up like a ball of rubber bands, another end bursts out and the struggle begins over again, until we learn to live in faith with untidy ends. If everything is clear then faith is irrelevant. We are not called to solve the mystery, but enter it.[26]

---

26 Christine Mallouhi, *Waging Peace on Islam* (Downers Grove, IL: Intervarsity Press, 2000), p.52.

RESPONSE:
Today I will value mystery because it enables me to feel God's love.

PRAYER:
Thank You Lord that though the world around us if full of suffering, it is more full of beauty and grace. Help me to trust You and value mystery.

July 1

OUR SACRIFICES, NOT OUR ACHIEVEMENTS

…now God is building you, as living stones into his spiritual temple. What's more, you are God's holy priests, who offer the spiritual sacrifices that please him because of Jesus Christ.

1 Peter 2:5

Open Doors colleague, Ron Boyd-MacMillan, shares the following insight from his teaching, "Why I Need to Encounter the Persecuted Church."

When I lived in Los Angeles, I was always stressed about one key question—am I fulfilling my potential? Everywhere I drove, I was surrounded by advertisements telling me that I was not earning enough, that I needed to have an "attitude transplant." I worried about whether I should take more courses in the elusive search for more success. My friends were actors and actresses desperate to attract the attention of some film producer, and working a couple of part-time jobs in the vain hope that someday, they will be discovered. I too always felt unfulfilled.

But is the purpose of my life really to maximize my potential? A visit to the persecuted soon cured me of that idea. This fact becomes clear—fulfilling one's potential cannot possibly be the purpose to life because so few actually get the opportunity to do so!

Look at the millions of Christians in China's house churches. All of them live lives in which—for want of a better term—they are trapped. They do not have choices. Because of their Christianity, many are denied access to education, or are barred from developing promising careers. I sat in a house church of seventy peasant Christians, and wondered, *How many great scientists, violin players, or philosophers could be in here, but they and the world will never know, because they never had the chance to study, learn algebra, or hold a musical instrument.*

Would God really make a world where only a tiny minority could fulfil their life's purpose, and doom the rest of us to a lifetime of frustration?

We were studying 1st Peter one night, and suddenly I had an insight while reading chapter 2 verse 5. It struck me: God makes each life that is yielded to him a living stone in building his temple. That's why we are alive. That's the purpose of it all. We are all made to become a stone in his spiritual temple, his eternal kingdom. And everybody gets the opportunity to become a "living stone" just by virtue of giving our lives to him. We are priests because we offer a sacrifice. That sacrifice is the only one we can make—that of our lives. And so we find the purpose for which God made the world—to build a kingdom of worshippers for Himself. That old man in the house church whose back is bent double from a life in the rice paddies is a living stone. That woman whose baby was taken away during the Cultural Revolution because she was a Christian is also a living stone. No one wastes their life who gives it to Jesus. They are placed into an eternal structure—the kingdom of God, and will rejoice forever in that status.

No one goes unfulfilled because God builds his kingdom on our sacrifices, not on our achievements.

RESPONSE:
Today I will be fulfilled as a "living stone" for God and offer Him the sacrifice of my life.

PRAYER:
Thank You Lord, that I don't need to spend my life seeking fulfillment other than in You!

July 2

PRAYER CHANGES THINGS

Let us then approach God's throne of grace with confidence, so that we may receive mercy and find grace to help us in our time of need.
Hebrews 4:16

Ages ago the prophet Jonah saw it happen. The population of the city of Nineveh (in the north of present day Iraq) repented from sin. A radical change came because he preached and God's Spirit worked. Almost on the same spot in the city of Mosul (modern Nineveh), the climate has changed too.

After 2003, Mosul became a city with increasing violence. Car bombs, attacks and all kind of violence are normal in this old city. Civilians of whatever religion and police and soldiers have been targeted. In the beginning of 2010, there was a significant increase in violent attacks on Christians. In the month of February that year, eight were killed in just ten days. This all caused an exodus of Christians.

"Thousands of Christians have left our city…and that hurts," shares twenty-one-year-old Dawud. "I saw a lot of my friends leaving too," the young Iraqi adds. His family has been Christian for generations, as is the case with many Iraqi Christians.

Open Doors worker, Daniel, says that as far as he knows the number of Christians dramatically dropped in the second biggest city of the country. Before the fall of Saddam Hussein, the number in Mosul was estimated at two hundred thousand of the one and a half million inhabitants. "We believe the number is now far less than one hundred thousand, many of them not living in the city itself but in Christian villages around."

"We started some years ago to pray for our city," Dawud continues. "It started small with just our family, but soon there were more believers coming to the prayer meetings. Now we pray weekly on Tuesdays and Saturdays from five till seven in the afternoon. Some fifty Christians in our city regularly participate," he says. "Because of our prayer, the city started to change. The situation is different now.

What I see now is that my generation doesn't want to leave, we want to stay. This is God's place for me. I'll stay; I will never leave. And if I will be killed, I will be killed."

"But," he goes on, "the situation is much better now. We can go out as youth again, even in the evenings. We can go to our meetings without being afraid, we don't feel insecure anymore." His father, pastor of one of the churches in Mosul, confirms that the climate in the city improved after they started praying as a church. With a smile on his face he adds, "We even saw Muslims becoming followers of Jesus."

RESPONSE:
Today I will rejoice in the ability I have to take every issue I face to the Lord and trust Him for the answer.

PRAYER:
Remember brothers and sisters who live in violent societies. Pray that fear will not drive them to leave.

July 3

PRAY THAT GOD WILL BE GLORIFIED

Now, Lord, consider their threats and enable your servants to speak your word with great boldness.
Acts 4:29

In Acts chapter four, Peter and John have been released from prison after many threats from the authorities. They return to the church and report. The church goes to prayer. But the remarkable thing is that they do not pray for protection but for boldness. We know God was pleased with their request because after their prayer the place in which they were meeting was shaken. Filled with God's Spirit they spoke the word of God boldly.

Four hundred Christian young people attended a three-day prayer conference in the mountains of northern Iraq in the summer of 2011. Six buses full of Christians came from violence-ravaged Baghdad. For the Christians from the south of Iraq, where persecution, kidnapping and bombs are a daily reality, the conference was like refreshing water. For three days they didn't have to worry and enjoyed being together with hundreds of other young believers in freedom. Christians from Baghdad, Mosul, Kirkuk, Basra and other cities came to the Open Doors sponsored meetings.

Behind the podium hung a huge banner with the theme of the conference. *As waters cover the sea, the glory of God will cover the earth.*

"That is the dream of God for Iraq and this world," said one the worship leaders, "and that should be our dream." Referring to the difficulties in the country he continued, "Tell in the middle of trouble about your hope, about God's dream. Know that in the middle of the heat, fruit ripens. God is preparing us for the harvest."

Many times during the conference, speakers referred to the persecution in the country and in other parts of the Middle East. Some of the churches lost many members during the last few years in Iraq. Due to the violence, Christians fled from the south of Iraq to the north, the Kurdish region or even to other countries. "Know that the church in Jerusalem was small too, but it changed the world," the speaker encourages the young believers.

One of the pastors said, "With this Arab Spring we're living in a very special time. We believe this is an historic conference. In the coming months big things are going to happen in this region. Focus on God; focus on His kingdom and God will do the rest."

Another speaker shared an experience from Egypt. "December 2010 and the beginning of January 2011 we had 40 days of fasting and prayer for Egypt in our church in Cairo. God said to us that what He was going to do would be awesome." Everyone knows what happened after that in Egypt.

"That was God's interference in history!" He expressed the way many Egyptian Christians saw the events of January 2011. "Ask for the impossible and it will happen," he said. "Pray for His desire. Look what happened in Acts when the church had a hard time. They did not ask for their own protection, they asked to glorify God's name."

RESPONSE:
Today I will pray that my circumstances and challenges will ultimately glorify God's name.

PRAYER:
Thank You Lord for boldness You give Your church in the midst of threats and violence.

July 4

DISCOVER YOUR HEROIC SPIRITUAL ANCESTORS

These were all commended for their faith, yet none of them received what had been promised...
Hebrews 11:39

Open Doors colleague, Ron Boyd-MacMillan, shares the following insight from his teaching, "Why I Need to Encounter the Persecuted Church."

It was early 1980's in a village in Czechoslovakia, and I had just given the pastor of a rural church a Bible in his own tongue. It was leather bound, with a gold zipper, and was the first complete Bible he had held. I remember him sniffing it, marveling at the leather smell, playing with the zip and being almost afraid to touch the thin precious pages. Then he began to talk to the members of the church. Pointing at me he said, "This gentleman is your heroic spiritual ancestor. Every time the Bible comes into a culture, it is a threat, and is opposed. So it takes men and women to risk all to bring it to us. This man has taken such a risk."

I was embarrassed, but he went on to say to me, "The Bible also came into your culture. It was also a threat. Tell me, who are your heroic spiritual ancestors?" I am ashamed to say I did not have a clear idea of who these men were in my country of the United Kingdom.

So I returned to my country with his challenge ringing in my ears, "Find out the story of how your Bible came to you, and you will discover your heroic spiritual ancestors."

What a dramatic story I uncovered. Full of spies, deaths and power politics. I learned so much about John Wycliffe, the first man to translate the Bible into English in the world of the 1300's, when most clergy could not even recite the Ten Commandments. He formed a cadre of guerilla preachers to comb the country, with hand copied versions of the Bible, a book banned by Parliament. Wycliffe died of a stroke from the strain.

In the 1500's, William Tyndale benefited from the invention of the printing press. He had to leave England to accomplish the task, never to return. At age twenty-nine in 1524, he settled in Cologne, and by 1526 was ready to smuggle 6000 copies of the Bible in English into Britain. The whole British naval fleet was put on alert, and boats were stopped and searched. First tens and then hundreds of the Bibles got through. The bishop of London tried another tack. He sought to buy the entire print run through an intermediary. His intention was to burn them all. Tyndale got wind of it, and approved the sale, saying, "Oh he will burn them. Well, I am the gladder, for I shall get the money from these books, and the whole world shall cry out upon the burning of God's Word." And so it was. He burned them, and Tyndale used the money to improve the translation and print more…at the church's expense.

Tyndale was captured by assassins and then strangled and burned in August 1536 for "heresy." His last words were, "Lord, open the King of England's eyes." This prayer was swiftly answered, and the English reformation was quickly fueled by a spate of translations. What a story it was. And what heroism from my spiritual ancestors!

RESPONSE:
Today I will thank God for my spiritual ancestors who brought God's Word to my land.

PRAYER:
Ask God if you may somehow, someday, be used to bring His Word to needy people.

July 5

STANDING STRONG

Be strong and take heart, all you who hope in the LORD.
Psalm 31:24

Until the fall of President Ceausescu in 1989, Romania was one of the most important countries for Open Doors Bible delivery ministry. We supplied countless Bibles and books—especially to Pastor Paul Negrut of the Baptist Church in Oradea. He later wrote to Brother Andrew and said, "In a divinely appointed network, we would receive a small number of Bibles to be distributed quietly and carefully among believers. Although the food supply was scarce, the Romanian believers treasured the Word of God more than anything in this world. When asked to choose between food parcels and Bibles, every Romanian that I know asked for Bibles.

"What Open Doors has done for us is better described in the words of a Christian lady who whispered to her husband, 'The angels have arrived.' Their little daughter heard those words and rushed into the next room to see the angels. To her surprise and disappointment, the 'angels' she saw were two bearded men casually dressed. The little girl had great difficulty reconciling her imagination about angels with the reality she saw. As strange as this looked for that little girl, this is the spiritual reality: for us you have been God's angels that brought us the Bread of Life."

Previously, Open Doors knew that the little Baptist Church of Oradea was likely to be knocked down at any moment as it was located in a slum clearance area. A new building was badly needed, because the little church was nowhere near big enough to accommodate all the believers anymore. However, the possibility of the church being granted planning permission for a new building was very slim.

At the beginning of 2005, we found that the little church still had not been pulled down, but it was no longer in use. A beautiful, big, new church had taken its place—a gigantic church, which seats 3,000. Every Sunday it is completely full, as it was in the past, right into the aisles. During the week, Bible studies are held for about 400 teenagers and young adults.

Dr. Paul Negrut's church is heavily involved in evangelism and missionary work, reaching to Central Asia, Russia and the Middle East. They even have a theological university where pastors receive training. Students come not only from Romania but also from the missionary fields. One student is from Yakutsk (Siberia).

But not all believers in Romania are getting on well. Pastor Paul says, "In my experience, 95% of the believers who faced the test of external persecution passed it, while 95% of those who now face the test of prosperity fail it."

But he also quickly analyzed the situation of persecution well: "It is not persecution itself but the lessons learned under persecution that make and keep the church and an individual believer strong in the Lord… what makes the difference is how we respond to persecution and how we respond to freedom."[27] Stand strong in the Lord!

RESPONSE:
Today I will prepare myself for the hard assignments in responding biblically to challenges.

PRAYER:
Pray for Romania that God will revive His church to stand strong in the face of prosperity.

27 Audrey Dorsch, "After the Persecution—What Then?" *Faith Today* *(November/December 1992), p.60.*

July 6

THE WORD OF GOD IS LIFE

"The grass withers and the flowers fall, but the word of our God endures forever."
Isaiah 40:8

Amir, a young Algerian man, was temporarily staying in an apartment of a friend while recovering from depression. His friend had moved out leaving only a few items behind, but unbeknownst to him, he had left behind his most prized possession, God's Word!

"While I was cleaning the apartment, I found a New Testament," Amir says. "This New Testament changed my life. I found the Lord Jesus Christ by reading the book." In the following months leading into years, he kept reading the Bible. Slowly, his depression lifted and the recovery and healing began to transform his life.

Amir continues, "One day I was watching Christian satellite TV and I saw the phone number of another Christian in Algeria. I immediately contacted that person and soon afterwards we met, which was great. This brother in Christ brought me into contact with a small group of believers, which I am attending regularly now. Praise to God for His healing and mercy. And thanks to the one who forgot his New Testament in the apartment."

Meanwhile, Brother Gideon is in prison in Eritrea with a group of other believers because of their faith. He says, "The government representatives came up with a new idea to ask us to stop our faith and sign an agreement that we will not read the Bible. We will not pray and not have a meeting of more than two people. If we comply with that, we will sign and they will release us from the prison. But I told them I will not. Because of the Holy Spirit's assurance in me I was ready to face anything...I said 'No, Christ is my life. As Paul said in the book of Ephesians that for me to live is Christ, and to die is gain.'

"They beat every part of my body...until I almost died. I was thinking of Jesus. What an honor for me to share his affiliation. I remember I said to myself inside, 'Lord, please forgive them. They don't know what they are doing to me, but I give you my soul to rest in your hand.'

"They took us to the prison again. After three months we had a Bible smuggled in without their knowledge. We tore the pages out of different Bible books and we distributed those to different cells.

"We chose four believers to take responsibility to do distribution of the parts of the Bible. I was one of those four chosen believers and it was my responsibility to coordinate all these things. Because there is no paper in the prison cells, I was using toilet paper to write verses of the Bible and send them to others. When the government agents searched our cell, they found all those verses I sent to the sisters. They asked 'Who sent those papers, those verses?' When they found it was me, they put me under severe torture for months. There was no part of my body without pain.

"One of the persecutors asked me a question. 'Why you are paying so big a price? Why don't you renounce your faith and live a peaceful life?' I replied, **"To me, the Word of God is life!"**

RESPONSE:
Today I will honor and prize God's Word and build my life upon its everlasting promises.

PRAYER:
Pray for those in prisons around the world who pay a huge price for loving God's Word.

376

July 7

OPEN AND CLOSED DOORS

"For my thoughts are not your thoughts, neither are your ways my ways," declares the LORD. "As the heavens are higher than the earth, so are my ways higher than your ways and my thoughts than your thoughts."

Isaiah 55:8-9

The Bible has much to say about open doors but many times — even as Christians — we seem to face obstacles on our path and in our ministry. Blocked doors can be VERY frustrating. Yet God often uses closed doors to advance His cause.

Bible teachers like Max Lucado remind us that God closed the womb of a young Sarah so he could display His power to the elderly one. He shut the palace door on Moses the prince so he could open shackles through Moses the liberator. He marched Daniel out of Jerusalem so he could use Daniel in Babylon.

And even Jesus knew the challenge of a blocked door. When he requested a path that bypassed the cross, God said no. He said no to Jesus in the Garden of Gethsemane so He could say yes to us at the gates of heaven.

It's not that our plans are bad but that God's plans are better.

A prayer is circulating on the Internet that expresses it this way:

> **He asked for strength that he might achieve,**
> **he was made weak that he might endure;**
> **He asked for health to do larger things,**
> **he was given infirmity that he might do better things;**
> **He asked for power that he might impress men,**
> **he was given weakness that he might seek God;**
> **He asked for wealth that he might be free from care,**
> **he was given poverty that he might be wiser than carefree.**
> **He asked for all things that he might enjoy life,**
> **he was given life that he might enjoy all things;**

He received nothing he asked for.

He received more than he ever hoped for.

His prayer was answered!

Blessed man!

The shortest distance between a closed and open door is the distance between your knees and the floor. The one who kneels to the Lord can stand up to anything.

RESPONSE:
Today I will accept that my blocked door doesn't mean God doesn't love me. Quite the opposite. I'll see it as proof that He does.

PRAYER:
Thank You Lord that You know best and have even better plans for me and my service for You. Help me wait patiently for You to open the right door at the right time!

July 8

SPEAK ON BEHALF OF THOSE WHO SUFFER

At my first defense, no one came to my support, but everyone deserted me. May it not be held against them.
2 Timothy 4:16

The Apostle Paul knew exactly what it was like to be alone, to be deserted by all who called themselves "brothers" and "sisters." A former colleague who has done considerable travel among the persecuted says, "It is hard to believe that Christians are the largest persecuted group in the world today. But it is even more difficult to believe that this is so seldom mentioned in our gatherings and church services. More Christians know the names of their favorite actors than their fellow believers who are in prison."

He continues, "With every trip something in my heart breaks as I hear the echoes of suffering:

- I remember the echoes of an Egyptian mother as she shared how her young boy was stuck in a haystack because she refused to deny Jesus.
- I remember the sounds of weeping as fellow students in Indonesia shared how Sariman, their co-student, was hacked to death.
- I remember the cries of anguish as we walked from church to church that was burned to the ground on the island of Lombok.
- I remember the tears of Rebecca in Iran as she showed the picture of her father who was stabbed to death for sharing the gospel.
- I remember the voice of Pastor Daniel in Vietnam as he shared how he was chained to the ground for six months.
- I remember the fear of Grace from Sudan as she shared how her church was attacked and her friend was shot through the head.
- Oh, I remember the cries of Caleb in Eritrea as he shared with tears how two dear friends were executed in front of him because of their faith.

- And I remember the tears of Joy in the southern Philippines as she shared how her fiancé was shot to death in their church in Mindanao.
- **But, most all, I remember the deafening sounds of silence every time I return home.**

RESPONSE:

How can I be silent today? How can I not speak on behalf of those who suffer? How can I desert those that belong to the same body that I belong to and who desperately need the encouragement of my intervention on their behalf?

PRAYER:
Lord, broaden my awareness of the needs of my suffering brothers and sisters. May I not be known for my silence.

July 9

TRAINING IN RIGHTEOUSNESS

Everyone who competes in the games goes into strict training. They do it to get a crown that will not last; but we do it to get a crown that will last forever.
1 Corinthians 9:25

A young Romanian Christian was called in to the secret police for interrogation. He had dreaded this moment. Fear gripped him throughout and he was unable to give a categorical rejection to the police offers of good treatment and security if he would only inform on his fellow-believers. He did not accept the offer either, but his inability to reject it unquestioningly brought personal agony.

He could not sleep that night because of his fear and guilt. The next morning led of the Holy Spirit, an older Christian came to visit the family. He was unaware of the young man's dilemma. Being a former prisoner for his faith, he was able to counsel the young man from Scripture about his situation. He built up the young man in fellowship, training him for the next ordeal.

It came the same afternoon when the youth was taken in for his second interrogation. The same thing happened and the young man was still upset by his answers. Again the older believer came to encourage him.

Three days of more interrogations passed. Eventually the young man was able to reject the police offer completely. With no further hold on him, the police let him go. Counsel, prayer and patient caring had brought him through and trained him in righteousness.

To maintain biblical integrity, let us consider training as a prescribed course in righteousness in which each individual is disciplined through practice to be obedient to God's direction for mankind and able to withstand the schemes of the devil.

People who commit themselves for a cause have a right to expect training in the job for which they have been selected. In some of the trades, this is called "apprenticeship." In medicine, it is known as "internship." In the military, it is referred to as "basic training." In

381

Scripture, it is referred to as "discipleship." However, in our modern day, training is often by-passed due to the pressures of time, need and a low value placed upon the office to be filled. This was not the case with Jesus in His selection and training of His disciples.

After calling His men to be **with Him**, he challenged them to commit themselves to following after Him—to be *"fishers of men."* Jesus then began to train them to become His kind of *"fishers of men."*

RESPONSE:
I want to be a trained disciple of Jesus Christ. I will submit to His guidance and discipline.

PRAYER:
Lord, help me to realize and accept Your "training" process as I follow You today.

July 10

EMPTINESS AND FILLING

As the deer pants for streams of water, so my soul pants for you, my God. My soul thirsts for God, for the living God. When can I go and meet with God? My tears have been my food day and night, while people say to me all day long, "Where is your God?"
Psalm 42:1-3

Ron Boyd-MacMillan writes in his epic volume, *Faith That Endures*:

I remember interviewing a former Muslim extremist in Egypt. He had converted to Christ in his early twenties and led a church for Muslim converts. This is illegal in Egypt, and the fellowship was betrayed to the police. Soon this young man found himself in prison. He was tortured. An electric cattle prod was pushed into his mouth. He was whipped and hung from the ceiling with his hands tied behind his back. But all this paled into insignificance compared to what other prisoners called "the experience." He was pushed into a stone box, a cube about five feet square. No light. No latrine. And he was left there for a month, food being passed through a grate every few days. Most prisoners went mad as a result of "the experience"—but not him.

He found Christ there, and the words he used to describe his experience are still the most brilliant description of the process of how persecution actually delivers more of God:

"In great suffering you discover a different Jesus than you do in normal life. Normally we are able to hide from ourselves who we really are and what we are really like. The ego is well defended. But pain changes all that. Pain and suffering bring up to the surface all the weak points of your personality. You are too weak to mount the usual defences, and you just have to gaze at what you are really like. I was a wreck in that cell. I was reduced to tears all the time. Crying, weeping, sobbing, wailing in the never-changing utter darkness.

"I came face-to-face with how awful I really was. I saw all the horrible things I had done, all the horrible things I was. I kept seeing myself again and again. But just as I was about to collapse into complete despair and self-loathing—and probably die—an incredible realisation burst into the cell like an exploding star. It was this: Jesus loved me even right then, as I sat in my own filth, weak, helpless and broken, empty and sinful. Even in that state, He loved me, and Christ rushed in and filled me, and the filling was so great because I was so empty."[28]

RESPONSE:
Today I realize that God can use persecution to draw people closer to Himself. I will "fix my eyes on Jesus" to accept my awfulness and His filling.

PRAYER:
Thank You Lord that You fill us when we are truly empty. Help me not to hide my real condition from myself and before You.

28 Ron Boyd-MacMillan, *Faith That Endures* (Grand Rapids: Fleming Revell, 2006), p. 319-320.

July 11

THE BEATITUDES

Now when Jesus saw the crowds, he went up on a mountainside and sat down. His disciples came to him, and he began to teach them.
Matthew 5:1-2

For the next nine days we'll look at Jesus' greatest training program—the Beatitudes. It is important to remember that each of the eight Beatitudes has a two-fold nature: a "knowing" and a "doing" response. We must not only know them, we must also respond to what we learn from them.

Eight times in the Beatitudes it says, ***"Blessed are…"*** To understand the Beatitudes, we need to know the meaning of those words. ***Blessed are*** refers to Jesus' evaluation of the kind of person He names in each Beatitude. Jesus was referring to *His esteem for that kind of person.* His meaning is, "I esteem highly any person who…." He was urging us to have that kind of attitude. His deeper meaning is, "All you who hear Me, choose to become like these kinds of people."

One noted author calls the Beatitudes, "God's radical reconstruction of the heart!" We must never consider that Jesus was promising happy conditions, as though He meant, "The one who is poor in spirit will feel good and always be joyful."

The first four Beatitudes focus internally—that is, they speak to the heart of the one who wants to obey God. They can be viewed as four stepping stones to becoming an obedient servant of the Lord Jesus Christ. They are: humility, mourning, meekness and hunger for righteousness.

The second four Beatitudes focus on the external behavior of the servant who follows Jesus. They are: mercy, purity, peacemaking and persecution.

This teaching has particular relevance for Christians who live under Islam. Restricted, deprived, regarded as second class citizens, laughed at, despised, often living in fear, many times persecuted, the words of encouragement are precious and give fresh hope of another place and time when things will be put right.

While in countries like Malaysia and Indonesia, there are greater freedoms and life is not so difficult, there are restrictions nonetheless. In others like Pakistan, Christians have suffered unjustly and are denied many basic rights. In Saudi Arabia, Egypt, Iran, Sudan, Nigeria and Morocco, the story is similar though the extent of suffering may vary. To all, Jesus gives this important message. We will look at each of the eight Beatitudes individually.

RESPONSE:
I will study Jesus' Beatitudes so that I live the way Jesus lived.

PRAYER:
Pray for Christians in Islamic countries that they will receive great encouragement as they seek to know and live the Beatitudes in their regions of restriction.

July 12

THE POOR IN SPIRIT

"Blessed are the poor in spirit, for theirs is the kingdom of heaven."
Matthew 5:3

Acknowledging our poverty in spirit is humility. It occurs when a man or woman realizes his or her own utter lack of resources to meet life and finds his or her strength in God. Such an attitude leads one away from attachment to things to attachment to God and heaven. The word for poor here means absolute, abject poverty. We can thus paraphrase the first Beatitude this way:

Blessed are those who have realised their own utter helplessness and inadequacy and who have put their whole trust in God. Such a person will humbly accept the will of God and thus become a citizen of the kingdom.

Christians especially in countries like Pakistan find this a great comfort, for the majority of them are road sweepers and do menial jobs that others will not do. They are denied better jobs often because they are illiterate. Their children have no access to higher education and so the cycle of poverty continues with little hope of a break. Surely this message is also for them. As they put their complete trust and hope in the Lord, they are assured of a place in the Kingdom of God.

A Chinese Christian woman, a leader in her church, was arrested and put in prison. Led of the Lord, she volunteered to do hard labour, cleaning the filthy prison cells on her knees. This humble work gave her opportunity to sing and share Jesus with the prisoners in each cell. Through her words and actions many prisoners came to know the Lord in a personal relationship.

RESPONSE:
Today I acknowledge my helplessness and inadequacy and place my complete trust in God.

PRAYER:
Lord, help me express true humility in practical ways today and show that my trust is in You alone.

July 13

MOURNING

Blessed are those who mourn, for they will be comforted.
Matthew 5:4

Mourning is the kind of grief that cannot be hidden. It can be a deep sorrow for our own unworthiness that leads us to trust the Lord as our total Provider, seeking His presence and counsel (authority). Such action is rewarded by the Father's gracious comfort.

It can also be for grief over the sorrow and suffering of this world. Blessed is the man who cares intensely for the sufferings, sorrows and needs of others. And so again we can paraphrase this Beatitude:

Blessed are those whose hearts are broken for the world's suffering and are deeply sorry for their sin and unworthiness, for they will find the joy and comfort of God.

As we meditate on this, what comes to mind is the need to mourn for the state of the church and Christians generally. In many countries, churches are weak and nominal, or are split by internal conflicts. There is need to mourn. There is need to mourn also for believers who have quit the struggle and crossed to the other side.

Mourn for the poor quality of preaching, the lack of prayer and the deficiency of spiritual power. Mourn for those who come to the church only to find they are unwelcome. Mourn for Christians unwilling to introduce the light of Christ to them. Mourn for a church hiding its light, too scared to let it shine. Yes, there is much to mourn for. Yet, the promise is, if we mourn, comfort will come.

A self-sufficient Bible trainer from the West, spent time in China with young leaders needing biblical training. He felt inadequate at first but later wrote, "As I left them, I wept. I wept because I had to go back to a world where God was not taken half as seriously. I wept to return to a church where if I do not insert enough clever illustrations, eyes glaze over and no one listens to my talks. I wept to go back to a world of unread Bibles and dry eyes. I wept to return to a lifestyle that would regard me as mad if I kept trying to rise at 4.30 a.m. for prayer. I wept because I really wanted to stay with those fifty teachers and learn to love God as they did."

389

RESPONSE:
Today I will repent of my self-sufficiency.

PRAYER:
Lord, I truly mourn over my own sin and unworthiness. And I mourn too for the deep and painful suffering that I see around our globe. May I receive Your joy and comfort.

July 14

THE MEEK

Blessed are the meek, for they will inherit the earth.
Matthew 5:4

Meekness is not to be confused with weakness. In Scripture, meekness means "power under control." In this context, the contrite, praying person is blessed with the indwelling control of the Holy Spirit and the inheritance promised to the believer even in conflict.

History shows that it is the people who have learned this, people with their passions, instincts and impulses under disciplined control, who have been great. (see Numbers 12:3 and Proverbs 16:32) Thus:

Blessed are those whose every instinct, every impulse, and every passion is under the control of God's Spirit! They will be right with God, self and others and enter the life which God alone can give.

Pray for this meekness when entering into dialogue with those of opposing positions. There will be times when patience and self-control will be sorely tested. There may also be times when the Spirit will suggest a change of direction in the dialogue or a strategic retreat that looks suspiciously like defeat. To be meek is to be able to willingly accept temporary defeat in order that there may later be victory in the Spirit.

A co-worker in China was struggling with the attitudes of a house church group who forbade hand-clapping during the singing of hymns. One leader complained bitterly. Every evening in the brothers' sleeping quarters, he would complain further. The group would then debate endlessly on whether or not clapping hands during singing was permissible. It was like the black smoke pouring out from the weeds.

This continued until the afternoon of the last day, when God used His Word, and the Holy Spirit did an amazing work. This brother stood up and admitted his wrongdoing. He asked God to forgive his ignorance, stubbornness and defensiveness. With his confession, Christ's love tore down an invisible wall. It was as if the Lord "broke down gates of bronze and cut through bars of iron." The response of the workers as they prayed together was, "The glorious King has come." Thank and praise the Lord. He was completely victorious.

391

RESPONSE:
Today I will quit calling the shots and surrender complete control to God.

PRAYER:
Lord, today I completely surrender to the control of Your Spirit in my life. Help me to be meek.

July 15

HUNGER AND THIRST FOR RIGHTEOUSNESS

Blessed are those who hunger and thirst for righteousness, for they will be filled.
Matthew 5:6

This attitude portrays a maturity of belief that shows a servant is ready for service. When completeness or wholeness is achieved, the servant receives the satisfaction of being used of God for that which they have been called, trained and equipped.

In ancient times, wages were very low and men often could not earn enough for the family to eat well. Water was also a precious commodity. The emphasis in this Beatitude is the passionate desire for the whole, for complete righteousness as a matter of life and death. Blessed indeed is the one whose most passionate desire is to love God and to love others as they ought. Thus:

Blessed are those who long for total righteousness as a starving person longs for food and as a person perishing of thirst longs for water, for they will be truly satisfied.

People of other faiths are impressed with those who take their faith seriously. They do not respect people whose religion is merely outward form, who are just "*weekend Christians*." Much of what they see is materialistic, that is, "carnal" or "worldly" (see 1 Corinthians 3). Christianity turns them off—the low regard for moral purity, the hedonism, the wishy-washiness, the unwillingness to suffer or make sacrifices, the fear of making a stand.

As Brother Andrew says, "How can Muslims respect a church that is in hiding?" Christians need to acknowledge their beliefs and be willing to suffer for their faith and convictions. A more complete righteousness will definitely have great impact. It will earn respect for our preaching the gospel.

During a visit to Indonesia, a coworker had the wonderful opportunity of participating in an Open Doors SSTS seminar held in an area of intense conflict. The constant presence of armed soldiers outside the building confirmed that this seminar was far more than theology – this was reality! More than 700 churches were already burnt to the ground and the church in the region was facing a severe onslaught.

On the second day of teaching, he remembers one pastor suddenly jumping up and with all his heart cried out, "My brother, please don't teach us to survive, teach us to be faithful."

RESPONSE:
Today I am so grateful for God's presence in my life that I yearn for more of Him.

PRAYER:
Lord I long for total righteousness so that the world will see more of Your faithfulness in me.

July 16

THE MERCIFUL

Blessed are the merciful, for they will be shown mercy.
Matthew 5:7

As we in humility recognize our "poverty of spirit," God in His mercy forgives and equips us. Having received mercy, we are expected to show it to others.

The biblical term merciful is related to the word for empathy, which means the ability to get right inside another person's skin until we see things with his eyes, think things with his mind and feel things with his feelings. This is what Jesus did for us in His incarnation. Thus:

Blessed are those who empathize with others until they are able to see with the eyes of others, think with their thoughts and feel with their feelings. The one who does this will find others do the same for him or her and will know that God did this for them in Christ Jesus.

How do we see our non-Christian friends? Can we see Muslims, for example, as real people groping in the semi-darkness, under the mere glimmer of light that a crescent moon provides, thinking that is all the light there is?

As we see them, mercy would be an appropriate word to describe our feeling and attitude as well as actions toward them. Just as we would go to the aid of a blind man heading in the wrong direction, so mercy should similarly drive us to go after them and show those who are willing to listen, the way to more complete light.

If we are secure in the knowledge that Christ is the Sun of Righteousness, then we do not need to prove anything but patiently and gently show others the way.

A relatively young man decided to work for the Lord in China. His father was not a Christian and very strongly opposed him. The son decided to attend a series of Christian meetings in one of the areas where he was serving. His father opposed so strongly that they quarreled before he left for the meetings. Then the son suddenly died while he was at the meetings.

The Christians there prayed and showed much concern. They knew that the news of the death would be hard for the father, so they asked a doctor to be there just in case the father needed him. When the father arrived and saw the love of the Christians, he gave his life to the Lord.

RESPONSE:
Today I will see others as Jesus sees them and I will empathize with them as though in their skin.

PRAYER:
Lord, help grow closer to You so that I will act like You, forgiving others and being sympathetic.

July 17

THE PURE IN HEART

Blessed are the pure in heart, for they will see God.
Matthew 5:8

As our mourning to God begins the transforming process of our new life in Christ, so our lifestyle of purity amid the impure can become the beginning of reconciliation.

This Beatitude necessitates the strictest and most honest self-examination. We are to do everything with pure, unmixed motives. This demands the death of self and the springing to life of Christ within the heart.

So, blessed are those whose motives are unmixed and who operate in purity. They shall be given a vision of God Himself. As we draw closer to Him through purity, we shall see Him more clearly, love Him more dearly and follow Him more nearly. Thus:

Blessed are those whose motives are absolutely pure and whose life is characterized by purity, for they will be able to see God.

The area of moral purity is one major concern of Muslims. Great stress is laid on modesty in dressing and purity of relationships between the sexes. But Christians seem so nonchalant about such issues. Is it because we do not care about purity? No. The difference is in our starting points. In the Muslim view, purity is from the "outside in." For the follower of Jesus it must be from the "inside out." Thus, Muslims seek to cleanse themselves knowing they are in need of cleansing, whereas we know Christ has already cleansed us.

But we tend to disregard the danger that dirt can pose to us and we become careless. What is important to realize is that a careless disregard for even the "appearance of evil" will lead people to wrong conclusions and cause them to stumble. It is not enough to say we are pure. We must be seen to be pure.

A co-worker in China was teaching a class of believers in which two antagonistic-looking groups of students sat across from each other, looking as if they were facing enemies. As he was sharing, some students started crying and others were repenting. He told them that if they needed to apologize to others, they should sincerely ask the Holy Spirit to work, and to move them, and to give them the courage to admit their wrongs to others. He said that God delights in pure hearted children, and He wants to use submissive, humble people. Everyone was hugging and crying. Everyone was confessing his or her sins to each other. The cleansing brought purity to their relationships.

RESPONSE:
Today I will seek to live my life in true purity before God with good motives.

PRAYER:
Lord, I can only live this way if I listen and respond positively to the reproving of Your Holy Spirit. Help me to be sensitive to purity issues.

July 18

THE PEACEMAKERS

Blessed are the peacemakers, for they will be called children of God.
Matthew 5:9

With the possession of a meek spirit, we are equipped to step into the midst of conflict and be ambassadors "waging peace" that passes all understanding. The richness of the New Testament word "peace" describes a condition of perfect and complete positive well-being. It also describes right relationships—intimate fellowship and goodwill between human beings. Peace comes not from avoiding issues but from facing them, making peace even when the way is through trouble.

Blessed are those peacemakers who produce right relationships in every sphere of life, for they are doing a God-like work.

Such actions may involve laying down one's life, like Jesus did, in order to reconcile men with God and break down barriers among men (Galatians 3:26-29). Are we willing to pay the price so that others might find peace with God? Are we willing to insist that all should hear the gospel and believe? In some conflict areas of the world, Christians call this *"waging peace."*

Our brothers and sisters in Israel and the West Bank—where "peace" is sought but very evasive—remind us that Jesus' high moral teaching is that we should not resist evil with evil (Matthew 5:39). Jesus is calling His followers not to respond in kind to the acts of injustice and dehumanization directed against them, but rather to respond with transforming initiatives. This unique perspective that He teaches contrasts with the "fight or flight" responses so deeply conditioned in human beings.

Dr. Salim Munayer is a wonderful example of such a peacemaker. The organization he founded takes groups of Christian Palestinians and Israelis on trips to the desert where they must work together in a situation that breaks down barriers and promotes trust relationships. Brother Andrew comments that this ministry doesn't "just talk about the problem between Palestinians and Jews. It brings the two sides together and provides the means for them to reconcile."

"Waging peace" involves: promoting love not hate; fostering unity among brethren; being a witness of a higher kingdom; and following the non-violence example of Jesus.

RESPONSE:
Today I will be proactive and "wage peace" in my sphere of influence.

PRAYER:
Lord, make me an instrument of Your peace. May I counter hatred with love and injury with forgiveness today.

July 19

THE PERSECUTED

Blessed are those who are persecuted because of righteousness, for theirs is the kingdom of heaven. Blessed are you when people insult you, persecute you and falsely say all kinds of evil against you because of me. Rejoice and be glad, because great is your reward in heaven, for in the same way they persecuted the prophets who were before you.

Matthew 5:10-12

With our hunger and thirst for righteousness comes the promise of persecution for those who take a stand for God. We have not been called to safety and comfort but to serve in the midst of conflict. Persecution is not to be strenuously avoided, for it is the result of righteous living. To avoid it, one would have to cease living righteously.

The early church went through much persecution for their faith in Christ. It affected their livelihood. They had to ask themselves, Should a Christian craftsman create idols for the temples? Or should a tailor sew robes for heathen priests?

Persecution affected social and family life. Most feasts were held in the temple of some god. A common invitation would be dining at the table of such a god. Even an ordinary meal in a home began with a cup of wine poured out in honor of the gods, like grace before a meal. Could a Christian share in such a meal like that?

Severe persecution meant being flung to the lions, burned at the stake, or being wrapped in pitch and set alight to provide light for Nero's palace gardens. Or it meant being sewn in animal skins and set upon by Nero's hunting dogs. Christians were tortured on the rack; scraped with pincers; had molten lead poured on them; had red-hot brass plates fixed to the most tender parts of their bodies; had eyes torn out; had limbs cut off and roasted before their eyes; had hands and feet burned while cold water was poured over other parts to prolong agony.

Most of us have never in our lives made a real sacrifice for Jesus. To have to suffer persecution is to walk along the same road as the prophets, the saints, and the martyrs. To suffer persecution is to make things easier for those who are to follow. To suffer persecution is to experience the fellowship of Christ, as Shadrach, Meshach and Abednego did in the furnace (Daniel 3:19-25). It is not always so dramatic, but it is nevertheless real. Most of us enjoy the blessing of liberty today because men and women in the past were willing to buy it for us at the cost of their own blood, sweat and tears.

RESPONSE:
I will accept persecution, whether mild or hot, which comes as a result of righteous living.

PRAYER:
Lord, encourage those today who are experiencing severe persecution for Your name.

July 20

BEING SALT OF THE EARTH

"You are the salt of the earth. But if the salt loses its
saltiness, how can it be made salty again?
It is no longer good for anything,
except to be thrown out and trampled underfoot."
Matthew 5:13

Jesus is making a statement of fact here when he says, *"You are the salt of the earth!"* It is not a command or wish list. It is to be reality here and now. The implication is that we are to be what God has already made us to be.

The context is Christians facing persecution. Their numbers are small and they are insignificant. Salt is cheap in some places and expensive in others. We have the saying that a man is worth his weight in salt! Its value may vary yet it has unusual properties that far exceed its value.

This is what should happen when Christians take their stand for God in society. That stand for good renders society infertile for the growth of evil and ungodly influences. When England went through revival under the ministry of the Wesley's and George Whitefield in the 18th century, a possible bloody revolution such as afflicted France was averted.

Usually it happens on a more moderate scale. Conversations moderated, consciences pricked, respect for others heightened.

The disciples of Christ do not remain silent about their faith. They do not hide themselves, but live and work in places where their influence may be felt. The light that is in them can then be most fully manifested to others so that they may see that the light of real Christian goodness. It is a light not of this world but coming from God, and may in consequence be led to give honor and praise to its Giver.

I was blessed to visit a seminary in Indonesia that reflects this teaching of Jesus. They are surrounded by a Muslim community where many live in poverty. Rather than live in an isolated enclave, the school and students serve this community with the love of Jesus. They teach literacy lessons; they provide first-aid medical care; they distribute food and clothing to the hungry and naked.

During an outbreak of violence by extremists against churches in the area, an angry Muslim mob approached the seminary one night chanting their slogans and waving their machetes. When they arrived at the buildings, they found a circle of Muslim people surrounding the campus holding hands in a large circle. They said to the extremists, "We will not allow you to destroy this school. These people help us and our children with all our needs. You may not harm them!" The mob disappeared.

Being salt and light in community also has its rewards.

RESPONSE:
Today I resolve to live my life for Jesus in a way that will positively "salt" my community.

PRAYER:
Help me, Lord, to stand for the good and be a salty influence for You in the world around me.

July 21

THE VALUE OF SALT

*Let your conversation be always full of grace, seasoned
with salt, so that you may know how to answer everyone.*
Colossians 4:6

At the end of His Beatitudes, Jesus stated that His followers were
to be salt and light in the world. Salt was highly valued in the ancient
world for four special qualities:

a. Its purity - glistening white and coming from the sun and
the sea, it was the most primitive of all offerings to the gods.
If we are to be salt, we must be an example of purity. In the
world, efforts to lower standards of honesty, diligence in work,
conscientiousness and morality are going on all the time. The
Christian must be the person who holds aloft the standard
for purity of speech, conduct and thought. Words cannot be
effective unless backed up by pure living.

b. It was inexpensive but precious - Christians may seem few,
insignificant and of no consequence to society. In 1 Corinthians
1:26-31, Paul addressed the early church with the concept that
though few in numbers, lowly and unimportant, Christians are
called to exercise godly influence over the whole of society.

c. As a preservative to keep meat from going bad - salt rubbed
into meat slowed the rotting process. Christians whose lives
exhibit "blessedness" will have a preserving impact upon a
society that, if left to itself, will rot and deteriorate. In Judges
9:45, Abimelech, after defeating the city of Shechem destroyed
it and scattered salt all over it. Spiritually, this is what the
Christian does when he takes his stand for God in society.
He makes that society, be it his friends in school, his fellow
students at college, his co-workers, or those with whom he
plays sports, less fertile soil for other ungodly influences. We
too can have a preserving witness, by being involved with this
world gone wrong, if we will pay the price.

405

d. To season food - salt brings out the distinctive flavor of food. The increase of God's people should increase the flavor of life in many different ways. By His very presence, Jesus raised the spirits of people. There was a quality about His life that could not be explained in natural terms. As our verse for today says, our speech especially should be seasoned with salt. In this context Paul also talks about not grieving the Holy Spirit. Since speech is linked to a person's spiritual state and has tremendous potential for building up or tearing down (James3:3-12), the constant reminder is to watch not only what is allowed to come forth but how it comes.

By our presence, participation and penetration of society, in our daily contacts in our neighborhood and community, we are to bring the flavor of Christ to an unbelieving world.

RESPONSE:
Today I will check my conversation and be sure I season it with the salt of purity.

PRAYER:
Lord, forgive me when I grieve Your Holy Spirit by what I do and what I say and how I say it.

July 22

THE LIGHT OF THE WORLD

"You are the light of the world. A town built on a hill cannot be hidden. Neither do people light a lamp and put it under a bowl. Instead they put it on its stand, and it gives light to everyone in the house."
Matthew 5:14-15

Jesus is also the great light of the world (John 8:12). Those who believe in Him are brought out of darkness into His light (Colossians 1:12-13) and in turn become lights also. In essence, they live the Beatitudes. What does light do?

   a. **It exposes dirt** - If Christians live holy and righteous lives, it will show up the unrighteous deeds of others (Ephesians 5:8-14). An example is that people who take bribes feel very vulnerable if there are others that don't. Christians who work in government offices can, by their uprightness and integrity, diminish the amount of corruption just by their very presence and principles.

   b. **It lights up the way so that we do not stumble** - If Christians walk by the principles of the Word of God, their lives take on a higher purpose and direction than that of self. This will not fail to attract the attention of a watching world. The world then is faced with a choice—to accept or reject such a model. To those who reject, that light becomes darkness. But for those who accept, that light illumines their lives and they will not make wrong choices.

   c. **It discourages works of darkness** - More crimes are committed at night than in the daytime.

   d. **It dispels fear** - When light shines, the phantoms of the night just fade away. People who are afraid of the dark prefer to sleep with the light on.

Light even enables discernment to be made—between friend and foe and between truth and counterfeit. It enables work to be done. Light enables plants to grow. Used in modern technology, it aids in telecommunications (fiber optics), helps to heal (lasers), and aids in publishing books.

The light of the gospel also blesses in so many ways. And Christians who walk in it can in turn help others by sharing the knowledge they have concerning life, death, sin, salvation, God, the devil, heaven and hell. For these are the issues that plague man on a wide scale and for which they are striving to find adequate answers. The light will be recognized, not just in words, but in "good deeds" which lead others to praise our Father in heaven.

In Kumasi, Ghana, African Enterprise has been organizing city-cleaning teams. Before an evangelistic campaign, Christians often ask government leaders if they can clean it up. Then they send out teams of people with makeshift straw brooms and pails of soapy water to scrub the city. Christian workers have cleaned hospitals, city parks, and government grounds before major outreaches to exemplify practical love.

RESPONSE:
Today I am determined to shine for Jesus—the true light of the world!

PRAYER:
Lord, I want my life to count for You and Your kingdom. Help me be a lighthouse for You.

July 23

PURIFIED BY THE REFINER'S FIRE

He will sit as a refiner and purifier of silver; he will purify the Levites and refine them like gold and silver. Then the LORD will have men who will bring offerings in righteousness...
Malachi 3:3

It sounds easy to say we will always forgive others but what happens in your heart when your own son is brutally murdered. How can God make good come from that terrible event?

For answers, we go (in two parts) to the southern Philippines where a decade ago Severino (Junie) Bagtasos, a young pastor, was sitting in the front row of his church in Alat listening to his sister conclude her Sunday message about heaven. Suddenly a man barged into the chapel. Two loud bangs were heard. Before anyone could make sense of what happened, Severino lay lifeless in a pool of blood. The killer made his escape as the distraught church members gathered around their pastor, killed instantly by gunshots to his chest and cheek.

His mother, Purificacion, says, "I miss my son. Junie was the most caring of all my children. He would always offer help when I was cooking. He would often ask me and his father advice whenever he was beset with difficulties in the ministry because his church members were older than him. I was blessed by Junie's sincerity and faithfulness in the ministry. Nothing could hinder him from going to his Bible studies. Heavy downpours and floods could not keep him from bringing the Word of God to those who needed to hear it. Death threats did not stop him."

There is not even a hint of bitterness as Purificacion speaks of that painful time. "During one of the services held at the wake of my son, my husband told the congregation, 'We forgive the person who killed our son. If that person is here, I want you to know that we forgive you. If he is not here, and if anyone of you knows him, please tell him that we forgive him. The God we serve is the God of love and we want to show that love to you.'"

But there were those who didn't share these convictions. She adds, "Some of my husband's relatives who were also Muslims got angry at him for saying this. They were eager to avenge Junie's death. It's part of their culture. But my husband restrained them and told them that our God is a God who also forgives. We chose to forgive our son's murderer."

Purificacion shares what she thinks now was one of God's reasons for her losing Junie. "After my son's death, many Christians whose faith had grown cold were ushered back to the Lord." Now after a decade has passed, she continues to see God's hand in it all. She adds, "I believe Junie's death was part of God's plan. It was His way of opening the doors that have long been shut. You see, before the death of my son, Chinese-Tausug believers were scattered all over Jolo [their island in southern Philippines]. Many of them stopped attending the worship services.

When my son began the work in Alat [a predominantly Muslim town], little by little these believers started to gather again. Junie, their pastor, loved them dearly and was truly passionate for the ministry. One by one they started coming to church again. Before long, these believers were on fire once more and got involved in the work of God." God's refining at work!

RESPONSE:
Today I will live in the awareness of God's refining plan for His Kingdom's expansion.

PRAYER:
Lord, purify Your church and help me to accept whatever consequences this will have.

July 24

THE OVERFLOW OF THE SPIRIT

May the God of hope fill you with all joy and peace as you trust in him, so that you may overflow with hope by the power of the Holy Spirit.
Romans 15:13

Yesterday we looked at the martyrdom of Severino (Junie) Bagtasos in the southern Philippines and we are listening to his mother, after ten years' time, explain what she has learned about the good that God's Spirit has brought from the painful loss of her dear son. Purificacion Bagtasos exudes the warmth of a mother and the spirituality of a woman of God. One would not think she'd experienced every mother's nightmare. She overflows with peace, courage and hope.

She says, "Through this tragedy, God paved the way for the distribution of the *Kitab Injil* [New Testament] in Jolo. A year after Junie's death, I heard over the radio an *Imam* [Muslim religious leader] preaching using the *Kitab Injil*! What's more amazing is that it is the Muslims themselves asking and distributing copies of the *Kitab Injil*, not the Christians!"

In 1986, thousands of Gideon Bibles were burned to ashes in Jolo. Ten years later and after Severino's death, a revived interest in the Bible grew among the Muslims in the whole island.

She adds, "I remember during the wake of our son, the church was filled with Muslims for the first time. We even had to put in additional benches to accommodate those who were still coming. We took that opportunity to preach and declare Christ to them. One way or another the seed of the gospel was planted in the hearts of all the Muslims gathered there. It will not return to the Lord void."

And so it was that Severino accomplished in death what he may not have accomplished in life—to preach Jesus Christ to as many Muslims in Jolo as possible.

Secondly, Purificacion talks about vengeance. "We never filed a case because we know God will avenge us and that is where we stand. It also spared us from the long process and uncertainty of obtaining justice. God has seen what had happened and He knows my son's murderer. I believe He will give us proper justice in His time.

"I feel compassion for them," Purificacion adds as she turns her thoughts to the Muslims they are reaching. Muslims believe that if you kill an enemy of Allah on the first day of Ramadan, the act will ensure your passage to paradise. Perhaps blinded by this belief, Junie's killer chose to commit the crime on the very day Ramadan started that year.

Purificacion never thought she'd outlive any of her children. She experienced dark and painful days. But she says, "The prayers and the letters of comfort sent by Christians around the world helped me and my family as we battled loneliness and depression over the loss of my son...We felt all the more encouraged to continue in the ministry God has entrusted to us."

Purificacion and her husband expanded their ministry after their son's death. They took over the Bible studies Severino used to teach. They felt empowered. She concludes, "I don't remember feeling fear. Instead of fear, we were filled with courage."

RESPONSE:
Today I want my life to be so filled with God's joy and peace that it will overflow to others.

PRAYER:
Remember to pray for ongoing strength and courage for Purificacion and her family.

July 25

EMPATHY WITH THOSE NEEDING COMFORT

Comfort, comfort my people, says your God.
Isaiah 40:1

In July, 2011 the world was stunned as peaceful Norway experienced a bombing in downtown Oslo and the shooting massacre at a youth camp outside the capital. When the dust settled, the shocking death toll stood at seventy-six. Letters and e-mails of comfort, support and prayers for the grieving families and nation poured into the Open Doors-Norway office. On July 25th our Norwegian Director sent out the following message:

On behalf of our people and nation, I want to thank all of you around the world who are praying for us and are sending words of comfort after the terrible acts that have shaken the nation.

A week ago my wife and I met the Ortiz family in Ariel, Israel. They experienced a bomb attack that almost killed their son Ami a few years ago. They gave us a cup with the Israeli and Norwegian flags on it, and an inscription from Isaiah 40:1, *Comfort, yes comfort my people!* The last days these words have become a message to our people, the Norwegian nation.

In Haifa we also met the parents of a Christian girl who was one of many victims after a suicide bomber killed dozens of Israeli school children on a bus some years ago. Every year they have a memorial day. They have buttons with the text: '**Don't forget – don't forgive.**' But the Christian parents said, 'We cannot wear that button. We do not want revenge or hatred to fill our hearts. We are called to forgive and love.' But of course, they will always have the pain.

It is not possible to find words that express the pain and sadness we feel after such cruel deeds. But we can already see good and beautiful things coming up. People are focusing on how to comfort and help each other. People cry together, and king, queen and prime minister show their emotions before the whole nation. Politicians from different parties are talking to another in a different way, and

413

people admire their good leadership in this difficult time. There are great discussions and wise speeches about the most important subjects. As a nation we have hard days, but also days of learning.

People come to church in a very humble way. It is a place for prayers, lamentations, hope, comfort and love in these days; a place to meet the Comforter and Saviour.

In Open Doors we frequently get information about terror against sisters and brothers from so many places in the world. Some times it feels 'far away.' But now we will hopefully understand more of the fear and threat every persecuted Christian faces in their lives.

Grace and peace! The staff of Open Doors-Norway

RESPONSE:
Thank God that He comforts us so that we can use His comfort to comfort others.

PRAYER:
Pray today for all brothers and sisters experiencing the fear and pain of terror and loss.

July 26

SPIRIT OF FORGIVENESS

"...For if you forgive men when they sin against you, your heavenly Father will also forgive you. But if you do not forgive men their sins, your Father will not forgive your sins."

Matthew 6:14-15

A Spanish father and son were estranged. The father later went to search for his son. When he could not find him, the father put this ad in the Madrid newspaper:

"Dear Paco, meet me in front of this newspaper office at noon on Saturday. All is forgiven. I love you. Your Father."

Saturday noon, 800 Pacos showed up at the office looking for forgiveness and love from their fathers.

Forgiveness is one of the most powerful actions that Christians can perform. The world does not understand the ability or reasons to do this because it is most unnatural in a dog-eat-dog world. There is also pain to be overcome because behind every act of forgiveness lies the wound of betrayal; but there is far more pain and emotional, social, physical damage done when we do not forgive.

An Asian Christian apologist says, "If I am asked what separates Christianity from other religions, or what's different about Christianity, aren't all religions the same when you get down to it?' one of the first things that I would say is bound up in this one beautiful word: **forgiveness**."

Peter asked Jesus how many times he should forgive a brother who sins against him. He thinks he is magnanimous and suggests seven times! Jesus makes his famous reply, *"...not seven times, but seventy-seven times."* (Matthew 18:22).

Jesus then shares a parable about a man who, after much pleading for mercy, was forgiven for much and yet would not forgive another person who owed him little. In the parable, the master throws the man into jail to be tortured until he pays back his large debt. Then comes

415

the conclusion: *"This is how my heavenly Father will treat each of you unless you forgive your brother from your heart."* (Matthew 18:35).

RESPONSE:
Today I will forgive others who hurt me because God has commanded it and because my own forgiveness depends on it.

PRAYER:
Lord, give me a spirit of forgiveness toward others who hurt me, just as You have forgiven me.

July 27

EXAMPLE OF JESUS

*"Father, forgive them for they do not know
what they are doing."*
Luke 23:34a

On January 23, 1999, 58-year-old Australian Baptist missionary Graham Staines and his two sons were burned to death when the vehicle they were sleeping in was doused with gasoline and set on fire, allegedly by members of a Hindu fundamentalist group, in the Indian state of Orissa. Graham Staines had been working with leprosy patients for thirty-four years.

Hundreds of millions witnessed Gladys Staines, Graham Staines' widow, forgive her family's murderers in the name of the gospel on Indian television—a scene which moved many to tears "and may have achieved more for the gospel in India than many years of missionary work," according to an Indian evangelist.

Describing her prompt forgiveness of the killers as a "spontaneous act," Gladys Staines says, "it took away the bitterness" that otherwise would have remained in her heart. Since the incident she has people coming to her door asking how they can become Christians.

The imagery she used was also powerful. **"Let us burn hatred… and spread the flame of Christ's love."**

Forgiveness is to be given even when it is not asked for. On the cross, forgiveness was one of the first words of Jesus. The soldiers doing the crucifying had not asked for forgiveness but Jesus realized their need of it.

Forgiveness can only be truly accomplished in the power of the Holy Spirit. But when given, it communicates most powerfully the love of God. And we are called to be like God, to bear God's family resemblance.

Forgiveness is a personal transaction that releases the one offended from the offense. The forgiveness required by the Scriptures is more than detached or limited forgiveness, it is full and complete forgiveness in which there is a total cessation of negative feelings

toward the offender and the relationship being restored has the
possibility to grow.

RESPONSE:
**Today I will show Christ's love by forgiving those who do not even
ask for forgiveness.**

PRAYER:
**Lord, may I be like You and through the power of Your Holy
Spirit forgive completely those who bring offenses against me.**

July 28

WHAT FORGIVENESS IS AND IS NOT

Bear with each other and forgive whatever grievances
you may have against one another.
Forgive as the Lord forgave you.

Colossians 3:13

To understand forgiveness we must realize what forgiveness is **NOT**:

- Forgiveness is **not forgetting**. Deep hurts can rarely be wiped out of one's awareness.

- Forgiveness is **not reconciliation**. Reconciliation takes two persons, but an injured party can forgive an offender without reconciliation.

- Forgiveness is **not condoning**. Forgiveness does not necessarily excuse bad or hurtful behavior.

- Forgiveness is **not dismissing**. It involves taking the offense seriously, not passing it off as inconsequential or insignificant.

- Forgiveness is **not a vague notion of 'tolerance'**. This is, at best, a low-grade parody of forgiveness. At worst, it's a way of sweeping the real issues in life under the carpet.

- Forgiveness is **not pardoning**. A pardon is a legal transaction that releases an offender from the consequences of an action, such as a penalty.

Throughout the Old Testament we read that only God can forgive sins. We hear David exclaim, *"He forgives all my sins…"* (Psalm 103:3). We also see examples of human forgiveness—even in pain—like Joseph forgiving his brothers for selling him into slavery. Joseph gains true freedom. He then names his son Manasseh, "one who causes to be forgotten."

In the New Testament we see Jesus, the Lamb of God, come into to the world to die for our sins. Through His shed blood we can once and for all receive ultimate forgiveness. This is the pure "gospel of grace." This forgiveness is a gift. We do not deserve it but God, in His grace, reached out to provide forgiveness to a dying world.

Then we read in the verse above the impact of this on those of us who have received that forgiveness. Its ethical challenge parallels "love your enemies" and "pray for your persecutors."

In the final analysis, forgiveness is an act of faith. By forgiving another, I am trusting that God is a better justice-maker than I am. By forgiving, I release my own right to get even and leave all issues of fairness for God to work out. I leave in God's hands the scales that must balance justice and mercy. I simply forgive others and leave them to God.

RESPONSE:
Today I will leave fairness and justice in God's hands. I will obediently forgive others just as the Lord forgave me.

PRAYER:
Lord, grant me the faith to trust You with the offenses committed against me. I will forgive.

July 29

FORGIVENESS IS FOR OURSELVES TOO

Forgive us our debts, as we also have forgiven our debtors.
Matthew 6:12

Corrie ten Boom often thought back over the horrors of Ravensbruck prison camp and realized that it was hard to find forgiveness in her heart—the true Christian attitude for the former Nazis that would reveal through her the Spirit's goodness. Where was love, acceptance, and forgiveness in a horror camp where allegedly more than 95,000 women died? How could she ever forget the horrible cruelty of the guards and the smoke constantly coming from the chimney of the crematorium?

A few years later, Corrie was speaking in a church in Munich, and when the meeting was over she saw one of the cruelest male guards of Ravensbruck coming to speak to her. He had his hand outstretched. "I have become a Christian," he explained. "I know that God has forgiven me for the cruel things I did, but I would like to hear it from your lips as well. Fraulein, will you forgive me?"

Conflict raged in Corrie's heart. The good Spirit of God urged her to forgive. The spirit of bitterness and coldness urged her to turn away. *"Jesus, help me. I can lift my hand. I can do that much."* As their hands met it was as if warmth and healing broke forth with tears and joy. "I forgive you, brother, with all my heart." Later Corrie testified that "it was the power of the Holy Spirit" who had poured the love of God into her heart that day.

Philip Yancey gives a pragmatic reason why we must forgive that seems very foundational: **forgiveness alone can stop the cycle of blame, pain as well as vengeance and violence**. The meaning of the New Testament word "**forgiveness**," he says, is literally "to release, to hurl away, to free yourself." The only way to break the chain or cycle of hurtfulness is to stop and ask forgiveness. This allows a relationship to start over and begin anew. The Russian writer, Solzhenitsyn, believed this forgiveness is what truly makes us different from animals. Only humans can perform that most unnatural act of forgiveness that transcends the relentless law of nature.

The only thing harder than forgiveness is the alternative. A teacher once told each of her students to bring a clear plastic bag and a sack of potatoes to school. For every person they refused to forgive in their life's experience, they chose a potato, wrote on it the name and date, and put it in the plastic bag. They were then told to carry this bag with them everywhere for one week, putting it beside their bed at night, on the car seat when driving, next to their desk at work. The hassle of lugging this around with them made it clear what a weight they were carrying spiritually, and how they had to pay attention to it all the time to not forget and keep leaving it in embarrassing places…Too often we think of forgiveness as a gift to the other person, and it clearly is for ourselves as well!

RESPONSE:
Today I will give myself the gift of forgiveness. Is there someone I need to forgive?

PRAYER:
Father, I pray today for the power of Your Holy Spirit to enable me to release any cycles of hurtfulness in my life by forgiving others.

July 30

THE FREEING BEAUTY OF FORGIVENESS

"This is how my heavenly Father will treat each of you unless you forgive your brother from your heart."
Matthew 18:35

In Ciudad Juarez, Mexico, a street-witnessing team became involved in an extraordinary situation. A young Mexican called Samuel would walk for two hours each day to join them and act as an interpreter. They discovered that Samuel's mother and sister had been murdered and that he witnessed the killings but, despite trying to intervene, was unable to stop them. He said he knew the man who did it.

He had a desire to go and avenge the killings, but then became a Christian and his whole attitude changed. He began a Bible study group now attended by twenty people. On the final night of the meetings, he saw the man he believed had murdered his mother and sister go forward to receive Jesus Christ as his Savior. Samuel made his way through the throng of people and shook his hand and welcomed him "into the Kingdom." Samuel was able to forgive him.

In Jesus' teaching, there is little doubt that, as a Christian, I MUST forgive those who have wronged me. Then our human, time-bound minds cry out with the loud fleshly inquiry—"WHY?"

Again Philip Yancey points out that through the process of forgiveness we realize we are not as different from the wrongdoer as we would like to think. And we end up linked on the same side.

In essence, God linked Himself with us humans in the incarnation. Somehow God had to come to terms with these creatures He desperately wanted to love. On earth, living among us, he learned what it was like to be human—yet without sin. But He put Himself on our side. God made Him who had no sin to be sin for us.

Forgiveness is a key component of the victorious, overcomer. This is the way of the cross to becoming "more than conquerors."

As a young Christian in Cambodia, Cham witnessed a Khmer Rouge soldier—a youth he knew from school—bludgeon his mother to death by hitting her repeatedly over the head with a wooden board.

Cham suffered from severe depression over memories of that incident for many months. But eventually the Lord helped him gain victory over it.

Ten years later, Cham was walking down the main street of Phnom Penh and saw that young man who had killed his mother. The young man was very fearful of revenge when he recognized Cham approaching him. With moist eyes Cham looked at him and said, "In the name of Jesus, I forgive you!" Cham was free.

RESPONSE:
I accept today that forgiveness is a must for me as a follower of Jesus.

PRAYER:
Thank you, Lord, for so many rich examples of the freeing beauty of forgiveness.

July 31

GOD'S CARE

Cast all your anxiety on him because he cares for you.
1 Peter 5:7

Ron Boyd-MacMillan shares the story of Sister Lin and family from North Korea. As Christians, she and her husband prayed for a child for years. After many years she finally conceived. They asked God for a safe delivery because it was now the severe famine period of the mid-1990's.

Her husband went to search for food but came home weeping. All he could offer her was bark from a tree to make soup. It was not enough to nourish a woman with child. Then her husband went further afield to find food and was shot to death by soldiers as he foraged food from the garbage bags on a train. She was now alone.

When contractions started, she lay on the ground and gave birth to a dead baby boy. She named him after her husband and buried the body. From there she began to walk north and crossed the river into China. A Korean Christian family in China nurtured her back to health.

Telling Ron her story, she asked, "Can I forgive God for making the world this way?" Many of us, if honest, would acknowledge that we often have doubts about God when we see the suffering and pain in our world, just like Sister Lin. But we should value our doubts because they end up bringing God close.

Ron answered her poignant question with another question, "Why are you still a Christian?"

Sister Lin replied, "First because my Lord died young and alone in excruciating pain without knowing why either."

Ron says, "It's true. Even Jesus on the cross asked 'Why.' God with all His power knows how to share our suffering too."

Sister Lin's second answer was, "I have gradually come to see that God's care is everywhere to be seen, if I can look beyond my own suffering." She pointed to the Christian family risking their own lives to help her.

Ron concludes, "She still feels the pain from her loss. The causes of her suffering have not been taken away. Neither has God given her an answer as to why He didn't save her husband and child. But she has taken her doubts to Him and entrusted the mystery of her suffering to Him because she trusts Him and He has come close."

RESPONSE:
Today I will look beyond the suffering I see around me and see God's love and care.

PRAYER:
Thank You Lord that You do care for Your creation and that in our moments of doubt You draw close and reveal the truth of Your love and care.

August 1

BOLD IN THE SPIRIT

My soul yearns, even faints, for the courts of the LORD;
my heart and my flesh cry out for the living God.
Psalm 84:2

Months ago a North Korean man successfully waded across the Tumen River into China looking for food, money and work in order to return later to his home country with help for his family. He was befriended by Korean-Chinese Christians (not an uncommon scenario among refugees there). As he sat in Christian meetings, an older woman said to him, "Receive the Holy Spirit or you can't go back into North Korea; it's too dangerous!"

After many discussions with believers, he confessed Jesus as Lord of his life and received the Holy Spirit. He packed Bibles along with his food cargo and crossed the river back to North Korea. Though it was a full moon night, there were no guards since everyone was watching North Korea play football (soccer) against Brazil in the World Cup games in South Africa.

As soon as he arrived home, he began talking about his new relationship with God. His family became irate. The young man's uncle tried to beat this "new idea" of God and Jesus out of him shouting, "How can you believe these things?"

The young man replied, "How can you not? Without God how do the sun and moon rotate?" The Holy Spirit gave words to the surprised young man. Soon the beating was forgotten and the uncle was listening intently. The whole family of this young man ultimately received Jesus as Saviour and Lord.

On returning to China for further training, he commented that unless people are filled with the Holy Spirit they should not go back to North Korea because the spiritual warfare is worse than ever.

He concluded, "Only with the Holy Spirit's help can we be bold. Pray for me that when I am caught I may be bold in my faith."

RESPONSE:
Today I will rely on the Holy Spirit to make me bold in my witness.

PRAYER:
Lord, my soul, my heart, my flesh, cry out to You for the filling and power of Your Holy Spirit.

August 2

FLEEING PERSECUTION

When you are persecuted in one place, flee to another.
Matthew 10:23a

One of the clear biblical responses to persecution is to flee. But it is not the only response. Thus it is imperative that the persecuted believer is sure that his running away is in the will of God. History is full of examples of Christians who relocated because of religious persecution.

The early Christians in Jerusalem were not obeying Jesus' orders in Acts 1:8 (evangelize to the ends of the earth) so God allowed an Acts 8:1 (persecution) to send them on their way. The original text indicates the persecution accomplished the will of God for as they scattered abroad, they went "gossiping" the gospel (Acts 8:4). The first meaning of the word "gossip" was "to chat" or "rehearse." The early Christians, when scattered by persecution, could not help but repeat the glorious message of the gospel to everyone they met.

The Apostle Paul left Damascus over the wall in a basket when a life threat was discovered early in his ministry. He was not just trying to avoid persecution, but he knew it was not yet God's timing for his life and ministry to end. That occurred years later in Rome.

Today an Egyptian Christian leader is in hiding because he has the highest price on his head—four times more than Osama Bin Laden ever had. Zakaria Botross' entire life story is that of defying death. The total price for his elimination (a fatwa), at last report, was one hundred million dollars. This is because his ministry to Muslims is so challenging, effective and productive. If his arguments cannot be countered then his voice must be silenced.

He was one of the most striking figures of the Coptic Orthodox Church. In 1964 he had a conversion experience which changed the direction of his ministry to thousands of people. Not only did Father Zakaria preach for conversions to Christ and to strengthen believers, he also effectively rebutted accusations against Christianity made by Islamic leaders. He is a scholar of ancient Arabic and knows the Koran and the Hadith (Islamic traditions) so thoroughly that Islamic scholars find it difficult to refute his teaching or counter his challenges.

His zealous activities could not help but attract the notice of the authorities of the State. He was removed from his church. Twice he experienced imprisonment for ministering to Muslims and leading them to faith in Jesus. He was accused of the ultimate crime, evangelizing Muslims and thereby inciting religious factionalism. Then he was deported and exiled from Egypt. His subsequent ministry in Australia and the UK was successful but not with everyone's approval.

Today as an elderly senior, he lives in hiding in the West because more than sixty million people—most are Muslims—watch his satellite TV programs and visit his website. Countless millions across the Arabic speaking world are turning to Christ annually because of his ministry.

Like the Apostle Paul, Father Zakaria runs and hides, not because he is afraid of dying, but by defying death has been able to have the most effective ministry in the world to Muslim people.

RESPONSE:
Today I will resolve to run from persecution only when I know it is the will of God.

PRAYER:
Pray for leaders like Zakaria Botross who have to live in hiding because of their effective ministry for the Lord and His church.

August 3

ENDURING PERSECUTION

"I will show him how much he must suffer for my name."
Acts 9:16

These are the words of Jesus to Ananias when Saul of Tarsus had an encounter with Jesus on the road to Damascus. Though Saul, who became the Apostle Paul, resorted to flight several times in his missionary work, he did not try to avoid persecution as a life style practice. Indeed in 2 Corinthians 11:23-27, Paul outlines and describes the repeated persecution he had endured for Christ.

The Bible and history are replete with examples of those who in the will of God refused to flee but stayed and endured the persecution to the point of self-sacrifice and even martyrdom.

A few years ago I was in Thailand for some organizational meetings. One of my colleagues brought a Vietnamese pastor to meet me who was in great anguish. His story touched me deeply.

Pastor Vin was at home in Vietnam one earlier evening when a parishioner knocked on the door. He had just met a sizable group of North Korean refugees who had trekked through China and become lost in the Vietnamese jungle. They were emaciated, ragged and fearful.

The Pastor invited the refugees to his home where they were fed and his people brought them adequate clothing. But what now? If discovered by the Vietnamese authorities, they would be repatriated to North Korea to certain death or life in labor camp. Their only hope was to seek asylum in neighboring Cambodia which did not have an extradition agreement with North Korea.

Then came a second knock on the door. It was the parishioner again. The Vietnamese authorities had been tipped off that North Korean refugees were in the area and were actively searching for them.

Pastor Vin knew the jungle route to Cambodia and knew what he had to do. Bidding his family farewell, he set off with the group of refugees and led them safely through the jungle to the capital of Cambodia where they successfully sought asylum as refugees.

But the Vietnamese authorities soon became aware of what the pastor had done. They notified his wife that he would be arrested and imprisoned immediately upon his arrival home. He fled further west to neighboring Thailand for safety.

The night I met him in Thailand he was in tears. His wife was scheduled for surgery the next day in the hospital back home in Vietnam. She so wanted him to be there with her during this trying time. Yet he could not safely return home. He was in a quandary. We prayed together that God would be with his wife in her medical emergency and give him wisdom to know what to do.

Later I heard from our colleague that Mrs. Vin's surgery was successful and that Pastor Vin, knowing what he would face, returned home to Vietnam. He was immediately arrested and placed under house detention. But he used his time at home discipling new believers.

Fleeing is not the only option when persecution strikes. There are times when God's will is for us to stay and face the music!

RESPONSE:
Today I will stay in tune with God's Spirit so that I will know what responses He wants me to make.

PRAYER:
Help me Lord to be aware of Your purposes in the events and challenges of my life.

August 4

APPEALING TO LEGAL RIGHTS

As they stretched him out to flog him, Paul said to the centurion standing there, "Is it legal for you to flog a Roman citizen who hasn't even been found guilty?"
Acts 22:25

The Scriptures illustrate responses to persecution in three primary ways. On the one hand is the command of Jesus to flee when it occurs and on the other, the stalwart example of those who stayed and endured, persevering through the challenges. In between is the example of the Apostle Paul (whose life responses exhibited both extremes also). When arrested in a mob violence scene in Acts 22, he appeals to his legal rights for protection from a needless beating. In Acts 25, he escapes almost certain death at the hands of the Jews and a corrupt judge by appealing to Caesar, again a right of his citizenship.

Pastor Abdias Tovilla studied law in order to help his indigenous people of Chiapas in southern Mexico who have been expelled from their homes simply because of their evangelical faith. He is following the model of the Apostle Paul who used whatever means possible to stand up to persecution.

You could say Abdias Tovilla practices two vocations—law and grace. Ordained as a pastor of the National Presbyterian Church of Mexico in 1981, Tovilla enrolled in the School of Law of the National Autonomous University of Chiapas the same year. He passed the bar exam in 1988 to become a licensed attorney and represent persecuted Christians. He resigned his pastorate in 1992 to be the Executive Secretary and Legal Advisor to the State Committee of Evangelical Defense for Chiapas (CEDECH), but is still a voting member of the Chiapas Presbyterian Synod and preaches on many Sundays at the invitation of local churches.

Abdias Tovilla has a concern for justice—especially for others. Dealing with injustice is also part of our Christian calling. Pastor Tovilla knows that those who speak out to denounce injustice are on the very front line of persecution themselves. He has gained some

433

support from Mexico's southernmost state Bishop who has appealed for an end to the violent and prolonged persecution of evangelical Christians by "traditionalist" Catholics. Bishop Felipe Arizmendi called for "no more expulsions nor divisions on the basis of religion" and asked that "there be no more destruction nor house-burnings, nor skirmishes, nor the shedding of blood due to religious, political, cultural or economic differences."

Over the past 30 years, religious intolerance has triggered the forced expulsion of some 35,000 evangelicals from ancestral lands in Chamula and other districts. Despite the unrelenting pressure, evangelical Christianity has grown steadily throughout Chiapas. Today, thirty-five per cent of the state population adheres to evangelicalism, according to census figures. Since the early 1980s, Open Doors has been working in Bible distribution, training and community development with a vision to contribute to reconciliation in the area.

RESPONSE:
Today I will speak out against injustice and discrimination of brothers wherever it occurs.

PRAYER:
Thank You, Lord, for brave brothers, like Abdias Tovilla, who stand for justice and truth.

August 5

FOUR-STAGE PROCESS OF PERSECUTION

Speak up for those who cannot speak for themselves,
for the rights of all who are destitute.
Proverbs 31:8

Jesus' basic communication theory in Matthew 12 is that people speak and act from the overflow of what is in their heart. Jeremiah and others remind us that the heart can be exceedingly wicked. One of Aleksandr Solzhenitsyn's famous statements is "The line of good and evil cuts through the heart of every human being."

Christian persecution within a country or state rarely happens suddenly or in isolation. It is most often a process. Some years ago Rev. Dr. Johan Candelin, who headed the World Evangelical Alliance's (WEA) Religious Liberties Commission recognized this and devised a three-stage process of what happens leading up to persecution becoming entrenched in any society. He labeled the three stages of downward spiral as *disinformation, discrimination* and *persecution*. Dr. Candelin later expanded it to a six-stage process with each of the three having a passive, then active, aspect.

Dr. Jim Cunningham and I included this process in the first edition of *Standing Strong Through The Storm* and in our seminars.

Some academicians and wordsmiths found it problematic to label the third stage with the same word as that of the process. So we began to wrestle with this issue from a sociological, historical and biblical perspective. We found interesting academic parallels. For example, in 1996, Professor Gregory Stanton, President of Genocide Watch, proposed an excellent model of an eight stage process of genocide. There are interesting similarities between this downward spiral and what psychologist John Gottman has labeled as the four most likely predictors of divorce.

When we accepted Jesus' four verb definition of persecution in Luke 6:22, we then found four clear biblical steps in understanding the downward spiral in the process of persecution: **opposition, disinformation, injustice and mistreatment**. We will look at these

435

four steps forming the acronym ODIM individually over the next four days.

Why is this important to you and me? Just today I read again the poignant words of German theologian Martin Niemoller written after he had been imprisoned for eight years in concentration camps as the personal prisoner of Adolf Hitler:

First they came for the Socialists, and I did not speak out because I was not a Socialist.

Then they came for the Trade Unionists, and I did not speak out because I was not a Trade Unionist.

Then they came for the Jews, and I did not speak out because I was not a Jew.

And then they came for me—and there was no one left to speak for me.

RESPONSE:
Today I will speak out for the rights of those who have no voice to speak for themselves.

PRAYER:
Help me, Lord, to be aware of the forces of evil that conspire against Your Kingdom.

August 6

THE PROCESS OF PERSECUTION-1: OPPOSITION

Consider [Jesus] who endured such opposition from sinful men, so that you will not grow weary and lose heart.
Hebrews 12:3

Whenever we ask audiences in free societies to word-associate "persecution," most responses are what we refer to as the "big three": torture, imprisonment and martyrdom. Many would agree that persecution is much more than the "big three" which are often only experienced in the final stage of the process of persecution.

Jesus repeatedly warned his followers that if the world hated Him, it would hate them also (John 15:18). In Luke 6:22, Jesus reminds his disciples that this opposition is a blessing. Not a blessing I ever hear many Christians praying for.

So the very basic and first step in this process is awareness that as a follower of Jesus, you can expect opposition, just as Jesus Himself experienced (Hebrews 12:3). He indicated that it will come from the world and possibly even from your own family and friends.

So do we walk around with a persecution complex, chip on our shoulder attitude, because of this? Absolutely not. The good news is that Jesus says we can live a life of joy in the midst of these troubles because He has overcome the world and so can we (John 16:33).

And this opposition is in every country and culture, not just those where severe persecution is being experienced. A few years ago Jim Cunningham and I wrote a little booklet about experiencing mild persecution right here in North America entitled *Red Skies @ Dawn* available at Open Doors offices. It is a dialogue between two young couples. Here's a relevant excerpt:

Sam responded. "Ultimately Satan, our real enemy, wants to destroy the church of Jesus Christ, wherever it's located. And Jesus Himself is the stumbling block to those who don't believe. When we say He is the only way, we are labeled as exclusivists and on this basis we are then considered intolerant."

Yvonne added, "I heard a program host on the radio the other day and he was obviously upset by this. When someone told him that Jesus is the only way to God, he shouted that we evangelicals are the scum of the earth!"

"Whoa," Sanjit reacted. "That's a little heavy, isn't it?"

Yvonne continued, "Well, he went on to say that it wasn't the belief to which he objected so much but he objected to the arrogance of any person claiming 'my way or the highway' and writing off the rest of the human race to eternal damnation."

All of this discussion clearly points out, "Sam concluded, "we are facing—and will face even more—attacks because of Jesus in us. Persecution may not be just for those brothers and sisters across the seas in places like East Africa and China, but perhaps even for us."

RESPONSE:
Today I will rejoice that in the face of general opposition to Jesus in me, I can be an overcomer like Jesus.

PRAYER:
Help me, Lord, to be aware of any opposition without it negatively affecting my witness.

August 7

THE PROCESS OF PERSECUTION–2: DISINFORMATION

Blessed are you when people…falsely say all kinds of evil against you because of me.
Matthew 5:11

This stage of persecution is characterized by unchecked ridicule and disinformation against a targeted group (Christian or others) most often spread through media. In this stage Christians are robbed of their good reputation and the right to answer the accusations made against them. Media, politics, entertainment, publications and schools are most often the avenues used to spread such insinuations or lies.

If disinformation about any group is disseminated long enough, no one will help in later stages because of this negative brain-washing about them. It essentially dehumanizes the person and is a pattern of thinking that may make it easier for milder wrongs to ignite a chain reaction of events. It creates an "us-versus-them" mentality.

A classic historic example is the gross disinformation the German Nazis spread about the Jews which then developed into a literal negative symbol when Jewish homes and businesses were marked with Stars of David and then targeted.

This also can result in verbal stereotyping. In the Rwanda genocide, the term "cockroach" became a negative classification of all Tutsi as conspirators against the government

There are many significant global examples of disinformation used against our Christian brothers and sisters. The influence and impact of negative television programs against Protestant Christians in an autonomous region in Central Asia is very strong. A local pastor was shown on TV and, without reference to any evidence, labelled "an enemy of the state." His family members' pictures were also shown at the same time causing them to be despised by their community.

Recently a Christian woman who was shown on TV was not able to continue her work in a kiosk in the market. Other vendors forced her to leave the bazaar.

One local pastor says, "Since the program is shown regularly on TV, persecution has become worse. Some people have left the church out of fear. When you start to preach (to the public), people close up and say, we have heard about you, we don't want to listen."

In North Korea, the entire society is controlled by propaganda and disinformation. Persecution is so severe that in many Christian families, children are not even told about the family's faith in Jesus until they are young adults because they are encouraged and expected to inform on their parents while in their school years. Christians are considered enemies of the state and the disinformation about this is wide spread.

Similarly, in countries like Laos, the government disinformation is that Christianity is an American religion being used to infiltrate their country rather than the former military methods. All Christians are thus portrayed as being traitors and working for America.

RESPONSE:
Today I will work for truth and quash all attempts at disinformation against followers of Jesus everywhere.

PRAYER:
Lord, grant Your blessing today on Your followers suffering from lies and untruths.

THE PROCESS OF PERSECUTION-3: INJUSTICE

In his humiliation he [Jesus] was deprived of justice.
Acts 8:33a

Christians experiencing persecution are following in the footsteps of their master, Jesus. In Acts chapter eight, Philip revealed to the Ethiopian eunuch that the passage from Isaiah 53 he was reading referred to Jesus who indeed was deprived of justice. Today in the Western world, we would describe His trial before crucifixion as occurring in a "kangaroo court!"

If disinformation about any group, including Christians, is disseminated long enough, no one will help when that group or person is discriminated against. Discrimination relegates Christians to second-class citizenship with inferior legal, social, political and economic status. Once discrimination takes place, no one will intervene when the mistreatment comes.

Examples of such injustice against Christians abound around the world: ID cards in a country where Christianity is an unacceptable entry in the religion column; daughters abducted because they are Christians; expulsion from the community just because they are evangelicals.

Christians in Pakistan are a small minority among a large Muslim majority and often face such discrimination. The problem is compounded by the fact that many Christians are illiterate and poor. One Christian teacher at a center training Christian women recently said, "We do face discrimination because we live in the midst of people who don't want us to move forward; people who keep trying to push us down so that we will always be in slavery."

But there is one repeated scene of injustice against Christians that occurs in Pakistan which brings me to tears. It involves young Christian girls. As a father of two daughters and having six granddaughters, I shudder every time I read news reports that describe Christian family injustice in this land. The stories usually work out this way:

Muslim women must marry Muslim men but Muslim men are

allowed to marry any woman they wish with the proviso that any children must be raised as Muslim. Consequently in Pakistan there are Muslim men who often desire some of the very beautiful young Christian girls in the community but realize there is no way their Christian families will agree to marriage. So these men resort to abduction.

The Christian father's only option is to go to court where the judge—usually a Muslim—hears the case and pronounces to the Christian father, "Your daughter voluntarily converted to Islam and voluntarily married this Muslim man so you are to have no more contact with her. One of the most recent cases involved two young Christian sisters aged thirteen and ten. In this case, the judge allowed the ten-year-old to return home to her family but not the thirteen-year-old.

Safwan, a secret believer in Algeria, found a Christian pamphlet between the paperwork given him at work and started reading it. Upon discovering him reading the pamphlet, his boss reported him to the police. Later that night the police visited him and searched his entire home. They found Christian CD's, several Christian movies and a New Testament. "It was clear to them that I had become a Christian. My boss fired me."

RESPONSE:
Today I will work toward justice for everyone in my own country and around the world.

PRAYER:
Lord, be with those experiencing discrimination today because they love and serve You.

442

August 9

THE PROCESS OF PERSECUTION-4: MISTREATMENT

For it has been granted to you on behalf of Christ not only to believe in him, but also to suffer for him...
Philippians 1:29

"When the process gets to persecution [mistreatment following disinformation and discrimination], no one will do anything because, 'You know they are bad people anyway,'" says Rev. Dr. Johan Candelin referring to his three-step process of persecution model.

Once the first steps in the process occur, mistreatment can be practiced without normal protective measures taking place. Persecution can arise from the state, the police or military, extremist organizations, paramilitary groups, anti-Christian sub-cultures and even representatives of other religious groups. The irony is that in many parts of the world, the accusations of the attackers turn the victims into the villains.

This stage is the end result and includes the "big three": torture, imprisonment and martyrdom which are most often the examples used for persecution. A specific example would be the imprisonment of hundreds of evangelical Christians in Eritrea without formal charges—many kept in metal shipping containers.

In Iran, a Christian couple were detained and physically and psychologically tortured for four days. The authorities even threatened to lock up their four-year-old daughter in an "institution." Twenty-eight-year-old Tina Rad from Teheran was accused of "activities against the holy religion of Islam," because she was reading the Bible with Muslims. Her thirty-one-year-old husband, Makan Arya, was accused of having endangered national security. Both of them had only been Christians for three months. Muslim converts meet together in small groups to talk about the gospel, to grow in the Christian faith and to encourage one another. They have made a vast transition from Islam to Christianity and they have a great need of training, security and a sense of belonging. The church tries to provide for this need and becomes the new "family."

When they were released, the threats started. "If you don't stop with your Jesus, next time we will charge you with apostasy," Tina was told. In Iran, this can mean the death penalty.

Jamaa Ait Bakrim in Morocco is also serving time for his faith. Moroccan Christians and advocates question the harsh measures of the Muslim state toward a man who dared speak openly about Jesus. An outspoken Christian convert, Bakrim was sentenced to fifteen years prison for "proselytizing" and destroying "the goods of others" in 2005 after burning two defunct utility poles located in front of his private business in a small town in south Morocco.

Advocates and Moroccan Christians said, however, that the severity of his sentence in relation to his misdemeanor shows that authorities were determined to put him behind bars because he persistently spoke about his faith. "He became a Christian and didn't keep it to himself," said a Moroccan Christian and host for Al Hayat Television who goes only by his first name, Rachid, for security reasons. "He shared it with people around him. They will just leave him in the prison so he dies spiritually and psychologically," said Rachid.

RESPONSE:
Today I will do everything possible to represent my persecuted brothers and sisters.

PRAYER:
Pray for Christians experiencing mistreatment and persecution around the world today.

August 10

THE SOURCE OF PERSECUTION

Then Haman said to King Xerxes, "There is a certain people dispersed among the peoples in all the provinces of your kingdom who keep themselves separate. Their customs are different from those of all other people, and they do not obey the king's laws; it is not in the king's best interest to tolerate them.

Esther 3:8

Today we feature the first in a series from a house church pastor's sermon in China:

The Bible is written to persecuted communities, and we must learn from each community the peculiar blessings and dangers of persecution. I would like to draw your attention to some lessons from the persecuted community in the time of Esther.

Esther was Queen of Persia sometime after 483 BC. She was a beautiful woman with a secret—no one except her adopted father knew it. It was her racial origin. She was a Jew.

There came a great persecution. In Esther 3:8, we read that the king of Persia's advisor says he should not tolerate a certain group of people. The king agrees, and issues a decree calling for the extermination of all Jews.

The Jews are devastated, including Esther. How they got into this situation, how they get out of it, and what happened afterwards all reveal great truths about suffering churches—of which we are one.

Where does persecution come from? What is its source? The text shows us clearly. Persecution is the result of pride. Pride on the part of the persecutor.

Haman is the culprit. He is humiliated because a Jew called Mordecai refuses to bow low enough to him. We are not given the reason why Mordecai would deliver such a calculated snub, but it makes Haman see red. Instead of just trying to get rid of Mordecai, though, he has to project his personal humiliation into something grand. He won't admit it's all just a personal grudge, but concocts an elaborate plan to get rid of all Jews because they are in breach of the king's laws.

His plan is a good one. The Jews are different, he says. True. They are so different, they are not good citizens, he adds. False, but the king is right to be suspicious of any group that seems to have other loyalties than just to him. It's the same in China. Our government persecutes us because we are different. We are honest, separate, and we have greater loyalties than just to the state. That makes us an object of suspicion.

But the root of it all is pride. The cause of the persecution was simply that Haman was angry. I have read that in Russia, the terrible persecutions that were visited upon the churches there came from the fact that Lenin's brother was shot by the Tsar's forces, and what galled him in particular was that a Russian Orthodox priest blessed the proceedings. He carried his personal hatred with him…It's a pride matter. It always is. The source of suffering is always found in human pride.

RESPONSE:
Today I will check my pride at the door and realize that God is still in control!

PRAYER:
Pray that prideful leaders will humble themselves to acknowledge the God of the universe.

August 11

SOLUTION TO PERSECUTION

"I will go to the king, even though it is against the law.
And if I perish, I perish."
Esther 4:16b

Today we have the second in the series from a house church pastor's sermon in China:

How is suffering overcome? Or if you like, what is the solution to persecution? A church father answered this way: "Pray as if everything depends on God. Work as if God were going to do his work through you." So when resisting persecution, we do everything humanly possible to lessen it. But then we also beseech God to put a stop to it. In the two comes deliverance.

You can see both sides involved here. On the human level, we see two characteristics coming to the fore especially—courage and cunning. Esther is the one who displays courage, by taking her life in her hands to enter the king's presence without an appointment. She says, "If I perish, I perish." What a brave woman! She's also the one who displays cunning, hatching a plan to entrap Haman. She throws a banquet, reveals her racial identity, and then exposes Haman as the man who wants to kill her.

Would it have worked? Who knows? Perhaps not. Haman did have great clout with the king as a trusted advisor, and Esther was merely a queen, and queens—as made clear here—are easily replaceable.

But it did work out, thanks to God. And this is the other side. We pray and pray that God will intervene. There is so much that is beyond our control. Our planning, our cunning, our bravery, is never enough. We need God's help. So the Jews have a time of weeping and repentance (Esther 4:1-3), and then God intervenes in an astonishing way.

An old pastor used to say to me, "I find that coincidences stop happening when I stop praying." The resolution of the book of Esther hinges on a massive coincidence, namely, that at the precise moment Haman expects to kill Mordecai, the king decides to honor Mordecai.

Both men reach each situation independently. Take the king, for instance:

- The king **just happens** to have a sleepless night before Haman will pitch his plan.
- He **just happens** to read the annals to get to sleep, and just happens to find the part that tells of a good deed of Mordecai.
- He **just happens** to decide to honor Mordecai the following morning at the very moment Haman comes into the room.
- He **just happens** to select the first person who walks into his room at that time to carry out his plan.
- That person is Haman, who **just happens** to be ready to ask for the head of Mordecai.

And through a misunderstanding, the king decides to put Haman to death, as he thinks Haman is molesting Esther when in fact he's only pleading. The point is, all this is outside human control. It's God's doing. But He worked within Esther's plan. And so the plan to persecute the Jews is foiled.

RESPONSE:
Today I acknowledge that there are no coincidences, just God-incidences!

PRAYER:
Help me, Lord, to be faithful and see evidences of Your control over my circumstances.

August 12

THE STRENGTH OF PERSECUTION

Indeed, we felt we had received the sentence of death.
But this happened that we might not rely on ourselves but
on God, who raises the dead. He has delivered us from
such a deadly peril, and he will deliver us again.
On him we have set our hope that he will continue to
deliver us, as you help us by your prayers. Then many
will give thanks on our behalf for the gracious favor
granted us in answer to the prayers of many.
2 Corinthians 1:9-11

The conclusion of the message on the book of Esther from a house church pastor in China:

I wish the book of Esther ended before chapter nine, but it does not. The book ends with the Jews taking revenge on all their enemies everywhere. They arranged a kind of amnesty for terrorism. For a day, they were allowed to kill anyone who had oppressed them and not be prosecuted for it. Thousands probably died. It was a kind of rough justice, but what does rough justice solve? It just makes the relatives of those slain burn with hatred, and they train their children to seek more revenge, and the weary cycle of bloodletting is accelerated.

I would apply this to the suffering church this way. Surviving a persecution situation involves desperation, but that desperation can turn into harshness and heresy if one is not careful. The terrible superstitions that came into the church in venerating the bones of martyrs were a response to persecution. Persecution brings martyrs. To revere martyrs is one thing. But to worship their relics as if they are a special lever to move the hand of God with—that is terrible.

Why is the book of Esther in the Bible? Because it tells us that God helps His people. If this decree had gone through, then a holocaust would have taken place and the will of God for the world would have been lost. We would have had no Bible otherwise. God was not going to let that happen, and He stretched forth His mighty arm to prevent it. The good news of His gospel must be spread. So reading about how

God intervened must have given great increase to a Jew's faith, as it increases ours too. God intervenes to save and get His will done. And His will is that all come to know Him and love Him.

So persecution can strengthen our faith, as we see God delivering His people powerfully and getting His will done.

I stand before you now, a living witness to the strength of suffering. We come out stronger, not because of our faith, but because we see God deliver us in mighty ways. We have to; otherwise we would be dead and gone. Praise God for persecution, for building His church no matter what the opposition.

Let us have the courage of Esther, and say, *"If I perish, I perish."* But let us remember that our courage is decisive only because God is mighty, and stretches out His arm to deliver us when we cry.

RESPONSE:
Today I will focus on God's deliverance and stand strong trusting Him for the future.

PRAYER:
Pray today for the Persecuted Church. Pray they will find their strength only in the Lord.

August 13

ENCOURAGEMENT

For everything that was written in the past was written to teach us, so that through endurance and the encouragement of the Scriptures we might have hope.
Romans 15:4

In Eritrea, Helen Berhane, with more than twenty other young women, was imprisoned in a shipping container that held only eighteen people. In her book, *Song of the Nightingale*, she shares what happened:

When [the guard] had locked us in and left, many of the women were furious and upset, and began to complain and cry. I tried to find ways to encourage them, and to make our situation more bearable. I encouraged everyone to sit on the floor in a circle and I began to speak to them.

'Remember that the walls of Jericho came down because of praises. If we keep complaining, we cannot win. Instead we must continue to pray, praise and sing. Satan wants to use discouraging words as a weapon against us, so we must continue to praise God in all circumstances.'

I could see some of the women nodding.

I continued, "When the Israelites were approaching the Promised Land they sent spies ahead. Many of them returned saying that the people were so huge the Israelites could not hope to beat them, and so they cried all night. But crying and complaining cannot solve our problems. Let us be like Caleb and Joshua. The larger our enemies are, the more of a feast they will make for us! Just think about the woman who suffered from bleeding and who believed that if she only touched the hem of Jesus' robe she would be healed. In the crowd she was the one who had faith and it was rewarded. We should not be like these people endlessly fighting amongst themselves. We should just reach out to Jesus and have faith.

This helped us to feel more accepting of our situation, and so we got into the habit of talking about the Bible, praying and singing in the container every day.[29]

RESPONSE:
Today I will pray, sing, and talk about the Bible rather than focus on my discouraging situations and relationships.

PRAYER:
Lord, may I use Your Word as an encouragement to endure with hope in You.

---

29 Helen Berhane, *Song of the Nightingale* (Colorado Springs: Authentic Media, 2009), pp. 38-39.

August 14

SELFLESSNESS

Do nothing out of selfish ambition or vain conceit, but in humility consider others better than yourselves. Each of you should look not only to your own interests, but also to the interests of others.

Philippians 2:3-4

Brother Andrew loves to tell this parable from the Middle East:

A certain man had two sons. One was rich and the other was poor. The rich son had no children while the poor son was blessed with many sons and many daughters. In time, the father fell ill. He was sure he would not live through the week, so on Saturday he called his sons to his side and gave each of them half of his land for their inheritance. Then he died. Before sundown the sons buried their father with respect.

That night the rich son could not sleep. He said to himself, "What my father did was not just. I am rich and my brother is poor. I have plenty of bread while my brother's children eat one day and trust God for the next. I must move the landmark which our father has set in the middle of the land so that my brother will have the greater share. Ah – but he must not see me; if he sees me, he will be shamed. I must arise early in the morning before it is dawn and move the landmark!" With this he fell asleep and his sleep was secure and peaceful.

Meanwhile, the poor brother could not sleep. As he lay restless on his bed, he said to himself, "What my father did was not just. Here I am surrounded by the joy of many sons and daughters while my brother daily faces the shame of having no sons to carry on his name and no daughters to comfort him in his old age. He should have the land of our fathers. Perhaps this will in part compensate him for his indescribable poverty. Ah – but if I give it to him, he will be shamed. I must awake early in the morning before it is dawn and move the landmark which our father has set!" With this he went to sleep and his sleep was secure and peaceful.

On the first day of the week – very early in the morning, a long time before it was day, the two brothers met at the ancient land marker.

They fell with tears into each other's arms. And on that spot was built the New Jerusalem.

RESPONSE:
Today I will focus on the needs and interests of others rather than on my own.

PRAYER:
Pray that this biblical attitude of love, humility and selflessness will pervade the church of Jesus Christ in the Middle East today and around the world.

August 15

LOVE YOUR ENEMIES

But I tell you: Love your enemies and pray for those who persecute you...
Matthew 5:44

Perhaps the most difficult of Jesus' commands is to love even our enemies. A true Christian always seeks another person's highest good—even when mistreated. Brother Andrew says **"The Christian's only method of destroying his enemies is to 'love' them into being his friends."**

Romanian pastor, Dr. Paul Negrut, was visiting an old friend in Romania named Trian Dors in his humble home. As Paul entered, he realized that Trian was bleeding from open wounds. He asked, "What happened?"

Trian replied, "The secret police just left my home. They came and confiscated my manuscripts. Then they beat me."

Pastor Paul says, "I began to complain about the heavy tactics of the secret police. But Trian stopped me saying, 'Brother Paul, it is so sweet to suffer for Jesus. God didn't bring us together tonight to complain but to praise him. Let's kneel down and pray."

"He knelt and began praying for the secret police. He asked God to bless them and save them. He told God how much he loved them. He said, 'God, if they will come back in the next few days, I pray that you will prepare me to minister to them.'"

Paul continued, "By this time I was ashamed. I thought I had been living the most difficult life in Romania for the Lord. And I was bitter about that."

Trian Dors then shared with Paul how the secret police had been coming to his home regularly for several years. They beat him twice every week. They confiscated all his papers. After the beating he would talk to the officer in charge. Trian would look into his eyes and say, "Mister, I love you. And I want you to know that if our next meeting is before the judgement throne of God, you will not go to hell because I hate you but because you rejected love." Trian would repeat these words after every beating.

Years later that officer came alone to his home one night. Trian prepared himself for another beating. But the officer spoke kindly and said, "Mr. Dors, the next time we meet will be before the judgement throne of God. I came tonight to apologize for what I did to you and to tell you that your love moved my heart. I have asked Christ to save me. But two days ago the doctor discovered that I have a very severe case of cancer and I have only a few weeks to live before I go to be with God. I came tonight to tell you that we will be together on the other side."

RESPONSE:
Today I will destroy my enemies only with love.

PRAYER:
God give me Your kind of love for my enemies—so they too will love You.

August 16

IDENTIFYING WITH CHRISTIAN PRISONERS

Continue to remember those in prison as if you were together with them in prison, and those who are mistreated as if you yourselves were suffering.
Hebrews 13:3

The letter to the Hebrews was written to first century Jewish believers in Jesus who were being persecuted. Some were so discouraged they were considering returning to Judaism. The writer encourages them to persevere because of the superiority of Jesus over everything and everyone else. And He will return to establish the ultimate kingdom.

Chapter 13 begins the author's final instructions. First we are to continue (repeated action) loving one another as brothers and sisters. This love is to be practical and reach out even to strangers who we are to entertain as we may not realize when one might be an angel. Then in our verse for today, our love is to extend to those who are in prison for their faith, even to the point of assuming we are in there with them. That makes a huge difference as to how we show practical love.

Russian Christian prisoner, Aleksandr Ogorodnikov, shares, "One night I was thrown into a cell with a broken window. The KGB was determined to do an experiment and freeze me. Later they would say, 'He broke the window in his cell and died of cold.' I felt despair. I thought to myself, 'Has God really left me? Am I really forgotten and neglected? Have my years of suffering been in vain?' "And in my despair I began to pray.

I usually pray silently, but this time I started to appeal to God out loud. 'God, have You left me?' My cries were bursting from a heart literally in utter despair."And right then, I suddenly felt a palpable physical warmth. Not the kind that comes from a heater, but like when a mother draws her freezing child to her breast, and warms him with her tearful breath of compassion. It was a very living, human warmth. It penetrates you, as if piercing you to the heart. And inside

457

your heart a spring opens up, out of which flows peace—a wonderful, magnificent, soothing peace. "I felt a very loving, brotherly touch—someone's caring hand touching my shoulder. I actually *felt it*.

In the morning, it was a shock to my executioners. They couldn't understand. I wasn't simply alive, but my temperature was the same as that of a normal person. I heard a doctor explaining to my executioners in the corridor, 'This is impossible! We can't explain it.' "It so happened that many people began praying for me. And that was exactly when they released me."

RESPONSE:
I will continue to remember my brothers and sisters around the world who are in prison for their faith.

PRAYER:
Lord, give the sense and touch of Your presence to those suffering for You in prison today.

August 17

SINGING TO THE LORD

One thing I ask of the Lord, this is what I seek: that I may dwell in the house of the Lord all the days of my life, to gaze upon the beauty of the Lord and to seek him in his temple…Then my head will be exalted above the enemies who surround me; at his tabernacle will I sacrifice with shouts of joy; I will sing and make music to the Lord.
Psalm 27:4,6

Brother Zhang, a young medical doctor and preacher in Zhejiang, China, refused to join the government Three Self Patriotic Church. He was arrested and spent eighteen years in prison eating poor food, being beaten and drowning in the stench of cellmates. He shares this testimony:

"The eighteen years were a tremendous spiritual challenge, which brought great blessings I never before thought possible in my life. Prison officials ordered me to empty the camp night-soil pit, the prison's cesspool. While I had little experience of physical labor, its hardship and suffering did not frighten me. Although most of the other prisoners dreaded night-soil pit duty as the most difficult task in prison, I accepted this assignment without complaint. The pit stored all the human excrement, both liquid and solid, from the entire camp. Once the pit was full, its human waste steeped until its foul contents were ripe enough to be used as fertilizer. Not only did I walk into this disease-ridden mess to remove it, but I had to breathe its stench as I scooped away each successive layer and dropped hundreds of shovel loads into collection buckets for others to carry to the fields.

"The night-soil pit's pungent odors lingered with the digger at least three days, literally surrounding him with an almost maddening stench. All the guards and other prisoners avoided the night-soil pit digger to escape being overcome by the lingering odor. One reason I could enjoy working in the night-soil pit was the solitude. Surrounded only by foul air and human waste, I could sing music of praise to God as loudly as I wanted. And the guards were never close enough to protest this otherwise objectionable behavior!

"One of my favorite songs during those days was 'In the Garden.' My Chinese night-soil pit was hardly the garden that the composer of that hymn had in mind! But God delivered great happiness to me to be able to sing His praises in such earthly misery."

RESPONSE:
Today I will sing praises to God no matter how terrible my circumstances turn out to be.

PRAYER:
Lord, may all Christian prisoners experience the joy of praising You in their trials this day.

August 18

PERSEVERANCE

You need to persevere so that when you have done the will of God, you will receive what he has promised. For, "In just a little while, he who is coming will come and will not delay."
Hebrews 10:36-37

The greatest example of Christian perseverance for me is Sister Alice Yuan from China. Her pastor husband, Allen Yuan, was imprisoned for almost twenty-two years for refusing to join the government controlled church in the middle 1950's. She says:

"When my husband Allen was sent to prison in April 1958, I was told that I would never see him again. I felt completely miserable and continually blamed God. The future looked so terribly bleak. I had the care of six children and my mother-in-law. I was only earning 80 cents a day. How could I keep my family alive on that?

"When it all became too much for me, one night I heard a voice: 'My child, I have everything in My hands. These things come from Me.' I replied, 'If these things come from You, please protect me and my family. Do not allow me to dishonor Your name. I want to serve You and glorify Your name'

"Then I received peace in my heart. I was encouraged by Psalm 68:19, *Praise be to the Lord, to God our Savior, who daily bears our burdens.* In those difficult years, people let me down, but God never abandoned me. But he did put me through trials.

"The first trial was the struggle to survive. I was only earning 80 cents a day. How could we get by on that? But God took care of us, in the same way that he took care of Elijah. He promised to be my shepherd and provider.

"One evening, my mother-in-law said that there was no food anymore in the house. The next morning, at five to six there was a knock on the door. 'Are you sister Alice?' asked a woman in her sixties, whom I didn't know. 'God wanted me to give you this.' She put a package in my hand and disappeared. When I opened the parcel I found there was rice in it and some other food and a banknote to the value of about four month's salary of a professor! Praise the Lord. Where man comes to an end, God begins! This was only one of the many miracles which kept us alive all those years."

Tomorrow we'll conclude her story of faithfulness and perseverance as well as God's miraculous care for His own.

RESPONSE:
Today I will not complain about discomforts but thank God for all His blessings!

PRAYER:
Lord, You desire faithfulness and perseverance. Help me develop these qualities in my life.

August 19

FAITHFUL PERSEVERANCE

"But my righteous one will live by faith. And I take no pleasure in the one who shrinks back." But we do not belong to those who shrink back and are destroyed, but to those who have faith and are saved.

Hebrews 10:38-39

Alice Yuan continues her testimony we began yesterday:

"The second trial came from the Communist party. Every day for nineteen years, I had to report to the police station, where for six hours, they put pressure on me. They said that I would never see my husband again, that I should divorce him and that I should give up my faith. With God's help I kept going. Praying with my eyes closed, I endured the interrogations every day.

"The third trial consisted of the hard work. After I had been pressured by the security police for six hours, I still had to work for eight hours to earn a living. I had to push handcarts filled with building materials. The carts were much too heavy. I was completely exhausted and was already tired before I started. In the winter, it was even worse. Sometimes I had to shovel cement up onto a floor above my head. The work was dirty, hard and cold, but I achieved my quota. The others were surprised and wondered where I got the energy from.

"The fourth trial had to do with my natural desires. I was thirty-nine-years-old when my husband was taken away. The authorities put me under pressure to marry someone else. All my papers would be changed, so that I could start a new life without all the difficulties. I was offered money and clothing. God loved me so much that He gave me the strength to resist all these temptations. When I prayed to God, He gave me everything I needed, and even more than that.

"My favorite text is Psalm 68:6, *God sets the lonely in families, he leads forth the prisoners with singing.*"

It is a miracle that her husband, Allen Yuan, got out of the labour camp alive. In December 1979, he was released after twenty-one years and eight months. He was then sixty-five years old, thin but still healthy. At an age when many people are enjoying retirement, Allan again took up his vocation as a pastor. He died on August 16th 2005 at the age of ninety-one. Alice joined him in heaven in early August 2010 to hear her own *"Well done!"*

RESPONSE:
I resolve to persevere, with faith in a good God, through all the trials that come my way.

PRAYER:
Lord, may all Your children experiencing severe persecution today be filled with faith and refuse to shrink back. Help me to emulate these great examples of faithful perseverance.

August 20

ENDURANCE AND ENCOURAGEMENT

May the God who gives endurance and encouragement give you the same attitude of mind toward each other that Christ Jesus had...

Romans 15:5

Zinaida Vilchinskaya was a grandmother at the time she was arrested in the Soviet Union while carrying Christian literature. She shares a poignant episode of how one believer can encourage another in endurance during difficult circumstances:

When the police first took me to the police station, I was put in a very cold cell with bare iron bunks. The guards took my scarf and my coat, and I lay on the bunk in just a dress. I was shivering, and I started to pray. When my cellmate saw me pray, she, too, got on her knees and said, "Oh, I can't stand it. I'm freezing too." She started to cry softly.

"Lord," I prayed, "if You want me to be frozen here, may Your will be done; just enable me to endure this with love, submission, and meekness. But You can help me. You can even take me out of here if that's Your will."

I lay back down and felt such warmth. I told the other woman, "Here, let me put my arm around you, and you'll get warmer." We warmed up together. Later when they transferred us to different cells, she told everyone in hers, "God warmed up Aunt Zhenya (as they called me) in our cell, and she warmed me up."

When a local pastor from South Sudan had the vision of starting a Bible School in an isolated area, he soon realized that the school needed help in feeding the hard working students. Each local congregation chose a number of young ladies to assist as kitchen workers. They fed at least seventy people daily and started a heartfelt tradition of singing Christian songs while serving the students.

Women from other congregations would also come to visit the students bearing gifts in the form of woven baskets, buckets filled with food and bundles of wood on their heads. The main purpose is encouragement and practical assistance. Their arrival is also identifiable with joyful singing. The humble services, gifts, encouragements and prayers of all these women have an uplifting effect on the students. It gives them the freedom to focus completely on their theological studies and become equipped for God's calling on their lives. Encouragement is a powerful gift!

RESPONSE:
Today I will seek to find ways to encourage others going through the same challenges I have faced.

PRAYER:
Lord, give me the mind of Jesus toward others in order that Your endurance and encouragement may flow through me.

August 21

LIVE EACH DAY AS YOUR LAST

[God] comforts us in all our troubles, so that we can comfort those in any trouble with the comfort we ourselves receive from God.
2 Corinthians 1:4

On that fateful Sunday morning in January 1996, Joy Dimerin's beloved fiancé, Severino Bagtasos, was killed when a lone gunman stormed into the church that he pastored and shot him twice. Severino was killed on the first day of the Islamic holy month of Ramadan, in the predominantly Muslim town of Alat on Jolo island, in southern Philippines. He had a zeal in reaching Muslims for Christ. Joy and Severino were supposed to get married in May 1997.

"By the grace of God, I am doing well and still enjoying the ministry," testifies Joy. She admits that feelings of loneliness and emptiness were the most difficult things she faced after her beloved Severino died. "I was afraid that I wouldn't find a godly man like him again," confides Joy. "I learned to see God's purpose in my life," Joy added. "I learned to accept whatever circumstances come my way and look at them as God's instruments in molding me and in making me a better person. Through [Severino's] life I learned commitment to the ministry and to prayer. Through his death, I learned to always be prepared to face the Author and Finisher of my faith. Through this tragedy, I learned to live each day as though it were my last."

Severino's killer was a Tausug. "God had intended it to be so," she says. As a Tausug she feels compassion for her people because they are blinded by their beliefs. She now serves the Lord by reaching out to them and the Sama Muslims of southern Philippines. "I have forgiven the one who killed Junie. It's hard to live with the hurt, the pain, and an unforgiving spirit, especially as I work with Muslims. I have learned to look at them the way God does. It's only through the gospel that they will change," said Joy with no trace of bitterness in her voice. The people who wanted Severino dead had the opportunity to hear the gospel during Severino's funeral service, perhaps the only time they would hear the love of Christ preached openly.

Joy received thousands of letters from all over the world through Open Doors, giving her words of comfort and assuring her of prayers being said for her. In a letter to her encouragers, she wrote, "Two years of being broken-hearted led me to spiritual wholeness." This was one of the paradoxes in her life. "I learned to be independent but dependent upon God, especially with regards to my daily walk with Him. I learned to be courageous and tough, but soft-hearted to the needy and suffering Christians." Perhaps, only those who have suffered can truly understand those who are suffering. And those who have experienced healing can truly empathize with those who are hurting.

Four years later, God brought Joy on staff with Open Doors. "I never thought that God would call me to minister to the Persecuted Church through Open Doors. God had allowed the great pain in my life for me to understand those who are in pain. He allowed me to suffer that I may best minister to the suffering."

RESPONSE:
I will live today as though it were my last: loving, forgiving, serving!

PRAYER:
Pray for Joy in her important ministry in the Muslim areas of the southern Philippines.

August 22

SINGING IN THE STORM

But I trust in your unfailing love; my heart rejoices in
your salvation. I will sing the LORD's praise,
for he has been good to me.
Psalm 13:5-6

The Psalmist expresses his praise in the context of asking God for deliverance from his enemies. His trust results in rejoicing which then results in singing God's praises.

A simple peasant girl from the countryside in China has used her musical creativity to encourage the house church movement all across China and touch the lives of millions of believers.

Xiao Min was born in a village in Henan Province in central China and has experienced much persecution. Though only receiving a junior high level education, she has been able to compose over 1,270 different hymns—both music and lyrics—that are sung by the Chinese churches in China and now throughout the world. They are known as the Canaan Hymns. Amazing creativity for a young lady with no musical training!

Xiao Min shares that twenty years ago many believers were arrested by the Chinese government. At that time, she prayed to the Lord asking if she could also be arrested and suffer together with these fellow believers. Soon after, she was indeed arrested and sent to prison. She says that she wasn't scared at all.

One summer day in prison when it was extremely hot she requested the guard to let everyone wash their hair. But she received a rude response telling her to ask the Lord Jesus to wash their hair for them. She used this discouraging response as an inspiration to write hymn number 56, "Lord, We Know Deeply" in the Canaan Hymns series.

In this hymn, Xiao Min sings:

Lord we know deeply that in every moment Your love never, never diminishes.

Lord we know deeply that in every moment, our only friend
is You.

Our hearts long for You, our hearts long for You,

Because You're the first in millions, no one can be compared
with You,

No one can be compared with you."

Not only was Xiao Min arrested because of her faith, she was also
persecuted by her family members. But she still testified to them that
God healed her sinusitis and that He is her Savior. She concludes,
"Even though we experience suffering, the Lord Jesus gives us
strength." Her strength enables her to sing to the Lord in the face of all
difficulties.

RESPONSE:
**Today I will sing praises to the Lord no matter how difficult the
journey.**

PRAYER:
**I ask, Lord, for the grace to be able to vocalize my trust and joy
and praise of You!**

August 23

JOY IN THE MORNING

Religion that God our Father accepts as pure and faultless is this: to look after orphans and widows in their distress and to keep oneself from being polluted by the world.

James 1:27

God's love compels us to feed the hungry, empower the poor, defend the weak and help those who are suffering. When we do these things, it includes encouraging and strengthening those persecuted for their faith in Christ. The church has often led the way in education and medical services in developing countries until governments or other local agencies take over.

Brother Andrew says that giving humanitarian aid is a picture of Jesus knocking at the door of our hearts (our lives) in Revelation Chapter Three. The doors of many hearts in the church are closed to acts of mercy and love in action. Therefore, Jesus stands knocking at the door of our hearts asking that we open that door and let Him in. His coming into our lives enables us to do acts of love.

"They killed my husband before my very own eyes. As if that wasn't enough, they destroyed everything by burning down our house including my dear husband's workshop." These were the words of Esther, the widow whose husband was killed by jihadists in Nigeria in January 2010.

For the mother of seven, life became unbearable. The house that her children called home no longer existed and the daunting absence of an income was an inevitable reality. To worsen their circumstances, the in-laws abandoned Esther and her children. Surrounded by walls of a room too small for eight people, depression threatened to overshadow her and Esther cried night and day, asking God for a way out.

She truly needed a shoulder to lean on. A friend told us her story and from there Open Doors provided financial support for this family. As a result the family was able to move into an apartment in a Christian area, with enough room for everyone. The new home lent enough space for Esther to even start working from home. She is a tailor by profession and hopes to rent a shop in the near future.

Esther thought it wise to take some of the money and start a vegetable garden on a small scale. The idea is to feed her family and at the same time generate an income from it. She is confident that her vegetable business will grow to the point where she will be able to send the children to school.

"If Open Doors had not come to my aid," Esther concluded with tears, "what would have become of me and my children? For all I know, we all would have been dead, either by the hands of Jihadists or hunger. As for my husband's killers—though it's been difficult—through your prayers and encouragement I've been able to forgive them."

RESPONSE:
Today I will live in awareness of those around me needing help and respond appropriately.

PRAYER:
Lord, give me Your compassion for people in need. May I be an agent of Your love today.

August 24

BE A GOOD STEWARD OF YOUR TRIALS

*Therefore, among God's churches we boast about your
perseverance and faith in all the persecutions
and trials you are enduring.*
2 Thessalonians 1:4

The Apostle Paul praises the church in Thessalonica for their faith
and love in the face of persecutions and trials. In essence he is telling
them that they are good stewards of their trials, not letting them
impact their faith negatively.

I recently heard gospel singer Lynda Randall express this same
thought of "being a good steward of the trials I face," as she
introduced her next solo "It is Well With My Soul."

The lyrics of this hymn were written by Horatio Spafford, a lawyer
of some prominence in Chicago. He and his wife Anna had one son
and four daughters, and were good friends of D.L. Moody and Ira
Sankey for many years. Mr. Spafford's children had come to Christ
through the influence of Ira Sankey's music. When the Spafford's son
died, the family went into deep mourning.

After two years of ministering to the homeless and needy people
of Chicago, Mr. Spafford thought his family needed a vacation. D.
L. Moody and Ira Sankey were in England holding evangelistic so
Mr. Spafford decided to take his family to England, where they could
vacation and also be a help to his friends Moody and Sankey.

He booked passage for his family on the ship *SS Ville de Havre*, but
at the last minute was unable to go with his family due to business.
He promised to follow them within a few weeks and they would all be
reunited in England.

As the ship sailed across the Atlantic Ocean, it collided with the
English ship *Lochearn*, and sank within 12 minutes. 226 lives were
lost, including the four Spafford daughters. Mrs. Spafford was rescued
from a floating piece of debris. When she arrived in Wales 10 days
later she cabled a message to her husband, "Saved Alone..."

Mr. Spafford booked passage on the next ship heading to England. As the ship crossed the area where the SS Ville de Havre sank, taking his daughters to the ocean's depths, Mr. Spafford felt the Holy Spirit fill him with a comforting peace. Leaving the ship's railing he went into his cabin where he penned the hymn that has soothed so many souls who have been brokenhearted...and one which I often hear sung in the meetings of the Persecuted Church:

When peace, like a river, attendeth my way,

When sorrows like sea billows roll;

Whatever my lot, Thou has taught me to say,

It is well, it is well, with my soul.

RESPONSE:
Today I will be a good steward of the trials I face…with faith, love and perseverance.

PRAYER:
Thank you Lord for Your faithfulness in all the trials I face. Help me not waste them.

August 25

NO TURNING BACK

Jesus replied, "No one who puts a hand to the plow and looks back is fit for service in the kingdom of God."
Luke 9:62

One of the blessings of teaching Standing Strong Through The Storm (SSTS) is the opportunity to meet special people in ministry who, though unassuming at first glance, have experienced deep riches in relationship with Jesus. Such a person I met in a jungle camp seminar in central Sri Lanka.

His English name was Samuel and he was a seasoned church planter. From Samuel I learned that church planting in a Buddhist country is no easier than anywhere else religious intolerance raises its head. I always thought Buddhism was a pacifist religion and philosophically it is. But try and plant a church in a dominant Buddhist community and you will see something different.

One day Samuel began to share with me about his ministry. He had been dedicated to the Buddhist temple as a young child by his mother just like his biblical namesake. As a young monk he was impressed by the witness of a Christian youth who led him to faith in Christ. He left temple life and felt called to be a Christian church planter. With his wife and two small children he moved to a new community and began to share Jesus. The villagers stoned his residence and when he would not desist, they burned it down.

He moved to another community and was attacked physically with severe wounds. In the next location the villagers schemed against him and his family. They cut the main posts of his home and worship center. At night they tied rope to the posts and pulled them out while the family was asleep. He knew God was with him. Two large structural beams fell down parallel to where the children were sleeping and neither of them was touched.

He continued on and I finally interrupted with the question, "How many times did this happen and you had to move on?"

Samuel smiled and answered, "Thirteen times!"

Of course, in my Western way of thinking I asked, "How could you continue on and persevere through so many attacks?"

He replied, "It's like the song we sang this morning at the SSTS seminar, *I have decided to follow Jesus, no turning back!*" And he quickly went on to say with a bigger smile, "Last month twenty-five people in my new community were baptized and I currently have another twenty-five in a baptismal preparation class."

Jesus gives strength to carry on and not turn back.

RESPONSE:
Today I resolve to not allow petty challenges dampen my commitment to follow Jesus.

PRAYER:
Thank You, Lord, for Samuel's testimony of Your faithfulness. Help me never to turn back from following and serving You.

August 26

REFINER'S FIRE

"...I will refine them like silver and test them like gold.
They will call on my name and I will answer them;
I will say, 'They are my people,' and they will say,
'The LORD is our God.'"
Zechariah 13:9

In 2004, my colleague and friend Dr. Jim Cunningham was in Ethiopia teaching Standing Strong Through The Storm (SSTS). His teaching assignments took him to the far western province of Gambella where many Christians of the Anuak tribe had been killed in recent fighting. The believers there told him about one of their pastors, Okok Ojula, who was in prison in the capital, Addis Ababa.

Okok had been head of the Bureau of Social Rehabilitation in Gambella. He was falsely accused of corruption and taking three million Ethiopian Birr. No evidence was presented so the trial was moved to Addis—three days away by bus—to a federal court. He had been sitting in jail for two years waiting for a trial date to be set! His wife Nuno and their six children were patiently waiting back in Gambella. They asked Jim to visit Pastor Okok in prison.

Jim went to the Administrator's Office of the main federal prison back in Addis to try and see Pastor Okok. "Why do you want to see him?" the administrator asked. Jim responded, "Because I was in Gambella, met his wife Nuno and their six children and I told them I would come and give him greetings from them."

He replied rather directly, "Why do YOU want to see him?" Jim looked him in the eye and said, "Okuk is a Christian and a pastor in Gambella, I am a Christian and a pastor in Canada. I want to meet him and pray with him!" At that moment the administrator's countenance changed. He turned to Jim and said, "You may meet him next door in the Deputy Administrator's office."

Okuk was brought in for forty-five minutes—with coffee provided—and they shared and prayed together! It was a great time of blessing for both men.

After three and a half years, Okuk was released from prison as a free man completely exonerated. He then shared with Jim by mail that he had earlier conformed his life around serving the Lord, resuming his education at the highest level, doing research work, and other valuable good things to help people. But he had never thought of imprisonment at any time. Time was very precious to him and he never thought of wasting it in prison sitting under a hostile situation. But having been in prison he learned many lessons.

Commenting about Moses' burning bush, he said, "Prison to me, is a place where the Lord can appear to us in flames of fire to refine us—but never 'burn us up.' I see that the Lord is more concerned with our **perfection** obtained through walks in all levels of patience, endurance, character, and hope in order to expel fear and self-centeredness in our lives—and prepare us to see and believe that He is God Almighty as He appeared to Moses. He intends for us not to put Him in our little box to use Him as an instrument to suit our release from the prison. [Rather] patience, endurance, character, and hope have to finish their work to perfection."

RESPONSE:
Today I will accept that God may have to put me through the refiner's fire to perfect me.

PRAYER:
Lord, build patience, endurance, character and hope into my life in Your way and purpose.

August 27

GOD'S ETERNAL LOVE

"I have loved you with an everlasting love;
I have drawn you with unfailing kindness."
Jeremiah 31:3

Yesterday we learned the first prison lesson from Pastor Okuk Ojula who was incarcerated on false charges for three and a half years in a federal prison in Addis Ababa in Ethiopia.

When Jim Cunningham was able to visit him in the prison, he told Jim that before the prison experience, he had centered his life on serving the Lord, pursuing his education to the highest level (he has an MA in economics from the University of Reading-UK), doing research work and other good things to help people. But he had never thought of imprisonment as having any spiritual or practical value. He commented, "Time was very precious to me and I never thought of wasting it in prison sitting for nothing under a hostile situation."

But God taught Pastor Okuk several lessons. The second one is that the depth of God's love for us is eternal. He says, "I was in prison for my **protection**. God put me in prison beforehand to escape the massacre of the elites and the educated people of my tribe in the Gambella region—the incident of December 2003 that shook the media world."

Genocide Watch reported that at least 416 Anuak people were massacred in December 2003 in Gambella led by Ethiopian government troops in uniform, but they were joined by other local tribal people from highland areas. Between 3000 and 5000 additional Anuak refugees fled into Sudan as refugees.

The pretext for these massacres was the ambush of a van on December 13th by an unidentified gang who murdered its eight occupants, who were U.N. and Ethiopian government refugee camp officials. There is no evidence that the killers were Anuak. The Ethiopian troops responded by murdering hundreds of Anuak civilians in Gambella and surrounding areas. They also burned their homes and raped the women.

Sources indicated that those targeted particularly were educated Anuak men, a tactic often intended to render a group leaderless and defenseless. To this day hundreds of Anuak Christians are still listed as "missing."

Pastor Okok is convinced that his imprisonment in Addis was God's love and protection because if he had been at home, he would have been a prime target because of his education.

RESPONSE:
Today I will walk in the assurance of God's love and His positive actions on my behalf even when they do not seem to be favourable.

PRAYER:
Pray for those brothers and sisters experiencing injustice without the understanding of God's purposes.

August 28

THE WORK OF MINISTRY TO OTHERS

Last night an angel of the God to whom I belong and whom I serve stood beside me and said, 'Do not be afraid, Paul. You must stand trial before Caesar; and God has graciously given you the lives of all who sail with you.'
Acts 27:23-24

We've been learning personal lessons from prison from Pastor Okuk Ojulu in Ethiopia as he shared them with Jim Cunningham.

He says, "The third lesson I learned is that imprisonment is for **ministry** to people in need. The thirty-six people who were imprisoned with me from Gambella in the Addis Ababa prison–777 kilometers (483 miles) away from our families–had no strong faith in the Lord.

"I began to realize that the Lord put me there to minister to these people, to feed them with the Word of God in the prison. I ended up baptizing some of them in the prison although I was not an officially recognized pastor, for no pastor was allowed to do this work in the prison."

I am always amazed at the positive lessons from reading prison memoirs of followers of Jesus. And so many times they come to this similar conclusion. They were there to serve others.

Mama Kwang of Project Pearl in China is a wonderful example. Carl Lawrence tells her story in his award-winning book, *The Church in China:*

As she sat quietly in prison singing a hymn, the Lord gave her a message: "This is to be your ministry."

"But," she objected, "I am all alone. Whom can I minister to?" She continued to pray that her ministry would be fulfilled. Suddenly an idea came to her. She stood up and called for the guard.

"Sir, can I do some hard labor for you?" The guard looked at her with contempt, mingled with surprise. No one had ever made that kind of request before.

"Look!" she exclaimed, "this prison is so dirty, there is human waste everywhere. Let me go into the cells and clean up this filthy place. All you have to do is give me some water and a brush."

Not to her surprise, she soon found herself on her hands and knees cleaning and preaching. She was looking into the faces of people no longer recognizable as human beings. Through continuous torture, they had lost all hope of ever seeing another human being who did not come to beat them.

"Oh, when they realized that they could have eternal life, they would get so excited. They would fall down on the dirty floor and repent of their sins, and do you know that very soon all the prisoners believed in Jesus Christ."[30]

RESPONSE:
Today I acknowledge that God can enable me to minister anywhere for Him—even prison.

PRAYER:
Thank You Lord that even in a filthy prison dungeon you give ministry opportunities.

30 Carl Lawrence, *The Church in China* (Minneapolis, MN: Bethany House Publishers, 1985), p.149.

August 29

REJOICE IN THE LORD

Further, my brothers and sisters, rejoice in the Lord!
Philippians 3:1a

We've been learning personal lessons from prison from Pastor Okuk Ojulu in Ethiopia as he shared them with Jim Cunningham.

He says, "The fourth lesson is to **Rejoice in the Lord always** in the prison.

"Prison means cutting off almost all your freedoms from the previous life. The devil is more pressing in the prison than anywhere in life, preaching negatives things to us. The most powerful tool for victory in our Christian lives in the midst of negatives is to preach positives to defeat the devil of negatives. In other words, it is to develop a positive attitude in a hostile situation like in the prison.

"In Philippians 3:1, it says, *Rejoice in the Lord!* Rejoicing in the Lord always enables us to approach the burning bush for a release from the prison. Let our prayer contain: "Yet not as I will, but as You will."

"I hope this kind of prayer can discipline us, and help make us approach the Lord very closely in the burning bush—the very place where we can hear a distilled voice from Him for the deliverance of many in their misery. The burning bush does not burn us up, but it makes us remove our sandals when we approach it."

Pastor Okok was released after three and a half years and God has rewarded his ministry, even his family. One of his daughters was chosen as Miss Ethiopia which paid for her education.

He continues to minister in freedom but with new perspectives based on his prison life.

Prison experiences are very personal and very impacting. I think that must be why I enjoy reading memoirs of Christians who have been in prison. They are so positive and uplifting compared to those of non-Christians.

I especially remember the prayer of a Christian brother who was in prison for years in Romania during the difficult years of the cold war.

483

He prayed:

"Lord, I look forward to the great day I see you and your family in heaven. I look forward to seeing the great evangelists standing before you. I look forward to the day I see all the missionaries coming home rejoicing with their sheaves. I look forward to hearing all the great singers of the world praising you. I look forward to seeing the great preachers of the ages standing before you.

"But Lord, I have one special request. When that day comes, allow me to be there in the clothing of a prisoner. I want to praise you throughout eternity in my prisoner's clothes to always remind me that I was a prisoner for you."

RESPONSE:
Today I will rejoice in the Lord in the face of all the negatives that Satan tries to throw at me.

PRAYER:
Lord, You are worthy of my praise and joyfulness no matter what circumstances I am in.

August 30

THE WITNESSING POWER OF THE HOLY SPIRIT

"But you will receive power when the Holy Spirit comes on you; and you will be my witnesses..."
Acts 1:8a

Prior to her Christian husband being released from prison in Iran, Maheen, feared that she might be arrested too. So she seriously prayed, "Dear Lord, I am not ready to go to a solitary confinement because of my Christian faith. It is such a closed and dirty environment. As you know I was born and brought up in a wealthy family and had a comfortable life. Please don't test me beyond my ability." She told God she would not be able to handle being arrested and mentioned her fear that she might give the names of all believers in the house churches to the police or even deny Jesus.

Three days later, the secret police knocked at her door. She said to God, "I have already asked you not to put me in this temptation. So whatever happens, it is not my fault. Because I had already told you that I am not a strong person and can't stand against these security people and can't tolerate persecution."

She said, "The police blindfolded me and took me to the solitary confinement. I was scared to death and felt sick as the place was very smelly." They put her in a cell and a few hours later brought her in for interrogation. She added, "I sensed the presence of the Holy Spirit very strongly. And I felt that God's peace came down on me and my fear went away."

When Maheen stood before the high official, she courageously testified of her Christian faith.

"It is an honor for me to talk to people about Jesus. I will be very happy to talk to you about Jesus and salvation too. Like all other people and Muslims, you also need Jesus in your life. Without Jesus a person does not have any peace and life is hopeless and without any purpose. Jesus laid his life down for you too so that you can have salvation and will not perish."

485

The official responded in anger, "Do you know what the consequence of all this will be for you? You can't evangelize me. It will cost you a heavy price."

On the third night the official came to her cell. Maheen was frightened fearing that he came to abuse her sexually or to beat her up. But the official told her, "Don't be afraid of me. I need your prayers. When you shared about Jesus with me, it had such a powerful impact on my life. I need to be saved. I need Jesus in my life. I believe God has sent you to come to this prison so that you can share about salvation with me. I am now completely aware of the fact that without Jesus I will be a miserable and hopeless person and I will perish. Please pray for me that I can be set free from this hell I live in."

Maheen had the chance to share about Jesus for three hours with him and at the end he repented of his sins and committed his life to Jesus. The official testified that for the first time he experienced the real peace and love of God in his life.

Maheen and her husband were both released from prison and are in touch with this official and his wife secretly. The wife of the official has committed her life to the Lord too.

RESPONSE:
Today I will walk and talk in the power of the Holy Spirit and trust God to use me as a witness wherever He places me.

PRAYER:
Thank God for the power of His Holy Spirit among committed brothers and sisters in Iran.

August 31

MARTYRDOM

Be faithful, even to the point of death, and I will give you the crown of life.
Revelation 2:10

In Ambon, Indonesia, a Christian youth camp was held in early 1999 with the theme "Soldiers of the Cross!" The camp was attacked by an angry group of Muslim extremists and a 15-year-old boy named Roy Pontoh was singled out for carrying his Bible and interrogated.

When asked, "Who are you?" he replied, "I am a soldier of Jesus Christ." The angry mob chopped at his left arm with a machete. The questioning continued, "Who are you?" And again Roy answered, "I am a soldier of Jesus Christ." Then they chopped at his right arm.

When they tried to force him to say, "Allahu Akbar," he replied, "As far as I know, Jesus Christ is the only Lord." Now the seething angry crowd cut open his stomach and demanded again, "Who are you?" With his last breath, Roy gasped, "I am a soldier of Jesus Christ." The mob cut off his head and threw his body in a ditch.

Martyrdom may be the end result of those who endure. In addition to Jesus, three martyrs are named in the New Testament—John the Baptist, Stephen and James. Some of the unnamed heroes of the faith mentioned in Hebrews 11:37 were also martyred.

Martyrdom is described as a legitimate response to persecution. This is not easily understood in our day and in our culture that specializes in personal "rights" and the avoidance of suffering. But a special crown is awaiting those who lay down their lives for their faith.

The appropriate response to persecution that one chooses depends on that person's intimate relationship with God the Holy Spirit and openness to His direction.

No doubt if you and I had talked to Roy Pontoh before his death, we may not have detected such bravery and loyalty to Jesus. Roy passed the hot water test with flying colors. He graduated to a special place with his Lord as a victorious overcomer.

Overcomers are like tea bags. You have to put them in hot water to know how strong they are!

RESPONSE:
Today I will live in faith and assurance that even in the test and threat of death I can be a victorious overcomer.

PRAYER:
Pray that all those who may face physical death today for the cause of Christ will walk in faith and realize they will never die.

September 1

RECONCILIATION IN THE MIDST OF PAIN

All this is from God, who reconciled us to himself through Christ and gave us the ministry of reconciliation: that God was reconciling the world to himself in Christ, not counting people's sins against them. And he has committed to us the message of reconciliation.

2 Corinthians 5:18-19

The first of September is a memorial day for the people of Beslan in North Ossetia as they remember the awful events of September first 2004. More than one thousand children and adults were taken hostage in School Number One and two days later more than three hundred and thirty of them were killed in the violence.

Memorial services are held and memories of the nightmare overwhelm everyone in town. Beslan's cemetery is unique; it has the youngest average age in the world (7-12 years old). The sight of so many graves of children deeply affects any visitor. One said, "People who do not live in Beslan have often forgotten the tragedy already, but as soon as you enter the city, you cannot escape the atmosphere of grief and deep mourning that is still enveloping the city."

When the tragedy occurred at School Number One, almost every family in Beslan was affected. A peculiarity in Ossetia is that nearly everybody is related to one another, so the catastrophe has affected many people in a personal way. Even those who were watching television during the event suffered diseases, heart attacks and strokes.

Pastor Taimuraz Totiev and his wife Ria had their five children at school; only the eldest daughter, Madina, survived the attack. Their four other children, Larissa, Luba, Albina and Boris, were buried on September 7, 2004.

The pastor's brother, Sergey Totiev, also had children at the school. Sergey and his wife Bela buried two of their children on the same day: Dzerassa (15) and Anna (9). Their son Azamat lost his sight in one of his eyes and is having surgery to save his other eye.

Both men are pastors of the Beslan Baptist Church. At the children's funeral Sergey spoke of forgiveness and advised people not to seek revenge, but to serve as peacemakers. His exact words were: **"Yes, we have an irreplaceable loss, but we cannot take revenge. As Christians, the Bible teaches us that we must forgive. Vengeance is in God's hands."** According to a Christian worker in the area, a demonic plan was broken when those words were spoken!

Since that time they have been doing everything they can think of to minister to families of the victims. Other churches and ministries have also taken up the enormous task of counseling and helping the survivors and the bereaved. Others decided to reach out to Chechen people (nationality of the neighboring terrorists) and are finding ways to minister God's love to them.

RESPONSE:
Today I commit to being a messenger of God's reconciliation through Christ—even to those who may cause harm to me or my family.

PRAYER:
Pray for the church to be an instrument of reconciliation and restoration in this volatile area of Central Asia.

September 2

THE PRIVILEGE OF CORPORATE WORSHIP

Sing his praises in the assembly of the faithful.
Psalm 149:1b

Open Doors colleague, Ron Boyd-MacMillan, shares the following insight from his teaching, "Why I Need to Encounter the Persecuted Church."

It's so easy to get fed up with church. For years I got very little out of church. The sermons were boring. The music was embarrassing. The fellowship was non-existent. The whole experience of worshipping with other people felt stale and pointless…Going to church in my country was an endurance test. Until I visited a Persecuted Church!

There were fifty of us squeezed into an upstairs room. The singing was hushed. The neighbors were hostile to the fellowship. Then a preacher stood up. An old man, with a wiry frame and wisps of hair springing from a mole on his chin. No sooner had he spoken a sentence than he broke down in tears. He kept saying, "I never thought I would have the privilege of preaching again." Then he would laugh, then cry again, great wails and sobs. Soon everyone was weeping with him. Except me. This went on for about half an hour, and I began to get very fed up with it all. He kept speaking a line, and my translator kept saying, "It's the same verse, it's the same verse." All this man did was repeat the same Scripture phrase, burst into tears, laugh, and then speak the very same phrase again. I thought, *"What kind of hopeless service is this."*

But afterwards I met the old man, and when I heard his story I repented of my attitude. He was a preacher, ordained in the late 1950's in China. He pastored a church for only six months before it was closed down. He was jailed, spending twenty years in prison. After he got out, he was very ill for a long time, but finally, at age 77, had the strength to speak again. I had witnessed his first sermon in 31 years! No wonder he broke down. I tried to imagine what it must have been like, holding the Word of God inside for 31 years, not knowing whether you would ever again preach. Then suddenly being allowed

491

to do so. How do you preach a sermon after a silence of 31 years? No wonder he was overcome.

He said, "I never thought I would get the privilege of speaking the Word to a gathered group of Christians with their Bibles open ever again. Through the long years of prison I thought that experience would never return. And when it came, as you saw, all I could do was choke out the verse that kept me going: *Sing his praises in the assembly of the faithful* (Ps149:1b).

I returned home with a transformed attitude. I began to walk to church with my Bible, praising Him for the opportunity. I went to the church early, walking the aisles and praying, thanking God for the building and the freedom to hold our service. When the preacher spoke, I thanked God that he had no fear. When the Bible was read, I thanked God for the men who took grave risks in the past to print and distribute this word in my language. When we sang a hymn, I sang out loudly, thanking God that I did not have to whisper in hushed tones.

Truly, what a privilege is corporate worship. The Persecuted Church rescued me from bitterness, and taught me to count my blessings I had taken for granted.

RESPONSE:
Today I will thank God for the privilege and freedom of corporate worship in my church.

PRAYER:
Thank You Lord for the freedom and blessing of praising You in my faith community.

September 3

HELP IN INTERPRETING THE BIBLE

Remember those earlier days after you had received the light, when you endured in a great conflict full of suffering.
Hebrews 10:32

Open Doors colleague, Ron Boyd-MacMillan, shares the following insight from his teaching, "Why I Need to Encounter the Persecuted Church."

Every pastor and Bible teacher works hard to understand the meaning of the Scriptures. They learn biblical languages, look up concordances, and consult commentaries, all in the hope of shedding more light on the key questions of interpretation:

1. who wrote this text and what did they mean by it?

2. who initially read this text and what did they make of it?

All good interpretation begins with the tools that answer these two primary questions. We are taught that these tools lie in the realm of scholarship, and most pastors take to their studies and their libraries accordingly. But there is another vitally overlooked tool that gives a key to the meaning of the Scriptures. The Persecuted Church of today represents the closest we can come to the original writers and readers of the Scriptures. You see, most of the Bible was written by persecuted people *for* persecuted people. By interacting with them, we gain unique insights into the original meaning of the Scriptures. We really need their help because what is obvious to a persecuted, biblical Christian, is no longer obvious to us. We inhabit a completely different universe. We need the persecuted to remind us of what life was like for the original New Testament community. The persecuted enable us in some small way to recover the "original eyes" of the first writers and readers of Scripture, and that can impact interpretation.

I remember a dear pastor from the West preaching about Jesus stilling the storm (Mark 4:35-41). His whole talk was on how Jesus could still the storms raging in our lives. He named storms like loneliness, misunderstanding, humiliation, persecution even. And he said, "Jesus can deliver you from every one of these storms, just like he did the disciples of old."

He was about to go on when an old man stood up. He was from a Middle Eastern country and had seen much suffering. He said gently and respectfully, "My dear brother, if you had been persecuted you would know the primary meaning of this passage. The point of this story is not that Jesus takes the storm away, but that there is no need to fear the storm if Jesus is in the boat." Everyone stared at him in silence. He added, "This passage is given to us for our comfort in the face of terrible storms, to know that Jesus is in the boat with us so that the storm will do us no harm." So that persecuted Christian—because he was persecuted—knew the meaning of the passage better than the preacher, *because* he was one for whom the passage was written.

RESPONSE:
Today I will read my Bible through the eyes and perspective of the persecuted.

PRAYER:
Lord, may Your Word come alive as I interpret it with the help of the Persecuted Church.

September 4

GLAMORIZING PERSECUTION

For just as we share abundantly in the sufferings of Christ, so also our comfort abounds through Christ.
2 Corinthians 1:5

Reg Reimer, a veteran missionary in Vietnam and with the World Evangelical Alliance counters the idea that some people express which glamorizes persecution and concludes it is therefore good. He says that deprivation, cruelty and dehumanization suffered by victims of persecution are NOT good but from the enemy! He writes in the book *Suffering, Persecution and Martyrdom: Theological Reflections*:

In Vietnam, for example, it is well documented that in the past 30 years Christians have been harassed, discriminated against, arrested without cause, starved, beaten, imprisoned, raped, dispossessed and chased from home and fields, and even killed for Christ's sake. Only the Evil One takes pleasure in inflicting these injustices on those made in the image of God!

In September 2005, a Vietnamese pastor was released from a terrifying 15-month imprisonment. He had been rotated to five different prisons, was sometimes in rooms with 100 criminals and other times in a solitary cell. He had been attacked by prisoners with HIV/AIDS. He confessed to feeling alienated from his family and his church after his release. The feeling worsened. Six months after release he uttered the words, "I only discovered real loneliness when I got out of prison. My colleagues, my own brother and even my wife don't understand and won't believe what I tell them." Persecution is not good!

People much prefer the more positive reports of those who seem to flourish in persecution. *It is truly amazing that for many, the persecution they suffer becomes a means of receiving grace!* They testify of God's strengthening presence in the harshest conditions. They report on God's miraculous provisions in times of extreme need. And so persecution and suffering become an occasion for God's comfort, often through others.[31]

RESPONSE:
Today I will resist the temptation to glamorize persecution and the persecuted. Instead I will pray unceasingly for those being traumatized.

PRAYER:
Lord please bring Your comfort to our brothers and sisters who are hurting from persecution today. And bless those who provide much needed trauma counselling for the Persecuted Church.

31 Christof Sauer and Richard Howell (ed), *Suffering, Persecution and Martyrdom: Theological Reflections* (Johannesburg, SA: AcadSA Publishing, 2010), pp.331-332.

September 5

REAL LIFE FORGIVENESS

"Do not judge, and you will not be judged.
Do not condemn, and you will not be condemned.
Forgive, and you will be forgiven.
Luke 6:37

Alexander Puerta has seen more than his share of tragedy. Raised on a small farm in Urabá region of northern Colombia, he was 17 when his father was murdered by an angry neighbour.

At 19, Alex nearly died of malaria. He called on a Christian evangelist to pray for him and experienced a miraculous recovery. That convinced him to accept Christ. He soon became a fervent evangelist himself and took a job at the Rancho Amelia banana plantation in Urabá.

A guerrilla army operating in the area mistakenly believed Rancho Amelia harbored a paramilitary squad. One morning in September 1995, they ambushed a bus carrying plantation employees, tied them up and threw them face down into a gully. The guerrillas then opened fire with machine guns on the helpless workers.

In the midst of the shooting, a bullet struck Alex Puerta at the base of his left eye, fractured his skull from the inside and exited, destroying his right eye and cheekbone. Amazingly, Alex did not lose consciousness, despite the excruciating pain and nearly suffocating in his own blood.

"The guerrillas came down the rows to find those who were still moving, finishing them off with a machete blow to the neck," he recalls. "They reached me and I told them that Christ loved them. 'This one's alive!' they said, and hit me twice very hard. They broke two teeth and cut off an ear lobe, but the machete did not penetrate my neck. Then they left.

"At that moment I heard a voice say, 'Fight for your life.' I felt such a strength and vitality that I succeeded in breaking my bonds. It hurt, but God gave me strength. When help arrived, they found me sitting up." Alex was the only victim to survive the massacre. Twenty-five of his Rancho Amelia co-workers, including several women, lay dead in the gully.

Survival has been difficult. Alex underwent five surgeries to rebuild his shattered face. Doctors told him that he would never see again. He remembers the long months of convalescence with nothing to do but sit at home with only the family dog.

Today Alex serves as a voluntary chaplain of Prison Fellowship, preaching in chapel services at the Bellavista National Penitentiary and counseling inmates. Some of the prisoners with whom he has shared the gospel are former guerrillas. At least one, he has learned, was involved in the massacre at Rancho Amelia.

Alex let it be known that he has forgiven each of the assailants who blinded him and killed his friends. "If one decides to follow Jesus, the foundation is forgiveness," he says. "Without it, there is no real Christian life."

Alex accepted an invitation from Open Doors to become a regular trainer for Standing Strong Through the Storm seminars offered throughout Colombia. Feedback from seminar participants indicates that Alex is particularly effective in teaching about forgiveness.

RESPONSE:
Today I will obey the Lord and forgive everyone who has hurt me.

PRAYER:
Pray for Alex as he teaches SSTS seminars in Colombia. Pray his students will also forgive.

September 6

FORGIVENESS IS NOT AN OPTION

And when you stand praying, if you hold anything against anyone, forgive them, so that your Father in heaven may forgive you your sins."
Mark 11:25

Our founder, Brother Andrew, says, "Forgiveness is the very core of the gospel message. I am a Christian only because God forgave me everything. There is no other ground on which to stand…not my repentance, not my praying the sinner's prayer. Nothing made me a child of God except God forgave. And He did it two thousand years ago through Jesus on the cross. Jesus took all that sin and nailed it to the cross and He says, 'Now, go, and put it into practice.'"

Poso, Indonesia is a beautiful place on a central island of the country. There we meet an elderly, physically weak, Christian mother who shares through her tears the tragedy that befell her seventeen-year-old daughter Alfita in 2005.

"My daughter Alfita was so beautiful. She loved Jesus, and she loved to sing. She loved spending time with her friends. One day, Alfita and three of her friends were walking to school. They always took a path that went deep into the jungle, far away from our village. Along the path grew beautiful flowers and my daughter loved flowers. That day, she and her friends, Theresia, Yarni, and Noviana stopped to pick flowers for their hair…"

The girls were all from Christian families. Three young Muslim men were waiting on the jungle path and savagely beheaded three of the girls including Alfita. The fourth girl, Noviana, survived her machete wounds.

The three men were tried for murder in the capital, Jakarta. Noviana and the families in question had to make witness statements. However, they first shook the hands of the murderers as a sign of forgiveness. Two years later, the suspects were sentenced to long terms of imprisonment.

The request for forgiveness came from one of the murderers. "It was very difficult to comply with this request," said the older brother of Noviana. "But we wanted to keep to Jesus' teaching and because of this, we are able to forgive. We hope that our step will also restore the peace in our town of Poso in Central Sulawesi."

The family members prefer not to talk about the day itself. During the hearing, Noviana again had to see pictures of her beheaded friends and answer questions by the prosecutors and lawyers.

Alfita's mother was severely traumatized by the murder of her daughter. She concludes, "All I could do was ask God for His peace, the peace that cannot be explained, that comes from trusting in Him. At the funeral He gave me that peace. Even though Alfita was brutally killed, I knew that she was safe in God's arms in heaven…After that, when I knew God's comfort in my heart, I was finally able to do as God commanded…so I let go of my right for revenge. I'm not bitter. I've forgiven the murderers and asked God to forgive them. I've prayed that they will realize what they've done."

RESPONSE:
Today I will confront my own trials and forgive those against whom I am holding anything.

PRAYER:
Pray for complete healing of the trauma in the lives of these four families in Indonesia.

September 7

FORGIVENESS CAN BRING HEALING AND RESTORATION

"You have heard that it was said, 'Love your neighbor and hate your enemy.' But I tell you, love your enemies and pray for those who persecute you, that you may be children of your Father in heaven. He causes his sun to rise on the evil and the good, and sends rain on the righteous and the unrighteous."

Matthew 5:43-45

The literal meaning of the word "forgiveness" in the New Testament is "to release; to hurl away; to free yourself." The only way to break the chain or cycle of hurtfulness is to stop and ask forgiveness. This allows a relationship to start over and begin anew. The Russian writer, Solzhenitsyn, believed forgiveness is what truly makes us different from animals. Only humans can perform the most unnatural act of forgiveness that transcends the relentless law of nature.

A young Iranian lady, we'll call Fatima, was full of hatred towards her mother-in-law. For fifteen years her mother-in law was her enemy and there was a great deal of enmity in the family.

Several times Fatima had even tried to kill her mother-in-law. Once she put poison in her soup hoping to kill her. The mother-in-law felt very sick after that and was taken to the hospital. The doctors took the poison out of her stomach and were able to save her life. On another occasion she had beaten her mother-in-law so badly that the ambulance took her to the hospital and again her life was saved. Other times she tried to kill her mother-in-law, but every time her life was saved miraculously.

The main reason for the hatred between Fatima and her mother-in-law was Fatima's marriage to her son. The mother-in-law had even gone so far as to contact different witches in order to bring a curse on the life of Fatima.

One day Fatima got hold of the *JESUS* DVD and watched it. The love of Jesus had a great impact on her life. When she heard one of Jesus' teachings that says: "Love your enemies and bless those who

501

curse you," she was deeply moved. She was especially touched by the fact that Jesus died on the cross for the sake of His enemies and even asked God to forgive them. At that moment Fatima fell on her knees and asked Jesus to come into her heart and change her. She turned over her entire life to Jesus. After that she sensed this deep love in her heart towards her mother-in-law.

After that experience, Fatima visited her mother-in-law taking flowers and sweets for her. She fell on her knees in front of her and asked for her forgiveness for all the bad things she had done against her. Fatima told her that her life was changed and Jesus had created a new love in her heart towards her. The mother-in-law in turn asked Fatima to forgive her for all the curses she had tried to bring into her life. She also gave her life to Jesus as the result of her daughter-in-law's evangelism. They entered into a beautiful relationship with one another from that moment onwards.

RESPONSE:
Today I will ask forgiveness—as Jesus said—of people I have hated and treated poorly.

PRAYER:
Thank You Father for Your example in loving the just and the unjust. Help me to practice this as Your son or daughter.

September 8

GRACE

Out of his fullness we have all received grace in place of grace already given.
John 1:16

We now consider the most important characteristic in the training of the disciple of Jesus Christ. That is the quality of living the Christian life with grace.

We use the word "*grace*" to describe many things in life:

- A well-coordinated athlete or dancer
- Good manners and being considerate of others
- Beautiful, well-chosen words
- Consideration and care of other people
- Various expressions of kindness and mercy

To show grace is to extend favor or kindness to one who doesn't deserve it and can never earn it. Receiving God's acceptance by grace always stands in sharp contrast to earning it on the basis of works. Every time the thought of grace appears, there is the idea of its being undeserved. In no way is the recipient getting what he or she deserves. Favor is being extended simply out of the goodness of the heart of the giver.

Also, grace is absolutely and totally free. You will never be asked to pay it back. You couldn't even if you tried. Grace comes to us free and clear with no strings attached. It is the act of unmerited favor — most often to the down and out.

Christ came down from heaven and he reminds us that the greatest in the kingdom is the one who serves. The ladder of power reaches up, the ladder of grace reaches down.

Dr. Donald Barnhouse said it best: "Love that goes upward is worship; love that goes outward is affection; love that stoops is grace."

Jesus never used the word itself. He just taught it and lived it. And it was written as a description of how He lived His life. The Apostle John describes Jesus' glory as "***full of grace and truth***" (John 1:14).

In a world of darkness and demands, rules and regulations, requirements and expectations demanded by the hypocritical religious leaders, Jesus came and ministered in a new and different way.

After commenting on His glory, John goes on to add, *"From the fullness of his grace we have all received one blessing after another"* (John 1:16). John and the other disciples became marked men. His style became theirs. They absorbed his tolerance, acceptance, love, warmth and compassion so that it ultimately transformed their lives. They too lived their lives demonstrating grace!

Thus grace is Christianity's best gift to the world. It's a force stronger than vengeance, stronger than racism, stronger than hate.

RESPONSE:
Today I desire to be a person like Jesus – full of grace and truth.

PRAYER:
Pray that God would fill your life with the ability to live with the grace of our Lord Jesus.

September 9

UNGRACE

The Word became flesh and made his dwelling among us.
We have seen his glory, the glory of the one and only Son,
who came from the Father, full of grace and truth.
John 1:14

Yesterday we concluded that "grace" is Christianity's best gift to the world! It's a force stronger than vengeance, stronger than racism, stronger than hate. But sadly to a world desperate for this grace, the church sometimes presents one more form of what Philip Yancey calls "*ungrace*."

Charles Swindoll in his book, *The Grace Awakening*, powerfully lists these enemies of grace as:

a. From without: legalism, expectations, traditionalism, manipulation, demands, negativism, control, comparison, perfectionism, competition, criticism, pettiness and a host of others.

b. From within: pride, fear, resentment, bitterness, an unforgiving spirit, insecurity, fleshly effort, guilt, shame, gossip, hypocrisy, and many more.[32]

Nothing has the power to change us from within like the freedom that comes through grace. And grace has very practical outworking in our lives.

a. A greater appreciation for God's gifts
Those who claim the freedom God offers gain an appreciation for the gifts that come with life: the free gift of salvation, life, laughter, music, beauty, friendship and forgiveness.

b. Less time and energy being critical or concerned about other's choices
When you begin to operate in the context of grace and freedom, you become increasingly less petty. You will allow others room to make their own decisions in life, even though you may choose

---

32 Charles R. Swindoll, The Grace Awakening (Dallas: Word Publishing, 1990), pp. 5-14.

otherwise. A grace-full Christian is one who looks at the world and others through "grace-tinted lenses."

c. More tolerant and less judgmental

When you are so involved in your own pursuit of grace, you'll no longer lay guilt trips on those with whom you disagree.

d. A giant step toward maturity

As your world expands, thanks to an awakening of your understanding of grace, your maturity will enlarge. You will become more like Jesus and you will never be the same!

RESPONSE:
Today I will determine to avoid those things that prompt "ungrace" in my life.

PRAYER:
Lord, I don't want to live any longer in the same old ways. Help me to become more like Jesus.

September 10

DISPENSING GRACE

And now these three remain: faith, hope and love. But the greatest of these is love.
1 Corinthians 13:13

How can Christians dispense grace in a society that is or seems to be veering away from God? As we noted in earlier devotionals, Elijah hid out in caves. On the other hand, his contemporary Obadiah worked within the system running Ahab's palace while sheltering God's prophets on the side. Esther and Daniel were employed by heathen empires. Jesus submitted to the judgment of a Roman governor. Paul appealed his case all the way to Caesar. In his book, *What's So Amazing About Grace*, Philip Yancey shares:

a. Dispensing God's grace is the Christian's main contribution

The one big thing the church has over the world is showing grace. Jesus did not let any institution interfere with His love for individuals. Here is where the fruit of the Spirit are so important in our lives. Jesus said we are to have one distinguishing mark—neither political correctness nor moral superiority, but—love.

b. Commitment to grace does not mean Christians will always live in perfect harmony with the government

Kenneth Kaunda, the former President of Zambia has written, "…what a nation needs more than anything else is not a Christian ruler in the palace but a Christian prophet within earshot." Jesus warned that the world who hated him would hate us also. As the early church spread throughout the Roman Empire, the slogan "Jesus is Lord" was a direct affront to the Romans. When conflict came, brave Christians stood up against the state, appealing to a higher authority. Through the years, this same energy continued. In all of this, we are to be wise as serpents and harmless as doves. All our actions—and even counteractions—are to be seasoned with grace. When we show just the opposite, then we must consider the wisdom of our choices.

c. Coziness between church and state is good for the state and bad for the church

Herein lies the chief danger to grace. The state, which runs by rules of ungrace—the entire "world" does—gradually drowns out the church's sublime message of grace.

The church works best as a force of resistance, a counterbalance to the consuming power of the state. The cozier it gets with government, the more watered-down its message becomes. Can you imagine any government enacting a set of laws based on Jesus' "Sermon on the Mount?" A state government can shut down stores and theatres on Sunday, but it cannot compel worship. It can arrest and punish murderers, but cannot cure their hatred much less teach them love... It can give subsidies to the poor, but cannot force the rich to show them compassion and justice. It can ban adultery but not lust, theft but not covetousness, cheating but not pride. It can encourage virtue but not holiness.[33]

RESPONSE:
Today I will operate in the world I encounter and in my church dispensing grace.

PRAYER:
Help me, Lord, to be a person who is known for my ability to live like Jesus—with grace.

---

33 Philip Yancey, *What's So Amazing About Grace?* (Grand Rapids: Zondervan Publishing, 1997), pp. 219-227.

September 11

GOD IS OFTEN MOST VISIBLE WHEN THINGS ARE MOST AWFUL

They plot injustice and say, "We have devised a perfect plan!" Surely the human mind and heart are cunning. But God will shoot them with his arrows; they will suddenly be struck down.

Psalm 64:6-7

During the tenth anniversary of the World Trade Center attacks of 9/11, many of the people who survived that fateful day were interviewed by the press. One was a man who lost his father to a heart attack as a young boy and outlived an IRA bomb blast in Britain as well as survived violent San Francisco earthquakes. Steve Gill was executive vice-president at Standard Chartered Bank and had just left his office in the World Trade Center for a breakfast meeting when he had to dodge the glass shards raining down from the North Tower after the plane had hit it. He successfully fled the scene on a ferry bound for Staten Island.

As a Christian, he has been repeatedly asked why God spared him but not thousands of innocent mothers, fathers, husbands, wives, brothers, sisters. He has no definitive answer. But when reflecting on lessons learned he says, "I saw that God is often most visible when things are most awful, whether it's Christ on the Cross or the World Trade Center attack killing three thousand people…I don't know why bad things happen. But I see that God is most present when things are at their worst."

There are a number of biblical examples. Perhaps Joseph's situation stands out most. Languishing in a jail on unjust charges, he is even forgotten by those he befriends and helps. At his lowest point, he is brought to Pharaoh to interpret a dream and becomes the second in command of the nation and saves his people and the Egyptian nation from starvation.

The Persecuted Church also testifies that God is most present in the worst of times. Pastor Wang Ming Dao spent over twenty-three years

509

in prison in China for his faith. On his release at eighty years of age he said of his imprisonment, "That was my honeymoon with Jesus!"

Muslim background pastor Medhi Dibaj in Iran spent seven years in prison with the last few years isolated in a small cramped cell. On his release he said, "The past few years have been the sweetest years I've ever spent with Jesus."

Liviu Georgescu was a teenager when his father, Costel, was distributing Bibles in Romania during the communist regime. Open Doors asked him what he thought of the time when his father was in prison for his faith. Liviu said, "It was a very good time, because then we had more time and opportunities to give Bibles to people and to talk about the faith. Now there is more freedom, but we have to work harder and put in longer hours in order to get by. This means that we have little time or energy for the faith. There is less interest as well."

God seems to be most visible when things are at their worst.

RESPONSE:
Today I will thank God for the difficult times and ask for help to see Him as visible in the good times.

PRAYER:
Thank You God for obviously being there in the darkest hours before the dawn of a new day or era.

September 12

THE REAL ENEMY

Be alert and of sober mind. Your enemy the devil prowls around like a roaring lion looking for someone to devour. Resist him, standing firm in the faith, because you know that the family of believers throughout the world is undergoing the same kind of sufferings.

1 Peter 5:8-9

Joshua Sauñe had not planned to speak at his brothers' funeral. Had he planned a speech, it certainly would not have been the one he delivered on that remarkable September day in 1992.

"Shining Path is not my enemy, Satan is my enemy," he told the mourners who packed the Presbyterian Church in Ayacucho, Peru. "The people who killed my brothers need Christ just as you and I do."

The funeral of Quechua evangelist and Bible translator Rómulo Sauñe, his brother Ruben and their cousins Josué and Marco Antonio, was one of the largest Ayacucho witnessed during the decade that the communist guerrilla army known as Shining Path terrorized the city. Nearly 5,000 people, the vast majority of them Quechua-speaking native Americans like the Sauñes, turned out to grieve the fallen Christians, murdered September 5.

God was there that day, too, performing silent miracles in the lives of several of the mourners.

Joshua was Rómulo's only surviving brother and had come immediately from his home in the United States when he heard of the murders. All during the long flight to Peru, Joshua seethed with anger. He later told a friend that, in the very moment he rose to address the crowd, God took away the hatred he felt for the Shining Path terrorists that had caused his family so much suffering. In its place, God gave Joshua a burning desire to carry on the evangelistic work that his brothers, parents and grandparents had faithfully performed.

"I suddenly saw [that] if I was going to fight Shining Path, I should fight with the Bible," Joshua said. "It was the first time I understood that."

Not long afterward, Joshua abandoned his successful art career in Arizona and moved back to Peru with his family to work with Runa Simi, the indigenous ministry founded by Rómulo and his wife, the former Donna Jackson. Between evangelistic campaigns in the Andes, Joshua and Missy Sauñe have worked to establish community self-help projects and schools for the widows and orphans of Shining Path violence.

RESPONSE:
Today I will publicly affirm that my only enemy is Satan and I will be alert to his tactics.

PRAYER:
Thank You, Lord, for the work you are doing in Peru as a result of Romulo's martyrdom and in the face of opposition from the enemy.

September 13

LOVE YOUR ENEMIES

***"For whoever wants to save his life will lose it,
but whoever loses his life for me will save it."***
Luke 9:24

One of the Anabaptists of the 16th Century who died in flames as a "heretic" was Dirk Willem. His story is particularly touching, because he forfeited a real chance to escape prison and death when he turned back to help one of his pursuers.

Dirk was captured and imprisoned in his home town of Asperen in the Netherlands. Knowing that his fate would be death if he remained in prison, Dirk made a rope of strips of cloth and slipped down it over the prison wall. An alert guard began to chase him.

Frost had covered a nearby pond with a thin layer of ice. Dirk risked a dash across it. He made it to safety, but the ice broke under his pursuer who cried for help. Dirk believed the Scripture that a man should help his enemies. He immediately turned back and pulled the floundering prison guard from the frigid water.

In gratitude for his life, the man would have let Dirk escape, but a Burgomaster (chief magistrate) standing on the shore sternly ordered him to arrest Dirk and bring him back, reminding him of the oath he had sworn as an officer of the peace.

Back to prison went Dirk. He was condemned to death for being re-baptized, allowing secret church services in his home and letting others be baptized as adults there.

The record of his sentencing concludes: "all of which is contrary to our holy Christian faith, and to the decrees of his royal majesty, and ought not to be tolerated, but severely punished, for an example to others; therefore, we the aforesaid judges, having, with mature deliberation of council, examined and considered all that was to be considered in this matter, have condemned and do condemn by these presents in the name; and in the behalf, of his royal majesty, as Count of Holland, the aforesaid Dirk Willems, prisoner, persisting obstinately in his opinion, that he shall be executed with fire, until

513

death ensues; and declare all his property confiscated, for the benefit of his royal majesty."

Dirk was burned to death on May 16, 1569. He showed love to his enemy and "saved" his life.

RESPONSE:
Love for our enemies even surpasses the love of our own lives. This is the Jesus way of the cross!

PRAYER:
Help me, Lord, to show love to those who are my enemies—even giving up my life.

September 14

LOVE FOR THE BRETHREN

Therefore, as God's chosen people, holy and dearly loved, clothe yourselves with compassion, kindness, humility, gentleness and patience. Bear with each other and forgive whatever grievances you may have against one another. Forgive as the Lord forgave you. And over all these virtues put on love, which binds them all together in perfect unity.

Colossians 3:12-14

Salim Manayer who heads a significant reconciliation ministry in Israel between Israeli believers and Palestinian believers tells this story in his newsletter of learning about true love for others in the body of Christ during a visit to Denmark:

I experienced something so beautiful. The love and acceptance of the Messiah through the lives of the people who took me around, opened up their homes, took me shopping, took care of me when I was sick and took time out of their busy lives to drive me from one end of the country to the other. I was so moved by their kindness, their hospitality, their compassion, their honesty and their love. Through long country drives they shared and explained to me their reasoning for various traditions and teachings.

And who were these people? Well, if you want to get technical they were Lutherans. Lutherans who belong to the state church – many of them pastors. Yes, we are different – I am an Israeli believer who does not hold to these traditions, but we are called to love each other in spite of our differences. Put all of these labels aside, these amazing people were my brothers and sisters, they are my family because we belong to the family of God and they embraced me as their family.

I was moved as I sat around the kitchen table drinking coffee after confirmation class with one pastor and while eating apple crisp on Rosh Hashanah with another pastor, attentively listening to them as they shared their passion to see the lost people in their communities and parishes find God and believe in him. It left an impression on my heart and encouraged and inspired me to reach the people in my own community.

Sometimes stereotypes and prejudices are there in the back of your head and you don't realize it until God places those same people you held stereotypes about in your face and they begin to show you the love God requires of his children...

Maybe I was sent to Denmark to impress upon, encourage, challenge and impart to the Danish believers to become reconcilers in their local communities; to bless them and show them that it is possible to break down the walls of bitterness and hatred, demolish their stereotypes and prejudices and to love their brothers and sisters. And yet, that is exactly what they taught me.

RESPONSE:
I commit this day to show true love to my brothers and sisters breaking down prejudices.

PRAYER:
Lord, I need Your help today to follow Your command to love all my brothers and sisters.

September 15

LOVE'S SACRIFICE

Greater love has no one than this,
that he lay down his life for his friends.
John 15:13

Jesus says the ultimate test of true love is the willingness to die for others—especially your friends. Of course, He personally demonstrated this Himself in giving His life on the cross for you and me. And today He continues to call those who follow Him to make this sacrifice as well. This classic war zone missionary story illustrates the point:

The mortar rounds landed in an orphanage run by missionaries. The missionaries and one or two children were killed outright and several more children were wounded including one girl about eight years old.

The medical staff who arrived to help soon realized that the young girl was the most critically injured. Without quick action she would die from shock and loss of blood.

When explained to the other children that a blood transfusion was imperative, the request for a blood donor met with wide-eyed silence.

Then one small hand went up and a young boy volunteered. He was quickly laid on a pallet, his arm swabbed with alcohol, and the needle inserted into his vein.

Through the ordeal, he lay stiff and silent but continued to sob later turning into steady, silent crying. The medical team kept asking if it was hurting but he would shake his head and continue to cry.

After a while the boy stopped crying, opened his eyes and looked questioningly at the nurse who took the needle out of his arm. When she nodded, a look of great relief spread over his face.

The boy had all along thought he was dying. He misunderstood, thinking that he was to give ALL his blood so the other little girl could live. And she was his friend.

RESPONSE:
Jesus calls me today to show sacrificial love—especially for those I consider friends.

PRAYER:
Pray that this depth of love will become a reality in the church of Jesus Christ and in your life.

September 16

LOVE YOUR NEIGHBOR

Give to the one who asks you, and do not turn away from the one who wants to borrow from you.
Matthew 5:42

The second part of the Great Commandment (Luke 10:27) is "Love your neighbor as yourself." Jesus then tells the story of the Good Samaritan. In this story Jesus defines our neighbor as anyone in need of help. This kind of love is very practical.

It was the middle of winter and the elderly Christian in prison had a badly infected ear. He thanked God that he had been able to keep his fur hat affording him some protection from the biting cold. At least he had a pillow at night.

One day one of his cellmates asked him for his fur hat. The Christian had been willing to share food with his cellmates, but felt he could not give up his hat. After all, he had an infected ear. He needed that hat.

Through the night he wrestled with his conscience. He was haunted by this Scripture: *"Give to the one who asks you, and do not turn away from the one who wants to borrow from you"* (Matthew 5:42).

After a night of prayer, he sought forgiveness before God and was ready to hand over his hat. In the morning he learned that during the night the guards had taken the cellmate to another prison with a more severe climate.

That same morning, the guards held a routine check of the cell and among the personal objects confiscated was the believer's fur hat.

He had tried to keep something that he was about to lose and God wanted to see the hat used for continued good with the other prisoner. Many years later, this believer remembered that lesson in Christian maturity which the Holy Spirit taught him.

RESPONSE:
Today I will live in the realization that people are more important than things.

PRAYER:
Help me, Lord, to not be tied down by my possessions but be open to sharing what You have given me with others in need.

September 17

STAND FOR WHAT IS RIGHT

"Blessed are those who are persecuted because of righteousness, for theirs is the kingdom of heaven. Blessed are you when people insult you, persecute you and falsely say all kinds of evil against you because of me."
Matthew 5:10-11

Jesus assures his followers there is blessing in suffering for what is right. This blessing may take the form of inner peace and joy. This is the meaning of the word translated "blessed" or "happy" in Jesus' teaching called the Beatitudes (Matthew 5:1-12).

The New Testament writer, James, indicates that pressures are blessings in disguise and should be responded to with joyfulness (James 1:2-3). The *MESSAGE* paraphrase translates the verses this way: *"Consider it a sheer gift, friends, when tests and challenges come at you from all sides. You know that under pressure, your faith-life is forced into the open and shows its true colors."*

Helen Berhane was severely persecuted in Eritrea's prison system because she would not deny her faith. No matter what they did, she refused to give in. She explains:

I told the chief, "I cannot abandon my faith. If you puncture a sack of grain, the only thing that pours out is the type of grain that was in the sack. It is the same with me. I can only say what is inside me; everything that is in my heart must come out of my mouth... The more you punish me, the stronger I will be. If you keep hammering on a nail's head it just becomes harder to pull out of the wall..."

I could not understand how they expected me to stop believing; it was impossible for me. In fact, the guards were making their own situation worse, because people began to ask what was so special about this religion that Christians refused to give it up, and they also believed. Our suffering became a glory for our faith...I am convinced that the number of Christians has doubled or tripled since they closed the churches. So perhaps God is using this terrible situation for his glory.[34]

RESPONSE:
Today I will stand for what is right because I know Jesus will be glorified and I will receive a blessing.

PRAYER:
Ask God to give strength and courage to those around the world being pressured to deny their faith today.

34 Helen Berhane, *Song of the Nightingale* (Colorado Springs: Authentic Media, 2009), pp. 70-71.

September 18

TURNING THE OTHER CHEEK

If someone slaps you on one cheek, turn to them the other also. If someone takes your coat, do not withhold your shirt from them.
Luke 6:29

An Open Doors colleague shares the following incident from an SSTS seminar in Indonesia:

I remember standing in front of nearly 800 pastors on the island of Timor facing a serious dilemma. Most of the pastors were victims of attacks by Muslims on the island of Ambon. They had lost homes, churches and even family members during these attacks. They were hurt, devastated and needed answers to the challenges they faced.

As soon as I started preaching, one pastor stood up and interrupted me: "Must we accept the persecution from the Muslims or must we retaliate? We are tired of forgiving just to be attacked again. We believe it is time to defend the honor of God and retaliate. What must we do?"

I understood perfectly the challenges. I had met those who were attacked and I have seen the scars on the bodies of those who simply accepted it. I understood there was no easy answer. Then another pastor interrupted: "No, pastor, tell this brother he is wrong. The Bible tells us to accept our suffering. We will dishonor God if we retaliate. Seventy times seven we need to forgive. Isn't this true?"

I looked at the pastors and replied, "The Bible is clear. You **MUST** retaliate!"

There was silence. I sensed the division. I could see the smiles on the faces of those who agreed and saw those who disagreed getting ready to leave the hall.

"Wait, brothers!" I intervened. "Before you leave, let me finish my sentence. Luke 6 teaches us clearly to retaliate, but in doing so, we need to choose our weapons. When someone curses you, you don't just accept it. You retaliate by blessing him. When someone mistreats you and persecutes you, you don't just accept it. You retaliate by praying for him. When someone takes your cloak you retaliate by giving your undercoat. When someone slaps you in the face, don't stand for it. Retaliate! Turn your other cheek."

The burden of just accepting suffering was broken. They were satisfied.

RESPONSE:
Today I will retaliate against attacks upon me using the spiritual weapons of Jesus.

PRAYER:
Lord, may I always remember how You want me to respond when others treat me badly.

September 19

WE DO NOT HAVE TO BE PERFECT TO DO GOD'S WILL

But we have this treasure in jars of clay to show that this all-surpassing power is from God and not from us.
2 Corinthians 4:7

Open Doors colleague, Ron Boyd-MacMillan, shares the following insight from his teaching, "Why I Need to Encounter the Persecuted Church."

While living in Hong Kong, I used to make a point of having dinner with many of the Open Doors supporters worldwide that gave up some holiday time to courier Bibles into China. Often in the course of their travels some of them would meet famous house church leaders and say, "To be truthful, I was a bit disappointed in meeting." They would add something like, "I thought these people would be remarkable saints, and of course they were, but they were also quite prejudiced, or rude, or had some other feature that I did not think worthy of a very spiritual leader." They assumed that the persecuted were "super-saints." But they are not.

It is a very unfortunate trend to idolize the persecuted. We assume that if a Christian survives twenty years in a stinking prison cell they are in a completely different spiritual category from ourselves. They are of course different in what they have experienced, but that does not necessarily make them more spiritual. As J.C. Ryle once put it, "Even the best of men are only men at the best." They often retain the blind spots and prejudices of their culture.

On one occasion I was taking a distinguished Bible teacher to meet a revival leader in Lanzhou, Gansu province. This Chinese leader had seen over 50,000 people come to know the Lord through his ministry over a ten-year period, but to our amazement he taught that "you can only come to faith on a Sunday." He had been taught Christianity by his beloved grandmother, who believed the Lord would only listen to pleas for repentance on a Sunday. We talked and argued about this, and eventually he threw us out shouting, "You just hate my Granny." I hear now, years later, that he has extended the "repentance period" to Saturday as well. Yet he is still an extremely effective evangelist despite this chronic, man-made obstacle he has erected to the grace of God!

Surely the great point is this: flawed as some Chinese leaders were, they did the will of God mightily. They labored in a country that has seen the number of Christians grow from less than one million in 1949 to over eighty millions today—the largest revival in the history of Christendom. God didn't stop pouring out his Spirit because his saints were imperfect.

If the persecuted teach us anything, it is that God will work through us even despite our prejudices, blind spots and eccentricities. If we offer ourselves, we will be used…as we are.

We do not have to be perfect to do God's will. Otherwise, no one could.

RESPONSE:
Today I will walk in faith thankful that I do not have to be perfect to do God's will.

PRAYER:
Thank You, Lord, that You can still use me with all my imperfections and blind spots.

September 20

SINGING IN THE SPIRIT

Let the message of Christ dwell among you richly as you teach and admonish one another with all wisdom through psalms, hymns, and songs from the Spirit, singing to God with gratitude in your hearts.

Colossians 3:16

Open Doors colleague, Ron Boyd-MacMillan, shares the following insight from his teaching, "Why I Need to Encounter the Persecuted Church."

Once I spent a week in the company of a famous female Chinese evangelist. Many characteristics that made her stand out; her courage, her long hours on her knees, her carefully cultivated simplicity of faith. But at the time, these were not the features that stuck with me and ended up transforming my faith. What actually impressed me about her was the same thing that impressed me about everyone else around her too. They were always singing. Singing hymns!

Three features of the singing were striking. First, the hymns themselves were not in the least profound. In terms of content, they lacked theological depth and poetic phrasing. Wesley or Newton would not have been proud of these offerings.

Second, they couldn't sing very well. Chinese are not renowned for their harmonic skills in any case. They warbled, croaked, and droned and screeched...all with a complete disregard for the tune.

Third, they sang primarily to themselves. Oh sure, they sang in groups and to each other, but the most of their singing was done by themselves, to themselves. But all this did not matter. The songs worked.

Travelling around with these persecuted believers made me realize I had forgotten how much Christians sing praises. For me, the only time I sang was in church or an occasional chorus at a home group. I had never really sung hymns to myself, or seen singing to another as a ministry. I didn't have a terribly good singing voice, and felt like I should leave it to those who were good at it. But after hearing everyone in the Persecuted Church of China singing virtually all the time, and seeing the difference it made to them spiritually, I wondered, *Why do I not sing by myself, to my own spirit, or see singing as a ministry of encouragement?*

So when I came back, I picked my seven favourite hymns. Ones like, "We rest on thee, Our Shield and Our Defender," and, "Breathe on Me Breath of God." I learned them, and during my quiet times, I sang to my spirit. And I found it to be true. A song lifts the spirit like nothing else. And as I read the Bible, I saw how central singing was to the practice of faith. The Israelites sing all the time in the temple; prisoners Paul and Silas sing in the cell; the early house churches sing to each other, and the Scriptures climax in the great throne visions of John in Revelation, and what is going on in that most hallowed place but the singing of a "new song".

Thank you Persecuted Church, for restoring a lost but key component of my quiet time.

RESPONSE:
Today I will sing to the Lord in my spirit and gain encouragement for service to Him.

PRAYER:
Lord, I ask You to help me be one who is always singing Your praises with my spirit.

September 21

DEALING WITH DIFFERENCES

"Master," said John, "we saw a man driving out demons in your name and we tried to stop him, because he is not one of us." "Do not stop him," Jesus said, "for whoever is not against you is for you."
Luke 9:49-50

The disciples complained to the Lord Jesus that some other men who were not of their group were ministering in Jesus' name. The disciples had forbidden them to continue, but Jesus rebuked them. The Lord had to deal with Peter very specifically through a vision and a dramatic experience before he could say, *"I now realize how true it is that God does not show favoritism, but accepts men from every nation who fear Him and do what is right"* (Acts 10: 34,35).

The Apostle Paul enlarged on this idea in Romans 14. He summarized his teaching when he said, *"Who are you to judge someone else's servant?"* (Romans 14:4). *"You then, why do you judge your brother?...for we will all stand before God's judgment seat"* (Romans 14:10).

We must be very careful about rejecting someone simply because they do not serve the Lord the same way we do. If we quietly go about the work the Lord has given us, we need not be overly concerned about how others feel led to serve Him.

In Eritrea, Helen Berhane experienced differences among believers even in the horrible conditions of the shipping container prison. She writes in her book, *Song of the Nightingale*:

It was an incredible experience to share my imprisonment with others who were also imprisoned for their faith. However, with Christians from six different denominations in one container, we often found that we disagreed. For example, there was one lady who was a traditional Orthodox Christian; a very strong believer. If I told a joke as part of my Bible teachings she disapproved, so she actually began to pray and worship alone, and even eat alone. I found it amazing that even in a container she would not socialize with Christians she perceived to be too worldly! Other people argued over how we prayed. Some people preferred to pray silently, while others would pray out loud, and in such a small space it was easy to see why this was a problem.

I had to remind them, "We are not in our churches now. In our own church halls we can do as we please, but here we must tolerate each other's differences. If we keep fighting they may send us to the underground prisons in the mountains, so we must be thankful for our freedom to worship together here, and not argue about the ways we used to worship when we were free."[35]

RESPONSE:
Today I will be very careful about rejecting someone simply because they do not serve the Lord the same way I do.

PRAYER:
Lord, help me to be humble in dealing with believers who see things differently than I.

---

35 Helen Berhane, *Song of the Nightingale* (Colorado Springs: Authentic Media, 2009), pp. 49-50.

September 22

SIMPLICITY OF THE CHURCH

And God placed all things under his feet and appointed him to be head over everything for the church, which is his body, the fullness of him who fills everything in every way.
Ephesians 1:22-23

Rene looked carefully both ways as he turned the corner. No one seemed to be watching. Wiping the perspiration from his forehead he glanced at his watch. He was five minutes early. He walked slowly around the block a second time to arrive at the large gate at exactly 7:14. He pressed the bell three times: short...long...short. It was the newly changed code to indicate he was a fellow-believer. The gate opened and closed quickly as Rene slipped inside. In two hours time there were several hundred believers gathered secretly in the basement for fellowship.

Rene sat quietly waiting for the others. He remembered reading in a magazine about a small group in China that gathered weekly in the back room of a small store to worship together. It was the era of the infamous Cultural Revolution. Since the believers could easily be overheard by anyone entering the store, they "sang" hymns together without words or music. Someone whispered the name of the song and they would silently move their lips and simply think of the words and music.

He chuckled out loud. The memory came of Pastor Wally saying, "We are an underground church like the believers behind the Bamboo Curtain, but the difference is that we can praise in full voice because the facilities are sound proofed. Not even our closest neighbour can hear us."

This is a description of a church group in Saudi Arabia - a country that has not had an official church in over fourteen hundred years. And yet many believers meet together secretly and at great risk all over the country.

The most common way for the church to express its faith in Western societies has been through the institutional pattern. Consequently, this is the only pattern with which many Christians are familiar. But this form can be easily eliminated by a repressive government, is difficult to maintain in other hostile environments, and may not be appropriate to local cultural needs. There are other options if you and your fellow believers were under the rule of those who were trying to repress Christianity.

RESPONSE:
Today I will accept that there are many forms of church to fulfill the five biblical functions of the church.

PRAYER:
Pray for those around the world who must meet in secret for worship services.

September 23

THE FORMS OF THE CHURCH

Day after day, in the temple courts and from house to house, they never stopped teaching and proclaiming the good news that Jesus is the Christ.

Acts 5:42

The place in which a church meets varies. The use of big buildings, complex organizations, involved programs, huge budgets that provide for schools, hospitals, orphanages and other social activities are only possible in financially strong unrestricted societies.

Although the Lord has blessed these activities in many places in the world, we must recognize that they are not essential to the existence of the church. In some countries these activities are forbidden by the government, while in others, the local economic situation makes them impossible. Still the church can thrive, because it is not dependent on these things. Serious problems have arisen when Christians have become confused on this point.

A number of years ago, for example, some Vietnamese leaders thought that their lack of funds for such things was the cause of the slow growth of Christianity there. On one occasion, the following conversation was overheard:

"Do you have communists in your part of the country?" the observer asked.

"Most assuredly. They are there," the leader replied.

"Are they growing in numbers and influence?" he then asked.

The leader hesitated momentarily, then admitted sadly, "Yes, they are growing very fast."

"Can you show me their meeting places and schools or introduce me to their leaders?" the observer continued.

"Certainly not," the leader said in disgust. "If they are known, they will be arrested."

"You mean they are secret, without buildings or property and still they grow in number?" the observer asked in amazement.

"Yes, you could say that," the leader responded.

"Then it must be that their growing influence does not depend on such things. If they can be wrong in their beliefs and still grow without money and buildings, why do you think the church of Jesus Christ needs these things?" the man concluded.

If God provides these things, then use them for His glory. If He does not, remember that the New Testament church had none of these things, but they turned their world upside down (Acts 17:6). The early Christians did not confuse the church's functions with methods. If they had done so, the church would have died in the bondage of Jewish legalism. The early churches were not encumbered by the presence of buildings, nor hindered by the lack of them. They met in public places, when they were permitted to do so, but when they were not, they went from house to house.

RESPONSE:
I will no longer confuse the forms of the church with the biblical functions of the church.

PRAYER:
Thank You Lord for those who use their homes as centers for Your worship and declaration of the good news of Your love.

September 24

THE BODY OF JESUS

And he is the head of the body, the church; he is the beginning and the firstborn from among the dead, so that in everything he might have the supremacy.
Colossians 1:18

In China, one small group of believers gathered weekly in the back room of a small store to worship together during the Cultural Revolution. Since they could easily be overheard by anyone entering the store, they "sang" hymns together without words or music. Someone whispered the name of the song and the group together silently moved their lips simply "thinking" the words and music.

In the Bible, the church is called "***God's husbandry***," "***the body of Christ***," and the "***household of Christ***" (I Corinthians 3:9; 12:13,27; Hebrews 3:6). It is also called His bride and a wife (Revelation 19:7-9; 21:2,9; Ephesians 5:22-33). These are all simple examples given to help us understand that the church is a spiritual entity, neither a building nor a human organization. This is probably the most common error in belief found among Christians. It is important that we realize that the church of Jesus Christ is basically and primarily spiritual.

When Peter confessed that Jesus was the Christ, the Son of the Living God, Jesus responded by promising to build His church on the solid "***rock***" of this great truth and that the gates of hell would not withstand it. (Matthew 16:13-18). According to the New Testament, a person who has recognized, as Peter did, that Jesus is the Christ, and who trusts in Him by faith as Savior and Lord, is "***born again***" (John 3:1-17).

This new birth is a spiritual experience that opens the heart to the Spirit of God. He enters that heart and dwells there. This believer is then a "***priest***" of God and enjoys direct access into the holy presence of God (I Peter 2:5,9; Hebrews 4:16). This relationship of an individual with Christ is clearly a spiritual relationship, and Jesus joins together individuals who have this faith in Him into a spiritual body—His church.

RESPONSE:
I will cherish my relationship with Christ and His body—the church.

PRAYER:
Thank You Lord for Your household of faith. Help me to understand its functions and walk and serve in expressing them.

September 25

FOR THE BENEFIT OF THE BODY

If one part suffers, every part suffers with it; if one part is honored, every part rejoices with it.
1 Corinthians 12:26

It is a beautiful picture when the church of Jesus Christ operates as the Bible teaches for the benefit of the body.

On January 21st 2007, Dimitri from Uzbekistan was arrested and subsequently sentenced to four years in a labor camp because of his "illegal religious activities." The labor camp in which he is being held is 850 kilometers from where his wife Marina and their three daughters live. They are allowed to visit him just a few times a year.

Marina is grateful for all the prayers for them and for all the encouragement which they have received through letters and cards.

"We've really experienced God's faithfulness. He's protected and blessed us, and He's always been close when we've needed Him. We want to thank God, because He doesn't leave us on our own. He helps us through tough times.

"I've visited Dimitri a few times and also taken the children with me a few times. His health is good and he's even trying to encourage others. They have to get up early in the morning to start work. Often he doesn't have the strength to pray, but then he senses that others are praying for him. He finds his strength in the Lord Jesus, tries not to become oppressed by the circumstances, and he thinks a lot about us. This helps him to survive.

"His Bible was confiscated by the guards and now he is writing out Bible texts from memory in a little notebook. In this way he has his own handwritten Word of God. He'd like to have his Bible back, but permission is still being refused.

"We're thankful for the many friends who are supporting us and writing to us at this difficult time. I'd also like to thank everyone for their many prayers. Now I'm coming to understand what the Bible means when it says, 'we are one body,' because 'if one part suffers, every part suffers with it.'"

RESPONSE:
Today I will not just think about myself, but function as a vital member of the body of Jesus.

PRAYER:
Lord, bless prisoners like Dimitri who today may be feeling lonely. May they experience the blessing of realizing they are part of Your body.

September 26

DEREGISTERING IN CENTRAL ASIA

And he is the head of the body, the church; he is the
beginning and the firstborn from among the dead, so that
in everything he might have the supremacy.
Colossians 1:18

"Our church is considering whether to relinquish our government registration," said Pastor Sergei to our SSTS seminar group in a restricted Central Asia country. No one knew how to respond. The seminar was being conducted in this pastor's church because it was the only one in the region registered with the central government!

"Why?" someone asked.

"Here is our reasoning," Pastor Sergei graciously replied. "We have a 'grandfather clause' that permits us to be registered even though we do not meet the current requirements to be registered. But I have to file a report with the government each month outlining the number of meetings, who attended and how much money we received from these meetings and people. I find it very difficult to give an accurate report, thereby possibly jeopardizing some individuals who attend our meetings, or to falsify the reports and thereby violate my conscience.

Pastor Sergei added, "I feel like I am working every day for the NSS (National Security System—former KGB). As a denomination, we are unprepared for persecution. I feel my people would be better prepared for persecution if we met in smaller cell groups and were not registered."

To register a church in this country, three conditions must be met: a list of at least one hundred members whose last names are Russian or Koreans but no one from one of the traditional Muslim tribal groups; a vote of 100% among the church neighbors favoring a meeting in their area; and a building, but few want to rent or sell a building to a Christian group—even if the neighbors approve!

"This is why we are thinking of deregistering with the government and going underground as smaller cell churches," concludes Pastor Sergei. Then he looks straight into your eyes and asks, "Do you agree?"

RESPONSE:
Today I reaffirm that Christ is the head of His church, not temporal authorities.

PRAYER:
Lord, give wisdom today to church leaders in countries where registration is so difficult and fraught with so many complexities.

September 27

NORTH KOREA TESTIMONY

And now, compelled by the Spirit, I am going to Jerusalem, not knowing what will happen to me there. I only know that in every city the Holy Spirit warns me that prison and hardships are facing me. I consider my life worth nothing to me; my only aim is to finish the race and complete the task the Lord Jesus has given me—the task of testifying to the good news of God's grace.

Acts 20:22-24

After Gyeong Ju Son, a young woman from North Korea, gave her moving testimony at The Third Lausanne Congress on World Evangelization in Cape Town in October 2010, the 4200 participants from over 190 countries, came away stunned—many moved to tears.

Born in Pyongyang, North Korea's capital, this petite 18-year-old is the daughter of a former high-ranking government leader—an assistant of the North Korean leader, Kim Jong-Il.

In 1998, when Gyeong Ju was at the tender age of six, her father suffered severe political persecution and the family was forced to flee to China. It was there that her parents came to know the amazing grace and love of God. After only a few months, her mother, pregnant with their second child, died of leukemia.

"It was in the midst of this family tragedy that my father joined a Bible study led by missionaries from South Korea and America, and after a time his strong desire was to become a missionary to North Korea," she says.

In 2001 her father was reported and arrested by the Chinese police, to be sent back to North Korea, where he was sentenced to prison. Desperately crying out to God during this time, his three-year incarceration only served to strengthen his faith. After his release he returned to China and Gyeong Ju Son was reunited briefly with her father.

"Not long after he chose to return to North Korea—instead of enjoying a life of religious freedom in South Korea—to share

Christ's message of life and hope among the hopeless people of his homeland."

In 2006 her father's work was discovered by the North Korean government and once again he was imprisoned. Not having heard from her father again, she assumes he has been publicly executed on charges of treason and espionage. This is often the fate of confessing Christians in North Korea.

Left in China, Gyeong Ju Son was adopted for a while by the family of a young pastor, and it was their love, care, compassion and protection that made a deep impression on her. When they left for America she was given the opportunity to go to South Korea.

RESPONSE:
Today I give thanks for brothers and sisters who serve Jesus at the cost of their own lives.

PRAYER:
Pray today for those believers still living in North Korea and committed to evangelism.

September 28

NORTH KOREA TESTIMONY – PART 2

Now if we are children, then we are heirs—heirs of God and co-heirs with Christ, if indeed we share in his sufferings in order that we may also share in his glory.
Romans 8:17

At the Third Lausanne Congress on World Evangelization in Cape Town in October 2010, North Korean Gyeong Ju Son shared her moving life story. Here is the conclusion:

While staying at the Korean Consulate in Beijing, waiting to go to South Korea, her life was dramatically and irrevocably changed when God came to her in a dream. She says:

"He had tears in His eyes. He walked towards me and asked 'Gyeong Ju, how much longer are you going to keep me waiting? Walk with me. Yes, you have lost your earthly father, but I am your Heavenly Father and whatever has happened to you, was because I love you.'"

Praying to God for the very first time, she gave Him her heart, soul, mind and strength, asking that she would be used at His will. A deep love for the lost people of North Korea and the need to bring the love of Jesus to them, has subsequently become her life purpose. She continues:

"I look back over my short life and I see God's hand everywhere. Six years in North Korea, eleven in China and now in South Korea. Everything I suffered: all the sadness and grief, all that I have experienced and learned; I want to give it all to God and use my life for His Kingdom. In this way I also hope to bring honor to my father."

Still a student, the intention of this young and vibrant follower of Christ is to go to university to study political science and diplomacy, and then work for the rights of the voiceless in North Korea. She concluded:

"Brothers and sisters here in this place, I humbly ask you to pray that the same light of God's grace and mercy that reached my father and my mother and now me, will one day soon dawn upon the people of North Korea, my people!"

RESPONSE:
Today I will continue to believe that God takes terrible situations and turns them into good.

PRAYER:
Lord, we pray that you will call many youths like Gyeong Ju to minister among the needy people of North Korea.

*To learn more about the challenges of following Jesus in North Korea, order the book **Escape From North Korea** from your national Open Doors office or from Amazon.com.*

September 29

I AM NOT AFRAID ANYMORE

One night the Lord spoke to Paul in a vision: "Do not be afraid; keep on speaking, do not be silent. For I am with you, and no one is going to attack and harm you, because I have many people in this city."
Acts 18:9-10

The Apostle Paul was experiencing great pressure and persecution while sharing the gospel in Corinth. With the encouragement of these "red letter" words from Jesus Himself, Paul gained courage to stay in Corinth for another year and a half teaching the word of God.

Known for its rich historical heritage and tourist attractions, Aurangabad is one of the very famous districts of Maharashtra, India. It has been an important place since ancient times because of its location in the famous Silk Route. The route traveled across the width of Asia to Europe. The city is named after the great Mughal Emperor Aurangzeb and is one of the fastest growing cities in India. Marathi and Urdu are the main languages spoken in the city.

During the first Standing Strong Through The Storm (SSTS) seminar, the participants expressed profound appreciation, gratitude and the need for more such seminars. So new sets of people were targeted in order to bring awareness and educate them on how to handle persecution when it comes.

The majority of the students confessed that they had never heard this kind of teaching before. Topics such as addressing religious intolerance were highly appreciated. While the participants were initially apprehensive of sharing their testimonies, they stepped forward after watching the persecution related movies and video clips, and boldly shared what God had done in their lives.

Pratima Pagare attended and commented, "I was always scared to death with the thought that fundamentalists will attack and stone us because we minister to people in the name of Jesus. I am so encouraged to come to this seminar and to hear the testimonies of people who faced persecution in their ministries and still went on. I was also strengthened by the teachings on how to stand strong in the midst of storms and this has driven away all my fears. I thank God and Open Doors for this."

Priti Alhad said, "I did not know what the content of the seminar would be, but gradually as the sessions went by, I considered myself privileged to be present here and be blessed by the teachings. I am not afraid of persecution but these teachings encouraged me and prepared me for the times of persecution…As I go from here I want to share this knowledge that I have gained here and create awareness among my church members and utilize these teachings in my ministry. I thank your ministry for organizing this seminar in our area.

RESPONSE:
Today I will keep on speaking and not be silent trusting the Lord for His protection and blessing.

PRAYER:
Help me Lord to lose my fearfulness and trust You when I face those who oppose me.

September 30

OVERCOMERS

*To him who overcomes, I will give the right to sit with me
on my throne, just as I overcame and sat down
with my Father on his throne.*
Revelation 3:21

Christians in areas of persecution have used many metaphors and similes to describe the victory of following Jesus and becoming an overcomer as He was. Here are some examples:

In the former Soviet Union, believers said:
Overcomers are like nails. The harder you hit them, the deeper they go!

In China believers said:
Overcomers are like bamboo. The more you cut them down, the faster and stronger they grow back.

In Iran believers said:
Overcomers are like rubber balls. The harder you throw them down on the floor, the higher they rebound!
and
Overcomers are like flowers. The more you crush them, the stronger and sweeter the fragrance.

In the Philippines believers said:
Overcomers are like stained-glass cathedral windows at night. Their true beauty is revealed only when there is light from within.

In India believers said:
Overcomers are like tea bags. You have to put them in hot water to know how strong they are!

You can be an overcomer! And you can stand strong through the storm!

RESPONSE:
Today I will be an overcomer standing strong through the storm.

PRAYER:
Pray that all Christians living under severe persecution will be encouraged and understand what it means to be an overcomer... as well as anticipate the many rewards Jesus promises to overcomers.

October 1

FORGIVE YOUR ENEMIES

And when you stand praying, if you hold anything against anyone, forgive them, so that your Father in heaven may forgive you your sins.
Mark 11:25

Hatred of her enemies is something Takoosh Hovsepian, the wife of an Iranian pastor murdered in 1994 no longer has. She says: "I've learned a lesson at God's University about how to love your enemies."

As a teenager, Takoosh prayed that she might be allowed to marry a pastor, so that she could spend her life in the service of God. Her wish was fulfilled, but the way would not be easy.

Her husband, Pastor Haik Hovsepian, was forty-eight years old when one day he did not come home. After twelve days, it became apparent that he had been killed at the behest of the Iranian government. About that time, four other Iranian pastors were also murdered in a cowardly way. They refused to sign an official declaration that they would not evangelize among Muslims.

In Iran, ninety-eight percent of the population is Muslim. After the Islamic Revolution of 1979 in particular, the problems for Christians became increasingly great.

Takoosh says, "During the revolution, hundreds of people threatened to set fire to the churches, which fortunately did not happen. The Islamic government does not want Muslims to go to church and evangelism among them is forbidden."

Pastor Hovsepian held important positions in the Iranian Church. On various occasions, he stated that he was willing to go to the utmost for his faith and for the church. His wife reflects, "Haik repeatedly said, 'We don't have to be afraid. We must trust in God.' But in my heart, I was afraid. Haik was full of love for people, even for his Muslim neighbours. They were welcome at the church; they knew that he would help them even in times of difficulty."

The day that Haik left to collect a friend from the airport and never came back is deeply engraved on the memory of the widow and her children. At the police station, the eldest son, Joseph, was only shown a photo of his father. According to the police, the body of Pastor Hovsepian had been found in an alleyway in Teheran.

Takoosh says, "I only had hatred in my heart, hatred for my enemies who had murdered Haik. I was not able to forgive them. I prayed with my lips, 'God, give me the strength to forgive,' but before I prayed, in my imagination I saw myself throwing mud at them. But one day a miracle happened. God taught me how I could forgive my enemies. I was asking for something which on the deepest level I did not want to ask for. But gradually, in a process of ups and downs which took months, God gave me the strength to pray more and more with my heart for those who had murdered my husband. God answered this prayer.

"Then I was no longer praying only with my lips, but from the depths of my heart. I had learned not only to trust in God and to lean on Him, but also how I can forgive my enemies."

RESPONSE:
Today I will forgive offences against me so God will forgive my sins.

PRAYER:
Pray for many Christian brothers and sisters of the Persecuted Church who have difficulty forgiving those who hurt them or their family.

October 2

CHRISTIAN PRISONER ENCOURAGEMENT

Your love has given me great joy and encouragement,
because you, brother, have refreshed the hearts of the
Lord's people.
Philemon 1:7

Twenty-nine-year-old Maryam Rostampour and thirty-two-year old
Marzieh Amirizadeh spent 259 days in Tehran's notorious Evin prison
in 2009 in Iran. They had to overcome the fear of life imprisonment
and the possibility of execution because they loved and followed
Jesus Christ. They had to remain strong through weeks in solitary
confinement, and endless hours of interrogation by Iranian officials
and religious leaders. They had to endure months of harsh living
conditions and debilitating sickness. In their first interview (with
Sam Yeghnazar of Elam Ministries), they shared what life was like in
prison and how they survived.

Marzieh said, "I would like to thank them [prayer partners] for their
prayers and support, and the letters they sent us. During this time it
wasn't just Maryam and Marzieh who were imprisoned, but all these
prayer warriors. This was a great encouragement for us. We felt their
presence alongside us. So please keep praying for those who are in
prison for their faith, believers in Afghanistan and Pakistan...Don't
think that your prayers are unimportant."

She added, "We heard that people sent us letters in prison, but we
didn't get any of them. Just hearing that people sent us letters, was a
great encouragement to us. And what's interesting is that the guards
who opened our letters, read the Bible verses and the prayers, and
were impacted. We know this because they told us and mentioned
some of the verses from the Gospel. I can't thank them [those who
sent letters] with all that is in my heart; I can say 'thank you,' but this
is not enough."

Maryam concluded, "I thank them. It's true we didn't see the letters
they sent, but we knew there was a large group supporting us.
This was a huge encouragement to us and helped us to stand firm.

We heard from our guards that forty to fifty letters were coming every day. They saw how Christians stood together to support their own. This was something that gave us hope."

Check our website for names and addresses of Christians in prison for their faith whom you can write to and pray for.

RESPONSE:
Today I will pray for and send letters to Christians in prison for their faith to encourage them in their persecution.

PRAYER:
Pray for hope and encouragement for Christian prisoners—especially those in solitary confinement—in places like Pakistan and Afghanistan.

October 3

PEACEMAKING IS VERY PRACTICAL

*Peacemakers who sow in peace reap a harvest of
righteousness.*
James 3:18

Jesus' instruction to His followers to be peacemakers is not as easily practiced in some areas of the world as we in the West might think. Tribal differences can cause deep divides.

In April 2011, Open Doors sponsored a Christian youth camp in the southern Philippines bringing together 115 youths, mostly believers from Muslim background (MBB's) from four different Muslim tribal groups. The goal of this camp was to show the youths that Jesus is the ultimate source of peace. When we have Him in our hearts, then, we can have peace within ourselves, with others and with our environment.

Every activity of the camp was also designed to foster awareness and appreciation of each other's tribal identity. Short drama presentations every night gave the youths a chance to tell their story. Bringing these ethnic groups to a point of understanding and acceptance was the crucial part of the camp. During Bible sessions, facilitators combined their lectures with tasks that encouraged campers to express their thoughts and feelings. They described their idea of peace, distinguished between peaceful and conflicting situations, and discovered their biblical responsibility as peacemakers taking after Christ's example.

While peacemaking starts with one's self, it does not end there. It must affect other people's lives. And so, the campers did community service in three neighboring areas during the camp. But the true litmus test for a peacemaker is when a conflict breaks out. The camp was on its homestretch when two campers from different tribes got tangled in a fight during the morning assembly. It was about to turn violent, until other youths stepped in. The two youths were brought to the camp director. Everyone was clearly upset as they streamed into the classrooms for the day's round of Bible sessions.

553

They were in for a surprise. An Open Doors co-worker shared, "The fight was staged. We wanted the campers to have an opportunity to apply what they had been learning so far. During the Bible session, we processed what happened. They realized that it brought out their biases and impatience; that some of their responses were condemning. They wanted to be a peacemaker, but they had yet to learn how to sow peace in times of conflict. It is a lifestyle."

It was an important lesson for the youths to learn, especially for those who lived in conflict areas. After the session, many campers approached the two volunteer actors and asked their forgiveness for judging and condemning them.

Then, the youths were given some time to write down their commitments to becoming a peacemaker. One fifteen-year-old said, "It'll be hard becoming a peacemaker, but I will try my best...The pastor taught us that becoming a peacemaker like Jesus comes with suffering. I must be prepared for that too."

RESPONSE:
Today I will take practical steps in being a peacemaker for Jesus wherever I am.

PRAYER:
Pray for young tribal Christians who struggle with Christ-like actions and responses in conflict situations.

October 4

GOD'S AMAZING GRACE

And now, my daughter, don't be afraid. I will do for you all you ask. All the people of my town know that you are a woman of noble character.

Ruth 3:11

When I think of God's grace in an individual's life, the story of Ruth comes to mind. And not just because Ruth was the name of my own dear mother. Ruth from the Bible was a widowed but faithful daughter-in-law whom God in His grace blessed with a new country, new husband and family. She is one of the few women (and a Gentile at that) mentioned in Matthew's genealogy of Jesus.

God's grace is also the key principle in so many people's faith stories. My co-teacher in Standing Strong Through The Storm (SSTS) seminars, Jim Cunningham, was teaching in Sri Lanka and learned first-hand of this amazing example. Names used are not their real names.

Arjuna, a young married man with a family, was part of a team of Christians running an orphanage in a rural village of Sri Lanka. One of the girls from the orphanage was sexually abused by a boy in the village. The police investigated and she identified the boy. The police then arrested the boy.

But the villagers rose-up-in-arms saying Arjuna sexually assaulted the girl and she just blamed the village boy to protect Arjuna. The villagers found and forced another girl to say she too was assaulted by Arjuna.

Arjuna was ultimately sentenced to fifteen years in jail where he subsequently led a number of other prisoners to Christ. One of those men who accepted Christ was Menika. After his release from prison, Menika went to seminary and became a church-planting pastor in a small rural town of Sri Lanka.

Arjuna continued in his prison ministry. He led another criminal to Christ who had committed a capital offence and was on death row. His name was Chandra. Before he was put to death, Chandra said to Arjuna, "I'd like to give the deed to my house to someone in ministry..." It just so happened Chandra's house was in the same small rural town where Menika was beginning to plant a church.

So Chandra gave his house to the "church-planting" former prisoner, Menika, redeemed by God's grace through Arjuna's being falsely accused and sent to prison. Amazing grace!

After six and a half years Arjuna was released from prison but because of the false charge against him was unable to work with children. He now has an ongoing ministry in the prisons of Sri Lanka.

Jim said to me, "This is not how most of us would have written the script, but—as in the life of Ruth—I rejoice in God's amazing grace and provision for all involved!"

RESPONSE:
I will praise God today for His amazing grace and provision in these lives mentioned and in my own life.

PRAYER:
Thank You Lord that Your amazing grace is so real, so available and so free.

October 5

HOPE FOR THE MIDDLE EAST

At that time the disciples came to Jesus and asked,
"Who, then, is the greatest in the kingdom of heaven?"
He called a little child to him, and placed the child among
them. And he said: "Truly I tell you, unless you change
and become like little children, you will never enter
the kingdom of heaven.
Matthew 18:1-3

In the summer of 2011, Musalaha held an Israeli-Palestinian summer camp attended by seventy Palestinian and Israeli children from Christian families. A visitor shares poignant observations:

For me, after six months in the Land, this camp gave me real hope like nothing else I have experienced. There was hope in the Bible studies, in the competitions, in the craziness and laughter, and in the worship. There was hope as the children were creative with their crafts and reckless in their play. There was hope as they were just being girls and boys – having fun, making friends, getting a break from the pressures of their everyday environment…

When they arrived, many of the children found friends they had met at last year's camp. A group of two Palestinian and three Israeli girls negotiated to be in the same room. Upon receiving permission, they pulled five bunks together to make one huge bed where they could sleep together…

At the camp I realized that I wasn't noticing who was Israeli and who was Palestinian. I saw my brothers and sisters from both sides of the conflict demonstrate a love of Christ and each other above their love of sticking with their side. Leaders cared for kids, loving and instructing them regardless of where they came from. We were all there as believers in Jesus, and as should more often be the case, during camp no other identity really mattered.

One day after craft time, a Palestinian boy from the West Bank proudly pulled me aside to show me his pencil case. On it, he had painted an Israeli flag. I am not sure how his parents would feel about

557

it, but it showed me how much more simple this situation is for the children. He loved his new friends and leaders and therefore had fond feelings about the place they are from...

As my coworker Tamara and I reflected on the camp, she said, "Innocence breaks down all this hatred that we have around us. You love the good things that you see in the other side. Like Jesus said, we should be little children."

For them, the "enemy" will never be faceless, inhuman, or distant. For them, the situation will never be easy or black and white. That is good. With open eyes they can help bring change. They are the hope.

RESPONSE:
Today I will look at the problems of our world through child-like eyes and see the challenges as Jesus sees them.

PRAYER:
Thank You, Lord, there is HOPE for even the greatest challenges of our troubled world.

October 6

DISCOVERING JESUS

And the things you have heard me say in the presence of many witnesses entrust to reliable people who will also be qualified to teach others.
2 Timothy 2:2

Camping experiences for me were always positive experiences. There you live and practice your Christian faith twenty-four hours a day. And that deeply impacts the campers.

Around the world, Open Doors sponsors camps—especially for discipleship training for young people. Twenty-three-year-old Roton is one of those youths who attended a camp in Bangladesh in early 2011 for young believers from Muslim background (MBB). He said, "To attend this camp, I traveled for seven hours. I walked thirteen kilometers before getting on the bus. It was exhausting, but I wanted to know more about Jesus."

In a brief encounter with Open Doors during the camp, Roton shared that he felt pressure when he was just a new follower of Christ. "Many times, my Muslim friends would ask me why my family and I became Christians. They wanted to know how much [money] we got for converting. They asked me if the people who converted me stepped on the Koran or ate pork. I lost all my Muslim friends; everyone hated me and my family."

Roton's father was the first believer in the family, and boldly shared his faith with others. He read from the Koran, searching for portions that mentioned Jesus. Later on, however, his eye sight deteriorated to the point of blindness. So, he asked young Roton to read to him every day some passages from the Koran that specifically talked about Jesus.

"I just followed what I was told to do. In the beginning, I was reading for my father. But after few days, I realized that I was becoming more curious to find the truth myself. Because of the witness of the Koran, I found myself believing Jesus as the Holy one, the Messiah. I became a Christian soon after; I gave my life fully to Jesus," Roton testified.

Discrimination soon followed Roton's new found faith. His religion teacher mistreated him. When the school principal learned of his conversion, he was watched and compelled to recite Muslim prayers. People questioned him about Jesus Christ, but all that Roton knew about Christ he learned from the Koranic passages he read for his father. It was time to learn more. Instead of succumbing to the religious pressure he experienced, Roton—with encouragement from his father—set out on a journey to learn more about his Lord and Savior.

"I am so happy to be in this MBB youth camp. It's my first. I saw that I am not alone! Many work together for Christ. In this camp, I discovered Jesus in the Old Testament. I will read the Old Testament more—together with the New Testament—so that I am prepared to answer questions people ask me. Someday, I want to study in a Bible school, so that I can help others who are on the same road as I am."

RESPONSE:
Today I will pass on to others all that I have learned and experienced in my relationship with Jesus.

PRAYER:
Pray for young believers around the world who are in the process of developing their knowledge and discipleship in following Jesus. Pray too for camp leaders and trainers.

October 7

CHOOSING NOT TO HATE

And hope does not put us to shame, because God's love has been poured out into our hearts through the Holy Spirit, who has been given to us.

Romans 5:5

Rami Ayyad was assassinated a few years ago on October 7th for his work as the head of the Bible Society in the Gaza Strip. His murder left his wife, Pauline, burdened with three young children and a heart full of hatred for his killers.

While Rami was locking up the bookstore owned by the Palestinian Bible Society in Gaza, a vehicle pulled alongside him, and several men forced him in the back seat. Rami, remaining calm and trusting in the Lord, was allowed to call his wife. "I'm going with some young men somewhere, but I'll be home soon," he tried to reassure her. That was the last time Pauline would hear her husband's voice.

Hours later, his body was found. He had been brutally tortured and shot twice, a bullet in the chest, and one in the head. A spokesman for the Palestinian Bible Society said, "He's a martyr for Christ." Pauline recalls, "I was so broken after the death of my husband, and I hated the people who did it."

There has been no progress in the hunt for Rami's killers. A local Christian commented, "Many of the Muslims believe that Rami was evangelizing people so it was okay to kill him."

In such an environment of hatred, Pauline's resentment festered. However, the Holy Spirit in His gentle but insistent way kept whispering to her until she could carry the hatred no further. "It was then," she recalls, "that the Lord poured over me forgiveness for those who killed Rami and those who I used to blame." Her heart was set free and she heard the Lord say, "It's not everybody who gets to be called a martyr's wife." Deep in thought, she reflected, "That's a great honor."

Brother King from International Christian Concern (ICC) writes, "Pauline's experience reflects that of the Persecuted Church in general. Abused, spat upon, beaten, tortured, raped, and killed, these believers suffer as Jesus did. Sometimes they respond in very human ways, but when they listen to and follow the Holy Spirit, a great power comes into them and they possess what they could not have imagined previously – peace, love for their enemies, and forgiveness for those who delivered only pure evil to their lives…This is the gift of the Persecuted Church. In the furnace of affliction, the Spirit of God is set ablaze in their hearts. In turn, their hearts become a beacon to all they come in contact with."

RESPONSE:
Today I will thank God for the gift of His Holy Spirit. I will listen to Him and follow Him.

PRAYER:
Thank You, Lord, for the example of Pauline. Strengthen her as she raises her children.

October 8

BEAUTY FOR ASHES

...and provide for those who grieve in Zion—to bestow on them a crown of beauty instead of ashes, the oil of joy instead of mourning, and a garment of praise instead of a spirit of despair. They will be called oaks of righteousness, a planting of the LORD for the display of his splendor.

Isaiah 61:3

This Scripture has special meaning to Christian women in Central Asia. Some of their "ashes" are: domestic violence, battering of women and sexual abuse, kidnapping of young girls (for marriage purposes) which is culturally accepted and (in some countries) honor killings. Trafficking and prostitution are a well-known phenomenon: many Uzbek girls find themselves in Thailand, Tajik girls in Dubai and Azeri girls in Turkey, without passports, without rights, forced into the sex industry. Central Asian women are often treated as objects of men's desire or as the possession of men.

Poverty is everywhere in Central Asia. It adds to the heaviness of life together with serious health issues, a lack of available health care and drug and alcohol addiction. Some of the Christian women have unbelieving husbands, and rejected by relatives, become social outcasts in their villages. Others have a husband who is on the run from the authorities, is in prison for his faith or is constantly monitored by the security police. How does she deal with all the pressure and what does she feel when there is a knock on the door? Add to this all the issues related to honor and shame, and the influence of folk Islam with its occult practices and curses. There are plenty of reasons to feel overwhelmed, overburdened and depressed.

Open Doors sponsors regional conferences for these Christian women in Central Asia. The impact of the women's conferences is like a ripple effect growing into ever widening circles. For many women who come, just to worship openly and to be able to sing loudly in a big group is already a great encouragement as many come from areas where this is not possible. During the conferences there is a lot of dancing, worship, and celebration.

Several years ago some Central Asian Christian women gained the vision for starting work among women in situations of domestic abuse, trafficking and prostitution. All that was learned at the conferences was shared at home with the women in their area. Plans and teaching resources were drawn up, local churches were challenged and equipped and a start was made with various projects that are of great value to the local community.

A pastor's wife, who spent three years in prison where she became a Christian, shared that she wanted to start ministering to women in prisons but she didn't know how to start. "Now I have an idea how to minister to women," she said after having attended the conference.

As God heals the pain and releases the women from their sorrows, He sets them free into a new love for Jesus and for ministry to others, both in the church and in society. They grow as mighty trees, providing shade and covering for others; all of this for the glory of God.

RESPONSE:
Today I will live in the freedom Christ brings and become a mighty shade tree of ministry.

PRAYER:
Pray for these women's conferences in Central Asia that God will bestow beauty for ashes.

October 9

DOUBLE PORTION OF EVERLASTING JOY

Instead of your shame you will receive a double portion, and instead of disgrace you will rejoice in your inheritance. And so you will inherit a double portion in your land, and everlasting joy will be yours.

Isaiah 61:7

Yesterday we looked at some outcomes from Christian women's conferences in Central Asia. When deep issues are discussed and prayed for, and when barriers of shame and dishonor are broken through, there are usually many tears. One participant said, "In fact enough tears have been shed to make many trees grow that we won't have any desert places left!"

As a result of God's healing movement new initiatives are born to bring healing to abused and rejected women and children in society: ministry in orphanages, to street children and abused children; outreach projects to women in prostitution, safe havens for abused women; involvement in politics to stop legislation on polygamy; preventive health care; teaching on HIV/Aids and caring for patients; involvement in pastoral care, intercession and prayer ministries; ministry to people in prison, etc.

There is a desire to not only participate in a conference, but also to use what has been learned and to develop more skills. Three young Uzbek women who had been to a conference before wanted to come back to be part of the prayer team, so that they can learn, and take back the skills to minister to their own women!

Others shared that they want to minister to other women when they go back home. Some churches used to have women's ministry but for some reasons it had stopped. After this training the women wanted to revitalise the women's ministry in their churches.

A speaker at one of the conferences says:

"In other countries, we saw Priscilla's—Christian wives who were standing beside their husbands in loving and serving the Lord. In Central Asia, we not only saw the Priscilla's, we also saw Esther's and

565

Deborah's—women who by themselves are standing strong in their faith and for God. Whether they are single or have an unbelieving husband does not stop them.

"The women we have met in that training seem to have Esther's character: 'If I perish, I perish.' They stand up despite the clear warnings of their husbands, neighbours or the authorities. They know the cost. One knew very well that her husband might lose his government job if a family member would be found witnessing for Jesus. She was warned by her husband to tone down her evangelistic zeal. But she could not keep herself from speaking of Jesus. Two others have marriages about to fail if it were not for their enduring stand as wives to keep the family intact. These participants are capable to lead other women even after just the first training."

As the women penetrate the walls of shame and break the silence, God fulfils His promise of Isaiah 61:7. Instead of shame and dishonor you shall have a double portion of prosperity and everlasting joy!

RESPONSE:
Today I want to receive a double portion of prosperity and everlasting joy from the Lord.

PRAYER:
Thank You, Lord, that You can turn shame and dishonor into everlasting joy!

October 10

GOD WILL NEVER LEAVE OR FORSAKE US

"Be strong and courageous. Do not be afraid or terrified because of them, for the LORD your God goes with you; he will never leave you nor forsake you."
Deuteronomy 31:6

"When I was pregnant with our sixth child," says Bahar from Central Asia, "my husband Bahtiyar fell ill and was diagnosed with stomach cancer. We often prayed for his healing and together with the few other believers in our village we looked to God for His help. Bahtiyar was also seeing a doctor, but not much could be done for him.

"Shortly before Bahtiyar's death several men from the village mosque came to our house and talked to him. They knew he had been a Muslim before and had become a Christian. Now, when he was so ill, they started debating with him and urged him to return to Islam, promising that they would give him a decent burial. Bahtiyar did not have to think about it at all; he refused to deny Jesus and sent the men away.

"He was with us for three more days; then he passed away and went to be with the Lord. It is our custom to bury our dead on the same day, so when my son went to the other believers in the village and told them that his dad had died they arrived immediately to arrange his funeral. They and other Christians from a nearby town did everything that needed to be done and really took good care of us as a family. According to our tradition Bahtiyar's body was put in a yurt so people could pay their respects.

"As we lived in a small village the news that Bahtiyar had died was out in no time and it did not take long before the Mullah and many men from the village came to the yurt and started to shout at the believers. "You can't bury him here in our cemetery, we don't want him here! This man has left our religion, he has betrayed us, and we don't want him to defile our cemetery. Find another place!" They were really angry and even threatened to burn our house and the yurt with

Bahtiyar's body. The believers called the police but it took a while before they arrived. Meantime they moved his body to Kisul, another village nearby.

"For a while I was completely confused and did not know what to do. Was God still in control? Was He watching over us as a family, over me? Here I was, pregnant with my sixth child, my husband had just died, we had so many problems burying him and the whole village, including my own mother in law, was against us. Where and how were we going to live?

"God has promised in His Word that He will never leave us, nor forsake us, and He never does. For a brief period I thought that God had left me, but fortunately that did not last long. Soon God reassured me of His presence, I rediscovered my joy in God and I trust that He is in control, even though things in our family have been very difficult this last year."

RESPONSE:
Today I will rejoice in God's reassurance of His presence and control of all things in my life.

PRAYER:
Thank You, Lord, that You are concerned about the smallest details of my life regardless of the circumstances.

October 11

I KNOW WHO HOLDS THE FUTURE

I will be glad and rejoice in your love, for you saw my affliction and knew the anguish of my soul.
Psalm 31:7

Yesterday we saw the faith of Bahar from Central Asia. Pregnant with her sixth child, she lost her husband, Bahtiyar, to cancer. But the Muslims would not allow her to bury him in the town. She continues her story:

"We were all desperately trying to find a solution. In neighboring Kisul, a plot of land had been given to the Christians to be used as cemetery, so the believers started to dig a grave. Before they had finished, a crowd of people arrived on horseback and in a truck. Three mullahs, many young men, even women and people from the village administration, were shouting and threatening the believers. The atmosphere was grim and the believers had to leave the area to escape a beating.

"We were not able to bury my husband that day. The next day the believers secretly took his body and took it to a completely different place, much farther away from our village and buried him there at a Christian cemetery.

"Bahtiyar's mother, with her addiction to alcohol, was targeted as the channel to put pressure on the family. She is seventy and not a believer in Christ. The Mullah convinced her that the family was a shame and blemish on the village and that she had to kick her daughter-in-law out of her house. She was very angry and told them to leave. She no longer even wanted to see her own grandchildren."

During the months that the family were trying to find a solution for their situation, they got a visit from a pastor who lives in the capital city. He had heard about their situation and inquired how they were going to live.

"How? I don't know! But one thing I know that God will not abandon us! He promised that in His Word and He is true to His Word. I think the pastor was touched by our situation; he started to help us and several other believers as well. They offered us a house in a nearby town. We were thrilled and we moved. Now we have our own place, with a small garden to grow vegetables. There will always be plenty of needs for the kids, but I have seen that God is faithful.

"When my little son was born I was so happy! Even though my husband is no longer with us, we make an effort to stay close as a family. The youngest ones do not realize yet that their dad has died; they think he has gone on a trip. We have not been able to visit the grave as we don't have a car to go the cemetery.

"I don't know what the future holds for us, but God is taking care of us. Thank you for praying for us. Pray also for the other families of believers who are still in the village and face hostility every day. Please pray for my mother in law; I would like to see the relationship restored, so that she can enjoy her grandchildren!"

RESPONSE:
Though I also do not know what the future holds, I will trust in Him who holds the future!

PRAYER:
Continue to pray for Bahar and her family, especially reconciliation with her mother-in-law.

October 12

THE BODY OF CHRIST AT WORK

...so in Christ we, though many, form one body,
and each member belongs to all the others.
Romans 12:5

Training for Christian women in Pakistan, where poverty and illiteracy abound, has proven to reflect the character of the body of Christ.

A student says, "It's important for me to be here so I can learn to read and write. Then I can read the Bible for myself, which is the most important thing for me. I want the gospel to spread throughout our country. Now I study hard and I can write my name. I intend to stand before the people and read the Bible by myself so that other people may be encouraged to learn to read and write in the same way.

One teacher named Gladys says, "I have a gift for sewing, cutting, and embroidery. The other gift God has given me is to share with other people and tell them about Jesus. That is the opportunity I have and that is what I am doing here. When I began here, I said to them, 'I am not educated. I can't teach anyone.' But then the Lord said to me, 'This is My work. I will use you.'

"We do face discrimination because we live in the midst of people who don't want us to move forward, people who keep trying to push us down so that we will always be in slavery. But the women testify to what God has done for them in their lives. From the time they first come here, I can see God changing their lives because the way they speak changes and they talk about the love they've been shown and how that has affected their lives. If someday a mother's children are Christian because I taught her, I would be so happy because I would know that God had done His work through me.

Another teacher reports, "I first came to the center to learn sewing skills. But my father took me out of the center. He sent me to work for a Muslim family who lived in Turkey. The family said that I should give up my faith because it was no good. I told them that God had blessed me through this faith, and that I could not find such a blessing anywhere else, and that my faith meant everything to me.

"Then one time, when their daughter was ill, they taunted me and said I better pray for her and see what Jesus would do. So I did pray for her, and she was healed. They knew I had prayed to my God for her and so they exclaimed, 'Glory to God! Surely your Jesus does answer prayers.'

Before I left them, I testified to them, and they said that my prayers work, but I told them, 'It's not my prayers. It is the Lord who causes us to pray and it is the Lord who heals.' And they had to admit that it was true, and that my God truly does work."

Another student concludes, "The Church is the body of Christ. We have to help each other to share the love of Jesus as He has shown us."

RESPONSE:
Today I will share my giftedness with others and help build up the body of Christ.

PRAYER:
Pray for the Open Doors training sessions around the world—especially among poor and illiterate Christian women.

October 13

I AM VALUABLE

I praise you because I am fearfully and wonderfully made; your works are wonderful, I know that full well.
Psalm 139:14

She hadn't laughed for nearly two years, ever since her father's tragic death in August, 2009. Even though she still liked sports and talking with her friends, Ruth's eyes didn't shine anymore, like other teenagers. And she never returned their laughter. Never again, Ruth thought, would she feel the joy she once had, before her father was killed. A fourteen-year-old girl at the time, she still believed two years later that she was to blame for the murder of her father, a well-known church leader in eastern Colombia.

The day the guerrillas shot him, he was waiting for her in an isolated place. Her parents had given Ruth permission to go play soccer. But she was late coming back, so her father had gone looking for her. Bitterness started to fill her heart, as she became angry with herself, convinced she had caused her father's death. At her fifteenth birthday party, she couldn't stop her tears from falling. "I don't want to live anymore!" she sobbed. Suicidal thoughts became part of her daily life, as she kept fighting with her sisters and wrestling with an unhappiness about everything that made her life unbearable.

Her widowed mother, who was receiving regular emotional and material support through Open Doors' program for martyrs' families, admitted that although all four of her children were struggling with problems over their father's death, Ruth's condition was the worst.

But God turned things around for Ruth in July, when she was one of thirty widows' children invited to an "orphan encounter" camp sponsored by Open Doors for children and teenagers from six different regions of Colombia. For three days, God used counselors to confront Ruth with the reality of her pain and start her on the path of healing.

At one point, she was asked to write down on some papers all the things that she wanted to fill her heart. "I want to fill my heart with forgiveness for myself, and for those who killed my father," Ruth wrote. Then she went on to tell the others what she had written, something that she had not had the courage to talk about publicly before. Together the children and teens sometimes smiled over what they'd shared, along with tears as they released their need to cry out their pain. As they faced the words of Scripture taught to them and prayed together, the walls that Ruth had built up in her heart started to fall down.

Overjoyed, Ruth said, "It is so hard to find people who really take care of me. I thought there weren't any! But now I realize that there are some, and even that I'm valuable for those who I don't even know! I would like to be a good Christian and serve the Lord with all my heart."

RESPONSE:
Today I will recognize that I am also valuable to God who loves me.

PRAYER:
Pray for the many children in the Persecuted Church who need emotional healing.

October 14

REJOICING IN PERSECUTION

"Rejoice in that day and leap for joy, because great is your reward in heaven. For that is how their ancestors treated the prophets."
Luke 6:23

This Scripture verse follows Jesus' statement about the blessings of persecution: hatred, exclusion, insult and rejection in Luke 6:22. This description is of persecution that is like Indian curry. It can be mild, medium or hot! And this verse parallels Jesus teaching in Matthew (5:12) about how we should respond when persecution comes our way.

Jesus does not just say accept it or receive it gracefully. He seems to almost go overboard in indicating that we should be glad and rejoice by leaping for joy when we receive this kind of treatment. Some would say Jesus goes over the top here.

The reason for rejoicing is because the persecuted disciple of Jesus is going to receive a great reward in heaven and is in the company of the prophets of old who also received this kind of treatment.

Can we realistically "jump for joy" in the face of persecution?

Pastor Richard Wurmbrandt was languishing in a Romanian prison cell after months of torture and now isolation. He was meditating on this Scripture and decided to make a literal application. So Richard danced —as much as anyone could dance in a cell three paces square— leaping about the room like a madman. The first time he did it, the guard really did think he had gone mad. It was one of the guard's duties to watch for signs that a prisoner's mind was beginning to crack under the strain of imprisonment, for if he went to pieces a prisoner would be of no more use for questioning. So the guard rushed off to his canteen and came back with a hunk of bread and some cheese and sugar, and broke the rule of silence as he tried to soothe this strange, laughing, capering figure. Richard ate the food gratefully. It was a very large hunk of bread, far more than he usually had in a whole week!

In his book, *In God's Underground*, Richard Wurmbrandt shares how encouraged he was at responding literally to Jesus' direction to react to persecution with great joy and rejoicing! He had received a reward on earth as well as in heaven.

RESPONSE:
Today I will respond to even mild persecution because of Jesus with great rejoicing realizing I will receive a wonderful reward in heaven.

PRAYER:
Thank you Lord that You expect me to take Your word literally. Help me to be joyful in the face of any persecution for You.

October 15

REJOICE IN PERSECUTION

He was in the world, and though the world was made through him, the world did not recognize him. He came to that which was his own, but his own did not receive him. Yet to all who received him, to those who believed in his name, he gave the right to become children of God...

John 1:10-12

The most recent edition of the famous prayer manual, Operation World, was published in November 2010 and was quick to highlight as a global trend, "...The rise in levels of persecution – especially for Christians." The editors of the Operation World explained why:

"The end of the European colonial era, the end of Christianity's status as state religion in most of the West and the resurgence of religious sentiments globally, especially fundamentalism, all mean that Christians generally no longer operate from a position of power or privilege. Christians are subject to persecution in much of the world. Evangelicals are subject to even more due to their proselytism and commitment to the uniqueness of Christ. The presence of persecution and hardship in the life of the church appears to be normative in Scripture; **contexts where persecution does not exist at all should be as much a cause for concern as places where it is intense**."

Open Doors' Dr. Ron Boyd-MacMillan concludes:

In the end, the rise of persecution is paradoxically for Christians something to protest and to celebrate, for as a Beijing house church pastor says, **"The church is always persecuted when it does something right...it shows Christ to a world that rejects him."** Persecution is the continual replaying of John chapter one verses ten and eleven: "[Jesus] came into the very world he created, but the world didn't recognize him. He came to his own people, but even they rejected him." And so in the challenging words of a Palestinian pastor, **"Every Christian must rejoice to be persecuted, and fight for Christ to be recognized in the midst of** suffering, for suffering is the gift by which we see our need of Him who came for us and loves us."

RESPONSE:
As Christians, persecution is a paradox: something to both protest and celebrate.

PRAYER:
Lord, help me to rejoice when persecution comes my way – whether mild, medium or hot! And help me to fight for Christ to be recognized in the midst of the suffering.

October 16

LOVE YOUR NEIGHBOR

You, my brothers and sisters, were called to be free.
But do not use your freedom to indulge the flesh;
rather, serve one another humbly in love. For the entire
law is fulfilled in keeping this one command:
"Love your neighbor as yourself."
Galatians 5:13-14

The Scriptures teach that God is committed to one major objective in the lives of all His people: conforming us to the image of His Son. What is the "image of His Son?" It is found in the words of Jesus, Himself, *"For even the Son of Man did not come to be served, but to serve, and to give his life as a ransom for many"* (Mark 10:45).

It then makes sense to say that God desires the same for us. After bringing us into His family through faith in His Son, the Lord sets His sights on building into us the same qualities that made Jesus distinct—a servant's heart and a giving spirit. It's so easy to lose sight of our primary calling as Christians. Even those who lead must do so with an attitude of genuine humility and an authentic desire to help others.

The best-known symbols of Christianity are the **cross**, the **icthus** (fish symbol), and the **dove** symbolizing the Holy Spirit. Probably the least known—yet most appropriate for the Christian—is the symbol of **the towel and basin**. The towel Jesus used when in humility and service, he washed and wiped his disciples dirty feet. Jesus instructed his disciples after washing their feet that they were to wash one another's feet.

J. Dudley Woodbury tells a poignant true story that occurred in the dismal refugee camps of Peshawar, Pakistan. The fighting between the Majahideen in post-Soviet Afghanistan and the rise of the Taliban resulted in thousands of refugees flooding into the camps near the border. Most of the children in the camps ran around barefoot in both the intense heat and intense cold.

A Christian organization brought in hundreds of sandals for the children but decided not to just distribute them but care for the children's feet as well. So they utilized as many Christian volunteers as possible who washed the children's filthy feet, put medication on their sores and prayed for them silently as they gave out the sandals.

As he tells the story, some months later a Muslim primary school teacher in the camp asked her students who the best Muslims were. One little girl raised her hand and responded, "The *kafirs*." (unbelievers).

After the teacher recovered from cardiac arrest, she asked, "Why?"

The little girl said, "The Mujahideen killed my father, but the kafirs washed my feet!"

Missions to the Muslims, he concludes, will be affected less by the flames of 9/11, or even the flames that started the Arab Spring, than by the inner flames that are ignited if we so follow our Lord.[36]

RESPONSE:
Today I will look for ways to serve others in genuine humility as a disciple of Jesus Christ.

PRAYER:
Lord, help me love as You did, serve others as You did and give of myself as You did!

---

36 J. Dudley Woodberry, "Muslim Missions: Then & Now," *Christianity Today* (September 2011), p. 36.

October 17

VALUE DOUBTS AND MYSTERY

No temptation has overtaken you except what is common to mankind. And God is faithful; he will not let you be tempted beyond what you can bear. But when you are tempted, he will also provide a way out so that you can endure it.

1 Corinthians 10:13

This is a Scripture passage that many use in discipling new believers. The New International Version of the Bible footnotes this verse with the reminder that in the Greek language the word "temptation" or "tempted" can also mean "trial" or "testing." It is a characteristic of the human condition that we often have doubts about God and we feel badly about them. But the story of Job in the Old Testament reveals that we should value our doubts because they bring God close.

Co-worker Ron Boyd-MacMillan tells the story of a missionary to Tibet at the time of the Communist takeover in China. He was imprisoned on the charge of being a counter-revolutionary. Every day for three years he thought he was going to be executed—a strain that ultimately broke him.

Daily he was taken outside and made to kneel down. They put a hood over his head and stated they were going to execute him. Then when he thought he was a goner, they pulled off the hood and laughed at his fear.

He was deprived of sleep and light; often placed in cells with hundreds of screaming people; demanded to renounce his Christian faith—all tactics of psychological torture. He said, "All I had were doubts: whether God was with me; whether God still loved me; even if was truly a Christian since I was so broken…I was raised never to question God and that doubt was a sin."

One day wanting to die, he finally prayed and said, "Lord, I have to talk about my doubts to you. I'm sorry it's all I have to talk about. But I just want to be in touch with you again."

That night he felt a warm breath in the dungeon, a comforting sweet breath. And he said, "I learned that nothing must keep me from talking to God. I knew from that breath that He even wants to know about my doubts.

Then he was taken to another cell which had a window and he saw the beauty of a colorful sunset. He wept. It was a picture God had drawn in majestic colors with the black ring of mountains in the distance looking like a crown of thorns. He commented, "The colorful sunset told me Jesus is still in charge...The world may be full of human suffering but it is more full of God's beauty and grace. That got me through. I took my doubts to God and realized His beauty. The next time they took me to a mock execution, I knelt and thanked God for the sunset I had seen. My sunset from my God! And when they took off the hood they saw no more fear—only a man at peace ready to die and meet his God.

RESPONSE:
Today I will talk to God even about my doubts, trusting Him to help me sense His loving presence.

PRAYER:
Thank You God that we can value doubt and we can value mystery assured that You still love us and care for us.

October 18

TRAINING A COLONY OF ANTS

For physical training is of some value, but godliness
has value for all things, holding promise for both
the present life and the life to come.
1 Timothy 4:8

Discipleship training is a significant part of the ministry of Open Doors. Today a report from one of those involved in receiving training in the house churches of Iran:

"I am proud to be an Iranian, but I have to say that daily life has not become easier lately. Three weeks ago I had a small talk with a Muslim in a park near a main street splitting Tehran north and south. We talked in veiled terms about religion and politics. At the end, the Muslim told me, 'It feels like a big prison, to be living here.' I agreed, but didn't dare to say so. I glanced away, thinking of my Christian friend arrested in December 2010 who is still in prison now.

"I realized that I have more freedom than many of my Christian brothers and sisters who are in jail. But after talking with this Muslim, I also realized that since I became Christian, I have even more freedom than he does! Even the Christians in Tehran's notorious Evin Prison have more freedom than Muslims do. It filled me with a feeling of sympathy and I thought about the lessons we had been learning. It's part of our discipleship training.

"That training really helped our house group. Together with my wife, we are the leaders of this house church, and every week we get together for at least one meeting. We rotate places and days but it is always in the evening. We study parts of the Bible, talk about the paragraphs that we like or don't understand, and then we try to apply this to our daily life.

"This sounds good maybe, but I often wonder if this is the right way to do it. How should I know? I became a believer six years ago, when I was seventeen. I don't feel qualified to call myself a leader. What do I know about the role of the Holy Spirit, about a Christian marriage, about explaining the Bible or studying the Bible in the right way? But others came to faith later, so I am the most 'experienced' of our group.

"The training helps us enormously to grow in our own leadership roles, but also motivates us to hand down the important things we learned to others. Now we know we have to stay close to the Word of God. Because it is easy to ascribe our own thoughts to the Holy Spirit, we learned how to test them against the Bible. The training also helped us open up and discuss untouched topics, like relationships in marriage and being a servant leader like Jesus was.

"Through this discipleship training, we've been so encouraged to know that people all over the world know about us and pray for us. This helps groups like ours to stay spiritually healthy, and grow in numbers, too.

"Even though believers in house groups like ours have to stay hidden and face a lot of difficulties, I think the church of Iran is like a colony of ants: most of them you don't see!"

RESPONSE:
Today I want to see new believers I know discipled in the Scriptures. I will do everything possible to teach and model God's Word.

PRAYER:
Pray for the discipleship training in Iran and other Islamic nations. Pray that house groups will continue to grow in their faith and reach out to others around them.

October 19

WHEN HOPE FADES, FAITH EMERGES

We wait in hope for the LORD;
he is our help and our shield.

Psalm 33:20

The hope of most female refugees from North Korea fades away shortly after arriving in China. Most do not want to flee to South Korea, because then they lose all contact with their family, and they are not in the position to support them anymore. And if they go to another place in China, it is only a matter of time before they are caught by either the police or human traffickers. And who knows what happens to them then?

So, is all hope lost? "No, there is hope," says co-worker Kun-so. She picks up a Bible. "And that hope is written in this Book. For in it are profound promises. There is a heaven. Jesus loves you. All tears will be wiped away. No more death, no more pain. The Bible can even be the key to a better life now.

"But we have to bring the hard, difficult, biblical messages to the surface. The Bible says that you have to bless those who persecute you. It means you have to love the husband that abuses you. I have seen improvement when a North Korean woman was able to love instead of hate. And I direct the women to how God feels about them, how precious they are in His eyes, about what Jesus Christ did for them on Calvary. Thanks to His sacrifice there is hope. I can point the women to the day that will come eventually. The day that our Lord will wipe away every tear from their eyes, the day that death shall be no more, neither shall there be mourning, nor crying, nor pain anymore, for the former things have passed away."

"After a while, we try to teach the women to forgive their Chinese husbands for their abuse. We tell them Jesus commands us to love our husbands. I know this is not easy to do. But we have seen that some women found the strength to do loving things for their husbands, and as a result slowly the husband started to change."

Moon lost her child through a forced abortion, only days before her due date. Moon still lives with the Chinese family responsible for killing her child. But she also came into contact with a female co-worker. The worker took care of Moon as best as she could. She befriended her, prayed with her and explained about God and His love for her.

"I will be forever grateful," shares Moon. "Thanks to you, I came into contact with God. As I learn more and more about Him through your Bible studies, I am grateful that this wonderful Being loves me. China and North Korea have not changed. I am still a person with no rights, and there is always the threat that the police will find me and send me back to North Korea.

"My situation is terrible, humanly speaking. But I feel like I am living in a whole new world, just because I know God. And I know my baby is with Him."

When hope fades, faith emerges.

RESPONSE:
Today I will place my hope in the Lord and trust Him to change the situations around me.

PRAYER:
Pray for North Korean refugees—especially women—who suffer severely often losing hope. Pray that they will indeed find hope in the Lord.

October 20

FACING TRIALS

Consider it pure joy, my brothers, whenever you face trials of many kinds, because you know that the testing of your faith develops perseverance. Perseverance must finish its work so that you may be mature and complete, not lacking anything.

James 1:2-4

James, in his letter to the early Christians, lists the qualities that many kinds of trials develop in us.

She stood outside the doorway of the church intrigued by the love and joy displayed by those inside. The missionary had asked her to come in, but she had politely declined. This was a hostile area in the Philippines, and her father had strictly forbidden her to have anything to do with "those Christians."

Unknown to the little Filipino girl, the missionary was praying fervently for her soul. Finally one Sunday morning, the little girl accepted the invitation to attend the Sunday school class. There she also opened her heart to Jesus and became a child of God. The missionary presented her with a beautiful white dress, representing the fact that Jesus had washed all her sins away.

The next Sunday the little girl was nowhere to be found. Concerned for the girl, the missionary travelled to her home village. Arriving at her home, she found the young, new believer lying in the dirt. Her white dress was torn, filthy, and soaked in blood. The girl's father hadn't shared the missionary's joy in his daughter's new-found faith. In a drunken rage he had beaten her, repeatedly kicked her, and left her to die.

The missionary gently lifted the fragile girl and carried her back to the church where a doctor rushed to help. But there was nothing he could do. He removed the ragged dress and cleaned her up, but her injuries were too severe. The missionary stayed with her, trying to comfort her during her final hour.

Upon regaining consciousness the little girl made an unusual request. She insisted on holding in her hand the white dress the missionary had given her. They explained that it was torn and soaked with blood and dirt. With the simple faith of a child she whispered, **"I just want Jesus to know that I was willing to bleed for Him."**

RESPONSE:
Today I acknowledge that struggles and trials are exactly what I need in my life. Without them, I would be crippled. I would never fly!

PRAYER:
Lord, cause my suffering to make what I really believe to be evident to others.

October 21

THE GLORY OF HEAVEN

Now if we are children, then we are heirs—heirs of God and co-heirs with Christ, if indeed we share in his sufferings in order that we may also share in his glory. I consider that our present sufferings are not worth comparing with the glory that will be revealed in us.

Romans 8:17-18

Suffering and persecution turn our hearts and minds to the glory that will be ours in heaven. Jesus promises a great reward in heaven to those who suffer (Matthew 5:12). Paul says above that the sufferings of the present are not worthy to be compared with the glory of the future, and Peter agreed (I Peter 1:6, 7; 4:13; 5:1-10). A Christian song when I was growing up says, "It will be worth it all, when we see Jesus." Those that are living today as spiritual "refugees" look longingly toward the eternal home.

Hebrews chapter eleven helps us to understand the history of this. In the first part of the chapter which is the "hall of faith" we see faith examples of power, life and vitality. Then in verse thirty-five the list changes to those who lost their lives—some through horrendous persecution. Yet all were commended for their faith.

In his book *The Barbarian Way*, Erwin McManus comments about this:

> All of them chose and walked the barbarian way, and they were blessed because they did not fall away on account of Jesus. They trusted Jesus with their lives, and they lost their lives on the journey. If you could interview any one of them, however, each would insist that even in the midst of suffering and hardship, he was most fully alive. They were not disappointed in God because they did not misunderstand who He was. They understood His call, and they chose it willingly. John the Baptist would join their number. Some barbarians survive the night in the lion's den; others experience their darkest night and wake in eternity.[37]

37 Erwin McManus, *The Barbarian Way* (Nashville: Thomas Nelson Publishers, 2005), p. 41.

RESPONSE:
Today I will rejoice in the glory of heaven that awaits and makes my suffering insignificant.

PRAYER:
Help me Lord to remember during the challenges I face here, that eternity with You is infinitely better.

October 22

WALK IN VICTORY

And we know that in all things God works for the good of those who love him, who have been called according to his purpose.
Romans 8:28

Our trust is not in a God who uses his power without a plan or at His whim. Rather our trust is in a loving, purposeful God who promises that all thing work together for good for those who love Him.

No one believes this any more than Kim Phuc. She is known as the picture girl from the Vietnam war. The Pulitzer Prize winning photo seen around the world was snapped on June 8, 1972 following a South Vietnamese napalm attack on Trang Bang village. Nine-year-old Kim is seen running down the road toward the camera, naked and screaming in pain.

Living in constant pain as a result of the horrific injuries she suffered, Kim recalls she was bitter and filled with hatred asking the universal question, "Why me? Why do I have to suffer like this?"

As a teenager, she encountered a Vietnamese Bible in a library. Impressed with Jesus and His teaching, she became a believer in 1982. She comments that it took years, but "God freed me from hatred and enabled me to love and forgive my enemies, to trust Him and to obey."

She still suffers daily from excruciating pain but she now finds purpose in that pain. "The pain reminds me daily to go back to the Lord in prayer," she says. "Then he gives me peace, energy, strength and grace to face each day…The pain is for my spiritual protection and I thank God for it."

Kim Phuc says she wants to change the way people see her; no longer the little girl crying out of pain, but now a young woman crying out for peace. She adds, "Now He uses my picture and my everyday life to glorify Him. Now I understand the purpose of why

I'm still here and why I suffer. It's to glorify the Lord. It's not about me. It's about Him!"

God has a plan and purpose for our life, and through our obedience to His teaching, He is going to work in us and through us that which will ultimately bring glory to God. With this kind of faith, we will see victory.

RESPONSE:
Today I will walk in victory because I will give every part of my being to glorify God

PRAYER:
Lord, help me to experience the purpose and meaning You have ordained in my suffering for You.

October 23

A DISCIPLE'S LOVE

"If anyone comes to me and does not hate his father and mother, his wife and children, his brothers and sisters— yes, even his own life—he cannot be my disciple."
Luke 14:26

A Christian medical doctor in China shares his experience when he refused to bow down or "kowtow" to an image of Mao because of his love for Jesus. After severe beatings did not succeed in influencing him, the authorities resorted to a more subtle strategy by getting his whole family to stand around him and weep. Here is the story in his own words:

I had seven children as well as my wife all surrounding me and weeping. Crying bitterly, my wife said to me, "If you don't kowtow you will surely die and then what will we do?" For three days they stood around me weeping until my wife's eyes were dreadfully swollen. "After you have died, what will happen to these children? Please, for the sake of your family, just kowtow." They cried and cried. I really did not know what to do. I felt that I had no more strength so I prayed, "Lord I have no strength left, what must I do?"

On the third day, the Lord's word [Luke 14:26] came, Hallelujah! There is no word of the Lord that is without power. The Lord through His Word filled me with the life and power of God. I said to my wife, "Stop crying. It's no use your crying. I am the Lord's disciple. For the Lord's sake I am ready to die!"

Then the day came when the authorities called me and said, "You had better consider your situation carefully. If you want to live, you must kowtow otherwise it will mean certain death for you. Tonight we will make you eat the "steel bean" (bullet). You will be executed! This is your very last opportunity!" And so he sent me back to think it over.

There was, however, no need for me to think it over. I was ready for the bullet. But the night passed without my being called. Next day I saw that outside folk were running hither and thither and I wondered whatever had happened to cause such alarm. Later I was to learn that immediately after I had left the office, black swellings appeared on the prison warden's legs and it was frightfully painful. Because he was the chief, all the doctors in the hospital were rushed to his side to give him aid. But within twenty-four hours he was dead.

The doctor was later released from prison and returned to his family and medical practice.

RESPONSE:
I recommit myself to the Lord. My love for Him will be even more than my love for family.

PRAYER:
Lord, help to prove my love for You above all others regardless of the circumstances.

October 24

SUPERNATURAL ANSWERS

But before all this they will lay hands on you and persecute you. They will deliver you to synagogues and prisons, and you will be brought before kings and governors, and all on account of my name.
This will result in your being witnesses to them.
But make up your mind not to worry beforehand how you will defend yourself. For I will give you words and wisdom that none of your adversaries will be able to resist or contradict.
Luke 21:12-15

During her years of imprisonment in Eritrea's wretched shipping containers, Helen Berhane was often interrogated and pressured to deny her faith. The Lord gave her supernatural answers each time as documents in her book *Song of the Nightingale*:

Yet another official visited and accused me of being anti-government. "Political agents are just using you," he said. "Why do you let them do this? Why do you risk your life to please other people and support their cause? Why make yourself a sacrificial lamb? Perhaps you are a genuine believer, but the ones who have asked you to stick so rigidly to this rebellious religion are just taking advantage of you for their political agenda."

I said, "If I may speak for myself: I have no other agenda but believing in the Bible. Since my childhood I have never had any other intention. This Bible is not new – my fathers and forefathers read it. I am reading the same Bible my grandfather read; the only difference is that he read it in *Geez* [old dialect] while I can read it in my language. He used to treat his Bible with special reverence and keep it in a sacred box, but I do not worry about handling mine. My grandfather went to church for fifty years but he didn't understand the Bible; we know it better because it is in our language. If you are trying to take us back to the days of the older generation, then you cannot care about what is best for our country.

595

Everything is changing and we have to adapt and move with the times. Each generation of inventors must bring new ideas, otherwise we will have nothing new and nothing will change or improve. In our generation, because we can understand the Bible, people are changing."[38]

RESPONSE:
Today I will trust the Lord for wisdom and words to answer those who challenge my faith.

PRAYER:
Lord, give me grace to answer all challenges against You and Your Word with Your love and wisdom.

38 Helen Berhane, *Song of the Nightingale,* (Colorado Springs: Authentic Media, 2009), p. 72-73.

October 25

THOUGH NONE GO WITH ME

"Do not suppose that I have come to bring peace to the earth. I did not come to bring peace, but a sword. For I have come to turn 'a man against his father, a daughter against her mother, a daughter-in-law against her mother-in-law - a man's enemies will be the members of his own household.'
Matthew 10:34-36

In the early morning of July 20, 1992 handicapped Pakistani Christian, Tahir Iqbal, died a martyr's death at age thirty-two in prison. He was charged with slander of the prophet Mohammed and desecration of the Koran. His death occurred under mysterious circumstances. According to fellow-prisoners Tahir vomited blood before he died which could point to poisoning or another form of violence. His stepmother declared, "Allah never forgives those who blaspheme against his holy prophet. Tahir received what he deserved."

When Tahir Iqbal, a direct descendant of the prophet Mohammad, became ill and paralyzed from his waist down as a young adult, his family abandoned him. It would be a foretaste of things to come. Christians befriended him and he gave his heart and life to Jesus.

Tahir was quite bold about his new found faith and this stirred up the anger of the imam at the mosque. The imam started a slander campaign against Tahir, which resulted in a Police rescue on December 7, 1990 when a crowd of Muslim extremists were out to murder him.

In order to protect Tahir he was transferred to the prison. He would never leave it. Tahir was under continuous pressure to return to Islam. "They want me to say that I was forced to change my beliefs, that it was because of money, or for a good job, or to get a wife. They must know that I only changed my faith because I did find the Truth."

His most famous statement when threatened with death was, **"I'll kiss that rope but I'll never deny my faith."**

When his pastor was notified of his death, he went to the prison. It turned out that Tahir's stepmother had already arrived to claim the body. Members of the church inquired the next day and to their shock they were informed that Tahir had been buried already. His stepmother had received and taken the body without a post-mortem. In less than 36 hours after his death Tahir received an Islamic burial ceremony performed by the same Muslim cleric who had demanded the death penalty.

Now he praises his Savior in heavenly glory, where all tears have been wiped away.

RESPONSE:
Today I reaffirm my commitment to follow Jesus even if none go with me.

PRAYER:
Lord, be with my brothers and sisters suffering unjustly in Pakistan today under the blasphemy law.

October 26

SACRIFICIAL GIVING

In the same way, those of you who do not give up everything you have cannot be my disciples.
Luke 14:33

Johnny Li, a former colleague and current missionary trainer in China shares about his meeting with two young pastors there:

As I entered the house, I surprised to observe the humble existence of these two mighty men of God. They were the leaders of house churches in their provinces, which had grown the past nine years to more than 200,000 Christians. They were both in their late twenties and even though they have been in the ministry since they were nineteen their enthusiasm reflected beautifully.

Everybody knew about the work of the Lord through these faithful servants. I also knew that they both spent several years in prison in extremely harsh conditions, but nothing prepared me for this humble home and modest lifestyle.

There were no furniture items, no ornaments, and no beds in the small house. Their clothes were hanging on the wall due to a lack of cupboards. The only furniture was a table and a chair to sit on. There was a blanket on the ground that was obviously used as the bed. Together we sat down and I started questioning them about their activities and work that was bearing much fruit.

"How often do you travel to neighbouring villages?" I asked.

"As often as possible," they replied.

"Where do you obtain your finances to do so?"

"We sell what we have," they replied and supplied me with an explanation to the question about the empty house which I dared not ask.

"We sold the chairs and we sold the cupboard," they continued. "And that supplied much-needed funds for our outreach."

"What happens when you have nothing more to sell?"

One pastor looked sadly down to the ground and answered softly,

"We find something else to sell."

"But what?" I kept on pressuring them. "You have already sold everything and have nothing left to sell. How will you raise money now?"

Then came the startling answer. "We sell our blood on the black market. We get about five dollars but the need is so great that we have to do something to tell the people around us about Jesus."

"How can you do this" I asked. "How can you justify selling your blood to send out missionaries?"

Without hesitation they answered, "We have no choice! The need is so great!"

RESPONSE:
Today I will not complain about what I lack but think of what I can sacrifice for Jesus.

PRAYER:
Lord, I reaffirm today my decision to follow You. I give You everything I am and have.

October 27

GOD FIRST

For I am not ashamed of the gospel, because it is the power of God that brings salvation to everyone who believes: first to the Jew, then to the Gentile.
Romans 1:16

Eighteen-year-old Nina lives in an Asian country where Buddhism is the faith of the majority. Since her mother is a devout Christian, she is constantly exposed to stories and lessons from God's Word. At school, her faith in Jesus Christ is often tested. Because Nina showed great aptitude at school, she was selected to be part of a team that would compete in a high school annual science competition. On the day of the competition, however, the Vice Principal, a very strict disciplinarian, decided to take the team to the Buddhist temple first. Nina fidgeted anxiously in her seat while aboard the school bus with her teammates.

As she tried to figure out what to do upon arriving at the monastery, the first of the Lord's Ten Commandments resonated in her mind—no other gods, except Him. *I can't disobey my God, after knowing who He is*, she thought. Nina felt trapped and confused. Obeying God meant disobeying the Vice Principal. Nina uttered a silent prayer. *"God, you changed the hearts of many kings before, surely you can do it again! Please Lord, speak to his heart!"*

When the team reached the temple, everyone entered except Nina, who stood at the gate. As Nina's teammates came out of the temple, the Vice Principal approached Nina with a stern look on his face. "Why did you not come in the temple with us?"

"Sir, I was born a Christian. When my mother gave birth to me, I was weak and at the point of death. Christians prayed for me and God heard their prayers," shared Nina.

"You could have just entered with us and not participate in the ceremonies," explained the Vice Principal, whose face and tone softened. Nina knew then that God had just answered her prayers.

"I did not have peace in my heart. I felt that I would be disobeying God if I entered the temple, sir," Nina responded. The Vice Principal did not pursue the matter any further; neither did he chide Nina for it. The team placed third during the science competition.

Nina testified during a youth training program that Open Doors organized. "I was surprised to see how God suddenly changed his heart; he rarely speaks that way to students. He is often firm and strong…His wife has had many miscarriages. I'm praying for his wife to have a baby soon. I'm also praying for him to know Jesus Christ. I'm sure it will happen someday!"

RESPONSE:
Today I will put God first in every situation I face.

PRAYER:
Pray for all young Christians who face the cultural challenges against putting God first.

October 28

THE WAY OF THE CROSS

And whoever does not carry their cross and follow me cannot be my disciple.
Luke 14:27

Two days before the SSTS Seminar in a restricted Central Asia country, Pavel, a Christian leader discovered the garage he was using to store restricted (illegal) Christian literature in the tribal language was broken into by youths and over 2000 pieces of literature stolen. Ironically, police discovered the literature being distributed at a nearby school by the mischievous youths and traced the ownership of the literature to Pavel.

He was "invited" to come to the police station. There he discovered that the authorities were open to receiving a bribe of one month's salary in exchange for having the remaining literature returned and the case closed. It was also suggested that because he was lacking the appropriate registration papers for being in this community, he should pay the money before the police "found some drugs in his home" and he be sent to jail for a longer period of time.

Pavel now had two choices: pay the bribe and redeem most of the stolen literature which had come into the country at great personal and emotional risk past many police checkpoints; or wait and see how God intervened to bring glory to His name even if it meant a fine or imprisonment. Pavel knew that to pay the bribe would open the door to a pattern of further blackmail, as the police would now own him as "their man."

During the 3-day SSTS seminar, the group met with Pavel and his wife and prayed with them each morning before he went to the police station for further interrogation in the afternoons. Pavel had to make a decision by the third day. As he left for the police station he told the group, "This SSTS seminar has changed my entire thinking on this matter. I am not paying the bribe. I am choosing 'the way of the cross.'"

Latest reports are that Pavel's case was resolved without a bribe and he is still active in effective ministry in his country.

RESPONSE:
Today I again choose to walk "the way of the cross" as I make my decisions and choices.

PRAYER:
Lord, help me never to choose the easy way of the culture but to walk "the way of the cross!"

October 29

WALKING BY FAITH

For we live by faith, not by sight.
2 Corinthians 5:7

Brother Wei from South-east Asia tells his story to a staff member of Open Doors. He is too shy to look at him directly. While he is speaking, he keeps his eyes lowered:

I'm forty-one years old and I'm a simple rice farmer. Twenty years ago, I became a Christian and in the past years, I've been in prison thirteen times because of my faith in the Lord Jesus Christ. The last time I was in a notorious prison, surrounded by a moat. In order to torment the prisoners, we were given rice mixed with sand. There were no toilets - we just had to find a spot somewhere.

I was arrested because I believed in Jesus and because I was active as a preacher. The punishment for this "crime" was two and a half years in prison, but I could be released sooner if I renounced my faith.

The guards constantly tried to force me to deny my faith. I was to sign a form which stated that I had "voluntarily renounced my faith" and that I would "no longer attend meetings." I was bound hand and foot and beaten, but I refused to deny my faith. My fellow prisoners mocked me and swore at me. They called me the "Jesus man." I wasn't allowed a Bible, and if I was caught praying, I was beaten.

After my release, as a result of the abuse I was no longer able to walk fast or to run. Sometimes I could no longer find the words to describe something.

Once I was back in our village, I heard that we had to leave because we hadn't been granted permission to go on living there. We were not allocated any land to work, the children were no longer allowed to go to school and the hospital was no longer willing to help us. Then we left and went to another district, where we had to start over again.

When the Open Doors worker asked him how he had been able to endure all this persecution, Brother Wei said, "I don't trust in what eyes can see, but I've put my trust in the Eternal, the Lord Jesus."

RESPONSE:
Today I will persevere through the challenges that come my way with faith in the Eternal God.

PRAYER:
Pray that all Christians being persecuted today will respond with this strong faith!

October 30

ADVANCING THE GOSPEL

Now I want you to know, brothers and sisters,
that what has happened to me has actually served
to advance the gospel.
Philippians 1:12

The Apostle Paul writes these words from prison but he assures his readers that prison in no way hindered the spread of the gospel, but actually advanced it. Then he states in the following verses that he is chains only because of Christ and because of his imprisonment, others have become bolder and fearless in sharing their faith. And the gospel advances!

Three middle-aged Indonesian Christian women were sentenced to three years in Indramayu prison, West Java, in September 2004. Dr. Rebekka, Ratna Bangun and Eti Pangesti were falsely accused of converting Muslim children to Christianity through their program called Happy Sunday.

There were four hundred men and twelve women in the prison. Rebekka, Eti and Ratna were the only Christian women. The other women were Muslims. Before the Christian women arrived in the prison, there was much unrest. Soon the prisoners got along together as friends. The three ladies were a great testimony to the women prisoners and also to the guards.

While in the prison, Dr. Rebecca said, "The most important thing for us to do daily is to become the living testimony of Christ's love among all the prisoners and to share the Word of God, even though we have to do it secretly. Only in His time will we be free from this prison, and when that day comes, we will have been purified as gold through this baptism of fire.

Ratna commented, "I sometimes feel that if I was outside this prison, I might be able to do many things for Christ. But then I realize how thankful I am to be here because we are able to share our lives with other prisoners. They are criminals, and they never heard the good news about Jesus and His unconditional love. God shows me that this is our opportunity to share the love of God.

Eti concluded, "I want my days here to become days with Jesus through my personal devotion, prayer and reading the Word of God. I want to serve Him in this prison because around us there are many souls trying to find the truth. I love to share the truth with other prisoners because it is easy to share with them about a God who loves them. They are looking for the answer for their troubled life. And the only answer lies in the truth of God's love.

"Being in the prison is not our plan. I believe it is God's will we are here, and the Holy Spirit helps us, encourages us and comforts us. The Holy Spirit leads us and God gives us strength to minister to the other prisoners. I believe many people in this prison will open their hearts to Jesus and many souls will be won for God's glory."

And that's exactly what happened. The three women even led worship services inside the prison. After three years, they were released and the other prisoners wept as they left. God even uses imprisonment to advance His kingdom.

RESPONSE:
Today I will pray differently for brothers and sisters in prison for their faith.

PRAYER:
Help me Lord to always trust Your plan – even when it seems difficult and overwhelming.

October 31

IN CHAINS FOR CHRIST

As a result, it has become clear throughout the whole palace guard and to everyone else that I am in chains for Christ.

Philippians 1:13

Authorities in Afghanistan arrested Said Musa on May 31, 2010, days after the local TV station broadcast images of Afghan Christians being baptised and worshipping the Lord. A Christian for eight years, he is married and the father of six. Before release from prison he wrote:

Hello my dear brothers and sisters, lovely and strong in faith. On Saturday I went to court, but my session was not held. I met then two persons. I became very happy when they introduced themselves [as my] defence attorneys…I immediately felt joy in my heart, like somebody gave me comfort, like stars, like lights. I one hundred percent believe it was the Holy Spirit healing my heart.

On Thursday some high officials came from the Attorney General's office. They asked me, "What is your name?" I introduced myself to them. After that they asked me, "Are you truly a Christian?" I replied to them, I am one hundred percent Christian. I believe in the Son of God Almighty, He is my Savior and Lord. I told them the only way to come to God is to have faith in Jesus Christ, He's the way, He's eternal life, He's truth, He's love, He's really God.

After that they asked me, "What is wrong with being a Muslim that you converted to the Christian religion?" I told them, it's the plan of God. God chose his people to complete his work on the earth. Muslim is not bad. The Christian people are never against any religion in the world. Our fight is just with Satan. We love our enemies, like ourselves. They joked and mocked me. "You want to make us Christians now?"

Today a new person came. He asked me, "Why do you not accept Islam; why is this religion better?" I replied to him, the golden thing is this, love your enemy as yourself. In which religion do you find this word? Just in Christianity.

He told me, "You know your punishment. It's death." I told him, I am one hundred percent ready for the sake of my faith. My Saviour gave his life for me. I am not afraid of a human; he just kills my body, but does not hurt my soul. I am afraid of my Lord and Savior; He will be able to punish my soul too. I told him I am holding on to my faith. I will never betray my faith. Without Jesus, what does the life in this world or the afterlife mean? Nothing!

RESPONSE:
Today I will pray for those like Said Musa who are truly in prison for their faith.

PRAYER:
Lord, may I have the strength and courage to confess You even under severe pressure.

November 1

BOLDER AND FEARLESS

And because of my chains, most of the brothers and sisters have become confident in the Lord and dare all the more to proclaim the gospel without fear.
Philippians 1:14

The Apostle Paul indicates that another reason why the gospel was actually advancing during his imprisonment was the bold courageous witness of other believers who had lost their fear.

Two Chinese itinerant evangelists who carried Christian books with them were arrested in Anhui Province during their ministry. The Public Security Bureau (PSB) put them in jail and beat them. The guard beat the face of one until it bled and then took his shoes away in the cold of winter. Then they poured cold water on him throughout the winter. He became deformed from the harsh treatment. Both were kept in jail for six months.

They had led two people to the Lord in that prison location before they were arrested, and when they were released from jail after six months, there were over one hundred new Christians in the area from the seeds that these men had planted. The two people that they led to the Lord spread the message to others. The work grew even while the itinerant evangelists were in prison.

In Addis Ababa, Ethiopia, fourteen Christians continued their witness while in prison by reading Scripture aloud. By the time they were released, they had read through the entire New Testament and forty-four inmates professed faith in Jesus Christ.

Pedro Pablo Castillo shares a similar situation in Nicaragua where half of the four thousand political prisoners became Christians. On the eve of their release, they prayed, sang and read Scripture to celebrate their pardon. Castillo returned to the jail to urge them to let Christ shine in their lives whether in jail or outside.

We shared earlier about Pastor Tu in Vietnam—leader of the fastest growing house church network. Pastor Tu spent three years in prison for his evangelistic ministry. When he was released, he found his house church network had grown three hundred per cent during his

611

imprisonment years.

I received a Christmas card from him the following year that read: **"...God greatly gives our church 20,203 more new believers this year. Hallelujah!"**

RESPONSE:
God's kingdom will advance when I overcome my fear and become a bold and courageous witness to the power of the gospel.

PRAYER:
Lord, help me to trust You fully and become a dynamic force in boldly advancing the growth of Your church.

612

November 2

STEADFAST TO THE END

And the God of all grace, who called you to his eternal glory in Christ, after you have suffered a little while, will himself restore you and make you strong, firm and steadfast.

1 Peter 5:10

Christians in northern Nigeria have suffered severely from physical attacks resulting in destruction of Christian churches, houses and shops. Hundreds of believers have been badly injured, many macheted to death, some burnt alive and even more shot dead.

Despite all that has happened in northern Nigeria, the Body of Christ is not discouraged, declaring instead they are willing to continue carrying the cross. One Christian articulated their commitment: "We will be steadfast to the end."

Another leader declared, "They destroyed our church buildings, houses and business centers, but the good Lord is comforting us. The Christians are growing in strength and total submission to God. Our challenge now is how to rebuild our churches and continue with the fellowship to encourage each other."

The affected families of pastors and church members have gone through unimaginable hardship after all they laboured for, all their lives, was destroyed within minutes. Many families were left unattended while some were able to move to refugee camps. Others are living under trees with their children, gazing at their destroyed houses and life belongings, shedding tears and calling for help in this desperate situation.

A lady who was crying inconsolably told Open Doors, "I have nowhere to go. All I have laboured for is gone, I cannot afford to feed my children, and life is difficult. I almost gave up, but I will continue to wait on God to come to my rescue."

"It is difficult to fathom the scale of destruction, but we have accepted it in good faith," said one pastor's wife who had lost her home. "It is nothing short of the fulfilment of the gospel. We love

613

these Muslims even though they hate us. They are not our enemies. We are only against the person behind their actions. We so much pray that they change their ways and accept Christ, so that we will rejoice together when we get to heaven."

The believers in the affected areas are now confronted with the challenge of how to rebuild their churches and lives, while facing the call of sharing love and total forgiveness.

A pastor who lost his church building commented, "We are always ready to pay the price for our faith. This added strength to our faith, no going back. We are going to encourage our people to see this from God's perspective. We want the world to know that what has happened in northern Nigeria…is even beyond politics. It is purely religious, and we need your prayers.

"Christ was rejected here on earth to the point that they crucified him on the cross for our sins; therefore, no amount of sacrifice for Christ would be too much. All we can do now is pray for the aggressors, because they do not know what they are doing. We will be steadfast to the end."

RESPONSE:
Today I will receive God's restorative help in being strong, firm and steadfast.

PRAYER:
Pray for brothers and sisters in northern Nigeria facing constant challenges to their faith.

November 3

NO TURNING BACK

"Whoever does not take up their cross and follow me is not worthy of me."
Matthew 10:38

In northern Nigeria, confessing Christ by word of mouth is not the only test of a believer's sincere submission to the authority of Christ—particularly one coming to Christ from Islam. A true follower of Jesus must be prepared to carry the cross, or else he falls away.

For 25-year-old Akin, his cross came quickly. His father and uncle took him from the home of one Islamic scholar to another, trying to convince him to compromise his faith in Christ. But all their efforts proved fruitless. Finally, as a last resort, Akin's family took him to an Islamic reformatory where he must either accept Islam, or die.

"There, I lived with thieves, murderers, alcoholics and drug addicts whose parents or relatives had brought them there to be rehabilitated. I did not belong there…Immediately, they had my hands and feet chained. The chains fastened on my legs were worse, as they joined the metals directly on my legs. They also beat me consistently. The experience was agonizing, but I had to endure, because I had seen the light in Christ and accepted it," said Akin.

"They maltreated us, but mine was more severe because the Islamic teacher told them I had blasphemed against the prophet of Islam," said Akin. "I wore the same shirt and trousers for nine months. I could not even wash them since I was chained, hands and feet."

After nine months in chains and under the cruel treatment of outcasts and the Islamic teacher, the Islamic teacher took Akin back to his father's house in the village. "My father was very upset and asked the Islamic teacher to take me back, since I had not recanted my faith in Christ," Akin said. But the teacher refused. "He handed me over to my father and left."

Because staying with his parents would mean his death, he immediately fled to a pastor's house for refuge. Akin stayed indoors for two weeks until the church relocated him to a more secure environment. Akin was discipled over the next two years, and then called into ministry.

Now in a Bible school, Akin still cannot go back home. The church in his village is small, with almost no means to support him. His Christian mentor is the only source of help for his school fees, books and provision of food.

"For me the battle continues, although I know it is Christ who rescued me," says Akin. "This is a constant reminder that Christ actually gave up his life for me…So my experience in that [Islamic reformatory] was just a part of the road that leads to eternity with Christ. He has told us the journey will not be easy, but we must press on, no turning back."

RESPONSE:
Today I will persevere in following Jesus no matter what obstacles I face. I will not turn back!

PRAYER:
Thank You, Lord, for the example of believers like Akin whose example imitates Yours in teaching me to follow after You, no matter the cost.

November 4

COMMUNITY EXPULSIONS

That is why, for Christ's sake, I delight in weaknesses,
in insults, in hardships, in persecutions, in difficulties.
For when I am weak, then I am strong.
2 Corinthians 12:10

My wife and I lived in Nova Scotia for twelve summers. Not far from our cottage is the museum, church and statue of Evangeline in Grand Pré, Nova Scotia commemorating the Acadian expulsion of 1755—a black mark in Canadian history.

When the British conquered Port Royal in 1710 after being ceded Acadia (Nova Scotia) under the terms of the Treaty of Utrecht, they found themselves up against a French speaking people who had developed a strong sense of independence against British and French rule. The Acadians initially refused to recognize British rule, wanting to keep their religious freedom and not wanting to be obliged to bear arms in the event of war. These conditions were accepted only in 1730 and, at that point, the Acadians were recognized as neutral subjects within the colony.

But in September of 1755, Charles Lawrence, the appointed governor of Nova Scotia, gathered the Acadians in the St. Charles Church in Grand Pre in order to read the declaration that they must relinquish their possessions to the British Crown and that they would be deported for their unwillingness to swear allegiance to the King of England. Unaware of what awaited them in the church, many Acadians were taken prisoner and deported to American colonies, France, and England, and several thousand died from drowning, misery, illness and starvation during the long ocean voyages. Families were separated and shipped out in different directions. Their farms and homes were burned so they would have nothing to return to.

Longfellow immortalized the tragic story with his epic poem about a mythical young girl, Evangeline, cruelly separated from her fiancé, Gabriel. They were reunited at his death bed.

Many other countries and cultures have sad memories of expulsions. One is ongoing today in Chiapas, the southernmost state of Mexico. More than 35,000 indigenous evangelical Christians have been expelled from their communities just because they are evangelicals and no longer taking part in their community's religious practices and rituals. They live in refugee-like camps.

One of those is Pascuala who was asleep when the community leaders came to burn her home. She woke up in time to warn her family. Fortunately one brother and sister were not there but the four children in the home were macheted, shot or burned to death as they tried to flee. Pascuala herself was shot and raped. She survived by feigning death. Weak and bleeding, she walked many hours to a hospital where her life was saved. But she says, "Since that time my desire is to help the people who are persecuted for Jesus because I feel their pain. I got in touch with Open Doors; they encouraged me to keep going with love. With their help I was able to get some supplies of embroidery thread for crafts to help other women…If God allowed me to live through my persecution, it is for one reason—to proclaim His name."

RESPONSE:
I will thank God for my challenges because they enable me to overcome and be strong.

PRAYER:
Pray for those still dealing with pain, separation and loss from community expulsions.

November 5

NEEDED: PATIENCE AND STRENGTH

*"I will rescue you from your own people and from
the Gentiles. I am sending you to them to open their eyes
and turn them from darkness to light, and from the power
of Satan to God, so that they may receive forgiveness of
sins and a place among those who are sanctified
by faith in me."*
Acts 26:17-18

These words of Jesus were spoken to Saul of Tarsus en route to
Damascus at the time of his conversion. Saul—later Paul—is now
sharing them with King Agrippa as a personal testimony. Though God
would rescue Paul, he still suffered many things for the sake of the
gospel.

One of the biggest challenges to remaining faithful under
persecution is the need to stay free from bitterness. Some forms of
persecution are particularly hard to forgive.

Elina's father is a pastor near Dhaka, Bangladesh. Extremists have
been trying to drive him and his family away. Elina shares her story:

"One night, I woke up because I had an exam the next morning
and I needed to study. When I had to go to the bathroom, there was
no one with me. Some boys came and they just moved onto me.
They touched me and then they took me away, but I couldn't scream
because they held my mouth.

"One of those two boys raped me while the other sat there. Then
I tried to run away, but I couldn't because they caught me again.
Then the other boy raped me. The boys said, 'If you tell somebody
about this, we will kill you.'" When she arrived home, Elina shouted
for her dad. The two of them brought her case to the police, but
they were told she had no proof. Elina and her father believe the
boys paid off the police, and they're still awaiting justice despite a
medical report confirming her story.

Elina says, "They did this because we are Christians. They don't want us here; they want us to be Muslims. They are trying to drive us out. It was difficult for me in those days. I just wanted to fly away or commit suicide, but my dad comforted me. He told me, 'Pray more and more, so God will give you more patience and strength.' It really helped me work it out…I have forgiven them; I have nothing against them in my heart."

Through the prayer and support of her family, Elina is finding God's strength amidst her pain. As a testimony to her Savior's redemptive power, Elina has extended His grace to the boys who violated her. Still, her journey to healing is far from over; a poignant reminder of the need to pray and send encouragement to our Christian sisters facing this heinous form of persecution.

In their response to persecution, Bengali Christians like Elina send a message to us in the West: a message of faith, hope and love—even for their oppressors so they might respond to the gospel of Jesus Christ and receive His forgiveness.

RESPONSE:
Today I too will pray for patience and strength to be a witness even to my enemies.

PRAYER:
Pray for young Christian girls like Elina who face great personal challenges to be a witness.

November 6

CHOOSING LOVE OVER HATE

Bless those who persecute you; bless and do not curse.
Romans 12:14

At the early age of eleven, Sam was living a pious Muslim life in the southern Philippines. He prayed at mosques on Fridays and fasted during Ramadan. Sam was the only one of his siblings sent to school where he excelled both in classroom and sports. He was everybody's favourite, popular and well-loved.

But everything changed one afternoon. After school, Sam passed by his grandfather's house who happened to be a Christian. He saw a maroon book with '*Kitab Injil*' (The Gospel) written on the cover. He opened it and started reading. "I was drawn to Jesus because his teachings were so different...Help the needy, obey and respect parents, do not be a false witness...they were not taught in Islam. Before that, I only knew to repay evil with evil."

So Sam committed his life to following Jesus and His teachings in the Bible. He was just a fifth grader then. Although he was the only Christian in his family, Sam's parents and siblings respected his new faith. But outside his home, among his friends, it was a different story. "You're a *kafir* (infidel)! You are not my friend anymore."

It was very painful for Sam to be deserted by his friend. His classmates at grade school kept a good distance from him. Some mocked him, calling him *kafir*. There were times during classes when kids would throw their shoes at him. They bullied him by writing stuff on his uniform, filling his bag with sand, and even punching him.

One day, a friend-turned-enemy yelled at him. "You Christians are filthy! Christians are garbage!" Sam cried and ran home. There were times when he was tempted to fight back, but he remembered the words of Jesus to love the enemies, to bless and not curse. In his heart, he prayed for those who bullied him and repaid them with a kind smile instead.

Sam, now seventeen, has endured physical harassment, insults, and discrimination from friends and school mates for boldly telling them that he is a Christian.

After Sam joined the Open Doors' discipleship program for MBB youths, he has become even bolder in seizing every opportunity to share his faith in Jesus. Sam knows that doing so might cost him his life someday.

"When I think of my friends, my heart breaks. I lost them, and though they turned out to be my enemies, I don't hate them. Instead, I pray for them that one day they will meet my Lord Jesus and be changed."

RESPONSE:
Jesus wants me to not repay evil with evil but rather love, bless and pray for those who are my enemies.

PRAYER:
Help me Lord to live among those who oppose me with the character of Jesus and respond to them with love and not hate.

November 7

FAITH IN THE MIDST OF ASHES

But now, this is what the LORD says…"Do not fear,
for I have redeemed you; I have summoned you by name;
you are mine. When you pass through the waters,
I will be with you; and when you pass through the rivers,
they will not sweep over you. When you walk through
the fire, you will not be burned;
the flames will not set you ablaze.
Isaiah 43:1-2

Twenty-eight-year-old evangelist Wako Halekie works in the town of Tuka Argiso in the border area between Ethiopia and Kenya. This small town is mostly inhabited by Borena livestock herders and is effectively divided between Oromia and Somali regional states. As a result both states are claiming ownership over Tuka Argiso. The federal government tried to hold a referendum to resolve the dispute, but they were unsuccessful.

Three years ago, Wako Halekie was assigned by his church to work as a missionary among the livestock herders in Tuka-Argiso. Despite their nomadic existence, Wako was able to plant three churches with an average of fifty members in each congregation. He attributes the positive growth to God's blessing on the ministry. But Islamic presence in Tuka-Argiso is growing progressively. Muslim missionaries from neighbouring villages are determined to Islamize all Borenas which rouses concern in the Christian community.

Wako says, "They regard my activities as an obstacle to their mission. I was alerted by some villagers about their antagonistic feelings towards me. Recently the Muslim missionaries criticised the Christian faith openly and tried to confuse our members."

On March 30th, 2011, Wako left home for a routine visit to new Christian converts. In the early morning hours of March 31st, one of the three houses at his residence was set afire. The fire spread to the second and third house where his wife, newborn baby and their two older children were sleeping. Both the first and second house burnt

623

to the ground. By the grace of God neighbours managed to rescue Wako's family from the blaze just in time before the third house's roof crashed in. None of their belongings were spared.

Mrs. Haleki said, "I heard a distant noise but thought I was dreaming. The next thing I knew, people broke through the door and dragged me and the children from the smoke. I was shocked and speechless." She was still recovering from the birth of their third child a week before.

Wako says, "I know the purpose of this fire was to destroy me and my family. But God intervened and saved my wife and children. God is faithful to His words! As it was written in the book of Isaiah 43:1-3; we will not fear their threats. God is our Redeemer. They thought I would leave the village, but I will not wave from the calling God bestowed on me. I took my wife's hands and together we stood in the midst of the ashes and gave thanks to the name of the Lord. By His grace I will continue serving Him right here in this village until the day He has helped me reach the entire village."

RESPONSE:
Today I will trust God to fulfill His promises even when going through fire and flood.

PRAYER:
Pray for Evangelist Wako and his family working in difficult circumstances and pressures.

November 8

FREEDOM IN FAITH

So if the Son sets you free, you will be free indeed.
John 8:36

During an SSTS seminar in Central Asia, we listened to testimonies of the participants who were mostly from Muslim background. We asked how long they had been followers of Jesus. The majority answered, "Nine years."

When we asked how they had become believers, they shared that there was a vicious religious civil war in their country nine years earlier. It had shown them the true colors of Islam and they turned to follow Jesus for the reasons listed below:

1. LOVE
   Jesus of the Bible teaches and exemplifies love and compassion.

2. WORSHIP
   They were attracted to the Christian love of singing and worshipping God with praise and joy!

3. FORGIVENESS
   Jesus shows how to forgive our enemies – feed them and give them water to drink.

4. JESUS' LIFE
   Jesus' teachings and His example are very attractive.

5.. WOMEN
   Jesus holds women in high esteem.

6. FAITH
   Jesus claims to be the way, truth and life. Salvation in Christ is by faith alone. No works or rituals or rules can save us.

7. TRUTH
   The gospel of Jesus Christ is "Good News" because He is the Truth. The gospel is based on Truth.

8. LIBERTY
   Christian expression is based on freedom and liberty in Christ. The Bible teaches the basis for such liberty.

These eight positive principles are a powerful affirmation of the uniqueness of Jesus Christ.

RESPONSE:
Today I will appreciate the uniqueness of the gospel and Jesus my Savior.

PRAYER:
Pray today that many more Muslims may come to faith in Jesus and follow Him fully.

November 9

AM I WORTHY?

***Whoever does not take up their cross and follow me
is not worthy of me.***
Matthew 10:38

Helen Roseveare is now an elderly lady who was a missionary to
Congo, Africa when I was still very young. I remember her holding
the audience of ten thousand university students spell-bound and then
in tears at Urbana '76. Her life story is a testimony to the grace of
God portrayed in the 1989 movie, *Mama Luka Comes Home*.

She is often asked by young people what she suffered for Jesus. Her
simple answer is, "During the Simba uprising in the Congo, I was
raped twice. Government soldiers came to my bungalow, ransacked it,
then grabbed me. I was beaten and savagely kicked, losing my back
teeth through the boot of a rebel soldier. They broke my glasses, so I
could not see to protect myself from the next blow.

"Then one at a time, two army officers took me to my own bedroom
and raped me. They dragged me out into a clearing, tied me to a
tree, and stood around laughing. And while I was there, beaten and
humiliated and violated, someone brought out the only existing handwritten manuscript of a book I had been writing about God's work in
the Congo over an eleven-year period. They put it on the ground in
front of me and burned it.

"I asked myself, *Was it worth it? Eleven years of my life poured out
in selfless service for the African people and now this?* The minute I
expressed that, God's Holy Spirit settled over that terrible scene and
He began to speak to me."

"'My daughter, the question is not *"Is it worth it?"* The question
is, *"Am I worthy?"* Am I, the Lord Jesus who gave His life for you,
worthy for you to make this kind of sacrifice for Me.' And God broke
my heart," Helen continues. "I looked up and I said, 'Oh Lord Jesus,
yes, it is worth it, for You are worthy!'" She concludes, "When you
ask the right question, you'll always know that He is absolutely
worthy of anything you can give Him or do for Him!"

Phil Callaway of *SERVANT* magazine once asked her, "Did you ever struggle to forgive those men?"

"No," she replied. "There was no sense of bitterness or even anger. I was overwhelmed by the sense that God was graciously using me in His purpose. All He asked of me was the loan of my body. The consequences were His. A year later when I returned to Congo and met the man who had humiliated me, I realized that I did carry some resentment and I wasn't sure I had forgiven him. But God led me to accept from Him the forgiveness that only God can give, and He gave me His peace again."[39]

Helen returned to Congo after all the above and continued her life of service for Jesus among the African people.

RESPONSE:
Today I will ask the right question, "Is Jesus worthy of the sacrifices He asks me to make?" Then I will answer affirmatively and take up my cross and follow Him!

PRAYER:
Thank You Lord for the wonderful trophies of grace, like Helen Rosevere, who encourage us in our walk with You Who are truly worthy.

---

39 Phil Callaway, "Is it worth it?" *Servant* (Issue 85, 2010), p.11.

November 10

PRAY WITH THE PERSECUTED

*You did not choose me, but I chose you and appointed you
so that you might go and bear fruit—fruit that will last—
and so that whatever you ask in my name
the Father will give you.*

John 15:16

The first request of us from the Persecuted Church is that we pray for them. And correspondingly, they are usually great models of people of prayer which we can emulate. But we often need to be reminded that they do not ask us only to pray *for* them but also to pray *with* them. If we only pray *for* them, we will pray for their safety and the termination of their persecution. They want us to pray *with* them which means we will pray for: the advance of the gospel in their land; that they will bear fruit that will last; and for perseverance and fearless courage in the face of suffering.

Pastor Samuel Lamb from Guangzhou, China, has an interesting prayer for severe situations of persecution which expresses his trust in a great God. He prays: "Lord, I rejoice in how You are going to work this out."

Moses Xie, a Chinese church leader who spent more than twenty years in jail for his faith, says that when asking visitors to pray for him he is really after three distinct outcomes:

"First, I want them to experience the blessing of prayer for themselves. They will go to God on my behalf, but they will receive a great blessing from being in the presence of God.

Second, I know that as they pray, their burden for the persecuted will increase, and as their burden grows, so their commitment to assisting us in all sorts of other ways will increase also. Prayer alone makes them be the body.

Third, I want them to release more of God's power into our situation through intercession, since I know that God has bound Himself not to act until we ask."

Today is a great day to glorify God in our lives and those of the Persecuted Church.

RESPONSE:
Today I will not only pray *for* **the persecuted but I will also pray** *with* **the persecuted.**

PRAYER:
Lord, may my life glorify You today and may I be a lasting fruit bearer who only desires that Your will be done.

November 11

REMEMBER

Then the LORD said to Moses, "Write this on a scroll as something to be remembered and make sure that Joshua hears it, because I will completely blot out the name of Amalek from under heaven."
Exodus 17:14

Joshua led the Israeli army in the fight against their long-time enemies, the Amalekites. Moses went up to the top of the nearby hill. As long as his hands were held up, the Israelis were winning. When he grew tired of holding up his hands, he sat on a rock and Aaron and Hur each held up one of Moses' arms till sunset when Joshua finally overcame the enemy.

The Lord instructs this event to be "remembered." It was to be written down—the first time in Scripture—as a permanent reminder. God's people are explicitly called to remember both God's deliverance and His judgment of the wicked.

The Bible records a number of events that people remembered. After Jacob's dream at Bethel, he used the stone pillow on which he slept as a pillar of remembrance. After the Israelis finally crossed the Jordan River into the Promised Land, they took twelve stones from the middle of the Jordan and set them up as a memorial about which they were to tell their children. Memorials help us to remember what God has done and enable us to trust Him for the future.

Esdras is a church leader in southern Mexico. He is also a lawyer and therefore is able to stand up for the rights of many indigenous people who are persecuted for their Christian faith.

He will always remember a significant event when God's protection was evident. He says, "I was visiting in Mitziton, an area where more than half of the community are Christians. The authorities wanted to turn two hundred Christians out of their homes and drive them out of the town. I intervened and was able to prevent them from having to leave. After this, I was publicly threatened with death. That day I was not able to return to my hometown and we spent the night in the home of a Christian. It was outside the town and there were no houses nearby.

"At about eleven o'clock in the evening, a strange sensation came over me. Something seemed wrong, but I didn't know what the matter was. At a quarter to twelve, two trucks turned up with twelve men. They were heavily armed with guns. I was completely alone with Marilene and our little baby. That day, we happened not to have any connection to the radio or mobile phone. I couldn't phone anyone and there was no chance of calling for help. The attackers came closer and closer. They called out, 'Now we've got him. He can't get away now. Now we're going to shoot him dead.'

"Suddenly something unexpected happened. The gardener, an old man who lived in the grounds, turned on the lights around the house. I hadn't asked him to do anything. When the attackers saw all those lighted lamps, they cried, 'Where have all those guards come from?'

"They slunk off and we were spared. Maybe they saw angels, who had come to guard us." Esdras now travels the world and remembers publicly God's great deliverance.

RESPONSE:
Today I will commit to remember the acts of God in my life and record them for the future.

PRAYER:
Thank You, Lord, for remembrance days we have of Your blessings and Your deliverance.

November 12

HOPE IN THE FACE OF REJECTION

Truly I tell you," Jesus replied, "no one who has left home or brothers or sisters or mother or father or children or fields for me and the gospel will fail to receive a hundred times as much in this present age: homes, brothers, sisters, mothers, children and fields—along with persecutions—and in the age to come eternal life.
Mark 10:29-30

A young lady from India who received Standing Strong Through The Storm (SSTS) training shares her poignant story:

Though I long to see my family, I cannot go home. I haven't been home in three years, ever since my family poured hot water on me to show their hostility. They were extremely upset when I accepted Christ as my Saviour as a teenager. I stopped worshipping idols and other gods that my family worshipped. I began to pray and read the Bible every day. My family, who kept food from me, even poured hot meals on me. They tore Bibles from my hand and burned them, six of them.

I was beaten severely for attending church services. One time so badly that I was half dead. While I was still on my sick bed I heard the voice of God saying, "Leave your family whom you love and follow me." It was a very difficult decision for me, but I agreed to do His word. So I told my father that I would be leaving for Bible college to study and learn about Jesus. On hearing my words he was furious and said that if I was to do my own will then I could leave for good. He demanded money that he had spent for my upbringing. It broke my heart.

Learning of the terrible condition I was in, an evangelist reached out to me with help and brought me to a Bible college supported by Open Doors. After a year I went home expecting my family to accept me. But they remained unchanged.

Two years later, my father attended my Bible college graduation in secret, coming in late to the back and leaving early. He did not want to speak to me. My family has only given me pain and sorrow and I think about it and weep.

But I believe in God's promise, *"Let your heart not be troubled, believe in God and also in me, there are many rooms in my father's house…I will come back and take you with me"* (John 14: 1-3). So one day I will be with Him in His heavenly home where there will be no more sorrow, crying or pain.

RESPONSE:
Today I will be encouraged that no matter what happens, following Jesus gives me hope.

PRAYER:
Pray for many believers, like the young lady above, who endure the pain of rejection.

November 13

IT IS HARDER TO LIVE FOR JESUS

Then Jesus said to his disciples, "Whoever wants to be my disciple must deny themselves and take up their cross and follow me..."
Matthew 16:24

Jesus' first call to those interested in Him was "Come and see!" (John 1:39). As His disciples spent more time with Him, Jesus' call became more demanding and required more commitment.

Here He calls those who would be His disciples to make the ultimate sacrifice and "Come and die!"

Jesus was the last person Sundar Singh was looking for as a late teenager in India at the turn of the 20th Century. After all, Jesus was the "foreign god" of the Christian teachers at his school. A zealous Sikh, Sundar had publicly torn up a portion of the Bible to protest its claims. One night as he prayed he became conscious of a light shining in the room. He looked outside to make sure it was not someone shining a light. Gradually the light took the form of a globe of fire and in it he saw the face of Jesus. Sundar threw himself on the ground and surrendered His life to Jesus.

The following months proved to be very difficult for Sundar and his family. Becoming a follower of Christ was not taken lightly by his family nor his community. He was excommunicated. He cut his hair, a gesture that did not make things any easier with his family who were convinced he had renounced his Sikh heritage.

A month after he was baptized in the year 1905, he took the vow of a sadhu. He gave away his meagre possessions, put on a saffron robe and became a barefooted wandering man of God. Among Christians the world over, this barefoot sadhu was later called the "apostle of the bleeding feet" because the soles of his feet were often covered in bloody blisters. The life of a sadhu is hard and entirely dependent on God. Sadhu Sundar Singh's needs were met entirely through the kindness of people he met wherever he went.

Sundar Singh is credited as the first missionary to cross the Himalayan Mountains to take the gospel to Nepal and Tibet. At thirty-six-years-of-age he made his last trip over the mountains. He never returned and is assumed to have been a martyr for Jesus.

In his diary left behind he had written, **"It is easy to die for Christ. It is hard to live for Him. Dying takes only a few minutes—or at worst an hour or two—but to live for Christ means to die daily to myself."**

RESPONSE:
Today I will do the "hard" thing: die to myself and live for Jesus and others who need His love.

PRAYER:
Help me Lord to live worthy of the calling as Your disciple. Show me the cross You want me to carry today.

November 14

NO ORDINARY LIFE

And if anyone wants to sue you and take your shirt, hand over your coat as well. If anyone forces you to go one mile, go with them two miles. Give to the one who asks you, and do not turn away from the one who wants to borrow from you.

Matthew 5:40-42

An Open Doors co-worker shares this personal experience from the Middle East:

The serenity of the pastor walking beside us seemed to calm the hustle and the bustle of the small village. He suddenly came to a stop, carefully looked around and then said, "Some time ago, exactly on the spot where you are standing now, a Christian brother was slaughtered to death because of his faith. He was abducted and brought here to be executed. Life in a mid-eastern village like this is not easy if you confess Jesus to be the Son of God. It could cost you your life."

I looked at this servant of Christ and asked him the obvious question "Why do you choose to live here? Why do you choose to follow Christ under such severe circumstances?"

Without hesitation he looked at me and his reply became a challenge and guideline for my walk with the Lord, even if it is in the safety of my home. He replied **"I refuse to live an ordinary life in Christ."**

As Christians we are called to refuse an ordinary life in Christ. We are commanded to reject worldly standards, to reject mediocrity, to reject compromise and to value people more than possessions, even more than our own lives.

To truly follow Jesus means His will is more important than my life. As well, while alive, I must adopt a lifestyle that puts people ahead of possessions, even one of my most valuable possessions—time! We tend to cherish stuff and comfort more than souls.

In the *Shepherd of Hermes*, an early church writing, we are urged, "Instead of fields, buy souls that are in trouble according to your ability."

RESPONSE:
Today amid the comforts of my environment I will refuse to live an ordinary life but seek to be more like Jesus.

PRAYER:
Lord, I want to live the Jesus way, valuing people more than things even to the point of sacrifice. Help me to escape the bonds of the ordinary Christian life.

November 15

PAYING THE PRICE

Pray also for me, that whenever I speak, words may be given me so that I will fearlessly make known the mystery of the gospel, for which I am an ambassador in chains. Pray that I may declare it fearlessly, as I should.
Ephesians 6:19-20

Martha was a young Chinese Christian engaged to be married but decided to postpone her marriage for two years to answer the call of God to deliver Bibles where they were urgently needed in her country. David Wang shares her story:

I recall meeting her once in the city of Xian. We had arranged to meet at 9 p.m., but she did not turn up until about 1 a.m. She was delayed because she had been delivering Bibles in a nearby village. But the local commune leaders discovered what she was doing. They beat her up, robbed her, and threw her on a deserted road. It was a miracle that she was able to make it to our appointment.

I noticed something was wrong with Martha. She was thin as a wire and her face was bloated. I asked, "What is the matter with you? Did they beat you up?"

"Oh, no," she said, "I've had this problem for some time now." Then she rolled up her pants to show me legs covered with stings and mosquito bites. As she traveled in the remote countryside of China, often she had to sleep in deserted huts or even out in the fields. She was literally eaten up by bugs and mosquitoes.

"Tomorrow we must go to a doctor," I urged her.

"No, no," she said, "I have to catch an early train tomorrow to go to Inner Mongolia. Where are the Bibles?" Her only concern was to get Bibles delivered!

In August 1983, Martha disappeared - as though she had just vanished into thin air. That was during China's 'Anti-Crime Campaign' when many people were arrested and executed throughout China. We became concerned for Martha.

639

Later we got a letter from her through her friends. It was not really a letter - just a little piece of paper. She had been arrested and charged for distributing "superstitious materials" in the People's Republic of China.

The little note read: "I don't know what the penalty will be, but please pray for me." She quoted Paul's words in Ephesians 6:19-20. A few weeks later, we received word that twenty-four-year-old Martha had been executed. She paid the price.

RESPONSE:
Today I will pay the price in serving Jesus in my area regardless of the risks.

PRAYER:
Lord, Martha's story humbles me. Help me love and serve You as much as she did.

November 16

TRANSFORMING INITIATIVES

But I tell you, do not resist an evil person. If anyone slaps you on the right cheek, turn to them the other cheek also. And if anyone wants to sue you and take your shirt, hand over your coat as well. If anyone forces you to go one mile, go with them two miles.
Matthew 5:39-41

When we read these verses about non-violent resistance we usually think this is a defensive directive of Jesus. For example, a leading church bishop in Nigeria, amidst severe Muslim-Christian conflict, has repeatedly been quoted in the press as saying, "We have turned the other cheek so many times, we have no more cheeks to turn!" This statement is often repeated by young people in the conflict zones of Nigeria who have become frustrated by Muslim attacks.

Palestinian Christians involved in peace, reconciliation and non-violence movements have helped me see this teaching differently. When Jesus teaches about *"turning the other cheek,"* it was an offensive—not a defensive—act of peace using a culturally relevant example of His day. A person who slapped another on the cheek normally used the back of the right hand as an act of insult by a superior to an inferior. Thus, by turning the "other" cheek, the one hit (the perceived powerless person) takes an initiative to force the aggressor to now return the swing and hit his face a second time. This time the "hit" must be with an aggressive open palm or fist thereby transforming the nature of the relationship. Very counter-cultural.

The Christ-like response of turning the other cheek says the person does not assume the inferior place of humiliation the striker had in mind but views himself as an equal. The supposedly powerless person has redefined the relationship and forced the oppressor into a moral choice: escalate the violence or respond with repentance and reconciliation.

Other transforming initiatives are to give your cloak when sued for your tunic and to carry a load for two miles for a person who can legally demand that you carry it for only one mile.

We all must seek "transforming initiatives" within our own particular context.

In the sixteenth century a renegade group of Christian leaders rebelled against their own religion. These dissenters called for the church to separate from the state and to reject all forms of violence. They waged their war with weapons of peace, and many died for their radical cause of calling Christians back to the way of Christ.

Known as "Anabaptists," they dared to think that Jesus should be taken seriously when he taught his followers to turn the other cheek, love their enemies, and do good to those who hate them. These "Inglorious Pastors" paved the way for all to lay down arms and acts of violence even at the expense of our own lives and liberties.

RESPONSE:
As a peacemaker for Jesus, I will seek out "transforming initiatives" wherever I see conflict.

PRAYER:
Lord, give me the attitude of Your peace and Your methods of not resisting an evil person that will prompt repentance and reconciliation.

November 17

RELEASE FROM CHAINS

Suddenly there was such a violent earthquake that the foundations of the prison were shaken. At once all the prison doors flew open, and everyone's chains came loose.
Acts 16:26

African Muslim, El Gasim, saw the sign of the cross one day while praying the usual five times a day in the prison where he was incarcerated. He changed positions but the cross wouldn't go away. This went on for seven days. He had no explanation for it, except that Christ was calling him to give his life to Him. A Christian pastor, also in prison explained that living for Christ would not be without suffering. They prayed together.

Other Muslim inmates saw El Gasim praying one day with another Christian prisoner and reported them to the authorities. When summoned to the superintendent's office, they openly declared their faith in Christ and received twenty-five lashes each, administered by a Christian warder. The other prisoner denied his new faith but El Gasim confessed Christ and said he would face the consequence, no matter what. This enraged the authorities. He was beaten, shackled in chains weighing over fifty pounds and put on death row to be hanged.

The imprisoned pastor had great compassion for El Gasim, knowing that if God did not intervene, he was surely staring death in the eye. He told him Paul and Silas' story, reminding him that he wasn't the first to be beaten and chained for the sake of Christ. The important thing to remember was that Paul and Silas prayed and praised God, when their chains fell off and the prison doors opened. The pastor confirmed that it could still happen today, because the power that worked then, was still at work today. They prayed together, earnestly seeking God's will.

The pastor retired to his room and continued praying. In the meantime, El Gasim, who then felt encouraged by the sharing, took the first step and to his surprise, the unexpected happened—the chain broke loose and fell from one of his legs. Bystanders, whose attention were drawn by the sound of the falling chain, watched in amazement as he took the second step—the same thing happened. A miracle had happened right before him and his other inmates. El Gasim went to the warder and told him, "Your chains are in the chapel, go and collect them."

Trembling and confused the warder informed his superiors of this strange occurrence. An emergency meeting was convened. The incident could not be ignored or laughed off as nonsense. There were too many witnesses. They decided that it would be best to let El Gasim go free, because if he stayed he would certainly convert others to Christianity. Sending him to another prison wouldn't help either, because even there they couldn't stop Christ from doing miracles.

RESPONSE:
Today I affirm my faith in a miracle working God who can release me from my chains.

PRAYER:
Pray for persecuted Christian prisoners who need to be released from chains today.

November 18

SOURCE OF PEACE

Peace I leave with you; my peace I give you.
I do not give to you as the world gives. Do not let your
hearts be troubled and do not be afraid.
John 14:27

Five Christian students were walking home from an Open Doors seminar in east Africa and passed a young Muslim man walking into the bush with a rope in his hand. He tied the rope around a tree. The students asked, "What are you doing?"

"I want to kill myself," he replied.

"Why?"

"I say my prayers five times a day and I read the Qur'an. I have money, a wife and children, but I have no peace. I want peace. That is my one big wish."

The students applied what they have learned and witnessed to this man named Keder. They told him that the Qur'an teaches that Jesus is a prophet but He is also the Saviour of everyone who accepts Him as Lord. He is the Prince of Peace. Keder left the rope in the tree and decided to give this Saviour a try. The students took him to church and after prayer Keder said, "I've found the peace I was seeking."

The following day Keder showed up at the seminar. A stranger wearing a Muslim hat scared the teacher at first but he continued. In the afternoon, Keder asked to give his testimony. "Until now, Islam was the only genuine religion for me because it was straightforward. I studied the Qur'an for five years and I did my rituals daily but none of that gave me peace. That is why I decided to kill myself. Then I met five of you Christians yesterday. I used to hate Christians, but when you witnessed and prayed for me, everything changed. Muslims are hurting without the knowledge of the Scriptures, therefore pray for them."

Keder is now secretly studying the Bible and attending church. He is the first Muslim in his area to accept Christ. His Bible study leader says that he attends regularly and arrives early to talk about Jesus before the Bible study starts. Jesus' peace makes him unafraid and he wants to witness. He is even prepared to die for Jesus.

RESPONSE:
Today I will rest in the promises of the Prince of Peace and not be fearful.

PRAYER:
Pray for Muslims who are hurting from the lack of knowledge of the Scriptures and the source of true peace.

November 19

POURED OUT LIKE A DRINK OFFERING

For I am already being poured out like a drink offering,
and the time for my departure is near.
2 Timothy 4:6

On the last day of an Open Doors seminar in South Africa, students shared how they thought the church should prepare for persecution. One man shared his son's story and its impact:

It was at the time when the pupils rioted, burning schools, churches, shopping centers, town councillors' houses and mercilessly attacking anyone whom they regarded as a 'sell-out.'

Each morning his sturdy, neatly dressed, thirteen-year-old Christian son wound his way through the mounds of rubble towards school, amidst the mocking of other youths wandering the smoke-filled streets. Later he would walk home, while the teachers, frightened by the threatening mobs, locked themselves in their homes.

One particular morning, after the family devotions, his parents watched as he walked off to school. At the school grounds, a mob blocked the gate. He walked undeterred through the gate and greeted them with a nod and a friendly smile.

He was in the center of the mob when they closed in around him blocking any further progress. One older gang leader, tall and powerfully built, grabbed the strap of his school bag and pulled him to a standstill. He glared at him and growled, "As a Christian you have always been on time for school, never late, never missing a day. You have always been praised by those 'sell-out' teachers for knowing and doing your school work in spite of our revolutionary slogan, 'liberation now, education later.' Today, you will have to decide for our revolution or else."

"I have decided to have nothing to do with your revolution," the boy replied unwaveringly. He remembered what his father taught on compromise in times of persecution.

647

With a curse the bully pushed him backwards into the mob. Blows rained on him and he tried in vain to ward it off, then a knife flashed in the sun, a second, and a third. Hours later, a policeman knocked on the door of his parent's home.

The father still lives in that house and preaches the love of Christ to the same community. Peace has returned to the township, but hardly a day passes without a passer-by, or a message scribbled on the garden wall, reminding him of that day.

The father says, "I greet them and smile at them in the hope that the testimony of my life and my willingness to forgive will eventually carry the light of Christ into their hearts, replacing the spirit of bitterness darkening their lives. I know by going back there to train the church leaders I am at risk of my life being *'poured out like a drink offering'* just like the Apostle Paul."

RESPONSE:
Today I will not live in fear nor compromise my faith no matter what Satan throws at me.

PRAYER:
Pray for courage for those whose lives today may be poured out like a drink offering.

November 20

LOVE IS THE ANSWER

He will rescue them from oppression and violence,
for precious is their blood in his sight.
Psalm 72:14

When a bomb ripped through a church in Alexandria, Egypt on New Year's Day, 2011, Christians across the Western world reeled with shock. Twenty-one believers were killed in the attack and many others were wounded. While Christians in the West watched the news reports with disbelief, local believers say the attack came as no surprise.

Responses to the vicious attack were varied. While some cried for revenge, others have responded differently trusting God to redeem these lives.

One explanatory story from Egypt is this:

Devil: "I just killed 21 of your family."

Jesus: "You didn't kill 21 of my family. You just sent them on ahead to me, and you mobilized the church to pray."

Brother Andrew writes:

What is your first thought when someone offends you? Anger? Indignation? Perhaps, if we're honest, our hearts even want to see some kind of retaliation or revenge.

But you know, Jesus is clear: revenge is not the answer. Love is. Especially when it comes to the Muslim world.

That's why, instead of retaliating when we read of a bomb attack against our fellow believers, I suggest our response should be repentance! Repentance that we have not prayed, have not cared, have not gone to the Muslim world to proclaim the true life and freedom we have in Jesus!

Let's keep asking God to truly change our hearts—that we might love, serve and pray more fervently…for the advancement of His kingdom and the glory of His name in the Muslim world and beyond!

RESPONSE:
Today I will seek to keep my eyes on Jesus and try to understand things from His perspective.

PRAYER:
Lord, change my heart so I am filled with Your compassion and thus love, serve and pray more fervently.

November 21

STAND FIRM AND STAND TOGETHER

But God has put the body together, giving greater honor to the parts that lacked it, so that there should be no division in the body, but that its parts should have equal concern for each other.

1 Corinthians 12:24b-25

As members of the same family we have the responsibility to come to the aid of another member who is suffering. The body of Christ is strong when each part is closely knit together. When one part suffers, all the other members suffer (1 Corinthians 12:20–27).

Members of the Persecuted Church who have been helped by others around the world have made comments like those of young Salamat Masih in Pakistan. He was charged with writing blasphemies against the Prophet Mohammed—even though he was illiterate. He was on death row until finally exonerated. After receiving cards from all over the world assuring him of prayers, Salamat said: "I never realized that I had so many brothers and sisters around the world."

A pastor who was attacked and hurt in Indonesia was so traumatized that he and the family left the area and the ministry. Before we judge him, perhaps we should ask if this pastor ever received enough encouragement and help from other churches and believers. Could it be that he felt so alone because there were not enough other people who cared for him?

Another believer from Hindu background in eastern Indonesia was led to the Lord by a doctor who prayed for him regarding his incurable disease and God healed him. He lost no time in joining a local church.

He said, "At that time, a lot of people accepted Jesus in my village, but they were afraid of the threats from their families. When they convert, village officials come to interrogate them. I, myself, have been interrogated many times after my conversion, and warned me not to convert others. But I was not afraid. I chose to keep my faith in Him no matter what happened." He experienced severe opposition and persecution from everyone he knew but he held fast to his faith. Open Doors then connected him with a group of other believers from Hindu background.

In November 2010, he and his family met a different kind of opposition that tested their faith. Mount Bromo erupted, covering hundreds of hectares of farmlands and plantations with volcanic ash. "Our livestock died, and we could not work on the farm…People around me ask why I can still smile and be happy. I just tell them that although I am poor and I face a lot of difficulties, I have Jesus. He gives me joy in my heart…Being with other believers reminds me that I am not alone. I am encouraged all the more to share the gospel with my people."

RESPONSE:
Today I will remember that I am part of a large body…a family that deeply cares for me.

PRAYER:
Pray for isolated believers that God will show them the reality of standing strong together.

November 22

LOVE YOUR ENEMIES

"You have heard that it was said, 'Love your neighbor and hate your enemy.' But I tell you, love your enemies and pray for those who persecute you..."
Matthew 5:43-44

Nigeria is divided religiously along the tenth parallel. On the north side Muslims are in the majority. On the south side Christians are in the majority. Along the border between these two groups much blood has been spilled repeatedly in recent years.

One pastor says, "We are facing persecution from our neighbors, the Muslims. They don't want to see the gospel progressing...and they feel envious that we have more church buildings...and our businesses are expanding as well."

Another pastor adds, "They see that they must stop the expansion of Christianity into the north, and that has to be done physically."

And a bishop of one church denomination is wearying from the many attacks. He is quoted as saying, "We have turned the other cheek so many times, we have no more cheeks to turn!"

One violent incident took place in Tudun Wada. It began when a young student was accused of drawing a picture of Islam's prophet Mohammed. All of a sudden the matter was taken seriously. They started burning churches and rioting with all kinds of weapons.

Nineteen Christians were killed that day, leaving behind mourning widows, family members and friends. Ten churches were burned. Thirty-six homes and one hundred forty-seven shops belonging to Christians were destroyed. But, God gave spiritual courage to His followers on that terrible day. And they refused to run.

Looking back on the situation, a pastor in the area says, "The churches that were destroyed...in fact there is none that has been rebuilt that is not bigger than what it was before. And the attendance by members has grown astronomically."

As soon as our Open Doors co-workers heard about the violence, they rushed to Tudun Wada to see the circumstances for themselves.

They provided for the spiritual, emotional and practical needs of the pastors and the entire Christian community.

Again the pastor comments, "They distributed to us Bibles and other reading materials. All of us pastors were very, very excited. We were happy."

Another added, "Open Doors through the Standing Strong Through The Storm seminar has lifted up our hearts, and has given us a heart of love for our enemies...Just like Jesus Christ said that we should pray for our persecutors...our attitude towards them is actually to pray for them, and love them."

The critically important need facing Nigeria is forgiveness. Christians are seeking to express it in tangible ways as they live out the love of Jesus Christ, just as He did two thousand years ago. He forgave the very people who nailed Him to a cross. That is the example Nigeria is witnessing today. And it is what will open the hearts of millions to the truth of the gospel.

RESPONSE:
I will be an example to others in loving, forgiving and praying for those who hurt me.

PRAYER:
Lord, bless the believers in central Nigeria today as they struggle responding to violence.

November 23

PAUL OF AFGHANISTAN

I have worked much harder, been in prison more frequently, been flogged more severely, and been exposed to death again and again. Five times I received from the Jews the forty lashes minus one. Three times I was beaten with rods, once I was pelted with stones, three times I was shipwrecked, I spent a night and a day in the open sea...
2 Corinthians 11:23b-25

The Apostle Paul suffered severely in his ministry of sharing the gospel in the first century. But Paul was always quick to point out that what others thought so terrible—his imprisonment—God turned into good. Rather than hindering the spread of the gospel, it actually aided its advance (Philippians 1:12-14). Paul's example was followed by many disciples down through the ages. You might be surprised to learn about one of these who lived in Afghanistan.

In Kabul, a brilliant young blind man who had memorized the whole Qur'an in Arabic listened to the gospel by radio and later publicly declared his faith in Jesus as his Lord. He became the first blind student to attend regular-sighted schools in Afghanistan. He graduated from University of Kabul with a law degree in order to defend Christians who might be persecuted for their faith. Some of his encouragement as a young believer came from a missionary from neighbouring Iran, Mehdi Dibaj.

Under the communist regime, Paul was arrested on false charges and put in a notorious prison where tens of thousands were executed. There was no heat in the jail during the cold winters. He had to sleep on the freezing mud floor with only his overcoat. A prisoner next to him was trembling with cold since he did not even have a jacket. Paul remembered John the Baptist had said, ***"The man who has two coats should share with him who has none."*** (Luke 3:11) He took off his only coat and gave it to the neighbour. From then on, the Lord miraculously kept him warm every night.

In prison, the communists gave Paul shock treatments to try to brainwash him. The electric burns left scars on his head. But he did not give in. God's grace was sufficient. After release from prison he kept mastering foreign languages and continued translating the Bible, writing and preaching...as well as discipling new believers. In 1988, Paul was kidnapped by a fanatical Muslim group and charged with apostasy because he became a Christian. He was beaten for hours with rods and ultimately martyred. But Paul's testimony lives on today as a trophy of God's grace. He is affectionately remembered as "Afghanistan's Apostle Paul".

You can read more about Paul in Dr. Christy Wilson's excellent book, *More To Be Desired Than Gold*, Gordon-Conwell Theological Seminary, 1994.

RESPONSE:
Today I will live biblically no matter what circumstances I may face knowing that God's grace is sufficient for me.

PRAYER:
Thank You, Lord, for the inspiring example of Afghanistan's Apostle Paul and his faithfulness in serving You to the end.

November 24

ASHAMED OF JESUS

Whoever is ashamed of me and my words, the Son of Man will be ashamed of them when he comes in his glory and in the glory of the Father and of the holy angels.

Luke 9:26

Young believers in the Lord in Muslim cultures often struggle with the issue of publicly declaring their new faith in Jesus. Shadiya is the youngest of five children in a Muslim family. At the age of eighteen she came in contact with a group of young people in the church of Pastor Jamil. During the summer of 2011, the church was visited by a group of other young Christians. During that time Shadiya decided to follow Jesus.

One day she forgot to hide her Bible and her younger brother found it. He asked his father about this striking book with a large cross prominent on the cover. Father was shocked. He soon found out that Shadiya brought the book into their house.

Initially dumbfounded by the hostile attitude of her father, Shadiya stood firm for what she believed. She admitted that she had become a Christian, that she received the Bible from some friends and that she no longer is a Muslim.

Her father interpreted this as denying her identity. This, in his opinion, was a betrayal of the entire family and the Muslim community. In other words, the shame for the family was unbearable. So in her father's eyes there was only one option; force Shadiya to deny her faith in Christ. "If you refuse to deny your new faith, you are no longer welcome in our home!" he yelled at her. Shadiya still held on to faith in Jesus.

The situation deteriorated even more after her father went to the mosque and shared the "apostasy" of his daughter with the local imam. They decided she had to deny her Christian faith openly and confess the Islamic faith in public. If she refused to do so, she would have to pay with her life. She would be stoned by the Muslim community.

She asked her apostate brother-in-law, Amir, for advice. He suggested that she do what they asked of her and remain a secret follower of Jesus. In her heart she could remain a believer in Christ, although she would openly deny her faith to save her life. Shadiya was not really convinced that this was the right thing to do and was full of doubt. In the end she followed the advice of Amir.

The prospect of becoming a martyr at the age of eighteen was now over but Shadiya remained doubtful about her decision. She and Amir asked Pastor Jamil what he thought about it.

"This could have been an opportunity for the whole family or the entire village to see God working in the life of an eighteen-year-old girl," he replied. "It is a great challenge to deal with our fear; still we should rely on Jesus, rather than basing our choices on fear."

The situation for Shadiya now seems less tense but the risk of escalation remains.

RESPONSE:
Today I will not allow fear to control me...especially regarding the public declaration of my faith.

PRAYER:
Pray for Shadiya and the people surrounding her. Ask our Father to further His kingdom through her and fellow-believers who are cautiously trying to help her to grow in faith.

November 25

RADICAL CHRISTIANITY

I counsel you to buy from me gold refined in the fire, so you can become rich; and white clothes to wear, so you can cover your shameful nakedness; and salve to put on your eyes, so you can see.
Revelation 3:18

Radical Christianity is a life-style, not just a mindset; radical Christianity is concerned with conquering, not cowering; with sacrifice, not superficiality; with victory, not verbiage; with scoring, not slumming; with penetration, not pandering. Radical Christianity is in first gear, neutral is nonexistent; radical Christianity is courageous but never constrictive constraining or cautious! Radical Christianity moves mountains; crosses Red Seas; pulls down walls; builds walls; walks on water; raises the dead; calms storms; feeds 5000 and walks through closed doors.

It suffers regularly; soars often; sweats daily; saturates everything and spreads everywhere. Radical Christianity calls sin black, hell hot, hypocrisy evil, Satan a liar and judgment sure. It doesn't back down, sit down or stay down. Radical Christianity doesn't depend on the strokes of others to keep it going. It doesn't acquiesce in the face of loud opposition, fold under pressure, wince under criticism, tarnish under time, die under duress, fade under technology nor rot under moisture. It doesn't rust, retreat, renounce, reconsider, return or renege.

Radical Christianity always lifts up Christ; knocks down barriers; marches over objections; overwhelms pessimism; gobbles up cynicism; and tramples down skepticism.

Radical Christianity gives lavishly; prays relentlessly; claims abundantly; works feverishly; preaches powerfully; serves lovingly; perseveres patiently and believes expectantly! Radical Christianity dares to challenge the prevailing standard to make it God's. It never plays to the grandstands; nor waters down its position; nor adjusts its principles, but rather is a thermostat that controls its surroundings, never a thermometer that merely adjusts to them. It is never big, popular, stylish, convenient, in vogue or in-step with the world. Its adherents are few; its sound clear; its philosophy unpopular and its rewards great. Its disciples aren't rewarded by this world but are those to whom Christ will say, "Well done!"[40]

A congregation of believers was worshipping in a Sunday service in Peru and a squad of heavily armed Shining Path rebels came rushing in. "We've heard that this group is committed to God. How many of you are willing to die for your faith? Raise your hands," he commanded.

Fearing they would be slaughtered, most of the congregation remained still. But a small number of believers tentatively raised their hands. The others were released and the commander said, "Those of you who raised your hands, stop worrying. We're not going to kill you. We just wanted to see who in the congregation believed enough in their faith that they were willing to die for it. That's the kind of radical commitment we're looking for."

RESPONSE:
Today I commit to being a radical Christian and give everything I am and have to Jesus.

PRAYER:
Pray for Christians in conflict areas who must regularly put their lives on the line.

40 Bob Moorehead, *Words Aptly Spoken* (Kirkland, WA: Overlake Christian Press, 1995), p. 17.

November 26

WHAT WOULD JESUS SAY TODAY TO THE PERSECUTED CHURCH?

I am coming soon. Hold on to what you have,
so that no one will take your crown.
Revelation 3:11

Today we share a message composed by Steve Haas for Prayer for the Persecuted Church:

To the angel of the church of the despised, incarcerated, separated, raped, and martyred; the Persecuted Church. These are the words of him who knows your patient endurance, understands your distress, and like you has been faithful to the shedding of his own precious blood.

You say you are isolated, cut off, that no one acknowledges your state. I see the terrors you face: the raids of your house churches in Laos, Indonesia, and China; the assault and murder of your leadership in Iran, India, and Chechnya...

I register every tear that is cried, record each longing conceived, hear each desperate plea confessed. I identify intimately with your plight. I have not forgotten you. Nor have many others who, although unfamiliar with the gravity of your suffering, draw hope and strength from your noble sacrifices for me. I have revealed your plight to your brothers and sisters in Christ and have called thousands of churches to pray for you and to serve you.

You say you are afraid. Recognize what you have that cannot be taken away. I have given you new life, an irrepressible joy, and an ever-present Spirit. Your transforming faith in me cannot be crushed but instead shines like a lighthouse, drawing those who sincerely search for the Way, the Truth, and the Life.

You say you are losing hope. Know that these afflictions are not the final word, that I am sovereign and just. In time, I will repay. Although these tribulations threaten to overwhelm you, I have prepared an eternal place of peace for you, a permanent sanctuary of refreshment and true freedom that begins the moment you recognize me as Lord and serve me as King. I am with you always.

Beware of those who come from outside your fellowship, who masquerade as teachers of the church but elevate personal comfort over godly obedience. Many travel from long distances and present themselves as spiritual masters of the faith, proclaiming that temporal health and security are your due. Do not listen to them. Theirs is a false teaching, only shackling you to the unrequited masters of greed and disquiet. In the midst of your suffering, I will prove to be your only true peace and anchor…

I delight in your resourcefulness with little, your dignity in suffering, your joyful endurance in the midst of adversity. It is these things that give witness to a power above all earthly kingdoms, a source of strength stronger than the might of any human power.

Remain faithful, and I will raise you up in victory. Patiently endure, for I will not tarry long.[41]

RESPONSE:
Today I reaffirm my commitment to be faithful and patiently endure until Jesus comes.

PRAYER:
Pray that the Persecuted Church will understand the deep reality of patient endurance.

---

41 Steve Haas, "What Would Jesus Say Today to the Church Enduring Persecution?" *Christianity Today* (October, 1999), **http://www.ctlibrary. com/ct/1999/october25/9tc073.html**.

November 27

PERSECUTION AND CHURCH GROWTH

On that day a great persecution broke out against the church in Jerusalem, and all except the apostles were scattered throughout Judea and Samaria.

Acts 8:1b

Pastor Samuel Lamb from southern China celebrated his 88th birthday in October, 2012. A quarter of his life was spent imprisoned for his faith. He still preaches several times on Sunday in his large house church and most week nights in Bible studies. His brilliant smile shines from a slight body suffering chronic disability resulting from 15 years confinement in a coal mine. "God gives me the strength I need," he says. He has never left China, fearing that if he traveled, the authorities would not let him return.

Lamb credits God for the faith to accept what has happened in his life. It has deepened his ministry. Lamb believes that sometimes God is more glorified through sickness and poverty than through health and wealth. Christians travel thousands of miles to discuss house church ministry with Pastor Lamb and visitors from around the world seek out his house church in Guangzhou, China, which gathers 3,000 members each week.

Pastor Lamb often refers to persecution and growth as intertwined. He is known for his quote, "Remember the lesson of the Chinese church: more persecution, more growth." As the pastor explains, "Before I was put into prison in 1955, this church's membership was 400; when I came out in 1978, it built up to 900 in a matter of weeks. Then after 1990, when everything was confiscated here and the church briefly closed, we re-opened and in a matter of weeks we had 2,000 members. More persecution, more growth—that's the history of the Chinese church, that's the history of this church."

Though the two are related, persecution in other parts of the world has not necessarily always brought church growth. North Africa is an example.

But the Bible, especially in the book of Acts, is clear that church growth will likely bring persecution. Each time the gospel made advances in Acts, persecution would break out. And in Acts 8:4, the persecuted and scattered believers went everywhere preaching the word.

RESPONSE:
Today I will accept the principle that sometimes God is more glorified through sickness and poverty than through health and wealth.

PRAYER:
Thank You Lord that You use all situations to grow Your church. Help me to be an active and eager participant.

November 28

RESPONDING WITH PRAISE

Be joyful always; pray continually; give thanks in all circumstances, for this is God's will for you in Christ Jesus.

1 Thessalonians 5:16-18

The overflow of singing praises amid great difficulties has tremendous spiritual power. Paul and Silas set the biblical pattern in the prison in Philippi (Acts 16).

Helen Berhane spent almost three years in the shipping container prisons of Eritrea. In her book *Song of the Nightingale*, she shares about the first time she and other women were put in an old metal shipping container that was very hot and filled with fleas and lice:

Everyone was very despondent, and many of the women were angry. They asked me what we should do and I knew they were expecting me to say that we should shout or bang the container, to let our captors know that we were not going to tolerate this treatment. But I remembered...[reading] about how Christians, like nightingales, could not be prevented from singing even in captivity, and I suggested that we sing: "We should praise God in spite of the fleas, in spite of the lice, in spite of the heat. We should thank God despite our circumstances." So I began to sing with them, and pray, and share the Word of God from memory.[42]

Pastor Ung Sophal sat in a filthy Cambodian prison badly beaten. His hands and feet were chained for five months. "Only my mouth was unchained," he said.

"...So I sang to God in prison all the time. Another prisoner heard me singing through a small hole in the wall, so I taught him the song—a bit at a time. He passed it on and soon eight of us were singing."

Archbishop Dominic Tang spent twenty-two years in prison in China for his faith. He reports:

---

42 Helen Berhane, *Song of the Nightingale*, (Colorado Springs: Authentic Media, 2009), pp. 36-37.

"Besides my prayer and meditation, every day I sang some hymns in a soft voice: 'Jesus I live for you; Jesus I die for you; Jesus I belong to you. Whether alive or dead I am for Jesus!' This hymn was taught to me by a Protestant prisoner who lived in my cell."[43]

RESPONSE:
Today I will respond to all the challenges of life I face with praise and thankfulness.

PRAYER:
Pray that all Christian prisoners around the world will also respond to their circumstances as those documented above.

---

43 Tony Lambert, *The Resurrection of the Chinese Church* (London: Hodder and Stoughton, 1991), p 179.

November 29

EVANGELISM FUNCTION OF THE CHURCH

"Therefore go and make disciples of all nations, baptizing them in the name of the Father and of the Son and of the Holy Spirit..."
Matthew 28:19

Johan Companjen, President Emeritus of Open Doors International, was travelling in the Philippines. Finding it extremely hot in his hotel room, he called for a staff person. "Is the air-conditioning not working?" he asked. "Oh yes sir," the man replied, "It's working. It's just not functioning!"

Jesus Christ ordained five functions for His church to be involved in for Him. We are to **evangelize** (Matthew 28:19); to **disciple** or train those who are evangelized (Matthew 28:20); to **minister** or serve people demonstrating God's love (Matthew 22:39; Ephesians 4:12); to **fellowship** together (Ephesians 2:19; Galatians 6:10); and to **worship** together (Matthew 4:10; John 4:23). In the Bible, there is not necessarily a priority order for these five purposes. They are all equally important.

Evangelism is one primary function. If we really have come to know Christ as Lord and Savior, we will want to share this wonderful experience with those we love. It sometimes seems hard or embarrassing to share the gospel with our friends and relatives. But if we really love them, and if we really believe that without Christ they will suffer for eternity separated from God, we will tell them no matter how oppressive the culture or the political situation may be.

Restrictions on the church cause new creative means of evangelism to arise. In a restricted country of Asia, one such creative method is to hire a bus and invite relatives and friends to a free outing to the beach. Once in the bus, the pastor with a hand-held loudspeaker starts preaching to his "captive audience" about the love of Christ. At the beach the sharing and fellowship continues...as well as a water baptism for new believers.

667

In Soviet Russia, a group of Christians took advantage of the funeral of a small daughter of one of the members to present a public evangelistic witness. On the way to the cemetery, they stopped every few hundred meters to sing triumphant songs of praise. The father of the dead child also gave a clear message of salvation in Christ. Many listeners along the way were deeply touched.

In Vietnam, Pastor Ho Hieu Ha spent over six years in prison for pastoring a growing church right under the noses of the unhappy authorities. But he felt that his imprisonment was not a waste because he used the time to witness to others who were also in prison. When he was released, he had led ninety-six people to Jesus and discipled them.

RESPONSE:
I am committed to sharing Christ's love with others. It is a primary function of the church.

PRAYER:
Pray for those in restricted environments as they creatively find ways to witness about their faith.

November 30

SHARE THE GOOD NEWS

Those who accepted his message were baptized, and about three thousand were added to their number that day.
Acts 2:41

Eight men sat in a small dimly lit room in a rural Chinese village home. Seven were preachers and their eyes were glued to the Bible held by the eighth man. It was a leather-bound zippered Bible with gold-edged trim on the pages.

The Western visitor suddenly became aware that the seven men were staring intently at his Bible. One of them generated enough courage to say, "What a beautiful Bible. May I look at it for a moment?"

"Of course," he replied. The Bible was gently handed from person to person as though it was made of eggshells. They asked how much it cost. And their faces fell when they learned it was the equivalent of twenty dollars.

Then the visitor received an inspiration. He decided to make this a personal ministry project. The qualification for receiving one of these Chinese Bibles should be so high that these leaders would be inspired to greater achievement. Yet, at the same time ensure that he would not need to provide a great number.

He told them, "If a person is mightily used by God, then I will bring him one of these Bibles."

"What do you mean mightily used of God?" the preachers queried eagerly.

Thinking fast he replied, "Those who have led at least 10,000 people to the Lord and discipled another 10,000."

To his astonishment the preachers burst out laughing. They said, "Oh, this is too easy. There are five of us here who can now qualify for your zippered gold-edged Bible, and we know ten more."

After his trip the visitor chuckled, "I'm bankrupt." But more seriously he added, "I've been working in China with house church leaders for many years. But one thing never changes...I am literally taken by surprise during each visit at how fast the church is growing."

RESPONSE:
Today I will take more seriously my responsibility in sharing the Good News of Jesus and fulfil the church's function of evangelism.

PRAYER:
Thank you Lord that Your church is continuing to grow quickly in China. May that be a reality in my country as well.

December 1

DISCIPLESHIP FUNCTION OF THE CHURCH

*"...and teaching them to obey everything I have
commanded you. And surely I am with you always,
to the very end of the age."*
Matthew 28:20

Another related function of the church is discipleship. Once we have
seen a friend or loved-one come to Christ we have a responsibility
to see that they grow in the Lord. In some cultures, if a person saves
another's life, that person becomes responsible for the one saved. This
is a good concept for the Christian. If we lead someone else into new
life in Christ, we are responsible to see that person learns what the
Bible teaches about the Christian life.

The Bible is so important to Christian growth that many Christians
want to immediately give a Bible to anyone they may lead to the Lord.
In some countries, like China or North Korea, faithful Christians have
carried on for years without Bibles, but it was very difficult. They had
to depend on Scripture verses that one of their members memorized
at some earlier time, or perhaps heard on a Christian radio broadcast.
The almost desperate hunger for the Bible among Christians who have
been cut off from it for an extended period, dramatically illustrates
just how important the Bible is to the Christian life.

If formal training centers have been closed, it is especially imperative
that local churches take very seriously their responsibilities to teach
(2 Timothy 2:2). This teaching may have to be done on a one-to-one
basis whenever a mature Christian and a young Christian can get
together.

There are many examples in the Bible of leaders being trained in
this way. Besides the clear example of Christ teaching His disciples,
we see Barnabas teaching Mark (Acts 12:25; 15:39), Priscilla and
Aquila helping Apollos (Acts 18:24-26), and Paul training Timothy
(Acts 16:1-3). Paul gives us the most detailed approach to "disciple"
a young believer. He taught first by example (1 Corinthians 4:16),
then he openly gave himself to his disciples, living with them and

671

sharing all he had (Acts 20:34). His relationship with them was not just "student/ teacher." Rather, he became very personally involved with them (1 Timothy 1:1-2). He gave them responsibilities while they were still in training, and kept in close touch with them even after they had become leaders themselves (1 & 2 Timothy and Titus).

In a prison in Sudan, a pastor quietly discipled a young believer from Muslim background as they were forced to work together. After his release, the young Christian became a dynamic witness for Christ.

RESPONSE:
Discipleship is another function of the church and is crucial in the life of a follower of Jesus.

PRAYER:
Pray for those in difficult circumstances—such as prison—trying to disciple new believers.

December 2

MINISTRY FUNCTION OF THE CHURCH

**...*to prepare God's people for works of service,
so that the body of Christ may be built up.***
Ephesians 4:12

Another function of the church is ministry. As Christians we need to be aware of the spiritual needs of others and sensitively seek to help them at every opportunity—both fellow-believers and non-believers. A word of encouragement or a small act of kindness may be the deciding factor in whether or not a struggling friend is able to stand against the enemy.

In a tribal area of northeast India, the poor Christians of one tribe made great sacrifices and took great risks to aid and encourage the new believers in another tribe after their leader, his wife and ten-year-old daughter were killed for their witness.

Ministry is demonstrating God's love to others by meeting their needs and healing their hurts in the name of Jesus. Each time you reach out in love to others you are ministering to them. The church is to equip the saints to do the work of ministry.

A co-worker and his family were visiting in the southern part of the Ukraine. As they entered the hotel after a tiring day in the streets, their daughter came sobbing into their room. "I saw a man today begging for money. He had no legs and was sitting on a skateboard. He looked so poor and lonely." The tears rolled down her cheeks. She truly felt compassion for a sight that they didn't even notice.

"I think Jesus wants us to give him a Bible when we see him again," she commented after they prayed together.

The following morning early, as they started their journey through the streets of Odessa, it wasn't long before she saw him. They knew that there was a certain amount of risk involved in handing out Bibles in the streets and thus didn't want to make it too obvious. He opened the Bible and slowly started paging through it. He reached down and took all the money in the handkerchief next to him and offered it to them.

They suddenly realized that he must be under the impression that they were selling the Bible on the black market and therefore the offer of all his savings. "Nyet, gift, gift," and they pushed back his hand with the money. He took the Bible, pressed it against his chest and then tears started rolling down his cheeks. He opened the Bible spending several minutes reading and paging through a book that he had obviously heard about but had never seen. They left him with hearts overflowing with gratitude.

Jesus made ministry so simple. It can be as easy as offering a thirsty person a glass of water in His name!

RESPONSE:
Today I will look for opportunities to minister to needy hearts in Jesus' name.

PRAYER:
Lord Jesus, I ask You to show me today those to whom I can minister in Your name.

December 3

WORSHIP FUNCTION OF THE CHURCH

"...Yet a time is coming and has now come when the true worshipers will worship the Father in spirit and truth, for they are the kind of worshipers the Father seeks. God is spirit, and his worshipers must worship in spirit and in truth."

John 4:23-24

All true believers recognize the privilege and responsibility to worship God. This worship begins when the Holy Spirit enters our being and grows and continues throughout our lifetime. Every believer should worship the Lord privately as well as gather together with other believers to worship whenever possible. We can worship the Lord because of who He is, because of what He has done in creation and redemption, and because of all that He has done for us individually.

Worship in Scripture seems to revolve around praising God. This is an act of the will not necessarily related to how a person "feels" or the immediate circumstances of life. In other words, we should praise the Lord even when things seem to be going wrong. This is an act of submission to His divine will and pleases the Lord (Psalm 67:3; Hebrews 13:15; Isaiah 12:1).

Worship is evidently a matter of attitude that may be expressed outwardly in prayer, various bodily positions (such as kneeling), singing, dancing, clapping etc. Music plays a very important part in the heartfelt worship of most believers. The form of worship should reflect the believer's cultural methods of showing adoration as long as it does not conflict with biblical guidelines.

Worship in the early church was simply an outpouring of thanksgiving from a heart that rejoiced in the Lord in complete disregard of circumstances. This type of worship cannot be stopped by anyone. A group of Christians in hostile surroundings can worship in this simple way without being limited to a certain building, a special time, or a prescribed program.

675

Worship is basically recognizing and declaring God's glory, holiness and worth. An act of worship is an expression of this recognition. The New Testament writers seemed to assume that all people knew how to worship. They give us few examples of how the early Christians worshipped. Participation in the Lord's Supper appears to have been their highest expression of worship. As they prayerfully remembered Jesus and His sacrificial death upon the cross for their sins, they were worshipping.

There are Scriptural references to other times of worship such as Peter's prayer (Acts 4:23-28), and Paul and Silas' experience in prison (Acts 16:23-25). Pastor Jack Hayford enjoys sharing the story about this as told by his favourite African-American preacher. Paul and Silas' prison cell singing was heard all the way to the heavenly throne room of God. He began to tap his toe to the music. And since heaven is His throne and the earth is His footstool, that toe tapping created an earthquake!!!

RESPONSE:
Today I desire every aspect of my life to declare God's glory, holiness and worth.

PRAYER:
Pray today for Christians in countries like North Korea who rarely have opportunity to express openly and publicly their worship of Almighty God.

December 4

FELLOWSHIP FUNCTION OF THE CHURCH

Consequently, you are no longer foreigners and aliens,
but fellow citizens with God's people and members of
God's household...
Ephesians 2:19

As Christians we are called to belong—not just believe. We are not meant to be loners but true members of his body—part of Jesus' family. It is thus important for Christians to spend time together to share their spiritual lives, encourage each other and have **fellowship**.

Satan brings all his efforts to bear upon Christians to prevent this fellowship. He realizes that believers need to help and strengthen each other, so he will try to prevent it by promoting indifference or by using the force of circumstances (Hebrews 10:24,25). Even informal or casual meetings can be used of the Lord for strengthening Christians, especially when formal meetings and large group fellowships are forbidden. Of course, large meetings can be useful, too. But normally, more help is given one-to-one in small "cell" groups where specific needs can be shared, discussed and ministered to in-depth.

Mona's story is a good illustration. It wasn't only that she was raped when she sneaked across the border into Malaysia. It wasn't simply because she sent her daughter back to Burma and had never seen her since she was a baby. It wasn't just the violence of those terrifying days in the '80's in Rangoon when students and soldiers clashed in the streets forcing her husband (then a student) and her to flee the country.

It was the thousand nights of loneliness. The trauma of the past haunted her. The papers she needed to stay in Malaysia legally. Papers that she could not acquire. The possibility of arrest and punishment by police.

The nightmares came on leathery wings of fear, dug their claws deeply and took up residence in her psyche. Her mind, once sound and clear, clouded with doubts and delusions: the sound of voices she did not know and horrifying images that would not go away.

But hers was not a life destined for darkness. The clouds were pulled away slowly, partly by the psychiatrist at the General Hospital, secured for her by the volunteers at the free medical clinic. Also by the kindness of strangers who reached out their hands in generosity.

It was the moment Mona was able to tell another woman in her own language of her troubles; this was when the first ray of light cut through the cloud and shone the possibility of hope into her circumstance.

Later, it was the time she spent with other women from Burma at the church. It was the songs they sang, the shared experience and language, the friendship, the food, the games.

Fellowship is life-giving to those who have been deprived of it.

RESPONSE:
Today I will seek to experience true fellowship in Christ.

PRAYER:
Pray for opportunities to support others who need a listening ear or a word of encouragement.

December 5

FULFILLING THE FIVE FUNCTIONS OF THE CHURCH

And let us consider how we may spur one another on toward love and good deeds, not giving up meeting together, as some are in the habit of doing, but encouraging one another—and all the more as you see the Day approaching.

Hebrews 10:24-25

In the summer of 2010, I led an excellent team of Open Doors staff and supporters on a visit to North Korea. We were allowed to pray publicly in the areas we visited and of course were presented with a formal church service on Sunday morning at one of the three churches functioning in Pyongyang. It was a well-executed performance — especially the choir. On its website, the Korean Christian Federation claims that there are ten thousand Protestant Christians in North Korea meeting at five hundred designated centers. In reality, Christians in the country experience tremendous challenges in worshipping publicly.

Brother Simon, the leader of the Open Doors work in North Korea, says that the true church must operate underground in the country. "They can't simply go to church to sing and to listen to the sermon. It is clear that being a Christian in North Korea is a lonely business."

Simon's thoughts turn to Sundays in North Korea. "It happens only sporadically that Christians consider themselves safe enough to meet together in small groups. Usually gatherings consist of only two people. For example, a Christian goes and sits on a bench in the park. Another Christian comes and sits next to him. Sometimes it's dangerous even to speak to one another, but they know they are both Christians, and at such a time, this is enough. If there is no one around, they may be able to share a Bible verse which they have learned off by heart and briefly say something about it. They also share prayer topics with each other. Then they leave one another and go and look for a Christian in some other part of their town or village. This continues throughout the Sunday. A cell group usually consists

679

of fewer than twenty Christians, who encourage and strengthen one another, plus one-to-one meetings in people's homes.

"Only if the whole family has turned to Christ is it possible to have something like a real fellowship gathering, as long as you keep your faith hidden from the neighbours. Besides this, it is sometimes possible to hold a meeting in remote areas with a group of ten to twenty people. Very occasionally, it is possible for Christians to go unobtrusively into the mountains and to hold a 'service' at a secret location like a cave. Then it may be the case that there are as many as sixty or seventy North Korean Christians gathered together."

In spite of severe limitations, believers can fulfill all five biblical functions of the church.

RESPONSE:
I will thankfully take my place in the assembly of believers to fulfill the church's functions.

PRAYER:
Thank you Lord for the faithfulness of Your church in North Korea against all obstacles.

December 6

LIFE SENTENCE

However, I consider my life worth nothing to me;
my only aim is to finish the race and complete the task
the Lord Jesus has given me—the task of testifying to
the good news of God's grace.

Acts 20:24

In a Sudan prison, Pastor Matta Boush was depressed as he faced thirty years on false charges. A visit from an Irish Catholic sister helped change his outlook. There were others in prison, she said, whose cases were far worse than his. She told him never to ask himself why he was there, but instead to ask for what purpose he was there. From that point Matta Boush began to minister to his fellow prisoners.

He began prayer meetings for non-Muslims and numbers grew quickly. One event at the prison made an especially strong impact. A prisoner, just prior to his execution, rather than being fearful, was calm and gave his testimony. He said he was not afraid to die because he knew he would go to heaven. This made such an impression that some of the Muslim guards became Christians.

He was transferred to another prison in the city of El-Obeid. Some Muslims objected to his ministry and prayer meetings so he was placed in solitary confinement for several months. Away from his God-given work and with too much time to think, depression overtook him again. But the encouragement of friends helped him through the hard times. Returning to the general prison population, he helped lead between 150 and 200 people to Christ.

Later Matta Boush was transferred to El-Khobar prison in Khartoum. There he was able to help build a prison chapel as well as continuing his ministry. In the next ten months, 200 people came to the Lord.

His sudden release indicated that the person ordering it had great authority. As a free man, he contacted churches and visited Nuba refugee camps. He was reunited with his three daughters. His wife, however, had married a Muslim man.

He began providing pastoral care for nine regional churches. He was faithful in sharing the Lord both in and out of prison. No sacrifice was too great to accomplish the goal.

RESPONSE:
Today I will sacrifice my comforts to accomplish the most important goal – sharing Jesus!

PRAYER:
Pray for pastors like Matta Boush in prison today around the world. Pray they will lose their own desires and accomplish the Lord's.

December 7

LOSE THE FEAR OF DYING

We are confident, I say, and would prefer to be away from the body and at home with the Lord.
2 Corinthians 5:8

Open Doors colleague, Ron Boyd-MacMillan, shares the following insight from his teaching, "Why I Need to Encounter the Persecuted Church."

There is a famous book called *The Denial of Death* by Ernest Becker. It is his contention that the whole of the Western world is really a gigantic playground to distract us from ever facing the fact that we will all die! Thinking about death is all but forbidden. Preparing for it is seen as a sign of morbidity. We arrange for the elderly to die out of sight in hostels and hospitals. And huge multinational companies produce products that promise to keep the effects of aging at bay.

Inevitably, when we are too scared to face death we end up being a slave to it. Even Christians can show the same dread of it as others. But an encounter with the persecuted can go a long way to diffusing this sense of dread.

Over twenty years of reporting on the Persecuted Church, I have interviewed literally hundreds of Christians who thought they were going to die for their faith. All of them—and I really do mean all of them—exhibited two amazing characteristics: they experienced unspeakable peace and joy in the midst of the pain as they began to feel death draw near; and they were as surprised as anyone that they were not afraid of death at the time.

Take Pastor You Yong, kidnapped by Islamic extremists from his church outside Madiun, central Java in December 2001. Furious that his church was full of Muslim converts, the extremists showered him with questions, trying to provoke him to attack them. They beat him and finally held a long machete to his throat. He assumed he was about to die. But what was going on inside Pastor You? Deeper than all the pain or fear? This is how he put it. "I was amazed that

683

throughout the ordeal I felt an incredible peace. I was also amazed at the answers I was able to give them. That verse came true—'when you are brought to trial, do not worry about what to say, for when the time comes, you will be given what to say' (Mt 10:19). The more they tried to provoke me, the more peace I felt."

And so when death reaches out its icy hand even in more everyday ways—when the plane hits an air pocket, or the results of the suspected cancer scan are due—I remember the experiences of my persecuted friends and I am strengthened to think, If they have been where I am about to go, and still testify that Jesus gives unaccountable peace, well, it is no tragedy to tread this well-worn path. Their experiences in the face of death help to take the dread away.

Of course, I know all this from the Bible, where Paul says that to be with Christ is "far better." And I have read that wonderful passage in Acts seven when Stephen has the face of an angel when he is stoned to death. But the truth comes with more power when a flesh-and-blood person who has faced death puts their arms around you and says, "You will have peace, and Jesus will be with you in the midst of it all." Death just cannot be that bad if Jesus is that great!

RESPONSE:
Today I will live in the peace of God that takes away the fear of dying.

PRAYER:
Thank You, Lord, for the encouragement of the persecuted to trust You in life and death.

684

December 8

OUR SPIRITS BLOSSOM WHEN WE SING

God sets the lonely in families, he leads out the prisoners with singing; but the rebellious live in a sun-scorched land.

Psalm 68:6

Open Doors colleague, Ron Boyd-MacMillan, shares the following insight from his teaching, "Why I Need to Encounter the Persecuted Church."

Chinese evangelist, Mrs Yang, was visited by another full time preacher who was very downcast. The preacher wanted to buy a tape player, but had no money. Mrs Yang sat down and just began to sing to him. Her voice was deep and scratchy, the tune barely discernable, the words simple: *I am a wanderer, my home is in heaven/ Life is fleeting/ Our home is in heaven/ In this world we have many trials/ And sadness and sickness/ True happiness is not in this world/ But in heaven.*

Mrs Yang sang as if before the Lord himself. Every word poured out from her core with total conviction. Tears rolled down her cheeks, her hands clenched the air, and she beat time on her hip. Soon the visiting preacher had joined in, and I watched them, roaring out the hymn together, smiles over both their faces. The preacher left, still with no money for his longed for tape player, but refreshed and encouraged.

Then again, I watched one morning as Mrs. Yang went out into the hills to pray. I followed her at a discreet distance. First she prayed for twenty minutes, then she sang, walking around, for another twenty minutes. For the next hour she read her Bible, making notes, planning the day's sermons. After that she sang again, for another half hour.

I confessed I had been spying on her, and asked "Why do you sing so much when there is no one to hear?" She said, "My father once told me, 'One of the sweet things about the Christian life is that you will do things because they are commanded, and then you will spend the rest of your life gaining deeper insight into why God's commands are so good.' So singing is a command. In the Psalms we are constantly exhorted to sing praises to our God. But as for why, I confess it is one of those wonderful mysteries my father told me about. You see, while in prison, I could pray and read Scripture, but nothing raised my spirits like singing. Maybe it's because singing somehow concentrates all of the body on the praise of God, but I have found it essential to the maintenance of a positive spirit."

Then she looked embarrassed. I said, "What is it? You were about to say something, but you have gone all reticent." She replied, "Well, it's just that an old lady told me something that really sums up the main reason I sing. She said, *'Our spirits are like flowers, and song is the sun. Just as flowers only truly open when the sun shines, so our spirits only blossom when we sing.'* I believe that. I don't know how, but it's true. Since my prison cell, I cannot do without song, and I am very frightened that as China gets more open, and the churches get more organized, we are going to leave the singing to the professionals. This would be terrible. The only way you can have a full blossoming spirit is to sing to it."

RESPONSE:
Today I will make my spirit blossom positively by singing to the Lord in the Spirit.

PRAYER:
Ask God to impact all Christians with this valuable insight of singing praises to Him.

December 9

GOD'S WORK IN CHANGING LIVES

Therefore, if anyone is in Christ, the new creation has come: The old has gone, the new is here!
2 Corinthians 5:17

The more you travel, the more you realize that God is at work changing lives all over the globe. Whether people have committed crimes against God (rebellion, blasphemy, hatred etc.) or crimes against society (murder, violence, theft etc.) or crimes against themselves (shame, guilt, despair etc.), He is able to bring about a complete transformation of their lives and fill them with His Holy Spirit.

Standing Strong Through The Storm (SSTS) teaching partner, Jim Cunningham, was sharing in a SSTS seminar with rural pastors in Colombia, South America. After the final session, Rauel (not his real name) approached Jim, almost shyly. With a warm smile and moist eyes, he extended his hand for what Jim thought was a handshake, but instead he gently offered a small piece of paper with some writing.

"For you, Santiago."

They hugged each other. Between Rauel's "No English" and Jim's "No Spanish" there was an unspoken bond of Christian love. They said their "good-byes" pointing heavenward as if to say, "See you again my brother!"

Jim's interpreter later translated the note. It read:

May the Lord bless your life and enrich your ministry. And may the angel of the Lord always encamp around you and all your family and nation. Take with you my remembrances and those of Colombia to the people of Canada.

Rauel.

"Do you know who Brother Rauel is?" the interpreter asked.

Jim shook his head "No."

"He used to be a guerrilla leader against the government forces," said his interpreter. "He came to faith as a follower of Jesus Christ a while back and this is his first time gathering with our pastors and leadership team. We earnestly prayed and had to have God's peace before inviting him here."

Jim concluded, "What an amazing story of God's grace. God is changing hearts—one at a time. Keep praying for peace in Colombia!"

RESPONSE:
Today I will praise God for His ministry in my life—and others—making changes and renewing my heart.

PRAYER:
Lord, we continue to pray for peace in countries like Colombia and in the hearts of those who struggle with injustice and inequality. And make me a totally new creation, I pray.

December 10

DELIVERANCE COMES THROUGH ENDURANCE

...if we endure, we will also reign with him...
2 Timothy 2:12a

Open Doors colleague, Ron Boyd-MacMillan, shares the following insight from his teaching, "Why I Need to Encounter the Persecuted Church."

Christian testimonies on the whole tend to be dominated by those who experienced wonderful deliverances: deliverances of healing, from cancer or other life threatening diseases, or deliverances from debt, or romance less marriages. Even when it comes to reporting on the persecuted, we read of Chinese house church leaders released from the grip of a deadly fever, or border guards with eyes miraculously blinded to the Bibles sitting in plain view on the back seat.

Yet it has to be said that deliverance stories—though they tend to grab the headlines—are not the norm. A dear old Christian in Beijing used to say to me, "Remember, for every deliverance story you hear, there are a hundred endurance stories." He was right. The story of the persecuted is primarily one of endurance.

I never saw this principle better illustrated than in the story of an old Chinese woman known throughout the world as "Auntie Mabel." A doctor in Beijing, she was well known for her bright Christian witness. She never married in order to look after a sick brother. Her family was wealthy. They lived in a large house in central Beijing. All that changed abruptly in 1949. Her large house marked her out as one of the landlord class. She was evicted from her house and forced to live in a garden shed, with just a stove, two deck chairs and an old bed.

The Red Guards—teenagers who were given power to direct the Cultural Revolution—began to visit her, beating her up, parading her in the streets, and forcing her to wear a placard with her crimes written on them. So thorough were the Red Guards that they erected a large sign outside her house declaring her a pariah because she had distributed "imperialistic literature." Mabel was shunned by neighbors, victimized daily by her work gang, and regularly beaten by Red Guards.

Many years later, she knew why she endured all this. In the early eighties, after Mao died, Mabel began to receive a stream of visitors saying, "During the Cultural Revolution, there was a large sign outside your house full of your crimes. One of them was that you had distributed Bibles. So I'm here on the chance that you have some left."

Amazingly that sign which made her life such a misery became the means of a new ministry. It kept people away from her during the Cultural Revolution, but afterwards, after she had endured, it drew them. A number of high-ranking members of the Communist Party in China today owe their faith to her endurance.

She reflected, "It's been nice to know why. It helps my faith. But it was hard. Every day was hard. I can't say I saw Jesus, or even felt him close most of the time. I just got the strength to keep going, and that was enough."

God can deliver us by transforming a situation, but more often He delivers by giving us the strength to endure the situation. That way, others are transformed as well as ourselves.

RESPONSE:
Today I will endure all challenges knowing that God has a purpose and I am in His hands.

PRAYER:
Thank You, Lord, for saints like Aunty Mabel who are such an inspiration and testimony.

690

December 11

FAITH IS NOT A SECRET

And pray for us, too, that God may open a door for our
message, so that we may proclaim the mystery of Christ...
Colossians 4:3

Some twenty-five years ago Boutros from a Middle East country
became a Christian. Since then he has revealed a big heart for
evangelism. Wherever he goes, he is always very open about his
Christian faith.

A couple of years ago he was arrested and questioned by the police.
They asked him if he had baptized people and he replied, "I told them
that I had baptized 1,000 people—the real figure at that time was only
700 but I increased the numbers because I knew I would probably
soon reach that number." Boutros is a secret believer that when guided
by God doesn't make a secret of his faith.

An Open Doors co-worker reported it was a great joy to meet him.
After a visit with Boutros he commented, "At his work place he has
a cross hanging. Everyone who comes to his place sees the cross.
Recently his chief started asking Boutros if he could go and work for
another company. Family members who work for the government told
Boutros' brother that certain people wanted Boutros killed. Our co-
worker asked him if he was afraid at all. He paused for a second and
then nodded and said, 'A little bit, now.'"

Boutros meets many people who want to know more about his
Christian faith. They ask him, because he openly and clearly is a
Christian. "I don't have enough time in the day to talk with them.
I have to work hard to make enough money for my living", he
apologizes. "I earn just enough to buy my daily food." But even
though he has to work hard, sometimes he can work and speak at the
same time. "Then I have long conversations about the Christian faith."

Boutros shared a vision he had recently. "I was lying in a pool of
water in a beautiful garden and all around me were many people that
I've known previously who had since left my country and were living
in other countries. All of them were praying for me. Through this I felt

691

that God was assuring me that many people around the world were praying for me."

Our co-worker was impressed and encouraged meeting Boutros. "What a great testimony of how God uses our prayers for the persecuted Christians. The prayers really are a comfort and support to the secret believers," he concludes.

After some prayer time together, Boutros and the co-worker moved to a safer place where no one would overhear what they were praying about. "It seemed important for him to have some form of physical contact, so we held hands and prayed for just a few moments before he indicated that we should get back. Although admitting that he was a little afraid at that moment, he seemed in a good mood, and very much encouraged by the vision he had of people praying for him. He did add though that he really needed prayer."

RESPONSE:
Today I will not keep my faith a secret but share openly with everyone I contact.

PRAYER:
Pray for Boutros and other secret believers who are so bold in sharing their faith and winning many to Jesus.

December 12

KEEPING FAITH SIMPLE

The LORD confides in those who fear him; he makes his covenant known to them.
Psalm 25:14

Open Doors colleague, Ron Boyd-MacMillan, shares the following insight from his teaching, "Why I Need to Encounter the Persecuted Church."

On his first visit to America, I took a Chinese Bible teacher to a Christian bookstore. I was not prepared for his reaction. I thought he would be overwhelmed by the variety of Bibles, reading aids, books and multi-media material on show. He was, but not in the way I expected. He stopped in the middle of the store, turned to me and said, "It must be very hard to be a Christian here."

"Why do you say that?" I asked.

"How are you going to keep your faith simple with all this available?" We walked around the store as he told me what he meant. He picked five books off the shelf. All had similar titles like *The Christian's secret of a happy life.* He leafed through them and said, "Each book seems to say there's a secret to living a happy life in Jesus. But their secrets are all different. They all say there is one secret, but each has a different secret? That's confusing."

"Well, that's just marketing" I explained a little defensively. But he went on. "Does that mean I have to buy all five books to really know Christ? That makes me anxious. What other secrets might I not be aware of? I have to buy more books. And soon, I would have more books than I could read, and I would not be happy, but guilty that I had spent money on all these books that I had no time to read."

He put the books down on the floor and said quietly, "In China, I prayed for God to bring me books. He did, but only at the rate of about four per year. So I read those books thoroughly. I copied out passages. I made summaries for teachers. I learned whole chunks by heart. These books really formed me. The point I'm trying to make is that if you have too many books, it's difficult to read one properly.

I'm not saying it's impossible, just hard. And this variety actually makes faith more complicated than it really is."

He taught me a daily habit he learned in prison. "Every morning when you wake up, don't get up, just stay in bed and for ten minutes thank God for anything that comes into your mind. It might be the wallpaper, it might be for friends, it might just be for life. Anything. Once you get going you discover that the world is full of grace, God's grace. With that attitude you are ready to live the day for God because you are overwhelmed at how generous God is to you."

It's so simple, and yet isn't there something in us that finds the simplest activities so hard to keep up? Maybe that is why we pack our lives with an infinite variety of routines and habits. Anything but just continually doing what is simple.

A Vietnamese evangelist said, "We are to stay in the first grade, grateful to Jesus, repentant for our sins, expectant of his coming. Don't graduate or you'll leave the basics behind."

RESPONSE:
Today I will live my life simply – back to basics of praising, praying, witnessing, awaiting.

PRAYER:
Help me, Lord, to stay in first grade so that I will never leave behind the basics.

694

December 13

SHARING FAITH UNDER PRESSURE

The Lord is not slow in keeping his promise,
as some understand slowness. Instead he is patient with
you, not wanting anyone to perish,
but everyone to come to repentance.

2 Peter 3:9

Twenty-nine-year-old Maryam Rostampour and thirty-two-year old Marzieh Amirizadeh spent 259 days in Tehran's notorious Evin prison in 2009 in Iran. They had to overcome the fear of life imprisonment and the possibility of execution because they loved and followed Jesus Christ. They had to remain strong through weeks in solitary confinement, and endless hours of interrogation by Iranian officials and religious leaders. They had to endure months of harsh living conditions and debilitating sickness. In their first interview (with Sam Yeghnazar of Elam Ministries), they shared what life was like in prison and how they survived.

Maryam commented, "When we were arrested most of the guards treated us badly, especially when they knew we had been involved in evangelism. They would curse us and would not let us drink water from the public tap or use the wash basin. But this changed and eventually they asked us to pray for them."

Marzieh said, "Some [prisoners] called us 'Dirty, unclean, apostates,' but their opinion changed and they asked for forgiveness. We had become an example to them and they would take our side."

Maryam added, "At Evin Prison the well-educated political and business prisoners called us '*Mortad Kasif*' (Unclean apostates). In less than a month everything changed. As they got to know us, they were curious about our faith, they respected us and called upon us to sort out arguments they had between themselves."

When asked if any prisoners came to faith, she said, "Yes. There were those who accepted Christ. When we were in Vozara [the first prison the women were taken to] we prayed the sinner's prayer with many of the prostitutes. They prayed themselves and we prayed for them. But there

695

were others who were too frightened to confess their faith. There were many who were impacted."

Even in prison, under tremendous pressure, it is possible to share one's faith.

RESPONSE:
Today I will resolve to use my freedom to share my faith with others in spiritual darkness.

PRAYER:
Lord may other Christian prisoners around the world have the courage and opportunity to share their love for You today.

December 14

LOVE MYSTERY

This, then, is how you ought to regard us: as servants of Christ and as those entrusted with the mysteries God has revealed.

1 Corinthians 4:1

Open Doors colleague, Ron Boyd-MacMillan, shares the following insight from his teaching, "Why I Need to Encounter the Persecuted Church."

However we splice it, the Christian life involves living with mystery. Many times the will of God is utterly incomprehensible to us. This is as it should be, since God's ways are so much higher than ours, but it doesn't make it any easier to live with. Living with mystery is hard.

Mystery should make us silent, humble, careful. We should not rush to explain what cannot be explained. But I remember on a visit to China meeting a famous house church leader. We were talking about revival. Revival is a mystery. Why does God bring it to some countries and not to others? We don't know. This leader said he knew: "Oh, there is no mystery to revival. Revival is brought about by persecution. You pray for persecution, and you will get revival later on."

But this is quite untrue, and one has to make allowances for persecuted Christians, for though they may know the history of their own churches well, they are often unaware of the history of the church worldwide. It is obvious that God has brought many revivals about without persecution. The Great Awakenings of 18th century America and Britain for example were brought about largely as a result of the preaching of Whitefield and Wesley. It is also obvious that there are places where persecution has not brought revival. One thinks of the whole of North Africa and the Middle East, which provided so many of our early church leaders like Tertullian and Augustine. Now there are only the sandy ruins of churches, and Islam.

Mysteries also should make us honest. We have to admit "we don't know" to God. But all too often we beg for answers we simply could not handle. But if I look at the *experiences* rather than the

697

explanations of the persecuted, I see that at the heart of mystery is not frustration, but joy and grace.

The same Chinese leader—so confident he knew the formula to revival—also shared a prison experience: "I had lost my church, my freedom, and I was starting to lose my health, and I cried to God, *Why are you letting me go through this?*" He received no formal answer, but said, "I felt a light within me that chased away the darkness, and I received the companionship of Christ. I cannot explain it any more than that, though God knows I have tried. It never comes out right. But the mystery of God's will was the means I rested on the bosom of Christ."

Mysteries appear dark, like black holes on the outside, but as we enter them, we are in for a wonderful discovery. At their center is not darkness, but light. This light is the light of Christ. Don't be afraid of a mystery. It is dark on the outside, but full of light on the inside.

RESPONSE:
Today I will not fear mystery but love it by entering to find the light of Christ.

PRAYER:
Lord, keep me silent, humble, careful and honest as I explore the mystery of Your grace.

December 15

TURNING FEAR INTO FAITH

Paul, a prisoner of Christ Jesus, and Timothy our brother,
To Philemon our dear friend and fellow worker—also to
Apphia our sister and Archippus our fellow soldier—and to
the church that meets in your home:
Philemon 1:1-2

The five functions of the church (evangelism, discipleship, ministry, fellowship and worship), as they were practiced in the New Testament, were frequently carried out in private homes. But the early church was not limited just to homes. They also used the temple, synagogues, lecture halls, open forums, riverbanks, ships and other places.

However, it is encouraging to realize that all the functions can be performed in a small house. In many restricted countries, this is the only available place. The New Testament specifically refers to five "house churches," and there were probably many more (Romans 16:3-5, 23; 1 Corinthians 16:19, Colossians 4:15; Philemon 1:2).

Believers from Muslim Background (MBB's) take great risks when attempting to meet together. They do so secretly in small groups of no more than ten or fifteen to avoid suspicion from locals. They change their meeting place each time they gather in order to cover their tracks. While some are fortunate to participate with their families, many come with fear because their Muslim relatives do not even know about their new faith.

Such was the situation of the twelve MBB's who quietly came one morning into a mountainside property in Central Java for a believers' gathering. It was special, because a baptism ceremony would take place the next day. The MBB's were excited and scared at the same time, more so for the four MBB's who came to be baptized. They are nervous as their families and neighbours still think of them as Muslims.

The gathering started at night. Beginning with worship songs, the room fills with warmth, slowly stripping away fear in the hearts and minds of the believers. After the singing, the MBB's and their children, sit on the carpeted floor. In their hands they hold the *Injil* and prepare for teaching. It may be a long while before they hear God's Word again—that is, if they get the chance to. If their faith in Christ is ever discovered, the prospect of attending the next gathering grows dim.

One MBB shares that since his conversion he experienced peace, especially when sleeping at night. No longer did he wake up the next morning with much anxiety in his heart. Fights at home ceased, and his wife noted a change in him. "My husband never shouts at me anymore. Our house is full of love now. I cannot stop thanking Jesus for changing my family. He is Almighty; He is good!" she said as she broke into tears of joy.

On the second day of the gathering, the MBB's stand at the side of a laundry pool as they witness the baptism of four more MBB's. They see tension vanishing from their faces as each comes out of water. The church can function in many forms and still be the church.

RESPONSE:
Today I will be thankful for the many ways I can gather with Christians to be the church!

PRAYER:
Pray for believers—especially MBB's—living in fear that can limit expression of faith.

700

WHAT'S YOUR STRUGGLE?

They have no struggles; their bodies are healthy and strong.
Psalm 73:4

Open Doors colleague, Ron Boyd-MacMillan, shares the following insight from his teaching, "Why I Need to Encounter the Persecuted Church."

I'm often questioned about the main difference between a persecuted Christian and a Western Christian. My answer has not changed in twenty years. In the Persecuted Church, Christians realize they are in trouble, and go to God about it. In the Western church, Christians forget they are in a fight, and even if they do remember, never manage to find the time to go to God about it.

Persecuted Christians know they are in a fight. Every day they struggle. Not being conscious of a daily struggle may be sure sign that one is losing the battle of life. The ancient Psalmist looked at the rich elite of Israel and said, *"they have no struggles."* They should have struggles if they wish to please God. But so many Christians in the world today seem surprised at the language of struggle today.

What struggles do the persecuted awaken us to? There is, first of all, *the struggle we are always in.* Everyone that visits persecuted communities comes away with a renewed appreciation of the spiritual battle we are always engaged in.

Secondly, there is, *the struggle we must awaken to.* A persecuted Christian in Palestine said, "When you become a real Christian, you get reawakened to the fact that 'the whole world lies in the hands of the evil one,' and this reflects in your own culture." She added, "What your culture worships, you have to struggle against." In her case, it was a worship of extremist terrorists, who risked everything to kill Israelis. In standing out against that, she struggled to communicate to her neighbors who thought she was being "unpatriotic."

We have to face up the same question. What is our culture worshipping? Is it, as Francis Schaeffer once said, "the god of personal peace and affluence," where we don't mind what goes on in the world so long as our space and prosperity is not affected?

Finally, there is, *the struggle we must create*. Brother Andrew tells the story of meeting Pastor Haik of Iran, who said to him in 1993, "Andrew, when they kill me, it will be for speaking, not for being silent." Haik was killed in 1994. If he had stayed silent about the treatment of his Christian friend, Mehdi Dibaj, Haik would be alive. But he chose to enter, even create, the conflict. The fact is we can avoid struggle if we want. Each of us has to make a choice to speak up, defy the powers-that-be, and bring a struggle into being. Otherwise Satan wins.

Persecuted Christians are always in a fight. They struggle all the time, against their own sins, against idolatries in their own societies, and against the orchestration of the evil one who is out to take our worship away from God. Yet these struggles should mark our own lives and churches as surely as the devil does not live exclusively in China or Columbia. This world is the place of struggle. What's your struggle? The persecuted force us to ask. Everyone ought to have one!

RESPONSE:
Today I will affirm and engage in the struggles I face in standing strong against the enemy.

PRAYER:
Thank You, Lord, for the struggles the persecuted awaken in me. Help me not avoid them.

December 17

GOD IS AT WORK IN HIS CHURCH

And in him you too are being built together to become a
dwelling in which God lives by his Spirit.
Ephesians 2:22

Daniel, a young "underground" house church believer from Muslim
background (MBB) would not attend the open church in his Middle
Eastern city because he felt its leaders were cooperating with the
government. Everything had to be secretive in the house church
meetings with no loud singing. It was risky meeting like this. Daniel
shares his story of discovery and what he learned from the experience:

"A few months ago, I was at the church leader's house. They
were old family friends and I was helping their kids to repair their
computer. The mother answered the door and men came into the
house. They were plainclothes police with papers that showed they
were from security and had authority to arrest. They took everyone's
phones, disconnected the internet, and gathered all of the computers
while they searched the house for Bibles. They found 300. They didn't
want to touch the Bibles, like they were dirty. They took the husband
and wife away in handcuffs.

"The leaders were still imprisoned when the police came to my
house about a month and a half later pretending to be postmen. In my
whole life, that was the first time I saw my father cry. They searched
through my room and took my computer, my books, my prayer
notebook, my written plans for our youth group, and my personal
Bible. They also took my sister's laptop and all of our cell phones. At
the end of their search, they told my parents that they were going to
take me with them. My mother was distressed, but I hugged her and
told her I would be back.

"They took me to the central prison. I was there for two weeks.
They only beat me the first day, but they still threatened me. For the
first week I didn't answer their questions, but the second week was
difficult. I was imagining my mom and dad—I had talked to my dad
and knew it was a more difficult time for them than for me. I still

wondered what I had done wrong and why I didn't have the right to praise my Lord.

"After two weeks they let me go after guaranteeing I wouldn't flee. About a month later they also released our leaders on bail. After that, they told me my case was still open and they could call me in at any time. We were uncertain of our sentence because they wouldn't hold a trial for around six months. Constant pressure. It was a pleasure to be persecuted for my Lord."

Asked what he learned from the experience, Daniel replied, "First, God taught me patience. Eventually, even though I was worried about my family, God gave me a chance to witness to my persecutors. I really don't hate them. I love them because they don't know what they're doing. They've been taught bad things, they're not bad themselves. I felt a responsibility to tell them about the light of Jesus that can break through their spiritual darkness…I want Western people to know that God is working in the Middle East, through persecution, deception, and difficulties."

RESPONSE:
Today I will be thankful that God can work through my fellowship of believers regardless of the level of freedom we enjoy.

PRAYER:
Pray for those in underground house churches who risk everything to meet and fulfill the five functions of the church.

December 18
FROM OBSTACLE TO INSTRUMENT

What, then, shall we say in response to these things?
If God is for us, who can be against us?
Romans 8:31

Open Doors colleague, Ron Boyd-MacMillan, shares the following insight from his teaching, "Why I Need to Encounter the Persecuted Church."

The Persecuted Church teaches us that everyone is either an *agent* of God's will, or an *instrument* of God's will. Everyone in this world has only two choices: they can choose to do God's will by co-operating with God, or they can choose to defy God and do His will unknowingly.

"Remember, our God is so great even the persecutors serve him," said a Chinese pastor wryly. He was referring to arch-persecutor of the Chinese church, Mao Tse Tung, who launched the fiercest anti-Christian campaign of the 20th century in the 1960's. Called the "Cultural Revolution," he swept away all churches, burned all Bibles, and imprisoned all the pastors.

Yet all he succeeded in doing was pushing the church deep underground, where it became embedded in the family structure and Chinese culture in a way 300 years of evangelism had failed to accomplish. From this fire emerged the world's largest revival – where the church grew from 1 million in 1950 to over 80 million today.

"We say," smiled the pastor, "that thanks to Mao—who thought he was annihilating the church—we have the greatest revival. He thought he was killing the church, but all the while he was doing pre-evangelism. God had the last laugh. Glory be to God—He always gets His will done."

This truth is also showing up in India. Since 1997 violence against Christians has increased greatly as a result of the election of Hindu extremists. Yet the effect of the extremism has been to drive thousands of low caste Hindus into the church. The more Hindu extremists persecute Christians, the more moderate Hindus are drawn into the church.

It is a glorious truth the persecuted awaken us to. Everyone ends up furthering the will of God! Even those who put obstacles in the way of the church serve God, because God just turns the obstacle into an instrument. This means that we must not despair when we think conditions for the flourishing of our Christian lives or our churches are less than perfect. Take your worst enemy or the one feature of your life, society or church that causes you most despair, then put your mind into gear and think—how would God work His will through this obstacle?

Are you childless? Maybe God is using that to give you a greater ministry, impossible with the responsibility of family? Are you powerless? Maybe God wants to show His glory and make you marvel? We may not get an answer, but it is a thrill to try, because we know everyone is either a willing agent or an unwitting instrument of the will of God.

He's too great, and He loves the world too much, for it to be any other way! God takes the obstacle, and makes it the instrument!

RESPONSE:
Today I will be an agent to accomplish God's will realizing He can make me an instrument.

PRAYER:
Lord, make me an instrument of Your will and work as I choose to cooperate with You.

December 19

BECOME A DISCIPLE

Then Jesus came to them and said, "All authority in heaven and on earth has been given to me. Therefore go and make disciples of all nations, baptizing them in the name of the Father and of the Son and of the Holy Spirit, and teaching them to obey everything I have commanded you. And surely I am with you always, to the very end of the age."

Matthew 28:18-20

Sixty-three-year-old Lena has established several secret churches in her Central Asia country. She now leads seven house fellowships which meet together in small groups. On several occasions she has had to cope with arrests. "One time police with guns entered the house where we were meeting with a group. We were taken off to the station. Of course we were afraid," says Lena. The reason why Lena can talk so "nonchalantly" about her arrest follows quickly. She does not necessarily see it as a problem, but as an opportunity to testify.

"I experienced how God took away my fear and gave me peace. Even more, I had the chance to tell the gospel to the head of police. While we were locked up there, I simply started to talk. I was given the opportunity to tell him what God had done for me," says Lena. "After some time, the man only said, 'Take your group away.'"

While she is telling her story, there is not a trace of fear, anger or bitterness to be found on her face because of the injustice. When asked how this is possible, Lena only has one answer. In God's Word, it says that for a long time there will be persecution, but that He will also grant a way out. She recalls Isaiah 41:10, which says, *So do not fear, for I am with you; do not be dismayed, for I am your God. I will strengthen you and help you; I will uphold you with my righteous right hand.* So Lena lives out her life in Uzbekistan, bearing in mind that God is watching over her everywhere.

She provides Bible teaching for Christians and has a heart for work with children and young people adding, "We have to do everything to help Christians to become mature believers." For example, Lena and other Christians try to hold annual children's camps where, for a few days, the children are introduced to the gospel through play. The enthusiasm of the children makes it clear that the camps are a success. But Lena and her staff encounter problems year after year. "It's difficult to find a suitable location, where we can receive the children in safety. And things remain tense: the police may always come and disrupt the camp."

Despite these difficulties, Lena does not give up. She sees the church growing and hammers home the missionary message of Matthew 28, in which Jesus calls on us to make disciples of all nations. This message is what Lena is living out, in the midst of persecution.

"We must understand that the church cannot grow without disciples," emphasises Lena. "Become a disciple!"

RESPONSE:
Today I will become a true disciple of Jesus using every situation—good or bad—to share my faith with everyone and encourage and train other younger believers.

PRAYER:
Pray for Lena and others like her growing the church of Jesus amid great persecution.

December 20

EVANGELISM OPPORTUNITIES EVERYWHERE

"In the same way, I tell you, there is rejoicing in the presence of the angels of God over one sinner who repents."
Luke 15:10

Pastor Joseph Bondarenko sat on the sunny deck of the Russian river boat as it pulled out of Tyumen in Siberia and headed north up the river. The leaves on the trees were already changing colour in a blaze of autumn beauty. But this was no Love Boat. On board this old river scow were over one hundred and fifty other Christians joining this adventure. The passengers were there to assist in a one-month evangelism outreach in northern Siberian cities—places where the gospel had not been preached before.

As Joseph soaked in the beauty of the sun and God's creation, he thought back on his early ministry years in the nineteen fifties and sixties. His aggressive evangelism in those days resulted in imprisonment three times. Yet there in those filthy prison cells, God was still present and his ministry continued. Joseph led so many to Christ in prison that they kicked him out each time. In total he lived nine years in a prison cell, isolated from his beloved wife, Mary.

He smiled to himself as he recalled that eventful day in 1989 when the KGB agent who had him imprisoned came to talk. The officer had been watching him for years and now articulated his desire to know Jesus too. Joseph's spirit leaped with joy as he thought back on the day that KGB agent and his family were baptized. Nothing is impossible with God.

He relived the many crusades in recent years when Open Doors provided as many as twenty thousand Russian Scriptures for new believers who responded to the call of God on their life.

And now with a group of musicians, preachers and follow-up personnel his vision for evangelism was continuing to be fulfilled; one whole month stopping and preaching at twenty cities along the main rivers of Siberia. At the end of the month, Joseph's "cruise-ade" had seen over 10,000 people pray the sinner's prayer and commit their lives to the Lord! And even more exciting is the fact that Christian young people were left behind in sixteen communities to do follow-up training and establish new churches.

On the walls of a hall in Joseph's church is the missionary journey history of this local body and the missionary vision maps. Joseph becomes very animated and excited as he traces the colour-coded missionary journeys for the past summers that young evangelists he is training had made into Siberia and onward toward the Far East. But more exciting for him are the dotted lines that lay out next summer's trip plans. They reached right to the Pacific Ocean!

Like his Master, Joseph went through much suffering and deprivation in his life. But like his Master, nothing gives Joseph more joy than knowing the angels in heaven were rejoicing.

RESPONSE:
Today I will recommit to share the good news of the gospel with everyone wherever I am.

PRAYER:
Pray that the many Joseph Bondarenko's of our world will continue to bear much fruit.

December 21

NEVER TOO OLD TO SERVE JESUS

The righteous will flourish like a palm tree, they will grow
like a cedar of Lebanon; planted in the house of
the LORD, they will flourish in the courts of our God.
They will still bear fruit in old age, they will stay fresh
and green, proclaiming, "The LORD is upright;
he is my Rock, and there is no wickedness in him."
Psalm 92:12-15

As I share with numerous audiences my experiences from years of ministry in Asia, I often try to drive home the point that the church in China teaches us that you can never be too young and never too old to serve Jesus.

Our Western church culture marginalizes youths until they have finished some level of higher education. And even worse, we marginalize those who are retired as now being "over the hill" and only fit to sit in a rocking chair for whatever years remain for them.

But repeatedly in the Old Testament, there are references to the elderly "still bearing fruit in old age!" And the Persecuted Church is replete with stories and testimonies giving evidence.

In 1997 I wrote a booklet titled *Great Bible Women of China* in which I share the story of five elderly Chinese Bible Women who completed long fruitful lives of service, finishing strong.

In his book, *Vietnam's Christians: A Century of Growth in Adversity*, veteran Vietnam missionary, Reg Reimer, shares the remarkable story of diminutive Mrs. Diep Thi Do. She and her pastor husband served as missionaries among the Stieng tribal people for twenty years. Just before Vietnam fell in 1975, her husband was captured by the communists and was never heard from again. She then did not dare do any tribal ministry except pray.

In 1981, emerging from the deep underground during the darkest years, she encountered some very discouraged Stieng Christians in the market. They begged her to be their missionary and pastor. She considered this a strong call from God and courageously called the

Stieng back into church groups. She often "stared down" resistance from communist authorities. She presided over the building of the largest church sanctuary in Vietnam. She performed all pastoral functions including marrying, burying, appointing leaders and administering the sacraments. Her bravery and her spiritual authority ensured that no one ever challenged her operating essentially as a bishop.

Reg Reimer concludes, "She described herself as 'only a little woman.' But her faith and trust in God made her a giant in the lives of thousands of Stieng Christians she had served for fifty-five years. More than four thousand came to attend her funeral and celebrate her life when she died at age eighty-four in 2008."[44] You can never be too old to serve Jesus!

RESPONSE:
Today I will acknowledge that disciples of Jesus can be useful for Him at any age—especially in their elderly years.

PRAYER:
Pray that elderly believers will realize the giftedness they have and can continue to utilize.

---

44 Reg Reimer, *Vietnam's Christians: A Century of Growth in Adversity* (Pasadena, CA: William Carey Library, 2011), p. 60.

December 22

THE BEAUTIFUL BRIDE OF CHRIST

I saw the Holy City, the new Jerusalem, coming down out of heaven from God, prepared as a bride beautifully dressed for her husband. And I heard a loud voice from the throne saying, "Look! God's dwelling place is now among the people, and he will dwell with them. They will be his people, and God himself will be with them and be their God. 'He will wipe every tear from their eyes. There will be no more death' or mourning or crying or pain, for the old order of things has passed away."
Revelation 21:2-4

Iraq is probably the last place in the world you'd expect to find an illustration of the beautiful bride of Christ. Yet on top of a beautiful plateau in the mountains of Kurdistan (Northern Iraq) a group of Arab Christians organized a prayer conference. More than five hundred Christians from all over Iraq, from all kind of churches including twenty local church leaders, came to pray for unity and peace in the country. "Oh God, unite our country again, bring peace to the Christians and strengthen your people," was the common prayer on everybody's lips. "This was a unique and wonderful experience for the Iraqi church," shares Joyce who was one of the participants.

Teachers and pastors gave lectures on humility and engaged the group in seeking the Lord Jesus Christ at first. "There was prayer for the country and prayer for the different pastors. And one of the highlights was the fact that local Iraqi pastors washed each other feet and that is a miracle in a country where there is so much division," Joyce adds. And she continues, "We prayed for God to give hope and life for individual Christians again; we prayed for individual prayer requests which were written down on paper."

Another pastor taught the group to love their country and to have a passion for the country. Joyce says, "Two young leaders from Baghdad were very much touched by this, since both of them had been victims of violence and kidnapping in Baghdad, because of their faith. They had problems in loving their country and the people in it."

One pastor shared, "Every six months we lose twenty per cent of our believers to the free world, and our main problem is also that so many Christian leaders are leaving. You just finish training young leaders and they leave. It is a pity and we are losing so many potential leaders."

Another Iraqi Christian shared with tears the experience of his kidnapping in Kirkuk. "God was with me and I felt that people around the world were praying for me, although I was amazed about that. God was with me and he brought me out."

In conclusion a pastor said, "Like Christ, the church in Iraq feels afflicted, not comforted and lashed by stones. And yet does the son of the king ever feel powerless? I do not think so; the presence of the comforter is in our midst in Iraq, so be brave and continue. The Holy Spirit in us is not just a power; He is God himself, who is with us. To God the church in Iraq is beautiful also; so let us love her and work alongside her to make her more so."

RESPONSE:
I will never lose faith that Jesus is developing His beautiful bride around the entire world.

PRAYER:
Pray that Iraqi Christians will continue to perceive themselves as Jesus' beautiful bride.

December 23

DEPORTATION MIRACLE

"Fellow Israelites, listen to this: Jesus of Nazareth was a man accredited by God to you by miracles, wonders and signs, which God did among you through him, as you yourselves know..."

Acts 2:22

In late 1992, "Wally" Magdangal, a Filipino Christian who for years had pastored a clandestine house church in Saudi Arabia, was arrested. His secret house church was unexpectedly penetrated by the "muttawa", the Saudi Arabian religious police.

Wally remembers reading in an Open Doors magazine about a small group in China that gathered weekly in the back room of a small store to worship together. It was the era of the infamous Cultural Revolution. Since the believers could easily be overheard by anyone entering the store, they "sang" hymns together without words or music. Someone whispered the name of the song and they would silently move their lips and simply think of the words and music.

He said, "We are an underground church like the believers behind the Bamboo Curtain, but the difference is that we can praise in full voice because our facilities are sound-proofed. Not even our closest neighbour can hear us." But they were betrayed and now Wally was en route to prison.

For three-and-a-half hours he was physically and mentally tortured. They slapped, boxed and kicked him on the face. Then using a long stick, they lashed his back and the palms of his hands. Then the soles of his feet. He could not stand without wincing and he describes his bruised body as looking like an eggplant.

Upon returning to his cell, Wally prayed for five hours thanking God for allowing him to participate in the sufferings of Jesus. Here are his own words: "Suddenly there was light. The cell was filled with the Lord's Shekinah glory. His presence was there. He knelt and started to touch my face. He told me, 'My son, I have seen all of it. That's why I'm here. I am assuring you that I will never leave you or forsake you.'"

715

Wally woke up two hours later feeling like a new man. He was amazed when he saw his body had been restored to perfect wholeness. No bruises, no cuts, no bleeding or blood stains. He adds, "God had completely restored me." This was a significant source of strength as he later repeatedly witnessed to his interrogators who were dumbfounded by his healing. Once after sharing his faith, Wally noticed the guard's countenance change. He was smiling. Wally said, "I could feel the Holy Spirit working already."

Wally (and his fellow-pastor) was spared scheduled execution on Christmas Day. Miraculously, at the last moment, they were released and deported home to the Philippines. Today he shares God's goodness and blessing around the world never forgetting that Christmas miracle.

RESPONSE:
Today I will thank the Lord that He still works miracles today, here and around the world.

PRAYER:
Pray for persecuted Christians who may be in prison today awaiting their miraculous release. Pray they will also be encouraged by the intimate presence of Jesus, Himself.

December 24

THE COURAGE THAT MADE CHRISTMAS POSSIBLE

"She will give birth to a son, and you are to give him the name Jesus, because he will save his people from their sins."
Matthew 1:21

Chinese evangelist, Brother Xi, was travelling one very cold Christmas Eve in the rugged province of Gansu. As he came to the next village he sensed something was wrong. He introduced himself as a bearer of good news. A small man interrupted, "Well we have only bad news here right now. A couple has just had their baby stolen." In the poorer areas of China, where couples are restricted to one child, it is not uncommon to have child snatching, even stealing babies for wealthy childless couples in the cities.

He stepped inside the house to find both husband and wife staring quietly at him. The couple's grief hung heavy in the air. He said, "I'm so sorry to hear about your plight, but I know someone who may help...God. Let me pray to Him."

There was no reaction on the couple's faces, so he went into prayer, feeling very uncomfortable indeed. "Dear Father, many years ago at this same time of year you sent a child into the world and rescued us all; we ask today that you will send back this child to us, and deliver this village from the sadness which grips it, Amen."

Suddenly the young husband spoke, "Shut up and go away. We have prayed to our gods and nothing has happened. Why should yours be any different?" He was grabbed from behind by the other villagers and propelled out of the village. "Don't you dare come here again!" they bawled.

He wandered the hills in a daze of humiliation, tears, and crying to God. Then he thought, *I went to that village expecting a hero's welcome, or at the very least, I relied on being a curiosity, quizzed and entertained by people who live very dull and isolated lives. Instead, I had only been treated a little like Christ was treated.*

717

Kneeling there in the snow, he knew what he had to do—go back to that village, knowing for sure he would be despised. This was to follow in the Master's footsteps. With a pounding heart he turned and began to walk slowly back towards the village. Suddenly, across the still late afternoon air, he heard a baby's cry coming from what appeared to be an old well shaft.

Sure enough six feet down was a little baby, wrapped in a thick blanket, lying at the bottom of the dry-well. He climbed down to hug some warmth back into it. It was a baby girl. Those who snatched it did not know it was a girl, and finding later that it was, left it in this old well to die.

He walked back to the village with the precious bundle of life. The villagers came running. They were amazed and overjoyed as they led him to the cottage of the poor couple, and the smile on the mother's face as he placed her baby into her lap was unforgettable. "Come, warm yourself by the fire" said the husband. They drew up a chair for him, and as the other villagers crowded round, he asked, "Who was that God you prayed to?"

What an invitation. Here he was, the honored guest, looking at thirty eager people, waiting with bated breath to hear the gospel. "Well," he began, "He came to earth in the form of a little baby, just about this time 2000 years ago..."

RESPONSE:
Today I will praise God that He is truly in control and can work out all situations for good.

PRAYER:
Thank God today for the coming of His Son to earth in humble yet powerful glory!

December 25

WHAT MADE THE ANGELS SO EXCITED?

Suddenly a great company of the heavenly host appeared
with the angel, praising God and saying,
"Glory to God in the highest heaven,
and on earth peace to those on whom his favor rests."
Luke 2:13-14

A depressed Chinese communist local party boss went to an official church to hear the preaching of a very sincere and learned elder he knew. Here is his story in his own words:

It was the first Sunday of December. I remember he talked about "The Angel's Song." After the service I spoke to him, "You know, I really can't see what all the fuss is about Jesus. He was a man of moral ideals, and died for his belief, but lots of other religions have such men, too." This elder smiled and said, "Are you looking for God?"

"I suppose I am," I admitted to him. He asked again, "Well, if Jesus doesn't seem to be up to much, what sort of God would you be looking for?" I answered slowly, thinking it through, "I guess a God who first of all is totally powerful, and then is also totally just or fair."

The elder probed again, "But how would you know a God like that was interested in you?" I said, "Then he would also have to be a God of love." The elder challenged me by saying, "If you find a God who is all three: powerful, just, loving, would you trust Him?"

"I might," I replied "but I would need to find an event that proved he was all three."

"Take this Bible," said the elder, handing me what I saw was his own copy of the Bible, "and come back to me if you find an event that shows God is supremely and uniquely all three."

I started reading the Bible and pretty soon I came across that verse the elder had preached on the morning I attended the church. "*Glory to God in the highest*." What was it that made the angels so excited? After all they had witnessed, what was so unique about the birth of Jesus?

719

I had little time to brood on this because my wife was expecting our first child. All went well with the delivery and I held the little warm bundle, gazing into his peaceful sleeping face. What perfection the baby seemed. As I looked, the more I was amazed by the sheer miracle of birth.

Had I really used the word "miracle" to describe the birth of my son? Then I thought, the miracle of the birth of Jesus had to be more than just a miracle of birth to impress those angels so much. I read on, and the Spirit of God gave light to my eyes. God had become a baby.

I looked for three characteristics of the God I would trust. Power. This had to be a greater act than the creation of the world. In the beginning God was merely bringing a world into being.

Love. God came! If He wasn't interested, He would not have bothered to come at all. After all, Jesus had a very hard life, not the kind of life that anyone would wish for.

Justice. God loved us so much, He came. He came Himself to redeem sinful man. Here was the meaning and glory of Christianity— all captured in the incarnation.

I wept and wept in my little study. I must have stayed on my knees for hours. When I looked at my watch, and suddenly noticed the date...it was the 25th of December...Christ's birthday! That Christmas was so real. I saw in the cradle the infinite power, justice and love of God supremely and uniquely illustrated. As long as I live, I will celebrate Christmas every day.

RESPONSE:
Today I will worship the God whose power, love and justice came in the form of His Son.

PRAYER:
Thank God for Jesus. Ask Him to help you celebrate Christmas every day!

December 26

HARVEST TIME IN CHINA

The shepherds returned, glorifying and praising God
for all the things they had heard and seen,
which were just as they had been told.
Luke 2:20

House churches in China love to celebrate Christmas—without Santa and the commercialization found in the West which, sadly, is now creeping into the profit-centric malls in China's cities. They revel in the opportunity to share about the coming of Jesus Christ and God's love to colleagues, friends and neighbors who usually do not mind attending special Christmas gatherings in the spirit of the season.

Increasingly, house churches plan elaborate programs with performances, such as ice-breakers, Christmas carols, dances and sketches—to till the soil of each heart—before culminating with an evangelistic message. Several rent public halls or banquet rooms in hotels and create a festive air with decorations of balloons, ribbons and artificial flowers.

Brother Kao says, "We found out that it was possible for us to rent meeting halls in some places that were usually used for wedding dinners. So, with the Christmas season fast approaching, we booked such halls at multiple locations in preparation for our Christmas evangelistic outreach," Kao continued. Then the church put together a program and began practicing hard on the short plays about two months before.

"There was this one hall that had just been used for a wedding banquet. When we arrived to put up our Christmas decorations, we found it was already beautifully done up so we merely added a few more Christmas touches. We had our church members invite their unsaved friends and relatives. Because Christmas is viewed as a Western celebration, many people are curious and open to finding out what it's all about, so they readily come."

The hall was packed with many first-time guests. The program began with the singing of some Christmas carols and everyone sang with gusto, even though they might not have understood what the lyrics meant. Then the plays followed, dramatizing the story of Noah and the flood, showing the depravity of man, and how only eight were saved. At the end of it, the pastor went up on stage, explained what the whole story meant and shared about man's need for a Savior before making an altar call.

Kao explained, "Each night at every location where we held this outreach program, an average of one hundred people would pray to become children of God. And because we had received the materials from Open Doors earlier, we were able to give each new believer a Bible and a book on the spot. We find that doing so helps them to further understand the decision they have made and enables them to grow in their new life in Christ."

"Please inform our brothers and sisters who are praying for us that we are putting the books you supplied to good use and giving them to new Christians," he voiced gratefully.

RESPONSE:
Today I will pray for those who have not yet heard the Good News about Jesus Christ.

PRAYER:
Thank God that house churches in China have such effective outreaches at Christmas time. Pray against hindrances and interferences from the local authorities.

December 27

BROTHER DUAN'S MIRACLE

Thanks be to God for his indescribable gift!
2 Corinthians 9:15

Brother Duan was an elderly house church leader in northern China. He was travelling with a group of believers today to hear a dynamic Bible teacher, Brother Wang.

Duan asked, "What age is this Brother Wang?" When they told him he was in his early forties, a great look of pain swept Duan's face. He said, "I once had a son. I knew him for only two months. Now he's dead. But had he lived, he would be forty-two today. My wife called him "Christmas' Child," since he was born at Christmas time. I called him "Isaac," because we had despaired of ever having a child, but ten years after we were married, along he came."

All looked at Duan as he continued, "I only saw him for two months." He then told them how he and his wife were greatly persecuted evangelists in the 1950's—both in great danger of arrest. So they offered their child to their enemy, two-fingered Wu and his wife who were childless.

Duan never knew what happened until he came out of jail in 1978. His dear wife had died in the terrible famine of 1958. Their son had indeed been adopted by Wu, but the entire family had disappeared under the rubble when a devastating earthquake hit in 1975. Said Duan sadly as they approached the meeting house, "God judged me for being so irresponsible with my little son."

There was a crowd of two hundred packed into the house, and many outside at the windows. When Brother Wang began preaching, Duan got a terrible shock. It was like hearing himself. There was a commotion as he clawed his way to the window and looked at the preacher.

Hearing the commotion, the preacher stopped. There was minute of shocked silence as both men looked at each other. The physical likeness was amazing. Duan began to apologize, "I'm sorry Brother Wang for interrupting your excellent message. You see, I had a son, who would be your age now. And if he had lived, he would have looked and sounded just like you."

Brother Wang began to tremble violently. Suddenly his legs buckled beneath him, and someone caught him before he fell down. Tears came into his eyes, and he whispered hoarsely, clutching his pounding chest, "Are you Daddy Duan?"

Everyone wept. Father and son were reunited after forty-two years. Wang had indeed been brought up by two-fingered Wu, who had been so impressed by Duan's act of giving that he became a strong believer. Wu used to say to him, "I'm not your real father. He is a great man of God, full of grace and love. He gave you to me, and I give you all my love, and the encouragement to put God first, just like your real father." Wang's adopted parents had moved away from the earthquake zone before the tragedy, and both died of cancer in their sixties. He became an evangelist, and tried to find his real father, but Duan had changed his name so many times to avoid arrest that he had proved untraceable, even to his son.

As father and son continued to hug and weep, the elder of the church stood up and declared, "It's December. We have *seen* our sermon tonight. *"Christ came into the world to save sinners"*—that is Christmas. Just as Duan handed his only son to the care of his enemy, so God handed over his own son to us sinners. Let us rejoice in their reconciliation and ours too."

RESPONSE:
Today I will rejoice in God's act of reconciliation in sending His only Son for me, a sinner.

PRAYER:
Thank You, Lord, that You cared enough to provide a way for my being reconciled to You.

December 28

SAMUEL AND HIS CRIPPLED SON

But when the set time had fully come, God sent his Son,
born of a woman, born under the law...
Galatians 4:4

Samuel was a schoolmaster in a small city in central China. One
night he overheard his head teacher praying, "Lord, please help
Samuel to love his son. It's so sad the way he treats him so cruelly,
cutting him off, refusing to spend time in the home, ashamed of his
crippled boy. Lord, we don't know what goes on in the mind of his
son, but we do know he is very sad. His wife says the boy weeps
all the time when the father comes in and leaves. He may not know
much, but he does know he's not loved, and doesn't know why."

Deeply moved by the prayer, Samuel went home late that night
and sat beside his sleeping son for hours, just stroking his hair and
whispering, "Forgive me."

Every night after that, Samuel stayed late at his son's bedside,
reading him portions of the Bible — a book he had found at school.
When he had finished a page, he would signal to the boy, who loved
to help by turning the page. They felt warm together. Soon his wife
joined them for the readings, and the family grew closer and closer.

Samuel sensed new feelings of love well up inside him as he read
the truths of the Bible. He felt a power to love his son more and more.
That's when tragedy struck. His boy was run over by a truck and
badly injured. There was nothing the medics could do. They took him
home to nurse him through to the end. Christians came and prayed for
his healing, but the boy continued to deteriorate. By this time Samuel
was praying to God, and crying out for Him to spare his son's life. But
in December, after a sudden power failure, the boy finally died.

Samuel asked the Christians to hold a service for his boy. A pastor
came and prayed, saying, "Lord, you knew this boy was going to die.
How kind of you to reconcile father and son before he died. Thank
you for your work of grace. And we thank you for your eternal work
too. You watched your son, helpless in flesh, die and grow cold — all

725

because you knew we could not love you otherwise, as we are so blind in our selfishness."

Samuel pondered the meaning of this prayer. He didn't understand it all. But he did get this: God had lost a son too. Unlike Samuel, God lost a son He had cherished, a son that was perfect. How much harder for God. He went to church the following Sunday in a nearby community where they were celebrating an event unknown to Samuel, called "Christmas."

Samuel testified on that very Sunday, "I see that I went through what God went through. He had a Son He loved, and watched Him die that life may come to everyone. I too had a son, but I did not love him. Then God broke my heart, so that I could love him. Then He took him.

"But I have life now, life that will last so long that one day I know I will be reunited with my son. And he will not be lame. And we will fellowship together, not in freezing rooms of fear and pain, but on beautiful planets of peace and harmony. I can love again, and this is the joy of Christmas for me. Even in my grief, with my son gone, I can love again. We can all love again!"

RESPONSE:
Today I will express my love for God even in the midst of any pain and loss.

PRAYER:
Pray for people who have suffered deeply and may feel God cannot forgive them.

December 29

GIVEN WHAT TO SAY

But when they arrest you, do not worry about what to say or how to say it. At that time you will be given what to say, for it will not be you speaking, but the Spirit of your Father speaking through you.

Matthew 10:19-20

It was early in the morning the day after Christmas. It was cold. Mehdi Forootan sat in the back seat of an undercover police car in front of his house in Tehran, Iran. An officer pointed a camcorder at him. "Do you know why you were arrested?" the officer asked him. "No," Forootan replied.

The officer turned off the camera and looked Forootan in the eyes. "I can beat you until blood is coming out of your mouth and every part of you. The next time I turn on the camera, you tell me why we are taking you," the officer said and turned the camera back on.

Forootan spoke of his faith in Christ, and he spent the next 105 days in Iran's harshest prison. On Dec. 26, 2010, authorities had arrested Forootan in a wave of persecution against Iran's underground church. More than three months later, he was one of a few who had not been released.

During one interrogation, an officer turned on a camcorder and pointed it toward him, demanding that Forootan tell him about his "crime." Forootan began to tell him how he had struggled with substance abuse as a teenager, "and how when I was in university I found Jesus and He saved me, and I have been free ever since. But he became angry and turned off the camera. He said, 'I asked you to tell about your crime, not evangelize us.'"

After months of trying to get him to write statements confessing a crime, authorities inexplicably released him. Forootan said his first month out of prison was one of the worst of his life. He couldn't speak to anyone of his prison experience for fear that authorities were watching and would re-arrest him. His parents had given the deed of their house to authorities as bail.

727

He and his fiancée decided it was best for him to leave Iran and go to Turkey as a refugee. For Forootan, this meant an illegal escape through the mountains, because authorities had confiscated his passport.

"I came out of Iran with 70 Afghanis," Forootan said. "I went to the mountains and walked in the mountains for eight hours, and after eight hours I came to Turkey...That was really hard, because I really love Iran, and I'm really sad about this land. Maybe I can't see my country again."

Many who follow Jesus in other lands make great sacrifices for the sake of the gospel. Despite harsh treatment—even prison with interrogations—they still love their home country. But during those interrogations, the Holy Spirit gives the right words to be spoken.

RESPONSE:
Today I will rest in the Lord realizing that when pressures come, He is with me and His Spirit will give me the right words to speak.

PRAYER:
Pray for those who like Forootan above are forced to leave the home land they love because of their witness to the gospel of Christ.

December 30

STAND STRONG THROUGH ALL STORMS

Blessed is the one who does not walk in step with the wicked or stand in the way that sinners take or sit in the company of mockers, but whose delight is in the law of the LORD, and who meditates on his law day and night. That person is like a tree planted by streams of water, which yields its fruit in season and whose leaf does not wither...
Psalm 1:1-3

Concluding Thoughts:

1. Ours is the Kingdom. No matter what setbacks we see or experience, in the end the Kingdom will revert to our Lord and we will reign with Him.

2. Ours is the victory through dying and living again – victory through being able to drink the cup of evil and injustice poured out and not being consumed by it.

3. Ours is the responsibility of caring for our suffering brethren, especially converts and those in countries more restrictive and repressive than ours.

4. Ours is the responsibility of reaching those who still sit in darkness.

5. Ours are the lives that should manifest purity and Christlikeness.

6. Ours are the hearts that should be willing to pay the price to bring peace and understanding among men and between men and God. Hearts willing to be proactive. Hearts willing to stand at the end of the day and having done all, stand.

7. Ours is the challenge to stand strong through all the storms we face and come through the fire refined and purified to walk the way of the cross before a dying world.

RESPONSE:
Today I will accept the challenge to stand strong through all the storms I may face!

PRAYER:
Pray for Christians living in severe persecution areas that refined and purified, they may experience all of the victory which is available through Christ.

December 31

DIFFICULT ASSIGNMENTS

Now what I am commanding you today is not too difficult
for you or beyond your reach.
Deuteronomy 30:11

It is possible! The Persecuted Church by example prove to us that it is indeed possible to lose everything...to suffer everything...to endure everything...yet maintain a joyful spirit and heart of love for the Lord.

So often our major shortcoming is simply to doubt that we could go through those experiences and come out of them as refined and triumphant as we have witnessed others in these devotionals. Jesus never promised that our life would be easy—just fulfilling. He never promised that things would be fair—only that He would be just.

Though we might think that life is too hard for these brothers and sisters about whom we've been reading, we have been given perhaps an even tougher spiritual assignment. Yet the principles in dealing with it remain the same.

Ruth Graham shared a convicting story about a Christian who had just arrived in a free country from years of persecution. He was appalled at the seeming casual commitment to Jesus and materialistic contamination of these Christians. And he said so. Sometime later he returned to visit the friend to whom he had spoken so bluntly when he first arrived. He asked if his friend remembered what he had said, the bitterness of his criticism. The friend remembered. The man stood silent for a few moments, reflecting. The friend tensed for a second attack.

"I have come to apologize both for what I said and the way in which I said it," he said simply. "I was merely afraid. I did not know how dangerous freedom could be. It has been a year now. And I am worse than those I criticized."

Then he added a significant statement: "It is more difficult to live the Christian life under freedom than under repression."

Iranian Christian leader Luke Yagnazar lives in the United States. He concludes, "It is more difficult to be a Christian in the USA than in Iran. There you are either a Christian or not!"

Pastor Samuel Lamb in southern China says, "We have physical persecution but you have materialism. Your lot is harder because we know what we are spiritually fighting. Many times you don't."

Another Chinese church leader adds, "Once you are chasing after money there is no time and energy for church affairs...And the government knows that materialism will destroy the church faster than persecution can...I tell my co-workers in China that the biggest enemy we're facing is no longer communism, it's materialism."

We must remember we are in a spiritual battle and we fight with spiritual weapons only.

RESPONSE:
Today I resolve to begin the New Year ahead accepting the more difficult assignment and putting God and His Kingdom ahead of all others and all else.

PRAYER:
Lord, help me accept the more difficult assignment putting You and Your Kingdom first.

Open Doors
PO Box 6237
Frenchs Forest NSW 2086
AUSTRALIA
www.opendoors.org.au

Missão Portas Abertas
CP 55055
Cep 04733-970
São Paulo-SP
BRAZIL
www.portasabertas.org.br

Open Doors
8-19 Brownridge Road
Halton Hills, ON
L7G 0C6
CANADA
www.opendoorsca.org

Åbne Døre Danmark
PO Box 1062
DK-7500 Holstebro
DENMARK
www.forfulgt.dk

Portes Ouvertes France
BP 40139
F-67833 Tanneries
Cedex (Lingolsheim)
FRANCE
www. portesouvertes.fr

Open Doors Germany
Postfach 1142
DE-65761 Kelkheim
GERMANY
www.opendoors.de

Porte Aperte
CP45
37063 Isola Della Scala, VR
ITALY
www.porteaperteitalia.org

Open Doors
32-22 Sang-do
2 Dong Dong Jag-Gu
Seoul 156-831
REPUBLIC OF
SOUTH KOREA
www.opendoors.or.kr

Open Doors
PO Box 47
3850 AA Ermelo
THE NETHERLANDS
www.opendoors.nl

Open Doors
P O Box 302 445
North Harbour
Auckland
0751
NEW ZEALAND
www.opendoors.org.nz

Åpne Dører
Magnus Barfotsvei 7
4633 Kristiansand
NORWAY
www.opendoors.no

Open Doors
PO Box 1573
QCCPO
1155 Quezon City
PHILIPPINES
http://ph.od.org/index.php

Open Doors
8 Sin Ming Road
#02-06 Sin Ming Centre
Singapore 575628
REPUBLIC
OF SINGAPORE
www.opendoors.org/ODS/

Open Doors
PO Box 1771
Cresta
Gautang, 2118
SOUTH AFRICA
www.opendoors.org.za

Puertas Abiertas
Apdo 49
18100 Armilla (Granada)
SPAIN
www.puertasabiertas.org

Open Doors
PO Box 48
701 40 Orebro
SWEDEN
www.open-doors.se

Portes Ouvertes
Praz-Roussy 4 bis
Postfach 147
CH-1032 Romanel-s-
Lausanne
SWITZERLAND
www.portesouvertes.ch
www.opendoors.ch

Open Doors
UK & Ireland
PO Box 6
Witney
Oxon OX29 6WG
UNITED KINGDOM
www.opendoorsuk.org

Open Doors
PO Box 27001
Santa Ana, CA 92799
USA
www.odusa.org

Open*Doors*
Serving persecuted **Christians** worldwide

733